King's College
Medieval Studies

XXI

King's College London
Centre for Late Antique & Medieval Studies

Director: Professor Julian Weiss

King's College London Medieval Studies

General Editor:
Professor Julian Weiss

Executive Editor:
Ms WM Pank

Editorial & Advisory Board:
Professor David Carpenter
Dr Serena Ferente
Professor David Ganz
Professor Simon Gaunt
Professor Judith Herrin
Mr Martin Jones
Professor Clare Lees
Dr Robert Mills
Professor Dame Jinty Nelson
Dr Karen Pratt
Professor Charlotte Roueché

Gautier d'Arras

Eracle

edited & translated by
Karen Pratt

King's College London
Centre for Late Antique & Medieval Studies
2007

© 2007 Karen Pratt

All rights reserved. No part of this publication may be reproduced, stored in a retrieval system, or transmitted in any form or by any means, electronic, mechanical, photocopied, recorded, or otherwise without the prior permission of the publisher.

ISBN 10: 0-9539838-3-8
ISBN 13: 978-0-9539838-3-4

A CIP record for the book is available from the British Library

Typeset by WM Pank, School of Humanities, King's College London

Printed in England on acid-free paper by
Short Run Press Ltd
Exeter
2007

Contents

Acknowledgments	vi
Introduction	vii
Gautier d'Arras – Author and Context	vii
The Relationship between Gautier d'Arras & Chrétien de Troyes	xiii
Résumé of *Eracle*	xvi
The Historical Heraclius, Byzantium & Gautier's Treatment of his Sources	xviii
The Genre of *Eracle*	xxiii
The Structure & Unity of *Eracle*	xxxi
Themes & Characters	xxxiv
A. Religion	xxxvi
B. The Court & Power	xxxvii
C. Women & Love	xxxix
Narrative Technique	xliv
The Extant Manuscripts of *Eracle*	xlviii
A. Manuscript *A*: Paris, Bibliothèque Nationale de France, fonds français 1444	xlviii
B. Manuscript *B*: Paris, Bibliothèque Nationale de France, fonds français 24430	l
C. Manuscript *T*: Turin, Biblioteca Nazionale, 1626 (L. I. 13)	li
The Language of *Eracle*	lii
A. Gautier's Language	lii
(i) Versification	lii
(ii) Dialectal Features	liv
B. The Language of MS *A*	lvi
(i) Scribe 1	lvii
(ii) Scribe 2	lviii
The Principles of This Edition	lix
The Major Differences between Raynaud de Lage's Edition & the Present Text	lxi
A Note on the Translation	lxiii
Select Bibliography	lxv
Text	1
Variants & Textual Notes	199

Acknowledgements

I am very grateful to the AHRC for the funding of an extra semester of sabbatical leave, enabling me to complete the editing of this text. I should also like to acknowledge my debt to the unpublished work of the late Sir Claude Hayes, whose papers were made available to me by the ever supportive and efficient librarians of the Taylorian Library in Oxford. Several colleagues have been extremely generous with their time and advice on this project, in particular Professors Penny Eley and Simon Gaunt, whose constructive criticisms of the introduction were invaluable, and Professor Glyn Burgess and Dr Roger Middleton, who came up with elegant solutions to my translation problems. I should also like to thank Wendy Pank for assiduously turning my manuscript into a handsome book. Finally, to my long-suffering family and friends I wish to express my love and gratitude for their support.

This book is dedicated to the memory of Professor Wolfgang van Emden, a much loved teacher with whom I first shared my thoughts on Gautier d'Arras.

Introduction

Gautier d'Arras's two extant works *Eracle* and *Ille et Galeron* have long been under the shadow of the romances of Chrétien de Troyes, his contemporary and rival. However, recent criticism has begun to appreciate Gautier's contribution to the emerging genre of courtly romance and his rhetorical elaboration of ideas about love, politics and religion in the twelfth century (Zumthor 1984, 161).[1] It is the aim of this new edition and translation of *Eracle* and of its companion piece *Ille et Galeron* (edited by Penny Eley and published in this series in 1996) to make Gautier's two works available for study by undergraduates so that they may discover a poet whose artistic skill has not fully been appreciated by scholars, but was recognised by his near contemporaries. In a thirteenth-century *Miracle de la Vierge* (Paris, MS Arsenal 3518, fol. 96b) 'Gautiers d'Arras qui fist d'Eracle' is mentioned in a list of good *menestrels*, along with Chrétien (de Troyes), La Chèvre, Benoît de Sainte-Maure and Guiot (de Provins?), and in the same century Meister Otte's *Eraclius*, a Middle High German adaptation of *Eracle*, bears witness to the European popularity of Gautier's first surviving romance.[2] Modern readers will find Gautier's witty realism, humour, psychological insights and innovative approach to gender particularly appealing, and the generic richness of *Eracle* makes it an ideal introduction to the study of early Old French narrative.

Gautier d'Arras – Author & Context

We know nothing about Gautier d'Arras, apart from what we can glean from his remarks in the prologues and epilogues to his extant works: *Eracle* and *Ille et Galeron*. Unfortunately though, these remarks are not easy to interpret. *Eracle* begins confidently with the author's name and with (according to some critics) an allusion to prior literary compositions:

> Se Gautiers d'Arras fist ainc rien
> C'on atorner li doive a bien,
> Or li estuet tel traitié faire
> Que sor tous autres doive plaire (1-4)[3]

---

[1] See the Select Bibliography for the full titles of works cited here in the form author, date, page reference.

[2] In the early thirteenth century the poet Chardry says in his *Set Dormanz* (54) that he will not be speaking about 'Tristram ne de Galerun' (Fourrier 1960, 312). This likely allusion to the eponymous heroine of *Ille et Galeron* suggests that Gautier's second romance was also well known, and possibly also that his work had some affinity with the Tristan material.

[3] *Eracle* has survived in three manuscripts: *A* = Paris, BNF, fr. 1444; *B* = Paris, BNF, fr. 24430; *T* = Turin, Biblioteca Nazionale, L. I. 13. My edition, based on MS *A*, is quoted throughout this introduction.

However, Gautier may not be referring here to previous writings, but rather to creditable works of a non-literary nature, or he may be hoping that his present *traitié* will be superior, not to his own earlier efforts, but to texts by other authors. He then flatteringly presents the 'bon conte Tibaut de Blois' (53) as the instigator (6, 86) of *Eracle* and as the generous patron of court entertainers, unlike other contemporary lords (30-46). In the epilogue, Gautier names himself again (6517), repeats the claim that Thibaut commissioned the work (6525), and now adds that his patron was 'Li fix au boin conte Tiebaut' (6524), thus enabling us to identify him as Thibaut V of Blois (1152-91), son of Thibaut IV.[4] Moreover, he states that the 'contesse ... Marie, fille Loëy' (6527-28), i.e. Marie de Champagne, daughter of Louis VII of France, sister-in-law of Thibaut and patron of Chrétien de Troyes, also encouraged him to write *Eracle*, and that 'Cil qui a Hainau en baillie' (6530), later named 'Quens Bauduïn' (6559), i.e. Baudouin of Hainault, incited him on several occasions to finish it.[5] The ensuing praise of Baudouin seems to suggest that Gautier had shifted allegiance from Thibaut to Baudouin (both referred to as 'princes'). Yet the author is clearly not settled, for his epilogue contains both expressions of hope in the generosity of his benefactor, and veiled threats, perhaps implying that he will move on if not properly supported.[6]

If there were any concrete evidence enabling us to identify his third supporter as Baudouin IV of Hainault (1120-71), we would have a firm *terminus ante quem* of 1171 for *Eracle*. Unfortunately, the internal evidence is ambiguous, and applies equally well to his son Baudouin V (1171-95). Lines 6556-58:

> Il est tous seus, c'en est la some,
> Nen a ne per ne compaignon,
> Ne ja n'ara se par lui non

seem to imply that Baudouin will be unique, unless he produces an equal himself, perhaps a son and heir. However, Baudouin IV had done this by 1150 and his son produced a male heir in 1171 shortly before inheriting the title, so at no point during the likely period of Gautier's activity could the poet reasonably imply that either of the two Counts Baudouin had not yet replicated himself (unless Baudouin V's son was simply too young to have proved himself yet). The poet's enigmatic words concerning friends:

---

[4] See also the variant reading in manuscript *B* after line 60. In presenting Laïs's seneschal positively in *Eracle* Gautier may have wished to flatter Thibaut V, who was the seneschal of France. This contrasts with the negative portrayal of Arthur's seneschal Kay in Chrétien's romances.

[5] The variant reading in *B* for line 6530 and the absence of lines 6537ff means that MS *B* suppresses any reference to Baudouin.

[6] Although in lines 6560-61 Gautier seems to be saying that he may soon apply himself to something new, i.e. a new composition, these lines could also suggest that he will place his hopes in another patron.

En dis et set ans et demi
Ne treuve on pas un bon ami (6543-44)

may be reminding Baudouin IV of long friendship, but they sound more like the admonishings of an older man to his young lord (Baudouin V, aged around 21 at the time of his accession), whom he may have known since childhood. Yet it is also possible that this is an allusion to Gautier's long association with Thibaut, or indeed the figure 17½ years could just be an arbitrary number representing a long time (Fourrier 1960, 194 and note 46).

Gautier's adoption of direct address and strong words in line 6559-66 is unusual, and may again imply a young addressee. On the other hand, his commendation of his patron's soul to the Holy Spirit in line 6545 (possibly a faulty reading, see the *T* variant) might refer to the late Baudouin IV, although he appears to be referring to his present benefactor. So, despite Fourrier's conviction that Baudouin V would have been more interested than his father in a 'historical' narrative like *Eracle* (1960, 193), the evidence is only slightly in favour of the son, and one wonders if Gautier's vagueness in his epilogue is designed to cover any contemporary lord of Hainault, all of whom were called Baudouin in the late twelfth century![7]

The two versions of *Ille et Galeron* copied in MSS *P* and *W* provide further information about Gautier's connections.[8] In the prologue to both there is a eulogy of 'l'empererris de Rome' (19), i.e. Beatrice of Burgundy, who married Frederick Barbarossa in 1156 and was crowned Empress of the Holy Roman Empire in 1167. In the epilogue to *W* (which is, according to Eley, a later authorial revision) Beatrice is named, but along with 'conte Tiebaut', the former having instigated the work, the latter urged its conclusion (Lefèvre edn, 6592w-92x). Finally, the epilogue in *W* states that Gautier 's'entremist/ d'Eracle, ains qu'il fesist ceste uevre' (6592-6592a).[9] The five occurrences of the verb *s'entremettre* in *Eracle* (1222, 1910, 1969, 4250, 4684) suggest that its primary meaning for Gautier was 'to undertake, to occupy oneself with' and that line 6592 in *Ille et Galeron* therefore states that *Eracle* was composed before *Ille*. However, some critics have argued that *s'entremettre* means 'embarked upon' (but not finished) and that it points to interwoven composition for the two works. Thus Gautier could have begun *Eracle* for Thibaut and Marie, turned to *Ille et Galeron* version 1 for Beatrice, completed *Eracle* for Baudouin, and then revised *Ille et Galeron* for Thibaut and Beatrice (Fourrier 1960,

---

[7] The absence of a patron called Baudouin from *Ille et Galeron* does not prove that the father was the patron of *Eracle*, but had died by the time the later romance was composed; indeed, this absence may simply indicate that Gautier carried out the threats expressed in the final lines of *Eracle*.

[8] See Eley edn, xii-xix. *Ille et Galeron* is quoted throughout from Eley's edition based on MS *P*, but Lefèvre's edition is used for significant variants from MS *W*.

[9] This line may also have been in *P*, see Eley edn, p. 223, n. 2.

204). Yet this theory overlooks the obvious allusion in the prologues to *Ille* in both *P* (180-84) and *W* (120-24) to the plot of *Eracle* (see Eley edn, xix), an allusion which would have been incomprehensible to an audience unfamiliar with the earlier work about Heraclius. Nor is it likely that Gautier was referring to an incomplete work which he was making known in instalments, despite the fact that once completed it would have been recited during several sittings. Indeed, the structural and thematic studies by Calin (1962), Lacy (1986) and Eley (1989) suggest that he did not compose *Eracle* in fragments, but had a unified conception of his work from the very beginning.[10] Those arguing that Gautier composed *Ille* before completing *Eracle* would have to accept the unlikely hypothesis that the warning against underestimating a colt with a shaggy coat was inserted into both *Ille* prologues at some later date once *Eracle* had been finished.

If we accept that *Eracle* preceded *Ille et Galeron* in its entirety, we can use the evidence of dedicatees to arrive at the following extreme dates of composition: 1159, the date on which Marie became Countess of Champagne on her marriage to Henri le Libéral (Benton 1961, 553-54) and 1184, the death of Beatrice. Many of the scholarly attempts to date the two works more accurately using the allusions to possible patrons fall into the trap of assuming that the mention of a new benefactor means that Gautier had changed patronage for some practical reason. Yet a close look at his words suggests that he may have accumulated protectors rather than replaced one with another (Fourrier 1960, 188-89). However, there is some plausibility in Eley's suggestion that the first version of *Ille et Galeron* was composed in the 1170s (after the death in 1171 of Conain IV of Britanny, the likely model for Galeron's brother)[11] and that Gautier sought the support of Thibaut V whilst Beatrice was away in Italy (1174-78), producing his second version around 1180. Just as plausible is Fourrier's idea (1960, 198-99) that Gautier received the commission for *Eracle* between August 1176 and April 1177 when Henri de Champagne, his wife Marie and Thibaut V met in Provins, whereas Baudouin (V) may have shown interest in Gautier's writing when he visited Troyes in 1179 to negotiate the betrothal of his children with Henri and Marie's son and daughter (Fourrier 1960, 203).[12] None of this can, however, be proved; it simply points to the frequent occasions

---

[10] In the plot summary of *Eracle*, 2903-14, I would not place too much significance on the words 'se jou puis' at the rhyme. It is unlikely that Gautier is here suggesting that he might have to abandon *Eracle* to compose *Ille et Galeron* first, but cf. Pierreville 2001, 12-13, and Fourrier 1960, 204-05. Nor is the absence from the prologue of any reference to Athanaïs suggestive of interrupted, fragmentary composition. The adultery episode forms an integral part of the 'testing of Eracle' theme which *is* mentioned in the prologue.

[11] Since the two references to the death of Galeron's brother are accompanied by the term *pieça* (3840, 4213), Fourrier (1960, 195) thinks that *Ille et Galeron* was composed some time after 1171. Similarly, the use of *ja* in line 69, 'Rome le vit ja coroner' suggests that *Ille et Galeron* was composed a while after Beatrice's coronation (Eley edn, xx-xxi). *Ja* in the sense of 'a while ago' is found also in *Eracle* (115 and 2579).

[12] Pierreville (2001, 15), on the other hand, thinks that Thibaut V may have commissioned

on which Gautier may have had the opportunity to obtain the patronage of the noble families of Blois and Champagne, whose support for a crusade to help the Byzantine Emperor Manuel I Comnenus towards the end of the 1170s was no doubt propitious for a work on the Byzantine Emperor Heraclius.

There are two further possible references in *Eracle* to historical events. The first concerns the imprisonment in a tower of Eleanor of Aquitaine by Henry II of England. If this is reflected in Laïs's harsh treatment of Athanaïs, it would give us a *terminus post quem* of 1174; however, the link is tenuous, and Gautier is more likely to be alluding to the literary topos of close-keeping by jealous husbands. The second is the fact that for a short while after his birth the future king Philippe-Auguste was called Dieudonné; this detail, if it was used by Gautier in line 225, would imply a date of composition shortly after 1165, when it was fresh in people's minds. Moreover, our poet may have wished to flatter the Capetian monarchy (related of course to his patron Marie) by comparing the young prince to Eracle.

More convincing at first sight though is the historical evidence adduced by Cowper (1949, 1954) in order to identify our Gautier with the knight Gualterus de Atrebato (or atrebatensis) who witnessed (or was mentioned in) over a hundred charters between 1160 and 1185, and who was a landholder and important officer of Philippe d'Alsace, Count of Flanders. However, the name Walter was common in the Middle Ages and any Walter hailing from Arras would have been called Gautier d'Arras. One might also have expected Gualterus to dedicate his works to his overlord Philippe, not to other nobles in his orbit. Moreover, the historical information about Gualterus does not square with the authorial image created by the narratives: of a poet largely dependent on patronage. Although the image could be fictional, Gautier's anxiety to reap his just rewards from his literary endeavours is clear from his use, in both epilogues, of the verb *emploiier*, which generally means 'to put to good use', but which in *Eracle* (502, 694 and 1002) has purely financial connotations:

Tuit li cortois, li afaitié,
Le doivent bien a Diu proiier,
Et que ge si puisse **emploiier**
Ceste oevre que je bien i aie
Et qu'ele en males mains ne kaie. (*Eracle*, 6518-22)

Eracle from Gautier ca. 1165 in the aftermath of the Second Crusade. His aim would have been to celebrate his brother's achievements in the Holy Land, where Henri had followed in the footsteps of Heraclius.

Mais l'uevre est molt bien **emploïe**
au quel d'ax qu'el soit envoïe'[13] (*Ille et Galeron*, Lefèvre edn, 6592s-t)

A more fruitful line of research by Cowper (1931) was to link Gautier with Provins, where the Counts of Champagne frequently held court. The depiction of Rome in *Eracle* may be influenced by locations and events in Provins: Athanaïs's round tower (possibly the octagonal Tour-de-César); the underground chamber at the old woman's house (the network of *souterrains*); the horse race (the *Cours aux Bêtes*); the Roman games (festivities accompanying the annual fairs). A particularly striking connection between *Eracle* and Provins is the fact that its main church was unusually dedicated to St Cyriacus, the Jew who helped to identify the True Cross (*Eracle*, 5123-202). The *Collégiale de Saint-Quiriace* was situated next to the Counts' palace, and Henri le Libéral and his wife Marie were its generous benefactors. Moreover, the timing of Provins's two annual fairs coincides with Feast Days associated with the True Cross: the May Fair included the Feasts of St Cyriacus (May 1st) and the Invention of the Cross (May 4th); the St Ayoul Fair began on September 14th, the Feast of the Exaltation of the Cross. Cowper's assertion that the eight-day Roman games in *Eracle* take place *just before* 'le feste Saint Jehan' (4218), and that this reflected the situation in 1166 and 1177, when Trinity Sunday fell just before June 24th, is not convincing (Benton 1961, 569). However, there is an interesting parallel between the stone market held on a Tuesday (737, 741) and the fact that the weekly market of Provins took place on that day (Pierreville 2001, 72). So, it is likely that Gautier composed *Eracle* with the religious interests and social calendar of his potential Champenois benefactors in mind.

Whereas our present state of knowledge does not allow the precise dating of Gautier's *oeuvre* or the identification of the poet with a known historical person, it is clear that the courts of late twelfth-century Champagne provided the milieu in which he operated, and that he must therefore have been a near contemporary and rival of Chrétien de Troyes (see below). They probably also shared the same influences. Delbouille's work (1973) on repeated rhymes employed by both poets, although based on rather mechanical statistical analyses, situates Gautier's practice close to that of Chrétien, but as an intermediary between him and earlier writers. Given that Marie de France's *Eliduc* provided a source for *Ille et Galeron*, the poet from Arras must have known her *Lais*.[14] Moreover, Beckmann (1963) has argued convincingly that Gautier was influenced by Thomas's *Tristan*. The enormous range of styles and registers evident in *Eracle* suggests that its author was familiar with all the vernacular genres: the *chansons de geste*, *romans antiques* (including the *lais* of *Piramus et Thisbé* and *Narcissus*), *fabliaux*,

---

[13] Note that Gautier plans to *send* his romance to both Thibaut and Beatrice; he is not a member of their court (Lefèvre edn, 6592c-92f).

[14] See Eley edn, xxx-xxxiv.

hagiography (such as the *Vie de Saint Alexis*), courtly lyric, as well as the *Conte de Floire et Blancheflor*, and perhaps Wace's and Benoît de Sainte-Maure's 'historical' writing.[15] Gautier's clerical education is clear from his use of Latin sources and classical rhetoric, and his inclusion of Latinate words (see below pp. xviii, xlvi and lvi).

Raynaud de Lage's investigation of the religious inspiration of *Eracle* (1974) concludes that Gautier was not just a cleric with excellent scriptural knowledge, but a man of the Church, to whom Christian discourse and doctrine had become second nature. However, despite their strong moral messages, his two surviving romances are also imbued with the language and ideas of courtly culture.

The Relationship between Gautier d'Arras & Chrétien de Troyes

Several critics, notably Raynaud de Lage (1971) and Pierreville (2001, 50-63), have been struck by similarities between the diction of Gautier d'Arras and Chrétien de Troyes, but it was long assumed that the latter (perceived as superior) had influenced the former. Morever, many critics favoured an early date for Chrétien's output, thus making him a precursor of Gautier.[16] Pierreville's re-examination of the question produced the following relative chronology: *Erec et Enide* – first part of *Eracle* – *Ille et Galeron* – *Cligés* – completion of *Eracle* – *Chevalier de la Charrete* – *Chevalier au lion* – *Conte del Graal*. However, this will need to be revised if we reject the theory of intercalated composition. In fact, her evidence (2001, 50-51) for the priority of Chrétien's first romance is very slim. The parallels between the description of festivities in *Erec et Enide*, 1989-2000, and *Eracle*, 3433-35, may result from influence in either direction or on both texts by Wace's *Brut*, 10823-32.[17] Moreover, if Gautier's boast during his narration of Eracle's conception:

---

[15] According to Eley (edn, xxxv), the version of Ille's wounding in manuscript W of *Ille et Galeron* is likely to be Andreas Capellanus's source for *De amore*, Book II, chapter 7, judgement 15. Any similarities between the *De amore* and Gautier's treatment of love in his romances are probably the result of Andreas humorously drawing on literary texts as sources of courtly exemplification; see Pratt 2007a.

[16] Of course the dating of Chrétien's romances is not firmly established; whilst the *terminus ante quem* for the *Conte del Graal* is 1191, the death of Philippe d'Alsace, Count of Flanders, the only solid *terminus post quem* (relevant to the *Charrete* and later works) is 1159, when Marie acquired the title of Countess of Champagne. Although some scholars have preferred an earlier dating, Hunt and Luttrell have both argued for Chrétien's main literary activity in the 1180s, which would make Gautier almost certainly his predecessor. See Claude Luttrell, *The Creation of the First Arthurian Romance: A Quest* (London: Arnold, 1974); Tony Hunt, 'Redating Chrestien de Troyes', *Bibliographical Bulletin of the International Arthurian Society* 30 (1978), 209-37.

[17] Wace, *Roman de Brut*, edited by I. D. O. Arnold, SATF (Paris, 1938-40).

> Si engenra en li celui
> Qui fist puis maint home esjoïr,
> Et dont il fait bien a oïr –
> De çou me puis je bien vanter. (206-09)

is an allusion, as Pierreville claims (2001, 57), to the last line of Chrétien's prologue to *Erec et Enide*:

> Des or comancerai l'estoire
> qui toz jorz mes iert an mimoire
> tant con durra crestïantez;
> de ce s'est Crestïens vantez. (23-26)

then Gautier has missed a trick in omitting any reference to Christianity or to his own name. While these may be independent boasts, it is likely that Chrétien is trying to outdo his predecessor by actually naming himself in a witty manner.

The evidence for borrowing by Gautier from Chrétien's *Cligés* is equally fragile. The resemblance between *Eracle*, 3520-40, and *Cligés*, 2783-800, 3112-23, is less striking if one retains for *Eracle*, 3525, the *A* reading *lanchier* (to shoot an arrow) and rejects the reading *rentier* favoured by previous editors, but probably the *lectio facilior* (easier reading) offered by the inferior *T* manuscript:[18]

Et se le **dient li auquant**	Ne dirai pas **si com cil dïent**
Qu'on depart bien sen **cuer en deus**	Qui an un cors deus cuers alïent...
Si l'envoie on en divers **leus**,	**I a de tiex qui dire** suelent
A ce c'on tient et a s'amie;	Que chascuns a le cuer as **deus**;
Mais qui çou fait, il **n'**aime **mie.**	Mes uns cuers **n'**est **pas** an deus **leus**...
Amors n'a cure de lanchier (*T*: **rentier**)	'Amors en li [Yseult] trop vilena,
S'ele n'a tout le cuer **entier**	Que ses **cuers** fu a un **entiers**,
Ne de cuer malvais a **parchon**,	Et ses cors fu a deus **rentiers**...
C'Amors n'a cure de **garçon**...	Car de mon cors et de mon **cuer**
Car ele est france et debonaire,	N'iert ja fet partie **a nul fuer**.
Et amans a tel cose a faire	Ja mes cors n'iert voir **garçoniers**,
Qu'il ne poroit faire **a nul fuer**	N'il n'i avra deus **parçoniers**.
S'il n'i avoit un poi **del cuer**,	Qui a le cuer, cil a le cors.'
Se ce n'estoit par grant usage.	(*Cligés*, 2783-84, 2798-2800,
(*Eracle*, 3520-28, 3533-37)	3112-14, 3119-23)

Not only are the verbal parallels highlighted above rather conventional, but also the sense of these two passages is quite different. In *Cligés* the narrator rejects the idea that

---

[18] Although the *T* reading *rentier* produces a richer rhyme with *entier*, it may be a scribal reminiscence of *Cligés* (3114) copied later in the same manuscript.

two hearts can reside in one body and then Fénice condemns the sharing of one's *body* between two men, whereas Gautier is denying the possibility of dividing up the *heart*. The rhyme *parchon/garçon* in *Eracle*, 3527-28, is similar to that in *Cligés*, 3121-22: *garçoniers/ parçoniers*, and in *Ille et Galeron*, 1285-88:

> Ne cuidés ja que garçonier
> Soient ja d'amor parçonier,
> Ne ja n'en seront parçonieres
> Celes qui en sont garçonieres.

(*Do not imagine that men of easy virtue could ever have a share in love, and love will never be shared by women of easy virtue*; Eley translation).

However, although the context in *Ille* refers to people of easy virtue, as does Fénice in Chrétien's romance, for Gautier the word *parçon* and cognates has the meaning of 'partaker in' in these cases. Thus the relationship between these passages from Gautier's romances and *Cligés* is unclear, and there may be a closer parallel between Chrétien's use of *rentier* (3114) and *parçoniers* (3122) and the rhyme *meteier/parçonier* in the *Roman d'Enéas*, 3827-28, for *meteier* and *rentier* both imply sharing.[19] The fact that Gautier uses the rhyme twice is no indication that he is the borrower (Pierreville 2001, 52-53).

While the influence of Chrétien on the love casuistry of Gautier's romances is unproven, and similarities may be the product of the influence of Thomas's *Tristan* and the *romans antiques* on both authors, two further details suggest that the Champenois poet was alluding to *Eracle* in his *Cligés*. First, the name of Cligés's cuckolded uncle Alis seems to be an inversion of Laïs. The latter name probably came first though, since it is justified by being rhymed with Athanaïs, the female name supplied by Gautier's source. Moreover, the enigmatic, and largely gratuitous reference at the end of *Cligés* to the Byzantine emperors' habit of locking up their wives is probably a humorous allusion to the cause of Athanaïs's adultery. In the same comic vein, Chrétien's praise of Marie de Champagne at the beginning of the *Charrete* parodies Gautier's eulogy of Beatrice in the prologue to *Ille et Galeron*. Gautier's omission of lines 79-88 in his revised version in MS *W* may well have been the consequence of his rival's jibes.

In my view, therefore, it is not necessary (pace Pierreville) to resort to the complicated theory of interwoven composition to explain the resemblances between the works of Gautier and Chrétien. The most likely solution is that the younger, ironic poet from Troyes enjoyed poking fun at his older, more moralistic contemporary from Arras. Whatever their relationship, it is clear that in order to understand the development of courtly narrative in late twelfth-century Champagne we need to bear in mind the interaction between these two writers.

---

[19]   Edited by J.-J. Salverda de Grave, CFMA, 2 vols (Paris: Champion, 1925 and 1929).

Résumé of Eracle

Gautier's prologue contains fulsome praise of his patron Thibaut and the latter's generosity towards court entertainers, followed by a plot summary (1-114).

There once lived in Rome a pious couple, Miriados, a senator, and his wife Cassine, who are childless after seven years of marriage. God answers their prayers by sending an angel who tells Cassine that she will give birth to a child, the most knowledgeable boy in the world. In accordance with divine instructions the child is conceived and born. He is baptised Eracle. Soon afterwards, an angel brings a letter for the child with further instructions. Having excelled in his education, Eracle is able at the age of six to read the missive, which informs him that God has bestowed upon him three gifts: special knowledge of precious stones, horses and women (115-278).

Miriados dies and Cassine suggests giving away all their wealth in order to save the father's soul. Eracle agrees; they distribute alms, found abbeys and then live a humble life of poverty and suffering. Cassine proposes to sell Eracle in order to fund more alms-giving. Her son agrees and suggests a price of 1,000 *besants* for himself. Eracle, with his mother's belt tied round his neck, is taken to market, where prospective buyers ridicule him. The emperor's seneschal, on learning of Eracle's special gifts, buys him. There ensue heart-rending farewells in which mother and son affirm their faith in God. Then Cassine retires to an abbey and Eracle goes to court with the seneschal (279-655).

The emperor is not convinced that Eracle is special and ridicules his seneschal's gullibility, but the boy confidently reiterates his powers and the emperor decides to test the first one by arranging a stone market. Ignoring all the obviously valuable stones on sale, Eracle buys one from a poor man who offers it for six *deniers* and receives forty marks. The emperor is furious, but Eracle claims that the stone protects its owner against water, fire and the sword. If he had paid too little for it, its powers would be lost. Eracle, aided by the stone, survives 'ordeals' by water, fire (the emperor joins in this test) and combat against an evil, envious opponent (656-1244).

Eracle rises in status and the emperor thinks of using him to find a perfect wife, but first his knowledge of horses has to be tested. The emperor arranges a horse fair and places his best steed among the animals present. Eracle chooses a shaggy colt and pays forty marks instead of the two and a half requested. The angry emperor agrees to a race in which the colt will run in relay against horses belonging to the emperor, the constable and the seneschal. The colt wins, but as predicted, is ruined by the effort, the marrow having seeped out of its bones (1245-1892).

Eracle, now the emperor's counsellor, is given the task of finding the perfect wife for his lord. All noble maidens in the empire are summoned to a bride show. The emperor informs them that his adviser will select a wife for him. The girls who have lost their virginity are especially worried. Eracle surveys the ranks of women, noting in particular representatives of seven female vices: avarice, lechery, inconstancy, loquacity, arrogance, nastiness, and the encouragement of flatterers. Eracle dismisses the women, who depart in anger (1893-2572).

By chance Eracle comes upon a young girl when riding in the old quarter of Rome. She is a poor orphan, but perfect in every way, and he promises her aunt that she will be empress. Eracle informs the emperor, who makes arrangements for his wedding, while the aunt gives her niece some moral advice. Laïs (now named) and Athanaïs wed; the emperor is very pleased with his bride, who wins the love and respect of her Roman subjects. Eracle is knighted, his past life now becomes common knowledge. After seven years of marriage, Laïs loves his wife dearly (2573-2968).

Rebels attack one of the emperor's cities and he prepares for a military campaign. Laïs decides to leave his wife in Rome under guard. Despite Eracle's attempts to dissuade him, the emperor places Athanaïs in a tower guarded by twenty-four elderly knights and their wives. He then leaves and besieges the city. In a lengthy monologue, Athanaïs expresses her grief and anger at such unjust treatment, vowing to change her situation if possible. She visits the Roman games, where she falls in love with the most accomplished participant, Paridés. Their monologues reveal that their love is mutual. Separation when the games are over results in violent suffering, expressed in a further monologue from each lover (2969-3996).

Paridés's 'illness' worries his relatives, who send for a worldly wise *vieille* living nearby. She recognises the symptoms of love and offers her services as go-between which, she claims, would bring success even with the empress herself. At these words, Paridés faints, his secret is revealed, and the old woman offers to help. The next day, she visits Athanaïs with a basket of cherries and at the end of a skilfully circumspect conversation discloses Paridés's love for her. The empress confesses her own love and promises to send the *vieille* a reward for her service and something for her lover. The old woman receives a pie in a silver dish, and at first believes the pie to be for her and the dish for Paridés. However, having angrily smashed the pie, she discovers the letter for the young man, and realises that the costly dish is her reward (3997-4448).

Paridés is asked to dig a chamber under the *vieille*'s house, where a good fire must burn, and to fill a hole in the street outside with water. On her return to the games, Athanaïs engineers a fall from her horse and is carried alone to the old woman's home to recover. The lovers meet in the underground chamber, but their joy is short-lived, for Athanaïs realises that Eracle will divine the adultery. Laïs is informed of his wife's infidelity and returns to Rome. During the lovers' 'trial' Eracle blames Laïs for his wife's sin and encourages the emperor to divorce Athanaïs and allow her to marry Paridés. Her dowry will be her father's lands (4449-5087).

The author intervenes to indicate a change of subject-matter, turning his attention to Eracle's mature exploits. Having narrated the legend of Judas Cyriacus and the Invention of the Holy Cross by St Helena, Gautier describes the situation in Eracle's day: Chosroes, a Persian king, sacks Jerusalem and seizes the Cross. He builds himself a 'heaven', where he produces various meteorological effects mechanically, places the holy relic in it and has himself worshipped as a god. The pagan ruler persecutes the Christians and murders Phocas, the emperor of Constantinople. Its citizens elect two new emperors, Eracle and an African. Eracle arrives in Constantinople first and becomes emperor (5088-5302).

Chosroes sends his son, who bears the same name, to attack Eracle and invade the Western Empire. An angel warns Eracle of the offensive. The armies meet at the River Danube and during a council of war, the emperor proposes single combat between himself and the pagan leader. Messengers are sent and Chosroes accepts. The combat is prefaced by failed attempts on both sides to convert their opponents to their beliefs. Eracle is victorious and Chosroes is thrown into the river. Most of the pagans are baptised (5303-5840).

Eracle presses on to Persia where he finds and worships the Holy Cross. He slays Chosroes the Elder. Having founded churches and distributed alms to the poor, he proceeds in triumph to Jerusalem. However, he fails to emulate the humility of Christ on Palm Sunday and miraculously the city ramparts close and block his way. An angel reproaches Eracle for his pride; the emperor humbles himself and prays. The walls separate and the Cross is replaced in the Holy Sepulchre. Chosroes's younger son is baptised and is given his father's land. Having thus instituted the Feast of the Exaltation of the Holy Cross, Eracle returns to Constantinople, where he reigns until he dies. A statue is erected there in his honour (5841-6514).

In his epilogue Gautier asks the Holy Cross to intercede for him. He mentions Thibaut of Blois, Marie of Champagne and Baudouin of Hainault as his patrons (6515-6568).

The Historical Heraclius, Byzantium & Gautier's Treatment of his Sources[20]

The deeds of the seventh-century Byzantine Emperor Heraclius, who reigned from 610-641, were known to clerics in the Middle Ages in two forms, in 'historically accurate' chronicle accounts and in more flattering liturgical or hagiographical texts. In the chronicle version, the sins of Heraclius overshadow his Christian feats. In the liturgical texts, Heraclius is presented as an exemplary Christian hero, whose one sinful

---

[20] For more information on this subject, see Fourrier 1960, 210-57, Walter E. Kaegi, *Heraclius, Emperor of Byzantium* (Cambridge: CUP, 2003) and http://www.roman-emperors.org/heraclis.htm, last accessed 3.7.07.

act is soon atoned for and whose recovery of the Holy Cross from the Persians was instrumental in establishing the True Faith in the Holy Land and beyond. Gautier's primary source for the mature exploits of his eponymous hero was a written work from the latter tradition: a Latin liturgical text found in an eleventh-century manuscript in Rheims library (Faral 1920). This *Passionarius ad usum Beatae Mariae remensis* contains readings for the 4th May, the Feast of the Invention of the Holy Cross, and includes the acts of Saint Judas Cyriacus. It also contains *lectiones* for the 14th September, the Feast of the Exaltation of the Cross. These describe Chosroes's attacks on Christians in the Holy Land, culminating in his theft of the True Cross from the Church of the Holy Sepulchre and his construction of a marvellous edifice or 'heaven' in which he is worshipped as a god. Heraclius, noted for his martial strength, educated speech and fervent Christian faith, sets out to challenge Chosroes's son and defeats him in single combat on a bridge over the Danube. After converting many Persians to Christianity, Heraclius seeks out Chosroes the Elder in his heaven, offers him the chance to convert, then cuts off his head. Having baptised Chosroes's younger son, Heraclius divides up the spoils of conquest between his army and a fund for the restoration of churches. He then takes the Cross to Jerusalem, where he is greeted by crowds waving palm fronds, but is prevented from entering the city when the walls close before him. An angel of the Lord compares his proud behaviour unfavourably to Christ's on Palm Sunday, but the walls part for Heraclius once he has humbled himself and the Cross is returned to its rightful place. Heraclius returns to Constantinople where he remains faithful to the Christian religion to the very end.

It is notable that the *Passionarius* does not include the more negative aspects of the emperor's life found in chronicle accounts. Omitted from it is the claim that Heraclius acceded to the throne of Constantinople on 5th October 610 by deposing the previous occupant Phocas, mutilating his body, then killing him. Also, towards the end of his life Heraclius suffered from dropsy and was accused of indulging in incest, heresy and astrology. His illness and inability to defeat the Moslems, to whom the Holy Land was lost, were interpreted as divine punishment for Heraclius's sins.[21]

Having chosen the version of Heraclius's life more appropriate to his literary aims, Gautier adapted his source quite faithfully, while amplifying battle scenes and passages of direct speech, thus enhancing further the dramatic impact of the liturgical text. For a narrative of the emperor's early life the poet from Arras drew on additional material of Byzantine origin, which he discovered in either written or oral form, perhaps when visiting Constantinople or through contact with travellers to the Eastern Empire. Gautier seems to have been the first writer to incorporate these extraneous elements

---

[21] Meister Otte, the thirteenth-century German translator of *Eracle*, adds these details to his adaptation in his desire to be more factually accurate (Pratt 1987, chapter XIV).

into a biography of the emperor Heraclius.

The first Greek motif used by Gautier concerns Eracle's conception, during which his mother obeys some rather unusual angelic instructions (148-69). Admittedly, there are biblical parallels here (the Annunciation; the story of Zacharias and Elisabeth, Luke 1: 5-16), which underline the religious vocation of the child conceived with divine aid, yet it has also been argued that these arrangements are reminiscent of the Byzantine mass. According to Fourrier (1960, 240-41), when the celebrant entered the Church of St Sophia, he would go into the holy of holies to sprinkle incense over the altar and to leave his gifts on it, in particular a silk cloth or *eilêton*, which was placed on top of the altar cloth or *endutê*, preventing the latter from coming into contact with the host. The priest would also cover the chalice and the patena with a large veil. Thus the conception of Eracle, which involves a silk cloth, carpet and cloak (148-214), takes place under similar circumstances to the mystical reincarnation of Christ on the altars of Orthodox Greek churches. What is more, the name given to Eracle's father by Gautier is Miriados, clearly a name of Greek origin, though the exact source has not been identified.

The events of Eracle's childhood are based on the folk-tale of the three gifts, a narrative which perhaps suggested itself to Gautier if he had heard both of the astrological powers of Heraclius and the talismanic quality of the statue in Constantinople which he believed depicted that emperor.[22] This archetypal tale, probably of Indian origin, concerns a slave who possesses an astonishing knowledge of precious stones, horses and people, and who is able, by placing his gifts at the disposal of a powerful ruler, to rise in fortune. Gautier's version, which shows some resemblance to the story of the three sons of the Sultan of Yemen from the *Thousand and One Nights*[23] and to the Byzantine *Ptocholeon*, seems to have passed through Arab and Greek hands before reaching France. The story of *Ptocholeon*, the Wise Old Man, exists today in three versions, the earliest manuscript, dating from the fifteenth century, seeming to preserve a much older story. In essence it tells of an old man reduced to poverty by Arab attacks, who encourages his sons to sell him into slavery to earn some money. The king's treasurer purchases him on account of his three gifts. Having bought a precious stone for a huge sum of money, the king asks the old man what he thinks of it, and the latter pronounces it worthless. This is confirmed when it is sawn in half and a worm is found in it. Later the king's prospective bride is pronounced worthless as she is the daughter of a Moslem and, when threatened, Ptocholeon reveals that the king is the son of a baker, a situation which his mother reluctantly confirms. Thus the old man rises to be the king's wise counsellor. Although the second test concerning horses is absent from the extant manuscript, there is internal evidence to suggest that it was originally present.

---

[22] See Fourrier 1960, 246. The statue was actually of the Emperor Justinian.
[23] http://www.mythfolklore.net/1001nights/scott/sultan_yemen.htm, last accessed 12.06.07.

The closest analogue to Gautier's *Eracle* from the *Thousand and One Nights* is present in the eigthteenth-century Tunis manuscript, but it seems to be based on a Byzantine source (Fourrier 1960, 217). Here the old man's *son* offers to be sold into slavery, which is the case in *Eracle*. However, the father refuses his offer and once he himself is purchased, he is able to distinguish for his owner between a valuable and worthless pearl, to choose the better of two horses and to identify the prince's origins. He claims to have read this information in the stars – again a link with Heraclius the astrologer. In Gautier's hands, however, this material becomes heavily Christianised. Eracle, called 'Diudonné' (225) at birth, proves to be the elect of God, whose powers and advice are at first questioned and then ignored. He is bought by the emperor's seneschal, who seems to symbolise the Good Christian of steadfast faith, whereas Laïs represents the doubting Thomas, who needs constant proof of God's powers. Meanwhile, the three ordeals Eracle undergoes also put *his* faith to the test. His rise to the position of emperor's counsellor is presented in the context of his increasing qualification to become Byzantine Emperor.

During the episode of the testing of Eracle, in which his ability to distinguish between appearances and reality is paramount, several elements seem to be Greek. The market at which Eracle chooses a precious stone for the emperor evokes Constantine's Forum in Constantinople as described by Robert de Clari in his *Conquête de Constantinople*, and the relay-race to test the colt may be a reminiscence of races held in the Great Hippodrome (according to Fourrier 1960, 241), rather than in the confined spaces of the Roman Circus. It may also reflect the Greek practice of distinguishing between colts and mature horses for racing purposes (cf. *Eracle*, 1551-86).

The bride show arranged to find the emperor a wife reflects a long-standing Byzantine tradition. Although this method of selecting a wife evokes in general terms the motif found in many medieval romances of the oriental ruler's harem from which he chooses his favourite mistress to be queen (for example *Floire et Blancheflor*), it reflects more closely the practice in eighth- and ninth-century Byzantium, whereby the empress was chosen from girls brought to Constantinople by their parents. They were assembled in the palace and the young prince, usually supervised by his mother, would select his bride. By this method Constantine VI was married to Maria in 788, Stauracius selected his wife in 807, and in 821 the twelve-year-old Theophilos chose Theodora, who later presided over her own son Michael III's selection of the woman who became St Irene. This custom seems to have died out by the tenth century, although there is a reminiscence of it in the fourteenth-century Greek romance of *Velthandros and Chrysandza*.[24] While Gautier may have taken the idea from the biblical story of Esther, it is more likely that he found it in a written source or heard about the custom either when in Constantinople himself or

---

[24] See *Three Medieval Greek Romances: Velthandros and Chrysandza, Kallimachos and Chrysorroi, Livistros and Rodamni*, translated by Gavin Betts (New York and London: Garland, 1995).

from travellers familiar with the Byzantine empire. Moreover, it is interesting to note that the historical events which may well have provided him with the episode of Athanaïs's adultery, an episode which follows immediately on the bride show in his romance, also include the selection of a bride who comes to court and takes the fancy of the emperor.

The story of the alleged adultery of the fifth-century empress Athenaïs (better known as Eudokia), the wife of the emperor Theodosius II, was familiar to historiographers of Greece in the Middle Ages and was represented by both a learned and popular tradition. It was probably the popular tradition which Gautier followed. According to the sixth-century writer John Malalas of Antioch, Athenaïs, daughter of the philosopher Leontius, came to Constantinople with one of her aunts to contest her brothers' inheritance of her father's property. Theodosius's sister Pulcheria was so struck by Athenaïs's beauty that she arranged for them to marry, once the girl had been baptised Eudokia. One day the emperor was given a magnificent Phrygian apple which he presented to the empress, but which she passed on to a young courtier called Paulinus, who in turn offered it to the emperor. When questioned, the empress lied, claiming that she had eaten the apple, so the suspicious emperor put Paulinus to death and divorced Athenaïs.

Perhaps Athenaïs's Christian name, Eudokia, reminded Gautier of Heraclius's first wife, Eudokia, thus giving him the idea of incorporating this narrative into his version of the life of Heraclius.[25] However, if this *was* his source, he has modified it substantially, for his Eracle is the cuckolded emperor's adviser, not the emperor himself, and the adulterous episode does not end tragically in *Eracle*. Moreover, Gautier locates Eracle's early life in a Rome ruled by the emperor Laïs, who is still alive when Eracle is elected Emperor of Constantinople. Thus he gives the impression that the empire at the time of Heraclius had two emperors, one in Rome and another in Constantinople, which reflects the situation in the twelfth century more closely than that in the seventh (and is also the case in his *Ille et Galeron*).

The influence of Byzantine history, literature, culture and customs pervades *Eracle* and since no composite source has been identified, it is likely that Gautier himself combined these disparate Greek elements into a cohesive narrative. One can only speculate as to why he undertook this task of compilation. It was possibly the result of his own interest in Byzantine material following travel abroad or conversations with travellers. More likely though it was in response to the interests of his patrons at the courts of Blois, Troyes and Provins that he composed a work on the emperor who recovered the Holy Cross from pagan hands. Links with the Holy Land were strong in Champagne, where the first Grand Master of the Temple, Hugues des Payens was born, and where Templar houses had been established in Provins and Troyes (Fourrier 1960,

---

[25] Or perhaps the fact that, according to the seventh-century *Chronicon paschale*, Athenaïs's father was the philosopher Heraclitus!

254). Henri le Libéral had himself been sent to Constantinople to be knighted by the Emperor Manuel I Comnenus in 1147 and was planning to take up the Cross around the time Gautier composed *Eracle*. Indeed, he returned from the Holy Land in 1181 with a relic of the True Cross. So Gautier's patrons' special interest in the True Cross, in St Judas Cyriacus and in Byzantium probably explains why the cleric they protected produced the Graeco-Byzantine romance of *Eracle*.

The Genre of Eracle

For modern critics *Eracle* is a romance, sometimes categorised further as a Graeco-Byzantine romance. This generic label clearly raises expectations in us about its form and content, yet Gautier's work does not fit easily into modern definitions of the genre. However, this may be because our conception of romance is based in particular on Arthurian romance from Chrétien de Troyes onwards and is less appropriate for early French narratives. In the following analysis of *Eracle* the term romance will be applied to those features in Gautier's work which twentieth-century scholars have identified as being the normal hallmarks of the genre: love and chivalric adventure, the evolution of the hero, sophisticated rhetorical elaboration, and tension between an idealising and an ironic, critical spirit.[26] The assumption should not be made, however, that contemporary poets would have recognized these features as belonging to a discrete genre. Besides, although Kelly has shown that the term *roman* is used 'generically' by medieval authors to refer to their compositions (*The Art*, p. 324, note 36 and especially Chrétien's *Charrete*, lines 2 and 7101), it is unlikely they were using the word as specifically as we do. This contention is supported by the fact that a range of terms is employed in *Eracle* to refer to the text, with the word 'roman' occurring only twice in the prologue: 'Assés vous dirai el romans' (95) and 'Si com m'orés el romans dire' (102). The scribal variation in these lines indicates that their meaning was unclear to contemporaries: line 95 in MS *A* reads 'es romans', whereas in *BT* it reads 'en roumans' i.e. 'in the vernacular'. This is also the meaning of *T*'s variant for line 102 'en roumanch dire'. The manuscript evidence thus questions whether Gautier was using the term *romans* generically or was simply distinguishing between the language of his work and that of his Latin sources. Moreover, even if 'el romans' did refer to his own composition, Gautier may be saying no more than 'in this narrative'. Indeed, he also calls *Eracle* a *traitié* (3) and its composition is described by the verbs *traire* (*B* variant, 3) and *traitier* (6517, 6531), perhaps evoking the Latin *tractatus*, an authoritative explanation of a point of doctrine. Most frequently, though,

---

[26] See Douglas Kelly, *The Art of Medieval French Romance* (Madison: University of Wisconsin Press, 1992); Simon Gaunt, *Gender and Genre in Medieval French Literature* (Cambridge: Cambridge University Press, 1995), chapter 2; and Tony Hunt, *Chrétien de Troyes: Yvain* (London: Grant and Cutler, 1986), 14-22.

the work is called an *oevre* (86, 114, 6521, 6525), a more general term with associations of craftsmanship, but also of good works, thus linking Gautier d'Arras's efforts with those of his illustrious protagonist Eracle. The courtly section contains the only allusion to a *contes* (2746), but this probably just means 'story'. It is doubtful therefore that any of the above terms is a synonym for romance as we now define it.

No generic terms are to be found in the scribal incipits and explicits either, the work is simply *about* Eracle:

A: 'Chest d'eracle l'empereour' and 'Explicit d'eracle'

B: 'AMEN d'Eracle'

T: 'Explichit del enpereour eracle'.

The manuscript context of the work does, however, yield a few generic clues. In MS *A*, *Eracle* is in the company of religious and/or historical works, bestiaries and scientific treatises; in *B* it is with secular romances, *contes*, a saint's life, and some religious and historical texts; in *T*, it is copied with romances, including Chrétien's *Cligés* (see pp. xlviii-lii below). The evidence for generic classification by the author, scribes, commissioners or compilers of manuscripts is therefore inconclusive, especially as some of the texts found with *Eracle* are equally difficult to categorise. Yet the work does seem to have been perceived by some as religious history, especially by the producer of *B*, who has inserted it, along with a saint's life and a crusading text, into a chronicle. Moreover, its Byzantine connections no doubt influenced the compilers of *A* and *T*, who included it with material about Cligés.

If *Eracle* is a *roman* in the twelfth-century sense of the term, its inclusion of very different source material in its three fairly distinct parts stretches to their limits any modern definitions of the genre. The *enfances* section draws on the Bible and hagiography in adapting the oriental folk-tale motif of the boy with three gifts. Gautier then switches to a more obviously 'romance' mode, intermingled with traditional antifeminist commonplaces, when Eracle's third gift is put to the test during a bride show. The adultery episode is dominated by the diction of courtly love, characterised by highly rhetorical monologues and interior dialogues, but the old woman in her role as *entremetteuse* is of Ovidian and *fabliau* origins (Pratt 2007b). In the final section, Eracle, the *puer senex* (wise boy) turned knight, metamorphoses into a precursor of Charlemagne, becoming the hero of a crusading epic. The religious atmosphere of the *enfances* returns at the end as Eracle is punished for his pride, then rewarded for his humility. Thus, a superficial reading of *Eracle* suggests that it is a generically hybrid text, with different episodes drawing on different genres, modes or discourses, each of which creates its own set of audience expectations.[27] Yet a closer reading reveals that even within these

---

[27] See Hans-Robert Jauss, 'Littérature médiévale et théorie des genres', *Poétique*, 1 (1970), 79-101.

episodes Gautier mixes major and minor registers, or what Kathryn Gravdal calls the generic dominant and interpretant.[28] The role of the interpretant or mediating tradition can be to encourage a reinterpretation of the dominant genre through intergeneric play. In fact, though, as Gravdal points out (13), all medieval literature is to some extent intergeneric, and as we shall see, *Eracle* provides us with a particularly rich example. Indeed, it forces us to redefine what we understand by twelfth-century romance.

In the following detailed analysis of the text's three sections several genre-related factors will be considered:[29]

1. the gendered presentation of the protagonists;[30]
2. the subject-matter and themes treated;
3. the diction, style and register adopted;
4. the relationship created between narrator and audience.

Although the term 'romance' will be used to refer to a mode of writing as defined by modern critics, we should not assume that Gautier's contemporaries would have recognised it as a discrete genre with characteristic, distinctive or constitutive features (Hunt, *Yvain*, 14-19). A degree of eclecticism may well have been a feature of early *romans*.

The narrative proper begins by creating in the audience the expectation of a saint's life. Although two noble characters worthy of any courtly or chivalric romance are introduced, the most prominent feature is their religious faith, and God is clearly a key protagonist. Intertextual allusion is to hagiographical works such as the *Vie de Saint Alexis* and to biblical accounts of pious but childless couples (Pierreville 2001, 20-24). Eracle's conception is dominated by the theme of obedience to God and the result is a child at first named Diudonné (225), then Eracle. Like the hero of chivalric romance, Eracle is an *élu*, a special person with a destiny to fulfil; unlike romance, and more akin to the crusading epic, is the sense that his destiny is not individual but collective, although his mission is not fully revealed until the third, more epic part of *Eracle*. His life is also in imitation of Christ; he is the *agnus dei* taken to be sold at market (429-32). The Christian tone of Part I is further enhanced by the many manifestations of the *merveilleux chrétien*:[31] miracles, angelic visitations, divine letters, and mysterious origins for the stone and colt which Eracle's powers enable him to select.

---

[28] See Kathryn Gravdal, 'Poem Unlimited: Medieval Genre Theory and the Fabliau', *L'Esprit créateur*, 23 (1993), 10-17.

[29] My analysis, based on the generic interpretants provided by the source material, divides the text into three parts: I: lines 1-1918, II: lines 1919-5087 and III: lines 5088-end. Gautier's own narrative divisions based on thematic content are considered below.

[30] Here Gaunt's arguments concerning the relationship between gender and genre will be borne in mind, although the intergeneric nature of *Eracle* problematises this relationship and would explain the complex, shifting treatment of gender in this work.

[31] A feature which links Parts I and III. For letters from heaven, see Pierreville 2001, 24-25.

Although the hero of *Eracle* is a man, Eracle's mother Cassine plays a primary role in Part I.[32] Her willingness to seduce her husband in the somewhat novel circumstances prescribed by the angel links her obedience towards God with that of the Virgin Mary. Her very active form of Christianity is manifest when she funds her alms-giving by selling all her inherited wealth and even her own son. This self-inflicted poverty is not only an extreme sign of her piety; it also challenges the concept of inheritance through the male line practised by twelfth-century feudal society and promoted by Arthurian romance. Indeed, patrilineage is frequently replaced in this work by real or symbolic matrilineage. Throughout Part I, Eracle remains his mother's son, largely uninfluenced by masculine values, even after arriving at the imperial court. His spiritual lineage is maternal, whereas lack of faith, the antithesis of him and his mother, is represented by the men at court. Similarly, the empress Athanaïs is presented as the spiritual heir of Cassine, descriptions of her piety echoing those of Eracle's mother (335-44, 2926-58, especially 127-28 and 2958). Two strong female subjects thus provide a link between Parts I and II, while the male protagonist seems to be gendered feminine through his association with them and their values.[33]

The diction of Part I is characterised by hyperbole and a moralising tone on the part of the narrator and pious characters. The language is gnomic, often expressing proverbial wisdom and Christian truths (Pierreville 2001, 323-32). Repetition of key phrases reminds one of more oral genres, especially sermons[34] and it is in Part I that the narrator's presence is most obtrusive in his role as story-teller and commentator on the action. Numerous verbs in the first and second persons underline the narrator's role in conveying a message to his audience and in creating a sense of community with them. This characteristic, usually associated with epic or hagiography rather than with romance, returns in Part III. The frequent use of the future tense in proleptic remarks emphasises the omniscience of the narrator, who, like God, presides over the action and knows the outcome. Thus the audience is reassured at moments of tension that God's elect will prevail. Similarly, Eracle's progress from gifted young lad to defender of Christendom is signalled by phrases beginning 'or est',[35] which convey narratorial approval and encourage the audience's participation in an exemplary narrative unfolding

---

[32] This accords with Gaunt's view that hagiography gives female characters more scope to act as subjects than romance; compare *Gender and Genre*, chaps 2 and 4.
[33] St Helena in Part III is yet another strong, pious woman in this work.
[34] Gautier's style is embellished by the use of enumeration, *frequentatio* and chiasmus, though there is a limited range of vocabulary used. Repetition of key phrases such as 'Fius, bien ait tele engenreüre!' (421, 571) and 'sainte est la vie que il mainent' (357; 648 in the singular) echoes the oratory of medieval preaching, while the commentary on Eracle's exploits provided by the common people is reminiscent of Beroul's *Tristran*. On the orality of *Eracle*'s diction, see Zumthor 1984.
[35] See lines 998, 1134, 1245, 1510-14, 1766, 1893-94, 1919, 2661, 2847, 2856.

before their very eyes (or ears) and presented largely in the present tense. Thus in Part I the moral lessons to be learned are made explicit, although digressions on the evils of envy continue into the 'romance' section of the narrative – not surprisingly given the role of envy at court, the setting which links Parts I and II of *Eracle*.[36]

Part II starts with a bride show, in which a new courtly tone combines with a continuation of the moralising of Part I, as the vice of each prospective bride is revealed. While misogyny and *courtoisie* are often bedfellows in Old French romance, Gautier seems to have separated out the material. The explicitly antifeminist remarks we associate with didactic literature are reserved for Athanaïs's defeated rivals.[37] On the other hand, the empress's adulterous love is treated more positively and with dignity. There is also a difference in the gender roles these women embody. The prospective brides are taken to the show by their male relatives, who remind them not to forget family loyalty should they win the crown (1978-91). Their role is that of female-as-marriage-pawn within patriarchal society, a role women often play in medieval romance. However, Athanaïs, being an orphan with only one pious *female* relative, is largely free of such patriarchal influences (2576-81). Indeed, she expresses this freedom most fully, becoming a desiring subject, in the very section of the narrative which is closest thematically to romance, the genre which so often objectifies married women. In this way Gautier's work and his female protagonist challenge the gender paradigms identified by modern critics in much twelfth-century romance (see Gaunt, *Gender and Genre*, 71-75, 187).

In the bride show located on the cusp between Parts I and II Gautier invokes misogynist commonplaces characteristic of the *fabliau* and didactic literature when he portrays Eracle examining and rejecting representatives of seven female sins (2163-2572). After much searching, the ideal bride is found in the most unlikely place, Gautier here seeming to confirm both Solomon's adage that a good woman is a rare thing (Proverbs 31: 10) and the Christian commonplace that an object of great inner worth is often unimpressive externally. Thus Eracle chooses the poorly dressed, pious Athanaïs. Although aristocratic marriages in the twelfth century were usually arranged rather than love matches, Gautier follows the new literary fashion of presenting conjugal partners as courtly lovers. Part II is dominated by 'romance' mode as both Eracle and Laïs become representatives of *courtoisie* – Eracle in the polite way he addresses the girl and her aunt (2619ff), and Laïs, whose handsome appearance suddenly seems worthy of note (2031-41), in his behaviour as lover. After the marriage, he becomes a jealous husband, stricken with an Ovidian-style passion. Laïs is thus a 'fin amant', whose normal sanity

---

[36] See lines 21-23, 77-84, 968-76, 1059-72, 1251-57, 1391, 1674-76, 1846, 2099, 2938, 3252, and Pratt 1987, 318-20.

[37] Apart from Paridés's comment on haughty women (3755-798b), provoked by his feeling of inferiority.

has been transformed into irrational behaviour by the power of love (2959-68, 2992-3009). Enjoying our sympathy for a short while, the emperor soon loses it when he rejects Eracle's advice, and locks up his wife. Now Athanaïs is the *mal mariée*,[38] who is allowed to defend her adulterous love in lengthy rhetorical monologues and interior dialogues typical of medieval romance. Although her narrative function is to prove the wisdom of Eracle, God's elect, thus providing a strong link with the hagiographical plot of Part I, Gautier has nevertheless created in her a female subject quite unlike the objects of desire and passive pawns used in Arthurian romance to cement homosocial bonding. With her sense of self wounded by unjust imprisonment, Athanaïs decides, even before seeing athletic Paridés, that she will not tolerate her situation (3313). Although she subsequently falls victim to Ovidian-style love, displaying the usual symptoms, the empress's love is predominantly courtly, an act of will, and her lengthy monologues become convincing rationalisations of her emotions. Gautier justifies her actions in courtly terms, even allowing her to conclude that God would approve of her love because it inspires courtly virtues in her (3710-22).

Irony, sometimes deemed a characteristic of romance, is surprisingly absent from this presentation of illicit love by the author of the strongly moralistic first part of *Eracle*. Indeed the happy outcome of the episode for the lovers mitigates against a critical reading of the affair. Moreover, audience sympathy and identification with the lovers (who are praised for practising the courtly virtue *mesure*, 4709-11) is won by evoking the traditional idea that only true lovers will appreciate their feelings (3809-42). The authorial omniscience noted in Part I is still in evidence in this section in the prophetic remarks on the pains of love (3476-78), and warnings to the audience that Laïs is about to be checkmated by his queen (4388-90). There are even moments when the narrator's exclamations seem to celebrate the lovers' joy: 'Cil est molt liés, ce poés croire' (4450) and 'Or sont li amant molt a aise' (4599; cf. 4486), the latter formulation echoing the approbatory 'Or est Eracles' phrase which punctuated the hero's ascent in Part I. In the light of this subtle narratorial bias, the activities of the elderly *entremetteuse*, though reminiscent of *fabliaux*-plots,[39] do not imply moral criticism of or ironic distance from the lovers' predicament.

The diction of Part II is primarily courtly, except for the dialogue with the *vieille*, which is sometimes bawdy and humorous, and the narrator's antifeminist comments during the bride show. The love interlude is above all dominated by monologues and internal dialogues, during which the protagonists describe their feelings and the empress analyses her possible courses of action. In their rhetorical sophistication and

---

[38] The literary type of the young girl married to a jealous husband, found notably in the *Lais* of Marie de France.

[39] See the popular tale of the 'bénitier d'ordure', which was originally an Ovidian tale used as a moral exemplum (Fourrier 1960, 229-30)

dialectical organisation they have much in common with the language of Chrétien's *Cligés* (Pratt 2007a), yet without the latter's irony.

So, Part II of *Eracle* shows many features of courtly romance, but is unusual in its treament of gender. For although Athanaïs's function in relation to the work's protagonist is to enhance the reputation for wisdom of the male hero, she dominates Part II of *Eracle* as she evolves into a desiring subject who drives the narrative forward, an *actant* in narratological terms whose courtly concept of love is justified and ultimately rewarded with marriage to her beloved.

Part III begins with a historical synopsis on the Invention of the Cross, in which we find another strong Christian female in the mould of Cassine and Athanaïs, namely St Helena. Gautier then describes Eracle's election as emperor of Constantinople. In relating the subsequent recovery of the Cross from the pagans, he gives epic treatment to source material taken from a Latin *Passionarius*. Here, as in many *chansons de geste*, Eracle's masculinity is tested in a wholly male environment. Indeed, in the epic section of Part III the female genealogy we noted in the hagiographical episodes of *Eracle* is replaced by a male one. First, Eracle has to overcome a father and son, the former worshipped by his people like the Antechrist, the latter a valiant warrior misguided in his beliefs. Second, Eracle, resembling a saint in that he has no heir, is succeeded by Chosroes' younger son, who is converted to Christianity and brought up as Eracle's protégé, thus evoking the symbolic paternity common in hagiography and *chansons de geste* (6421-26).[40]

Epic motifs (Pierreville 2001, 302-03) in this section include council scenes, the exchange of hostages (5597-98), the arming of the hero (5599-5613), attempts before battle to convert the opponent (5632-5703) and unchivalric behaviour in battle (5774, 5791-92, 5816-18). Although the metrical form of the octosyllabic rhyming couplet may have contributed to the suppression and modification of the more formal aspects of epic discourse, epic diction is represented by exaggerated boasts (5634-36), prayers to God (5729-38) and the ironic image of 'aigre sausse' (5812) to refer to an epic blow.[41] By employing 'les nos' (5426) to refer to the Christians, Gautier's narrator creates in the audience the feeling of a community of believers, characteristic of crusading epic and hagiography. *Eracle* ends on a homiletic note with the punishment of Eracle for his moment of hybris. The language becomes biblical and proverbial as the moralising,

---

[40] See Sarah Kay, *The Chanson de Geste in the Age of Romance* (Oxford: Clarendon Press, 1995). This detail is added by Gautier to his Latin source. The historical Heraclius was succeeded by two sons who seemingly bore his name: Heraclius-Constantine, then Heraklonas. Gautier's Eracle is childless, but the problem of succession has been solved by implying that the emperor's adoptive son, the pagan given the Christian name Heraclius, took over the imperial mantle.

[41] See Jean Rychner, *La Chanson de geste. Essai sur l'art épique des jongleurs* (Geneva: Droz, 1955) and Pierreville 2001, appendix 6.

intrusive narrator of Part I returns. There is also a return to the feminine gendering which was noted in the earlier hagiographical section. When confronted by the walls of Jerusalem closed before him, it is noteworthy that Eracle's prayer for divine forgiveness does not invoke male biblical figures, but Mary Magdalen (6301). Moreover, his fear that future generations will curse the child of his mother's womb suggests that he sees himself primarily as his mother's son, the reference to his father coming as something of an afterthought (6319-23). Finally, in donning a hair shirt (6242) he is imitating Cassine's pious behaviour in Part I (649).

Although the division of *Eracle* into three discrete parts has facilitated this analysis of their respective generic interpretants, it is clear that Gautier employs a variety of discourses and intertextual allusions within the different sections, resulting sometimes in a blurring of the sectional boundaries. Thus Cassine is presented as pious, but also courtly (120), and the horse race to test Eracle's choice of a mount is introduced by the epic phrase 'Biax est li tans et clers li jors' (1639). A certain narrative cohesion is created when in Part II Athanaïs, falling from her horse as a prelude to her act of infidelity, invokes the Holy Cross (4537), which dominates Part III. Likewise, although she seems to change from pious to adulterous queen, her speech on sin and the role Eracle will play in her discovery (4605-27) reveals some consistency in Gautier's conception, not only of her character, but also of the eponymous hero and the message he embodies throughout the work. Indeed, the hagiographical tone with which *Eracle* begins returns at the very end, making it a generically symmetrical text (Lacy 1986, 228-29).

While *Eracle*'s 'generic hybridity' as analysed above makes it difficult for modern scholars to classify, this was probably not an issue for Gautier's contemporaries, who seem to have used the term *roman* very broadly. Given the historico-biographical nature of *Eracle*, however, one could argue that this work most comfortably fits the genre of historiography, which in the twelfth century included texts such as the *Brut*, *Rou*, *Enéas*, *Thèbes* and *Troie*, works often designated by modern critics as romances, although other generic terminology is used by their authors. Indeed, set mainly in Rome and drawing on at least one Latin source, *Eracle* seems to exemplify Jean Bodel's second type in his famous taxonomy based on the *matières* or content of medieval literature:[42]

> Li conte de Bretaigne sont si vain et plaisant,
> Cil de Rome sont sage et de sens aprendant.
> Cil de France sont voir chacun jour aparant.
>
> (*The tales of Britain are so frivolous and amusing; those of Rome are wise and teach us good sense; those of France are shown to be true every day*).

Eracle would thus be a didactic, exemplary work of history (Wolfzettel 1990b), whose

---

[42] Jean Bodel, *Chanson des Saisnes*, 9-11.

moral is more important than its historical accuracy. Significantly, historiographical features such as veracity claims (5125, 6173-80),[43] the invocation of written sources (5119, 5126, 6089-90, 6100-01, 6435) or eye-witness accounts (1282), plus a high degree of geographical and chronological precision are to be found mainly towards the end of *Eracle*. Elsewhere, different modes dominate. Given 'the intergeneric nature of the medieval text' (Gravdal, 'Poem Unlimited', 13) it may be better to resist applying generic labels to whole works. All one can say is that the dominant of *Eracle* is historico-biographical narrative, while the generic interpretants for each part would be hagiography, courtly romance and epic respectively.

To conclude, Gautier's *Eracle* is a *roman* in the sense that it is a vernacular narrative in octosyllabic rhyming couplets, a 'texte narratif non chanté'.[44] It partakes of and alludes to a network of medieval literary traditions: historiography, epic, hagiography, folk-tale, antifeminist didactic writing, the *fabliaux* and courtly romance. In its narrative aesthetic it is closer to the *romans antiques* ('Cil de Rome') than to the Arthurian romances of Chrétien de Troyes ('Li conte de Bretaigne').

The Structure and Unity of Eracle

Eracle's 'generic eclecticism' resulting from the inclusion of disparate source material led earlier scholars to underestimate the artistic achievement of Gautier d'Arras (see Calin 1962, 275 for a summary of disparaging remarks on Gautier's romances). However, modern critics, notably Calin (1962), Lacy (1986), Eley (1989) and Wolfzettel (1990b) argue that *Eracle* does not consist of a loosely connected series of exciting episodes, but that it is carefully constructed and unified by certain key themes. Authorial interventions scattered throughout the text further suggest that Gautier made a conscious effort to organise and harmonise his subject-matter.[45] The lengthy plot summary in the prologue (87-113), in listing the highlights of Eracle's life, demonstrates that he intended his protagonist's biography to confer unity on the whole work. Then, just before the courtly interlude, Gautier draws his audience's attention to Eracle's later role in the recovery of the Cross, thus forging a link between the *enfances* and mature exploits of his hero (2900-02). These proleptic comments are accompanied by a first-person intervention in which Gautier claims obedience to his subject-matter or the *histoire*, while reserving for himself an authoritative control over the *récit* or order in which he relates events (2903-14). Rejecting interlace (*entrelacier*, 2903), he nevertheless follows Laïs briefly on campaign. However, another authorial intervention (3215-23) marks his return to the

---

[43] Other uses of the term *voir* are rather conventional: 2917, 2932, 3827.
[44] Paul Zumthor, *Essai de poétique médiévale* (Paris: Seuil, 1972), 159.
[45] According to Lorenza Arzenton Valeri (1990) Gautier's romance derives its authority more from the active and intrusive authorial persona he creates than from source references.

main focus of his story – the feelings of the imprisoned empress. The marriage crisis resolved, Gautier finally turns his attention to Eracle's crusading exploits. At this point Part III is clearly separated from the rest of the work by another comment in the first person on textual organisation:

> Il n'afiert pas a ma matere
> Que je plus die de Laïs,
> De Pariden, d'Athanaïs;
> Iceus vos lairons ore em pais,
> Si vos dirons d'Eracle humais (5088-92),

a plot summary, and a reference to a Latin source:

> Se bon vous ert a escouter,
> Bon me seroit huimais a dire
> Coment fu puis et rois et sire,
> Et par quele aventure avint
> Que il Coustanioble tint,
> Et le veraie Crois conquist...
> Signor, nos lisons en latin... (5110-15, 5119)

'Hu(i)mais' (5092 and 5111) is clearly an authorial marker of structural division. It also occurs, as one would expect, at the end of the prologue, just before the narrative proper: 'Humais voel m'oevre commenchier' (114). However, its occurrence in line 2746, 'Huimais commencera li contes', just as Athanaïs is about to be married, is more surprising. Raynaud de Lage (edn, xiii, xv) takes this to be the beginning of Part II (dedicated to the empress's love story), Part III starting at line 5093.[46] In fact, line 2746 affords a tantalising parallel with Chrétien de Troyes's 'premiers vers' at a similar point in the plot of *Erec et Enide* (1796), and it seems that Gautier, like Chrétien, views the bride-winning section as a separate narrative unit from the turbulent events of married life. Both authors may also be signalling a change of source here and pointing explicitly to the joins in their *conjointure*.[47]

However, for those critics concerned to demonstrate the thematic unity of *Eracle*, a structural division at line 2746 is problematic (Lacy 1986, 230). As Calin (1962) and Eley (1989) have argued, the themes of faith and doubt provide a unifying thread throughout the work, and this is signalled as early as the prologue (98). God's elect, the boy with three gifts, is at first disbelieved, then put to the test, and eventually proved right.

---

[46] Zumthor (1984, 195) suggests that the word in lines 2746 and 5092 marks possible breaks in the oral recitation of the text over three sessions.

[47] See Kelly, *The Art*, 17 and 319, *conjointure* being for him the artful combination of different elements into a harmonious whole. According to Lacy (1986, 230), the *conte* is a self-contained episode which Gautier has integrated into a longer narrative

From this perspective the episode of Athanaïs's adultery constitutes the final section of Eracle's *enfances*, the ultimate proof of the young man's veracity and wisdom, which qualify him to be the Christian emperor who will recover the Holy Cross.[48] Thus *Eracle* is thematically bipartite: the *épreuves qualifiantes* of the emperor's early life (115-5091) are followed by his mature exploits (5092-end), culminating in the *épreuve principale*, the recapture of the Cross.[49] Yet as we have seen, the work is generically tripartite, the interpretant of each section being dictated largely by its main source. Despite the bipartite macro-structure, the material in the *enfances* half is organised in threes: for each of Eracle's gifts there are three stages: he makes a claim, is greeted with disbelief, yet is proved right; to provide evidence the emperor organises three events: two markets and a bride show. Three ordeals verify the stone's powers; the colt is tested in a relay race against three opponents. Moreover, there is gradation in the difficulty of the tests: each ordeal becomes more dangerous and each rival horse faster (1727-28). Although the testing of the ideal wife takes a different form, it fits into the general pattern: whereas the stone is not harmed during the ordeals, the colt is ruined by premature racing and the empress by her imprisonment – both outcomes predicted by Eracle.[50]

In the second half of the romance it is Eracle's own faith in God that is tested, and although he succumbs momentarily to pride, neither Eracle nor Christendom suffer permanently. It is here that another important unifying theme identified by Wolfzettel (1990b) is revealed: Eracle's biography exemplifies the importance of election over birth, for his story is that of the self-made man who succeeds on account of his God-given talents and clerical discernment rather than because of the advantages of lineage.[51] Thus *Eracle* differs enormously from Arthurian romance, which tends to celebrate inherited aristocratic virtues and demonstrates how young knights can win land and honour through chivalric exploits and/or marriage. Although it is important that Eracle has noble parents (2856-60), he inherits nothing from them (apart from their piety), secures a position at court because of his wisdom and is elected Emperor of Constantinople thanks to his reputation for justice (5093-5109, 5265-68). Eracle therefore functioned as an exemplary figure for all those ambitious men from more humble backgrounds who sought advancement at the courts of kings and dukes in twelfth-century Europe.

---

[48] It is therefore important to Eracle that he is not falsely accused of advising the emperor to lock up his wife (5017-44). Two erroneous corrections in the edition by Raynaud de Lage (3652-54, 5017) obscure Gautier's insistence that his hero should be seen as blameless (see pp. lxii-lxiii below).

[49] The terminology is taken from narratology, which analyses the adventures of the Arthurian hero in terms of *épreuves*. See A. J. Greimas and J. Courtés, *Sémiotique: dictionnaire raisonné de la théorie du langage*, I (Paris: Hachette, 1979), 304.

[50] This ternary arrangement anticipates the three crosses of Part III.

[51] It is noteworthy that Athanaïs too is 'elected' (2758) and that the same meritocratic ideal is present in *Ille et Galeron*.

Although Gautier's idea of a *bele conjointure* (beautifully structured narrative) was not exactly that espoused by his rival Chrétien, an organising principle is definitely at work in *Eracle*, and from it emerges a clear moral message concerning the virtues of Christian faith. Whereas many modern critics prefer the classicising aesthetic of *Erec et Enide* or *Yvain* to the more baroque approach to style and content of Gautier, the latter's eclecticism and preference for detail rather than overall narrative cohesion may actually be more representative of the aesthetics of twelfth-century fiction than the iconic romances of Chrétien de Troyes.

Themes & Characters

In common with most medieval writers, Gautier subordinates the presentation of character to the investigation of topics of contemporary interest. For example, although there is some detailed psychological analysis of his lovers' emotions, the poet's main concern is to explore the nature of love. Indeed, many of his characters are representative types, and their depiction is dictated to some extent by the intertextual models Gautier is exploiting. Thus Cassine and Miriados are exemplary of the pious but childless Christian couple common in hagiography, Laïs is both the ruler susceptible to bad advice and later the married courtly lover whose possessiveness leads to alienating his wife (a type known from courtly romance and from some of Marie de France's *lais*); the old woman is a stock literary character, the go-between we find in the *fabliaux*; and even the eponymous hero exemplifies the true faith and service to God which characterise the protagonists of hagiography and the crusading epic (see *The Genre of Eracle* above). Although he is occasionally disappointed that he has not been able to find what he is looking for, Eracle never abandons his trust in God and never really suffers from crises of conscience or moral conflicts. Thus he differs from the heroes of Arthurian romance, whose characters are moulded by the challenges they overcome during their quests and who evolve into mature individuals.[52] In fact, the main characters in *Eracle* are barely individualised; instead they fall into two groups: those who embody the values promoted by Gautier, and those antagonistic to them. They thus have much in common with the positive and negative *exempla* associated with medieval didactic texts and history writing. This section will therefore focus on themes, with character being treated primarily as a vehicle for the discussion of ideas. However, Gautier's depiction of women and love will be analysed more thoroughly, since it involves deeper psychological investigation, and it is in the presentation of Athanaïs and Paridés that his subtle understanding of human psychology and gift for character portrayal emerges.

---

[52] Although Eracle rises in status, his character does not really change. God's punishment of him before the walls of Jerusalem merely corrects a temporary fault; it does not trigger the sort of maturation process undergone by Chrétien's Yvain.

Gautier's *Eracle* treats several topics which were being debated by clerical court authors in the twelfth century. Many of his themes relate to Christian doctrine and morality, and here his message is orthodox and traditional. However, Gautier's concerns are also secular and political, especially in relation to the allocation and use or abuse of power. No doubt his association with the courts of powerful French nobles and his precarious position as a poet dependent on their patronage made him particularly interested in the evil machinations of courtiers. The castigation of court vices including envy, slander, flattery and avarice fits well with the Christian morality he preaches and Gautier shows how much more dangerous these qualities can be in those who advise rulers. Through the leitmotif of appearances and reality (Schmitz 1992) the superficiality of court life and the inability of some rulers to discern what is right and good are satirised. By contrasting the perspicacity of Eracle with Laïs's poor judgement, Gautier encourages his audience to consider which qualities are vital in those who wield power.

The abuse of power in a domestic setting is the theme of the central section of the romance, in which Athanaïs's adultery is explained by her husband's desire to control her, but also by his lack of trust in her and in the advice of God's elect. Although the overarching theme here is the demonstration of Eracle's wisdom, the bride-winning and testing section of the romance contributes in interesting ways to the medieval debate on women and love. After the bride show episode, dominated by traditional antifeminist tropes and much moralising, Gautier provides a sympathetic and far less judgemental analysis of Athanaïs's ethical and emotional conflict. Moreover, in allowing his lovers the happy ending afforded by marriage, Gautier is one of the few twelfth-century writers to seem to condone adulterous courtly love, at least in certain circumstances.

Eracle is also interesting for the themes it does not treat. Chivalry, the staple of Arthurian romance, is barely discussed by Gautier. His hero's masculinity is not constructed by means of marvellous adventures, trials of strength and feats of prowess. Eracle is a clerical, rather than chivalric, hero. His main characteristics are his excellent judgement and faith in God, which enable him during his 'ordeals' to endure tests of a spiritual and mental rather than physical nature. Even in the epic section, Eracle's prowess in battle is not given prominence (there is more talking than fighting!). Indeed, his victory is attributed to inspiration from the Holy Cross (5740-41) and, as the angel makes clear, to God's help in answer to the emperor's prayers, not to the latter's personal strength (6213-17).

A. Religion

Both Gautier's narrator and his 'good' characters frequently adopt a moralising tone and employ gnomic language usually inspired by the Bible to promote orthodox Christian teaching. The importance of faith in and obedience to God are exemplified by Eracle's parents (during their son's conception and Cassine's arrangements after the death of her husband), by the horse owner for believing God's messenger (1456-80) and by Eracle himself (469-72, 821-26, 850-59, 1016-21), who never succumbs to despair, although he is sorely tested over the bride show (2573-74). The superiority of believers over doubters, whether pagans or those who ridicule God's elect, is demonstrated by the emperor's defeat of his pagan enemies in battles resembling judgements of God, and by the youth's silencing of the slanderers at court and neutralisation of any power they had over Laïs (1880-82). The Christian values of hope, humility, poverty and charity are embodied by Cassine, Athanaïs and Eracle. Both mother and son are keen on almsgiving and treating the poor with dignity (340-42, 643-44, 6238-40, see in particular Eracle's attitude towards the stone and colt owners, 865-76, 1455-92) and both found religious establishments (337-39, 6053-60). Athanaïs, before her imprisonment, represents an exemplary Christian sovereign (2927-58). The ideal life in imitation of Christ is in particular espoused by Cassine (357-60, 648-50), and although Eracle's imperial duties make retreat from the world of politics impossible for him, he still practises religious observances such as prayer (5729-38, 5767-69, 5897-5943, 6271-6338) and self mortification (6242-43). Moreover, in being compared to the lamb of God (429-31) and to Christ on Palm Sunday (6087-6232), he is presented as a type of Christ.

Gautier portrays the individual Christian's relationship with God as personal, for God communicates directly with his elect through letters and angelic visitations. This bond, modelled on the feudal relationship of lord and vassal with its emphasis on reward for service, dominates the words of both characters and the narrator (170, 316-18, 327-34,[53] 585-87, 610-14, 853-59, 1474-76, 2950-52, 6411-15 and 6467-78). Yet although God rewards the faithful (the economic vocabulary of profiting from investments – especially the use of the verb *accroire* – is striking here), success in this life is in God's gift, and the good Christian should always be aware that what has been lent to him (602-04) could easily be taken away. It is particularly important for those in power to be grateful for God's favour and use it wisely and humbly, as Athanaïs pledges to her aunt (2766-69, 2773-78). This, of course, is the lesson that Eracle learns before the gates of Jerusalem (6185-6232).

Finally, the Crusading message that belief must be translated into action when the lives of Christians are in peril is made explicit by the angelic messenger sent to the

---

[53] Here Gautier is expressing the orthodox view that the benefits of prayer for the dead can be transferred to another if the deceased has already reached paradise, cf. 6467-78.

emperor (5323-78), who, in defeating the pagans and winning back the Holy Cross, is presented as God's instrument on earth for the propagation of the Christian faith (6456). Thus, *Eracle* can be read as an exemplary Christian narrative, offering both positive and negative examples for the contemporary audience to follow or resist.

B. The Court & Power

As early as the prologue to *Eracle* Gautier takes the opportunity, while flattering his patron Thibaut, to criticise those envious courtiers and lords who fail to indulge in the courtly virtues of distributing largesse to entertainers and exhibiting good humour during festivities, and who promise more than they give (21-46, 65-67, 75, 77-84). Later, during the depiction of Eracle's initial reception at the imperial court and gradual rise in status Gautier focuses not only on the emperor's scepticism, thrown into relief by the seneschal's trust in God's elect, but also on the envy which motivates Eracle's enemies (968-80, 1059-72, 1251-57, 1391-95, 1674-76, 1846; Pratt 1987, 318-20). It becomes clear that vicious courtiers damage their own prospects of salvation (1829-44) and their lying, slander, flattery and bad advice influence rulers to the possible detriment of everyone (Castellani 1990; cf. the role of the evil barons in Beroul's *Tristran*). Eracle points out the shameful consequences of bad advice in lines 1375-80, and much of Part I is taken up with the hero proving his word against those of ill-motivated enemies such as his opponent in the trial by combat (1172-82, 1191-96, 1239-44). Once Laïs has accepted the youth's veracity and promoted him, the narrator is no less scathing about the courtiers' positive response than he was about their negativity. For their affection is not sincere, being born out of a desire to curry favour with their lord. Thus Eracle, like a man's dog, is not mistreated whilst his lord is well disposed towards him (1897-1904, cf. 1504-18).

A corollary to his satire on courtiers' vices is Gautier's criticism of less than perfect lords. *Eracle* demonstrates that with power comes responsibilities and warns that power can corrupt. Athanaïs is aware of this as she is about to embark on her role as empress (2773-78), reiterating the Christian view that the gifts of fortune (power, status and wealth) are lent by God to be well used. Similarly, the relatives of the girls attending the bride show warn them against forgetting their families once they are successful, and this leads to moralising on the importance of a noble heart in the powerful (1983-2008). Most importantly, though, the plot of *Eracle* shows that a ruler must choose his advisers carefully and act on their advice. Clearly Laïs is a negative exemplum in this respect. Although he appears to ask for counsel, he is merely seeking approval for a course of action already decided upon (3010-3162, especially 3065ff). When Athanaïs commits adultery, as predicted, Eracle fears for his reputation because he is familiar with the evil men who frequent courts and can ruin a virtuous man's name:

> «Sire, fait il, des hui matin
> Fu le cose par assoumee
> Dont j'arai male renomee,
> Et a grant tort, mais mençoignier
> Et gengleor et losengier
> Heent adiés ceus qui bien font;
> Ja des malvais ne mesdiront,
> Ançois lor tienent por ce pais
> Que il meïsme sont malvais.» (4740-48)

However, the wise counsellor eventually manages to convince Laïs to accept some responsibility for the adultery (4972, 4999) and to be merciful towards the lovers. In a long moralising speech (4961-5044), whose main theme is 'I told you so', Eracle defends his reputation and notes ironically that lords tend to believe unworthy counsellors more readily than those concerned to preserve their honour (4982-92). So, through the figure of Laïs, Gautier satirises rulers who have inherited their power (2032), but go on to abuse it, offering the elected emperor Eracle as a more effective role-model.

Eracle is shown to have the potential to be an ideal ruler while still a member of Laïs's court (2915-24) and is elected on account of his many qualities (5093-5109).[54] He behaves wisely during the campaign against Chosroes, choosing single combat to spare the lives of his men (5478-84). Not only does he ask for the counsel and support of his men, as was expected of a feudal leader (5440-48), but the fact that their advice is sound marks him out as a worthy sovereign. Despite his one lapse, his lack of humility on entering Jerusalem with the Holy Cross, he is aware that the consequences of his actions could harm others (6315-26), thus displaying the responsibility and *caritas* necessary in a good leader of men and exemplary Christian. On the other hand, the pagan 'god' Chosroes rules his people with fear (5509-12, 5571, 5581-84).

Thus, through the characters of Eracle and his negative counterparts Laïs, Chosroes and the evil courtiers, Gautier offers a meditation on the politics of the court and the qualities required in a Christian ruler worthy of his station. At a time when primogeniture governed the transfer of power and authority in many regions of medieval France, *Eracle* presents the alternative model of the self-made man whose intellectual, moral and chivalric gifts qualify him for high office (Wolfzettel 1990b).

---

[54] These lines are reminiscent of the oft-repeated commonplace that the ideal medieval king spares the fallen and subdues the proud.

C. Women & Love

Laïs's desire to take a wife gives Gautier d'Arras plenty of opportunity to rehearse the commonplace arguments against marriage so prevalent in medieval didactic literature. In this vein the narrator states that choosing a spouse is an important, but dangerous matter if one selects the nettle rather than the rose (1266-70). Later, during the bride show, the narrator makes the traditional link between women and Eve's fall (2083-90), caused, he argues, by covetousness. Indeed, the noblewomen present all seem to be guilty of this sin (2091-95), and of envy (2099-2103), and they are also too quick to criticise God's elect (2197-2200). Furthermore, the chastity of many seems to be in question (2109-29), with Gautier employing humorous euphemisms to describe the degrees of innocence and knowledge of these so-called virgins. However, the poet reserves his most scathing wit and misogyny for the seven women Eracle examines more closely and who seem to represent seven female sins: avarice, lechery, inconstancy, loquacity, arrogance, nastiness, and susceptibility to flatterers. Above all, Gautier associates women with deception, insisting in particular on the deceptive beauty of females, which can hide deeper vices. Using Eracle's ability to see beyond the surface in order to elaborate upon the theme of appearances versus reality, the poet uses a series of comparisons which are very unflattering to women. The latter are like the fox hiding in the shadows (2239), the brass beneath the gold, the lead under the silver (2214-15), for all that glitters is not gold (2244). The emperor seems to share this low opinion of women when he accuses them in rather uncourtly fashion of coveting the role of empress, and predicts that they will behave like children should they be disappointed in their quest (2139-62). That Athanaïs herself later makes a similar comparison between women and children (3901-04) merely betrays Gautier's clerical misogyny, which is patent in the numerous generalisations and proverbial expressions about women found in *Eracle*.[55]

In contrast, the initial presentation of Athanaïs is entirely positive; but this is not surprising since she has been selected by Eracle to be the emperor's wife because she is so exceptional. Athanaïs is presented as an ideal empress just before her husband's fateful decision to lock her in a tower (2811-46, 2927-58).[56] However, it *is* surprising that the empress's response to her unjust treatment, adultery with a young man, is narrated without Gautier's usual moralising. Indeed, rather than punishing his aberrant heroine, he rewards her with marriage to her lover.[57]

---

[55] See Pierreville 2001, 317-19, for a list of gnomic phrases relating to women.

[56] Chrétien's Enide too is described as an ideal queen-in-waiting immediately before the marital crisis produced by Erec's dereliction of his knightly duties (*Erec et Enide*, 2406-29) and in both romances it is the husband's excessive love for his wife which seems to be the cause of the problem (*Erec et Enide*, 2430-32; *Eracle*, 2959-68).

[57] Happy endings are granted to Guigemar and his lady in Marie de France's *lai*, but more often adulterous liaisons in medieval romance lead to much suffering (Lancelot and Guinevere) and death (Tristan, *Yonec*, *Equitan*).

Pierreville (2001, 191-241) reads Part II of the romance as critical of courtly love and of the empress, 'dont l'évolution suggère au contraire une dégradation et un avilissement' (191). She argues that the adulterous relationship is characterised by suffering and fear, that it is carried out in degrading circumstances, aided by the bawdy old woman, and that the lovers are simply concerned to satisfy their sexual desires. In this way, courtly love, masquerading as a superficial veneer for animal passion, is being satirised by Gautier, along with all the other superficial aspects of courtly society, such as beauty and largesse.[58] However, while it would be difficult to believe that Gautier condoned adulterous love, in my view he is not condemning the lovers as strongly as Pierreville contends, but has instead given them lengthy monologues accompanied by some narratorial commentary through which their motivations are explored and their actions explained, even justified, in courtly terms. In fact, as Wolfzettel shows (1988), he has produced a largely sympathetic account of how an active heroine responds to marital injustice and loss of freedom.

Gautier's depiction of Athanaïs's distress is full of psychological insight, as is the advice given by Eracle, but ignored by Laïs, namely that virtuous women commit folly when they lose their self-respect, that they respond better to trust than to mistrust, and that self-control is always more effective than imposed chastity (3030-50, 3079-3125). Because the empress's behaviour has been predicted by Eracle, it seems almost justified, especially as in her monologues she echoes the reasoning of God's elect. Athanaïs's concept of the marriage bond is very similar to that between lord and vassal or between God and Christian: unlike God, her lord and husband Laïs has not rewarded her properly for her service (3273-80, 3344-60) and has thereby dishonoured her. Having received no explanation for her imprisonment, her sense of injustice is unbearable. Thus Athanaïs's infidelity stems from her husband's ill-treatment of her, and begins prior to her meeting with Paridés. Not only does Gautier anticipate modern psychoanalysis by implying that desire precedes the object of desire, but he also presents the empress's love as a conscious act of will, a symbolic, psychological liberation from the physical constraints of the tower. In this respect his heroine resembles Marie de France's *mal mariées*, for example the lady in *Yonec*.

Athanaïs's first major monologue of 133 lines (3227-3360), located at the midpoint of *Eracle*, is introduced by the narrator, whose words seem to support the empress's view of herself as a victim of injustice (3223-26). Contrary to expectations, her lament contains no internal dialogue, no traditional conflict between the heart (normally representing desire) and the conscience. This is because her heart represents a laudable sense of self worth rather than a morally problematic love; her conscience is given no words

---

[58] Given Gautier's apparent status as a poet dependent on patronage, I think it unlikely that he is being critical of courtly largesse.

to speak because Athanaïs has nothing on her conscience. Outraged, her heart seems totally justified in its decision to change her situation:

> Miax ameroie en me cemise
> Estre a honor et a delivre
> Qu'enpereïs a honte vivre!
> A honte sui je voirement,
> Qu'on cuide qu'il soit autrement;
> Autrement seroit il, mon voel! (3308-13)

By the end of her monologue Athanaïs's heart has convinced her that it would be immoral to remain faithful to her husband, a master who fails to reward good service (3317-20). This leads logically to the conclusion of her second monologue, in which she admits that a liaison with Paridés would be foolish, yet ultimately defends her right to love a man who will treat her honourably, invoking personified courtly values to support her inclinations as if they were moral virtues approved of by God:

> Mais cui Amors tient asés prés,
> Orguel li taut et felounie
> Et fausseté et vilonie,
> Et si l'estruit de grant largece,
> De cortoisie et de prouece;
> Et s'en amor a un mesfait,
> Ces coses font vers Diu bon plait,
> Qu'il aime honor et cortoisie
> Et fine Larguece est s'amie.
> Or amerai, si serai large,
> Car Amors fine le m'encarge
> Que je le soie, et jel serai,
> Et sor içou si aquerrai. (3710-22).

While Gautier probably did not believe that courtliness was a substitute for Christian virtue or a real justification for adultery, it is nevertheless the case that Athanaïs's love impels her later to defend her lover altruistically when threatened by punishment (4817-26) and it seems that God does look kindly upon her by allowing her to marry Paridés (5045-70).

A crucial passage for our understanding of Gautier's view of the adultery is the narrator's intervention as the empress sets off for a tryst with her lover. Discussing her motivations, he asks whether her behaviour represents 'folie ou hardemens' (4510). He concludes that she is undertaking folly in a daring manner: 'Et ceste dame dont je di/A en folie cuer hardi' (4515-16).[59] However, this solution contains an unresolved paradox in that he has already defined *hardemens* as proceeding out of *savoir*, not *folie* (4513-14). It seems therefore that while disapproving of Athanaïs's plans, Gautier cannot help but admire the courage of her convictions. Moreover, unlike most medieval heroines she is literate (4378-83), thus sharing an important skill with the author himself.

The love experienced by the protagonists in *Eracle* is Ovidian in nature (Pratt 1987, 305-17) and has elements in common with the passion depicted in the Tristan romances by Thomas and Beroul, and with the codification of love in Andreas Capellanus's *De amore*. Although no arrows are explicitly mentioned (but cf. 3525), the lovers are presented as victims of an all-powerful, aggressive force (3630), falling in love simultaneously through the eyes (3493-94, 3727-30). Until reciprocation is confirmed, the anguish produced by hope and fear is amply expressed through the monologues of the two lovers (3499-3511, 3543-3722, 3736-98b, 3867-3919, 3927-96), who suffer the Ovidian symptoms of paleness (3997), sleeplessness (3817-18), loss of appetite, sobbing and shaking (3925-26). Lamenting provides them with the only form of relief, yet this is not available to Athanaïs because she is so closely guarded (3849-60). Paridés, on the other hand, is tormented by the thought that the empress's high social status will prevent her from loving him (3755-98b). The narrator not only focuses on their suffering, but through parallel syntax (3723-28) emphasises the equality and reciprocity of their love, which is the hallmark more of Tristan-style passion than of courtly love, since the latter tends to give the lady the upper hand. Nevertheless, Paridés is presented as a vassal to Athanaïs's lord when he affirms his gratitude for the gift of her body in a gesture of homage often associated with courtly relations (4633-34).

Although Gautier shares much of his love casuistry with his fellow twelfth-century authors (Pratt 2007a), he does seem to take issue with his rivals ('li auquant', 3520) when debating the possibility of giving one's heart to one's beloved whilst continuing to function (3517-40). He disagrees that the heart can be divided in two, stating instead that love will not make do with less than the whole heart. Yet whilst Chrétien in *Yvain* (2658–59) argues that when the lover loses his heart to his beloved, he fashions a replacement heart from hope, Gautier claims that Love, because she is 'france et debonaire' (3533), occasionally releases her grip to allow the lover to go about his ordinary business.

At the point when the love is consummated (an episode Pierreville considers to be rather sordid), Gautier's narrator asserts, without any hint of irony, that only those who have experienced love will appreciate what his protagonists are experiencing (4588-92). In my view, the love scene is reminiscent of Marie de France's *lais*, in which victims of

---

[59] Cf. the heroine of the lay of *Narcisus et Dané* (edited and translated by Penny Eley at http://www.liv.ac.uk/soclas/los/narcisus.pdf), 472-74. Athanaïs's courage and initiative are reminiscent of Dané, Thisbé and Iseut in the various Tristan poems.

arranged marriages give their bodies freely to genuine lovers, without the need to play the courtly game of deferral in order to enhance their pleasure. For Athanaïs, Paridés is a genuine lover, whose nobility of birth, body and heart make him worthy of her (3618-27).

When Laïs returns, he cannot understand why his wife, whom he has lifted out of poverty, has sacrificed the honour of being empress to her foolish desire (4771-4802, 4911, 4945-60). Paridés is also accused by him of bringing dishonour upon both the emperor and his wife. However, as is clear from the empress's earlier monologues, the lovers and the emperor possess different concepts of honour. For the latter, it involves wealth, power and status; for the former, justice, integrity and love, summed up in Paridés's words: 'Ne quit pas que cil muire a honte/Qui muert por fine amor veraie' (4914-15). Eracle also identifies the emperor as the person who has acted most dishonourably in this affair (4987, 5005-06), thus supporting the empress's view. So, not only is Athanaïs exonerated because her husband has disregarded God's elect (the main point of this episode in *Eracle*), but also because she is shown to have a superior understanding of *honor*, a concept dependent upon respect and trust rather than status and possessions. The couple's concept of *fin'amor* (4913-44), a compulsion which cannot easily be broken, is similarly contrasted with Laïs's possessive love (2959-68, 2983-3009). Unable to contemplate life without Paridés, Athanaïs tries to save him, by offering herself for punishment alone, and by claiming that she is, in any case, rotten goods unworthy of the emperor (4843-67). Her anguish when she is forced to name Paridés provokes pity in those present (4877), and this no doubt reflects the response Gautier was aiming at in his audience – sympathy rather than moral censure for the woman whose potential excellence is ruined by the behaviour of her husband and his refusal to take Eracle's advice (5073-85).

In this episode Gautier has produced a convincing psychological drama and at the end of it he takes the unusual step in twelfth-century romance of giving the adulterous empress a divorce supervised by the pope (5010) and the freedom to remarry (Pierreville 2001, 238-41). In this respect, he differs from contemporary writers who tend to punish adulterous queens,[60] but also from contemporary religious teaching, which allowed the husband to remarry if his wife committed adultery, but not the wife herself, who usually took the veil.[61] In both of his romances Gautier has found humane, realistic solutions to the crises experienced by his protagonists.

---

[60] See Peggy McCracken, *The Romance of Adultery: Queenship and Sexual Transgression in Old French Literature* (Philadelphia: University of Pennsylvania Press, 1998).

[61] Ille is also allowed to remarry, but only after Galeron has become a nun (*Ille et Galeron*, 5305-11).

Standing at the crossroads between the *romans antiques*, the Tristan romances, Marie de France's *Lais* and Arthurian romance, Gautier d'Arras's *Eracle* is a key document for our understanding of debates around religion, politics and love in twelfth-century France.

Narrative Technique

Significantly Gautier d'Arras uses divorce and remarriage as a realistic solution to the adultery of the empress. Not for him are the ingenious, magic remedies of the Tristan legend, Arthurian romance or Marie's *Lais*. Indeed, as Fourrier's study of 1960 shows, Gautier was an important exponent of the realist mode, which came fully to fruition in thirteenth-century French literature. *Eracle* is characterised both by a desire for verisimilitude (*effet de réel*) and by the inclusion of many borrowings from the real world (*effet du réel*). The former is achieved through the accurate observation of the details of everyday life; convincing portrayal of character; the avoidance of the supernatural (except for the Christian *merveilleux*); and a preference for precise temporal and spatial indications. The latter consists of identifiable geography and references to real historical people and events (Pratt 1987, 248-49).

The horse race is an excellent example of Gautier's eye for credible detail. The positioning of Eracle's three opponents is carefully described (1556-63), the horses' physical response to exertion is painted convincingly (1629-1765) and the effect on the colt of premature exercise (1884-90) seems to betray an intimate knowledge of equine physiology on the part of the poet. Similarly, Gautier avoids giving a heroic, but implausible account of the siege warfare that takes Laïs away from his wife. Instead he claims more realistically that only cutting off their supplies would defeat the inhabitants of the town (3201-11). While there is some courtly idealisation, especially in the descriptions of festivities at Thibaut's court in the prologue, in the finery associated with the bride show (2013-19, 2057-64), in the splendid entertainments of the Roman games (3430-38, 3799-3800), and in the physical portraits of the lovers (2582-93, 3479-90), one is mostly struck by the realistic portrayal of the minor, lower class characters such as the stone and horse owners and the old woman. Not only does Gautier show sympathy for their economic plight (836, 1449-58, 4255-56), he also adapts their dialogue to the situation. Whereas the impoverished stone owner exhibits a certain amount of deference towards Eracle (862-73), the colt owner addresses him as one would a child (1421-48). Similarly, the *vieille* in her conversations with Paridés uses colourful language appropriate to a woman whose wide experience has given her expertise in human psychology and relations between the sexes (4139-80).[62]

Psychological *vraisemblance* is the hallmark of Gautier's treatment of the lovers, but he

---

[62] For further information on this figure, who anticipates the *vieille* in the thirteenth-century *Roman de la Rose*, see Pratt 2007b.

also shows insight into the behaviour of ordinary people: the reluctance of the emperor's *sergant* to pay the stone owner is described concisely but effectively 'A un qui fait molt grouçanment/Faire li fait son paiement' (877-78), while the colt owner's fear that his newly acquired riches might be stolen from him is captured visually and economically in the line 'Muçant s'en va outre la gent' (1497). Gautier's account of the *vieille*'s anger on receiving the pie, before realising that the costly dish is for her, is a masterpiece of witty realism, her words conveying magnificently first her disappointment, then her overblown gratitude (4427-40, 4443-48).

There is plenty of evidence (see Pierreville 2001, 291-92, 295) for a realistic approach to time and place in *Eracle*. Gautier structures his narrative chronologically and invokes real locations for the action. Although he sometimes conflates the practices of seventh-century Rome and Byzantium with those of twelfth-century France, he differs from contemporary writers in preferring authentic history to the mythic past of Arthur and he includes real place-names rather than those of Celtic Britain. However, some temporal references may be symbolic, especially in those sections of the narrative influenced by the Bible and hagiography, for example the seven years during which Eracle's parents pray for his conception (141). Nevertheless, Pierreville's appendix 1 shows that the chronology of events in *Eracle* is wholly plausible. Moreover, even the oriental exoticism of Chosroes's heaven (5225-42), which at first sight resembles the Celtic marvels of Arthurian romance, proves to be the result of human endeavour, not the supernatural. Thus, in contrast to Chrétien de Troyes and Marie de France, Gautier is primarily a realistic writer, even presenting divine interventions as natural events in the life of God's elect.

The tone of *Eracle* is generally sententious, the text containing a high proportion of gnomic expressions (Pierreville 2001, 323-32), placed in the mouth of both characters and the narrator. However, this didactic tone is lightened by passages of humour and irony (Pierreville 2001, 349-51). Gautier produces amusing euphemisms and metaphors when referring to sexual activity (2112-14, 2338-39, 2381-82, 2410-12, 4176-77, 4582) and ironic expressions in the context of battle, a normal feature of epic diction (5291-92, 5812-13). His characters also employ humour, for example when the seneschal jokes that Eracle weighs the equivalent of a thousand *besants*, but that normally he does not buy items by weight. Further humour is produced by the ironic repetition of a term used by another character: thus, the narrator sarcastically repeats the word *giu* ('Quant acointié li ont lor giu', 1237) used earlier by the giant who challenges Eracle to combat ('Un noviel ju vous cuiç aprendre!', 1170) and Eracle later indulges in humorous repetition of the term *cuidier* to point out how false the beliefs of Chosroes the Elder are (6008-12). Examples of irony of situation are to be found during the bride show, when a girl's confident «Tu serras coronee, amie» (2282) is undermined by our knowledge that God's elect can read her thoughts, or when Chosroes the Elder threatens to kill Eracle outside his 'ciel' to preserve the sanctity of a place already defiled by his very presence as a false god (5993-98).

Gautier's familiarity with the medieval *artes poeticae*, which he would have acquired during his clerical education, is obvious in all aspects of his style (Pratt 1987, chapter XI). Amongst the difficult ornaments (*ornata difficultas*) at his disposal we find metaphors, metonymy,[63] synecdoche,[64] periphrasis (paraphrase; 1946, 3656, 5459), antonomasia (a descriptive phrase to replace the name of a character; 320, 445, 1338-39, 2363), *distributio* (a concept expressed by the collocation of contraries or the listing of complementary terms),[65] and hyperbole.[66] Figures of diction include anaphora,[67] anadiplosis (the immediate repetition of words at the end of one clause and at the beginning of the next; 1614-15, 3312-13), chiasmus,[68] epizeuxis (the immediate repetition of a word; 1713), *annominatio* and polyptoton (the juxtaposition of words similar in sound or related etymologically; verb annomination),[69] synonymy,[70] and *interpretatio* (extended synonymy by means of parallel constructions; 191-92, 3723-26). Figures of thought are represented by *expolitio* (elaboration of an idea using various syntactical structures; 1839-44, 4929-32), *frequentatio* (accumulation; 2155-62, 4827-34), personification (of *amors, avarisse, envie*, etc.), litotes (1520, 2603-04, 6141-42), antithesis (1766, 2545, 2753-54) and oxymoron (314, 595).

In particular, passages of direct speech, which constitute 45.15% of the text (Pierreville 2001, 299) are highly rhetorical. This is especially true of monologues, which sometimes turn into internal dialogue as characters employ dialectical reasoning in order to try to arrive at the truth. A good example is the following stichomythic speech, in which Paridés interrogates himself on the improbability of the empress loving him. Here he employs repetition, polyptoton on the verb *cuidier* and *correctio* (repetition in order to contest, 3750):

– Si est, espoir, por tes biaus iex.
– Or esce folie et orgiex
Quant tu cuides ne ne cuidas
Que fust por toi! – Je ne cuiç pas;
Ainc ne cuidai que fust por moi.

---

[63] Lines 244, 361, 1956, 5135, 5143, 5635.
[64] Lines 1895, 4325, 4789, 5813.
[65] Lines 127, 745, 2250, 3704, 4005-06, 4544.
[66] To exaggerate: lines 120-21, 133-34, 2166, 2256, 5871; to diminish through expressions of minimal value: 34, 783, 3984, etc.
[67] Lines 2286-87, 3557, 3902-03, 5663-65.
[68] Lines 316-17, 319, 580-81, 1601-04, 3913-16, 4929-32.
[69] Lines 2992-3008, 3709-22, 4508-19; polyptoton: 1779-84, 2252-55, 3576-78.
[70] Lines 442, 1779-80, 1931, 2668, 5509-10.

– Esta en toi! – Que dis «en toi»?
Las! je ne puis en moi ester;
Mes cuers ne se velt arester,
Ains m'a relenqui des hui main,
Et si m'a mis en autrui main; (3745-54; cf. Athanaïs's words, 3673-75)

No less rhetorically elaborate are passages of narratorial commentary. Here the complex relationship between fear, love and madness is reflected in the weaving together of related terms. Note especially the anaphora, *annominatio*, antithesis, paradox, personification and repetition:

Tos jors estuet que crieme i ait,
Que fins amans tos jors se crient
De perdre ce c'a ses mains tient,
Qu'il a tos jors crieme en amor:
Qui ne mescroit, ainc n'ama jor!
Et sages hom meïmement
Se crient tous jors molt durement,
Mais ja nus hom sages nen iert
S'il fait tout ce c'Amors requiert.
Mais se folie n'est pas teus
Com est folie natureus,
Car teus est de molt sage ator
Qui molt est faus en fine amor,
Et tel folie et tel savoir
Font en amor paour avoir. (2992-3006)

On the other hand, the few descriptions Gautier includes are banal (Pratt 1987, 210-31; Pierreville 2001, 248-53) and although they show some influence of rhetorical training, there is little variation in the vocabulary used to describe beautiful persons and objects (e.g. 2587-93, but cf. 5869-90 on Chosroes's 'heaven'). Our poet seems to tire of describing warfare too (3215-20), preferring instead to lavish his rhetorical skill on the exploration of emotions or exciting events such as the horse race.

Yet Gautier does show great inventiveness in his choice of imagery, employing similes and metaphors taken from botany (1268, 2383, 3123, 4267, 4831-32), zoology (2239), games (4388-90, 4586, 5978-79), agriculture (2390-92, 3330-32, 4864-66), metallurgy (1840-44, 2214-15, 4827-30), precious stones (2719), ornithology (3882-93, 4610-11), medecine (2299-2300), warfare (1998) and so on. Some of his most unusual images are found in the context of love (Pierreville 2001, 304-08; Pratt 2007a): Paridés accuses Amors of choosing only feeble victims and compares it to a man who jumps over a hedge at its lowest point (3975-77), and then to a painter who has dyed his heart yellow:

> 'Amors, ainc mais ne fus si male,
> Mais molt est gaune te tainture;
> Amors, tu ses molt de painture,
> Tu en as si mon cuer vestu...' (3980-83)

The rhetorical complexity of Gautier's compositions suggests that he was a literate cleric operating in a written culture. However, as Zumthor (1984) has shown, *Eracle* contains many stylistic features designed to enliven oral recitation. For example, the many first-person interventions and second-person forms of address (Zumthor 1984, 174-77), along with a high proportion of direct speech (1984, 189) and proleptic remarks (1984, 198), create a strong bond between the narrator (embodied during performance by the author himself or by a court entertainer or *jongleur*) and the audience. Adopting some of the techniques of the medieval sermon, including the incorporation of an authoritative gloss within the narrative (Zumthor 1984, 168), Gautier conveys his moral message most effectively. Yet the lively pace and variety of tone and register in *Eracle* ensure that his audience is not only instructed, but also entertained.

Gautier d'Arras's first extant work is a historical exemplum with a strong Christian message, expressed in long passages of gnomic verse whose oral quality is designed to retain the listening audience's attention. However, it is also a subtle psychological romance, embellished with pleasing rhetoric and enlivened with realistic, down-to-earth detail and fine wit.

The Extant Manuscripts of Eracle

Gautier's *Eracle* has survived in three manuscripts, two in Paris and one in Turin.

A. Manuscript A: Paris, Bibliothèque Nationale de France, fonds français 1444[71]

This vellum manuscript measures 285mm by 230mm and has an eleventh-century hide binding bearing the words: BÉRENGIER | TRADUCTION DE LA BIBLE | ETC. It now has 329 folios, which have been renumbered in Arabic numerals, but the gaps in earlier roman pagination indicate that several original folios have been lost and many of the following 24 items are consequently incomplete:

Fols lv-6v	: List of contents
1) Fols 7r-27r	: *Le Roman de sapience. Genesis* by Herman de Valenciennes
2) Fols 27r-46r	: *Vie de Jesus-Christ d'après les Evangiles*
3) Fols 46r-60r	: *Li Passions notre seigneur Jhesus Christ* and other works attributed to Berengier

---

[71] This manuscript was number 7534 in the catalogue prepared by Nicolas Clément in 1682 and number 32 in the catalogue of manuscripts from Mazarin in 1668.

4) Fol. 60r-61r : *De l'Avenement Antecrist*
5) Fols 61r-65r : *Des xv. Signes del jour dou jugement* by Berengier
6) Fols 65r-66r : *Li sermons au puile* by Berengier[72]
7) Fols 66r-71r : *De l'Assumption Nostre Dame* by Herman de Valenciennes
8) Fols 71r-75v : *L'Orison Nostre Dame* by Herman de Valenciennes
9) Fols 75v-77v : *Dou plait de sapience et de folie* by Gerars (incomplete)
10) Fols 78r-115r : *De Phisike, le premier livre* = *Le Régime du corps* by Aldebrandin of Sienna (incomplete)
11) Fols 115r-26r : *De Karlemaine le bon roi* (Old French translation of the *Pseudo-Turpin*)
12) Fol. 126r-26v : *Li lignie des rois de france*. The last entry mentions Philippe-Auguste and his son Louis (VIII, 1223-1226)[73]
13) Fol. 126v : *Li Nombre des eages dès Adan dusques à Crist*
14) Fols 127r-54r : *D'Eracle l'empereour* by Gautier d'Arras
15) Fols 154v-67v : *L'Orison ke Dex fist* = *Miserere* by Renclus de Moiliens
16) Fols 168r-70r : *Li Ver de le mort* by Helinand de Froidmont
17) Fols 170v-217v : *L'Ymage du monde* by Gautier de Metz
18) Fols 218r-27v : *Li Livres de Karité* by Renclus de Moiliens
19) Fols 228r-40v : *Li Livres estrais de philosofie et de moralité* by Alart de Cambrai (incomplete)
20) Fols 240v-56v : *Li Bestiaires devins* by Guillaume le Clerc (incomplete)
21) Fol. 257r-v : *Del Arbre del monde* = *Le Dit de l'unicorne et du serpent* (incomplete)
22) Fols 258r-65v : *Li Bestiaires d'amours* by Maistre Richart de Furnival (incomplete)
23) Fols 266r-78v : *Des .vii. Sages de Romme* (incomplete)
24) Fols 279r-329v : *De Marke, le fil Cathon* (continuation of previous work, incomplete)

Items 1-13 and 22-24 are written in two columns; the other items, including *Eracle*, are written in three, forty lines per column. Large blue and red initials alternate. In this manuscript, Gautier's *Eracle* is in the company of various religious works, two bestiaries, scientific treatises (with diagrams) and a translation of the *Chronique de Turpin* (pseudo-history). It may well have been included on account of its didactic, religious and historical nature. It is interesting to note that in manuscripts *A* and *T Eracle* and the

---

[72] Items 1-6 constitute a biblical compilation by Herman de Valenciennes, although some items are attributed to a certain Berengier.

[73] This gives us a *terminus post quem* for this copy, i.e. a date before which it could not have been made. However, since other manuscript copies of this work also end with Louis VIII, this fact does not provide us with a *terminus ante quem* for this manuscript.

story of Cligés are associated. The latter is mentioned at the end of item 23: *De Marke, le fil Cathon* in A, while T contains Chrétien's *Cligés*.

Manuscript A is dated by Henri Omont and by Cesare Segre as late thirteenth century and its language shows evidence of Picard influence (see below).[74] It seems to be a compilation of authors who hail from towns not far from Gautier's Arras: Valenciennes (Herman), Molliens-Vidame near Amiens (Renclus), Amiens (Richard de Furnival) and Froidmont near Beauvais (Helinand). This copy of the text, containing 6574 lines, has served as the base manuscript for Guy Raynaud de Lage and the present editor.

B. Manuscript B: Paris, Bibliothèque Nationale de France, fonds français 24430 (Sorbonne 454)

This is a large-format, parchment manuscript measuring 337mm by 255mm, bound in red Moroccan leather and bearing the arms of Cardinal Richelieu. Its 181 folios contain the following items:

1) Fols 1r-59v   : *Roman de Cléomadès* by Adenet le Roi
2) Fols 59r-80r   : *Chronique de Rains* (Rheims)
3) Fols 81r-112v   : *Vie des Pères du desert* (including list of contents fols 81-82)
4) Fols 113r-16r and 151r-69r : *Chroniques de Tournay*
5) Fols 117r-124r   : *Vie, en vers, de S. Eleuthère ou S. Lehire* (Bishop of Tournai)
6) Fols 124r-44r   : *Eracle* by Gautier d'Arras
7) Fols 145r-50v   : *Lettre de Jean de Villiers sur la prise d'Acre* (post 1291)
8) Fols 170r-75v   : *Li Contes dou rois Flore et de la bielle Jehanne*
9) Fols 176r-78r   : *Li Contes dou roi Constant l'empereur*
10) Fols 178r-81r   : *Li estoire dou roi Labiel et du roi Laban son père*

Omont dates this manuscript as late thirteenth-, early fourteenth century, while Albert Henry, the editor of *Les Oeuvres d'Adenet le Roi*,[75] dates it as late thirteenth century. Whereas all other items begin on a new folio (this leads to a considerable waste of parchment), *Eracle* begins immediately after item 5 and, like its predecessor, is written at first in two columns in the same hand. However, the scribe changes to three columns over the page (124v), thus most of *Eracle* and the whole of the *Roman de Cléomadès* are written in three columns, while all other texts are in two. The contents and dialectal features of B suggest that it was copied in or near Tournai (by more than one scribe possessing a rather messy hand) and Gautier's poem as presented in this manuscript contains more Picard forms than one finds in A. Moreover, the text of B is shorter (6498

---

[74] See Henri Omont, *Catalogue des manuscrits français de la Bibliothèque Nationale*, Paris, various dates and Cesare Segre, *Li Bestiaires d'amours di Maistre Richart de Fournival et li response du bestiaire* (Milan, Naples, 1957), xli.
[75] Bruges, 1951, 133-34.

lines) in that it ends at line 6536 and therefore does not attest the full epilogue offered by *A* and *T*, nor does it mention the name Baudouin. In manuscript *B*, *Eracle* is in the company of secular romances, *contes*, religious and historical works. It is notable that it is inserted, along with a local saint's life and a crusading text by the Grand Master of the Knights Hospitallers, into a chronicle about Tournai.

C. Manuscript T: Turin, Biblioteca Nazionale, 1626 (L. I. 13)

This large-format, parchment manuscript contains 146 folios and the following six items, of which Gautier's *Eracle* is the first:

1) Fols 1-22r   : *Eracle* by Gautier d'Arras
2) Fols 22r-27v   : *Le Blanc Chevalier*, a lay by Jean de Condé
3) Fols 27v-35v   : *Le Chevalier a le mance* by Jean de Condé
4) Fols 35v-108r   : *Sone de Nansay*
5) Fols 108r-29r   : *Cligés* by Chrétien de Troyes
6) Fols 128v-46v   : *Richars li Biaus*

In this manuscript too *Eracle* is written in three columns. Although Pasini and Mazzatinti claim that *T* dates from the thirteenth century, Scheler argues that this copy must have been produced in the first half of the fourteenth century since it contains works by Jean de Condé, who was still active in 1337.[76]

Unfortunately, this manuscript was involved in the 1904 fire at the Turin library and is now only legible under ultra-violet light. The columns of writing nearest to the spine have been partially destroyed. However, Löseth's pre-fire edition of the poem contains a fairly comprehensive list of variants from this manuscript. Since his reading of manuscripts *A* and *B* can be shown to be extremely accurate, it is felt that recourse to Löseth's critical apparatus for variant readings from *T* is justified. *T* offers the shortest version of the romance (6349 lines) and Scheler suggests that it was wilfully shortened by its scribe. The copyist (or one of his predecessors) seems to have deliberately 'corrected' or 'improved' readings which are attested by *A* and *B*, and omits lines which he no doubt considered to be superfluous. *T* frequently has recourse to the *lectio facilior* (easier reading) and sometimes produces complete nonsense. Here *Eracle*'s companion pieces are all secular and fictional.

---

[76] Josephus Pasinus, *Codices manuscripti bibliothecae regii taurinensis Athenaei. Pars altera* (Turin, 1749), 468-71; Giuseppe Mazzatinti, *Inventari dei manoscritti delle Bibliotheche d'Italia*, vol. 27, *Torino* (Florence, 1922); A. Scheler, 'Notice et extraits de deux manuscrits français de la Bibliothèque royale de Turin', *Bulletin du Bibliophile belge*, 1 (1866), 246-79, 343-74, and 2 (1867), 405-16. For a recent description of this manuscript, see Stewart Gregory and Claude Luttrell in K. Busby, T. Nixon, A. Stones, and L. Walters eds. *Les Manuscrits de Chrétien de Troyes/The Manuscripts of Chrétien de Troyes*, 2 vols (Amsterdam and Atlanta: Rodopi, 1993), 67-95 (91-92).

T was written by one East Picard scribe throughout, contains works by an author possibly connected with Valenciennes, certainly with Hainault, and the final folio contains 12 lines of verse mentioning Valenciennes. It is therefore another local, Northeastern French production.

From our brief study of the three surviving copies of *Eracle* it emerges that they were all produced in the same region and contain works by 'local' authors. Although the manuscript contexts of Gautier's work might indicate how it was perceived generically by his near contemporaries, the evidence is somewhat contradictory, perhaps resulting from the generic hybridity of *Eracle*.

The Language of Eracle

Given that the three extant manuscripts of *Eracle* were copied by scribes whose dialects may not have matched that of Gautier d'Arras, our only evidence for the dialectal features of Gautier's own language is to be found at the rhyme or, assuming that the author wrote in regular octosyllables, in cases where dialectal variations would have affected the syllable count.[77] Refining the conclusions of Heimer (1921), Hayes (1935-39) concluded that Gautier was Picard, but did not live in Arras. The most obvious Picard features of MS *A* are attributable to the scribes, not to the author;[78] Gautier's language has much in common with the increasingly influential Francien, but contains some characteristics of the North and North East. This mixed dialect betrays a probable Champenois domicile and intended audience. Since non-standard features are less obvious in *Ille et Galeron* than in *Eracle*, it is likely that the latter was composed first.

A. *Gautier's Language*

(i) *Versification*[79]

Gautier writes in octosyllabic rhyming couplets, achieving in *Eracle* a high percentage of rich and leonine (disyllabic) rhymes, the latter particularly frequent in the final epic section of the romance, e.g. *esmondee : fondee*, 6053-54. Particularly impressive are his trisyllabic rhymes, e.g. *soit amendee : pieça mandee*, 4047-48, *me venisses : me tenisses*, 6009-10, and the even richer *a fait departir : c'a fait dessartir*, 6049-50. There are examples of broken rhymes: *devin : de vin*, 653-54, *d'ire : dire*, 1675-76, *amot : a mot*, 4015-16; homonymic rhymes (the same word with different meanings or different grammatical functions): *estre* (= verb) *: estre* (= noun), 355-56, *amer* (= bitter) *: amer* (= to love), 3913-14, *conte* (= count) *: conte* (= account), 23-24; words rhyming with one of their compounds:

---

[77] According to Hayes (1935-39, Introduction, 42), Gautier's verse is very regular.
[78] For more information on the Picard dialect, see Charles Theodore Gossen, *Petite grammaire de l'ancien picard* (Paris: Klincksieck, 1951).
[79] For further information on this subject, see Heimer 1921, 12-25; Delbouille 1973; Pierreville 2001, 280-83.

proumetre : metre, 75-76, *lire : eslire*, 1965-66, and grammatical rhymes. The latter can develop into the rhetorical devices of *annominatio* or polyptoton (the repetition of etymologically related words in different morphological or verbal forms), which in the following examples are combined with chiasmus to create emotional highpoints in the narrative:

> Mais li jors est molt desirés
> Dont il s'est griement consirés,
> Et cele griement consiree.
> Tost vient li feste desiree (4493-96)

> Li varlés est molt angosseus,
> Et angossant va li espeus,
> Et molt angossant vait l'espeuse;
> Gens ne fu mais si angosseuse. (4887-90)

> Tant durement te peuç amer
> Que je te fis dame clamer
> De canc'on m'a signor clamé,
> Et or as autrui enamé! (4947-50)

While Gautier's versification is on the whole rich and varied, he has included in *Eracle* a few identical rhymes: *cose : cose*, 1411-12; *celui : celui*, 1903-04; *senés : senés*, 5105-06. He rigorously observes the syllable count of words, preserving the disyllabic endings of learned words, e.g. *engenreüre*, 137; *terrïens*, 224. Yet he cleverly exploits the flexibility provided by the syllabic variability of the following lexical items: *lors*, 70/*lores*, 3651; *adont*, 4786/*adonques*, 6439; *dont*, 6565/*donques*, 457; *cel*, 685/*icel*, 2336; *tel*, 2384/*itel*, 992; *cil*, 1144/*icil*, 1043; *ainc*, 1/*ainques*, 1119; *premiers*, 3386/*premerains*, 5279; *encor*, 6181/*encore*, 5492; *or*, 6309/*ore*, 4260; *verté*, 4796/*verités*, 3560; *veraie*, 4537/*vraie*, 5121; *mont*, 5579/*monde*, 5858; *Esperite*, 268/*Esperis*, 2928/*Espirt*, 2664/*Esperit*, 25; *ne* (elided)/*nen*. Variety is also achieved by employing standard and dialectal forms of parts of speech (see below): the first person plural endings *–ons/–omes*; the third person singular present indicative *compere/compre*; the pronouns *ele/el* and the possessive adjectives *vostre/vo*. While *come* is used in elliptical comparisons, *com* is used elsewhere, except in line 3113, 'come le face'. *Nïent* (sometimes spelt *noient*) is disyllabic at the rhyme, e.g. 3518, 4843, but can be monosyllabic (spelt *nient*) in the body of the text, e.g. 802, 841, 1789. Gautier was therefore a careful versifier; those lines identified by Zumthor (1984, 188-89) as hypometric or hypermetric are likely to have been scribal, and have been corrected in the present edition.

Brisure du couplet, whereby one sentence ends and another begins in the middle of a couplet, is to be found in the *Roman d'Enéas* (12% of verse), but is employed quite extensively in *Eracle* (19%).[80] This technique is particularly useful in dialogue, in which a change of speaker coincides with the second line of a couplet. However, as the following conversation between Eracle and his mother shows, Gautier does not always break the couplet, but sometimes interrupts the line, producing stychomythia:

> – Et jou si aim l'ame mon pere
> Tant con le moie, douce mere.
> – Fix, jel verrai dedens tierç jor
> Se tu l'aimes de bone amor;
> Je le verrai. – Vous? En quel guise?
> – Fix, que m'en valra le devise?
> – Si fera, mere, voirement,
> Car je ferai vostre talent.
> – Se le tenoies, fix, a bien... (297-305)

Along with *brisure du couplet* Gautier employs *enjambement* to propel the narrative forward and for dramatic revelations, e.g.

> Il ont paor que nes deçoive
> Peciés, c'aucuns les aperçoive. (4603-04)

cf. 266-67, 275-76, 1884-87, 6494-98. Although Zumthor (1984, 186-87) argues that our poet does not use this technique very frequently, it nevertheless contributes to the lively pace of Gautier's writing, thus enhancing the aural reception of his romances in a court setting.[81]

(ii) Dialectal Features

Much of Gautier's language coincides with standard literary Francien, but it does display (if only sporadically) the dialectal features listed below, with the relevant dialects shown in bold using the following abbreviations:[82]

N = Northern, NE = North Eastern (i.e. Wallonia, Artois, Picardy and part of Normandy), E = Eastern (i.e. Franche-Comté and Burgundy), P = Picard, W = Walloon.

---

[80] Pierreville (2001, 355-58) provides a list of occurrences in *Eracle*. See Warren (1906-07, 662ff) for the statistics, which seem to show that Gautier's practice is to be placed between the *romans antiques* and Chrétien's *Erec et Enide*, in which the proportion of broken couplets rises to 37% in the latter part of the text.

[81] Zumthor (1984) does not include the examples given above, but cites lines 227-28, 3172-73, 5374-75, 6313-14.

[82] Although the exact pronunciation of Old French is not known, and our knowledge of the phonology comes from the somewhat unreliable evidence of changing graphies used by scribes, I have attempted in the following to convey the approximate value of Old French phonemes by employing the International Phonetic Alphabet.

1. There is some syneresis (contraction) of two vowels in hiatus into a diphthong or long single vowel. Gautier uses both uncontracted and contracted forms, e.g. *miedi*, 2366 and *midi*, 4353; *desgeünee*, 4133 and *juner*, 4033; *mooule*, 1863 and *moule*, 1887. **NE**
2. Non-elision of *li* (feminine article), c.g. *Li ante*, 2747. **NE**
3. There is the archaic use of *nen* for *ne* (preventing elision before a vowel), e.g. 1300, 2453, 2725, etc. **N**
4. Tonic blocked [e] > [a] is attested by the dialectal form *asme*, 4182, rhymed with *pame*, 4181, but cf. *esme*, 5846. **E**[83]
5. Gautier's regular distinction between nasal *e* and *a* ([ã] and [ɛ̃]) is not Francien, e.g. *estrument : nïent*; *quant : auquant*, 3517-20. However, there are several exceptions: *espandre : prandre*, 1887-88 (and variants *tendre : atendre*) and *Ille et Galeron*, 998-99, *espandue : entendue*. Gautier also rhymes *dolans* and *noient* in both [ã] and [ɛ̃], e.g. *besans : dolans*, 417-18, but *gent : dolent*, 3315-16; *vivant : noiant*, 1193-94, but *noiens : laiens*, 1595-96; these are all rhymes acceptable in Champagne. **NE (but not a rigid rule)**
6. Gautier usually distinguishes between tonic [ai] and [ɛ] at the rhyme, although he follows Francien practice in confusing the sounds in *estre : mestre*, 915-16; *aresne : resne*, 1417-18; *terme : lerme*, 3991-92. **NE**
7. [e] does not rhyme with [ɛ]. **NE**
8. [ie] +[ə] > [iə]. Although the scribe uses the contraction *ie* for [ieə] all the time, Gautier has only one example of [ieə] rhyming with [iə]: *acomplie : covoitie*, 5373-74. However, in lines 2953-56, *abeïe : obeïe* and *proisie : envoisie* are treated as separate rhymes, yet the metre of 2956 indicates that the second couplet contains contracted forms. The syllable count of lines 2365-66, 5281-82 also suggests that the reduction of the triphthong is characteristic of Gautier's language. **NE, especially P**
9. Gautier rhymes [ɔi] < [ei] with [oi]; Chrétien does not and this develops in Francien later. *Eracle* may therefore be the first text to show this Northern feature, e.g. *croistre : connoistre*, 13-14; *connois : nois* (< nive), 1461-62. **N**
10. Loss of final *n*, e.g. *ronchi* (< runcinum) *: merchi*, 1521-22. **N**
11. Gautier has *n* rhyming with palatalised *n*, e.g. *frarin : lin*, 3453-54. **N, esp. Anglo-Norman**
12. The frequent rhyme *povreté : verté* in 867-68, 4795-96, 4957-58 attests to the metathesis of *r* by Gautier (i.e. *vreté*). **P**
13. Usually the final dental is effaced in the past participle, but the *t* is preserved in *samit : arramit*, 3431-32 and *forfait : lait*, 3229-30. **P**
14. Gautier rhymes final [s] with [ts] (sometimes spelt *z*) on several occasions, e.g. *senescaus : descaus*, 89-90, 995-96; *vous : sous*, 1027-28; *vous : trestous*, 1481-82. **P**

---

[83] This example may not be valid, however, as *asme* could be the product of syneresis.

15. Gautier has the Northern form *engiens* (rhyming with *biens* 5647-48) instead of *engin* (cf. also 1589-90, *engieng : tieng*). **N**

16. *Doing* (1st person singular of *doner*) *: joing*, 4633-34 (instead of *doins* in Francien). **N**

17. *compre* (3rd person singular) *: derompre* (infinitive*)*, 6243-44 (but cf. *compere*, 4715). **Possibly P**

18. Gautier employs the first person plural ending *–omes*, 319, as well as *–ons*, *–on*. He favours *–ons*; *–omes* is not necessarily Northern; *–on* (e.g. 6116, *oon*) is **Norman or Anglo-Norman.**

19. The present subjunctive form *kaie : aie*, 6521-22 (instead of *chiee*) is **Walloon.**

20. The new weak preterite form of the verb *croire* is dialectal, e.g. *creï : gehi*, 4623-24 (instead of *crut*), cf. *mescreï*, 4726. **NE**

21. Intertonic *e* is effaced between *n* and *r* in the future tense of 1st conjugation verbs, e.g. *donrai*, 875, 1479, etc., *comperra*, 5190. **NE**

22. Mute *e* [ə] is included as a vocalic interconsonantal glide in the future tense of other conjugations, e.g. *saverés*, 518 (but *savrés*, 287); *venderés*, 470; *perdera*, 734. **N, especially P**

23. Gautier shows the reduction of [ie] to [i] in *adevancir* instead of *adevancier*, e.g. *agencist : adevancist*, 5357-58, but cf. *avancier* in *lanchié : avanchié*, 3213-14. **NE**

24. Whilst *ele* is the most common form of the pronoun, *el* occurs in 330, 570. **NE**

25. The possessive adjective *vo* is found for *vostre*, 1390, 2355, 4093. **P**

26. The unstressed pronoun is elided with a following vowel, e.g. *Ardés m'en fu*, 918; *Laissiés me ens*, 4227 (the syllable count indicates that *me* and *ens* are elided here), but cf. *Giete moi a honor de ci*, 5730. **P**

Gautier shows a liking for technical, Latinate words (*mots savants*) which lend *Eracle*, especially towards the end, a strongly clerical tone. Examples are: *societé* (standard OF *soisté*), 4242; *perdission*, 3702; *firmament*, 5660; *humelité*, 6111; *generasce*, 6127; *passïence*, 6271. He also cultivates archaisms, using the old form *manguist*, 4391, and the archaic construction *de es le sien*, 2782.

B. The Language of MS A

Two copyists, identified independently by Hayes (1935-39) and Wolsey (1972, 57-60), produced manuscript *A*. Scribe 1 was responsible for the majority of the text: lines 1-1507, 1559-88, 1621-934, 2017-276, 2675-740, 2831-5537, 5547-6568; Scribe 2 copied lines 1508-58, 1589-1620, 1935-2016, 2277-674, 2741-830, 5538-46. An almost foolproof way of distinguishing between them is that Scribe 1 writes *Dix* = *Dius* (but also *Deu/s*, 124, 3132, 4648, 5246) whilst Scribe 2 writes *Diex* = *Dieus*. Scribe 1's habit of doubling consonants as in 2088, 2198, 4342, etc., has been noted in the rejected readings, as have the change-overs from one scribe to another.

In addition to these orthographic variations and the dialectal differences listed below, Wolsey (1972, 57-60) also distinguishes the scribes chirographically (i.e. by their handwriting). Scribe 2's ampersand (the symbol for 'and') and his abbreviation for *est* differ from Scribe 1's, as do some of his initial capital letters. Moreover, the second copyist makes more errors than the first, but these cannot be explained by the hypothesis that Scribe 1 was working from dictation at this point, for they are more consistent with faulty copying from a written exemplar. If the whole manuscript was copied by a single scribe, then the chirographic variations would be due to a change in writing equipment, and the orthographic differences would suggest a change in model text. The more likely explanation, however, is that there were two scribes employed on this manuscript.

(i) Scribe 1

The following features suggest that Scribe 1 was Picard, perhaps Walloon (examples in bold indicate where Scribe 2 shares the particular characteristic):

1. The reduction of the diphthong [ai] > [a] made *ai* and *a* interchangeable for Picard scribes. Hence *–ai for –a* and vice versa, e.g. *cuida* (corrected to *cuidai*), 3749; *Mis ai* (corrected to *Mis a*), 4185.

2. *Le* used instead of *la* for the feminine article and pronoun almost passim. Also the possessive adjectives *me*, 48, **2300** and *se*, 77, **2311**, 3001 for *ma* and *sa*.

3. Tonic [ɛ] is diphthongised when blocked, e.g. *pucieles*, 2024; *Biele*, 2065; *apriés*, 6406, but never at the rhyme.[84]

4. In the Northern region the triphthong [ɛau] was differentiated to [iau], e.g. *biax*, 385, 2749; *damoisiax/aus*, 1308, 3804/**2507**, 3458, and the diphthong [ɔu] was differentiated either to [au] or [eu], e.g. *talt* (< tollit), 79, 4699; *fals/faus* (< follis), 458, 5842/763, 1175, 4783 (but both scribes also have *fous/fol/fols* and at the rhyme we find *fols : clos*, 5225-26; *fous : vous*, 1027-28); *cals*, 5743 (for *cops*, cf. 5754); *vaura*, 6076; *valt*, 727 (*voloir*).

5. *c* or *g* plus *a* do not palatalize, giving [k] and [g] (spelt *c/k* or *g* not *ch* or *j*), e.g. *caitif*, 5231; *cambrelens*, 69; **cambre, 2300, 2605**; *gambes*, 5610.

6. Scribe 1 inserts no interconsonantal glide (*d* or *b*) between *m'l* (spelt *nl*), e.g. *ressanle*, 1157; *ensanle*, 4460; *assanler*, 4713; or between *n'r*, e.g. *reponre*, 5185, but Gautier rhymes it with *confondre* and therefore does not share this dialectal feature.

7. Reduction of triphthongs [ieu], [yeu] > [iu], [y], e.g. *Diu* passim; *liu*, 5669; *pules*, 6034; *fu*, 1041, 1091, but *feu*, 1023, 1037, 1058, etc. is more frequent, and always at the rhyme (e.g. 559).

---

[84] In this section differing practice at the rhyme indicates that Gautier does not share all the dialectal features of the scribe.

8. There is metathesis of *r* (*er* > *re*) in *fremetés*, 283 and (*re* > *er*) in *mousterroies*, 3960.
9. While Gautier distinguishes [s] and [z] at the rhyme, Scribe 1 rhymes voiced and unvoiced *s*, e.g. *gentelisse* : *francise*, 2005-06.
10. The scribes employ the variant forms *tes* < talis, **1545**, 3701, 6141; *dues* < dolium, 569, along with the more usual *teus*, 799, 804 and *deus*, 3303.
11. Preconsonantal *s* > *r*, e.g. *varlet* (passim) for (*vaslet*, spelt *vallet* by Scribe 2 in 1508, 2342, 2350); *dervee* (for *desvee*), 3398.
12. Picard verbal forms include *querra*, 1607 (*croire*); *venra*, 1752, *venrés*, 1862, *venrai*, 5932 (*veoir*); *veïr*, 3501 (*veoir*); *demanç*, 4346; *cuiç* (passim); *prisent* (preterite, but rhymed with *eslirent*), 5265-66; *fisent* (but rhymed with *ensevelirent*), 6481-82.
13. The Picard stressed pronoun forms *jou* and *çou* are characteristic of Scribe 1, while both scribes use *je* and *ce*.

(ii) Scribe 2
The second scribe, who is generally less careful than the first and omits more words (see lines 2415, 2427, 2441, 2477, 2511), has the following distinguishing features:

1. *c* palatalizes before *e* or *i* to give [tʃ] (spelt *ch*) as in *merchi*, 2631, instead of Scribe 1's *merci*, 3346; *ichi*, 1556, instead of *ici*, 4197; *teche*, 2418, 2434, 2438, etc., instead of *tece*, 496, 704; *riche(s)* 2731, 2762, instead of *rice(s)*, 151, 338, etc. (but Scribe 1 has *riches* in 2836); *achenés*, 2325, instead of *assenés*, 858, 2689. Cf. also *Achater*, *achaté*, 1525-26, instead of Scribe 1's *acater* and cognates, 343, 458, 4858, etc.
2. Blocked tonic [ɛ] is not diphthongised (see 3 above), e.g. *bele*, 1944, 1968, 1976, rather than *biele*.
3. Scribe 2 sometimes retains the liquid in *chevals/cevals*, 1552/1616, instead of *cevaus/x*, 94, 1315/1264, 1280, etc.; *bials*, 1535, instead of *biaus/x*, 3011/1481, 1549, etc.; *bialtés*, 2358, but cf. *biaus*, 2624.
4. Scribe 2 employs the standard form *Diex*, *miex* rather than the Picard *Dix*, *mix* of Scribe 1; cf. also *lieu*, 2413.
5. He uses *laier* in 2524 instead of *laissier*, 3026, 3961, 4628, etc.

In contrast to the practice of nineteenth- and even some twentieth-century editors, I have not as a rule corrected dialectal scribal forms in my edition, nor have I standardised the language of the text. *Eracle* as presented here is both an interesting literary document and a valuable resource for the study of Old French as it was developing in the twelfth and thirteenth centuries, i.e. during the lifetimes of the original poet and of the scribes who preserved his work for posterity.

The Principles of This Edition

This edition has benefited greatly from the scholarship of the four previous editors of *Eracle*: H.F. Massmann (1842), E. Löseth (1890), Guy Raynaud de Lage (1976) and Claude Hayes (1935-39), whose papers are deposited in the Taylorian Library, Oxford. It has also taken into account the corrections proposed by the reviewers of Raynaud de Lage's edition: Burgess 1978; van Emden and Pratt 1978; Ménard 1978; Roques 1979 (see also Roques 1981); as well as the comments made by Eskénazi (translation, pp. 39-43). I follow these scholars in choosing MS *A* (Paris, BNF, fr. 1444) as my base manuscript. The text of *Eracle* it offers was copied by two fairly careful thirteenth-century scribes,[85] who have omitted fewer authentic lines than the copyists of MSS *B* (Paris, BNF, fr. 24430) and *T* (Turin, Biblioteca Nazionale, L. I. 13).[86] MS *A* has occasionally been corrected by a later hand, whose readings have been silently adopted if they are merely correcting obvious errors. Lines repeated in error by the scribe of *A* have simply been ignored.

Raynaud de Lage (edn, vii-viii), citing an unsubstantiated claim by Löseth, contends that the coincidence of readings in *AT* suggests that those manuscripts represent a copying tradition distinct from *B*. Consequently, he argues that *T*'s agreements with *B* against *A* are significant, since they indicate original readings. However, he admits to having corrected *A* more than he would have liked, especially when *BT* agree against it. My research into the manuscript filiations (Pratt 1987, 17-42; see also Hayes 1935-39) suggests that *BT* belong to a separate family from *A* and that the German adapter of *Eracle*, Meister Otte, used a French source close to MS *B* for his *Eraclius*. This information has not unduly influenced the establishment of the present text, for the frequent interventions of Raynaud de Lage and the sort of composite edition produced by Löseth in 1890 are no longer acceptable. However, where *AT* agree against *B* in a way unlikely to be fortuitous, I have attempted to retain the *A* reading, even if the *B* reading makes more obvious sense (offering the so-called easy reading or *lectio facilior*); the translation affords the opportunity to suggest a plausible meaning for *A*'s *lectio difficilior*. While the agreement of *BT* against *A* is not significant (and often represents an innovation or error), I am aware that some *A* readings preserved in this edition may not be original. The possibly superior *B* and/or *T* readings are given as such in the variants listed at the end. Any authentic lines omitted by *A* additional to those included by Raynaud de Lage have been inserted using alphabetical ordering (e.g. 1860a, etc.) so that my line numbering does not diverge from that present in the secondary literature

---

[85] See Hayes 1935-39, Introduction, 34 and his edition, and Wolsey 1972, 57-60. The change-over between Scribes 1 and 2 is indicated, along with rejected readings, at the foot of the page in my edition.

[86] See Variants &'Textual Notes at the end of my edition for an indication of lines absent from MS *A*.

referring to the CFMA edition.

The editorial approach adopted here is to emend MS *A* minimally, usually only when it is obviously corrupt and makes no sense. The *rimes douteuses* listed by Hayes (1935-39, Introduction, 38) have not been corrected automatically, unless *A* is likely to be in error (see lines 1328, 3155, 3808, 5524). Thus the linguistic features of Gautier and his copyists are largely preserved. Rejected readings from *A* are footnoted. Hypo- and hyper-metric lines have been corrected, but the text has rarely been adapted to obey our concept of Old French grammar (especially the 'case system') unless the manuscript lesson is really ambiguous. Abbreviations have been expanded as follows, taking into account the practice of the two scribes when writing these words in full:

mlt is rendered by *molt* (as in l. 3055 where *molt* is written out in full);

⁊ is usually expanded to *con* except in *commencer*, *comme* and *comment*, where there are more examples of the form with *m*; also *compere* (as in *comperra* in 5190) and *combatre* (as in *combatant* in 5402);

ō is expanded to *on* except in *hom*, *preudom*. C'ō is usually written out as *c'on*, but can appear as *c'om*;

abbreviations for *nous/vous/nos/vos* have been expanded according to the practice of the scribe in the immediate context.

To aid the modern reader I have distinguished between *u* and *v*, *i* and *j*, and I have made sparing use of diacritics (accute accent for stressed *e*; dieresis on individually pronounced vowels in diphthongs or triphthongs; a cedilla under sibilant *c*; an apostrophe in *nen* when an obvious antecedent is present). Capital letters have been used for the beginning of each line (although the scribes are inconsistent here), for God and for obviously personified abstract nouns; this is sometimes a matter though of fine judgement. Numerals have been written in words for ease of reading (especially at the rhyme), but I have retained the graphy *x* for *us* in words such as *Dix* (= *Dius*), *fax* (= *faus*), etc. An indent marks a new paragraph where MS *A* has a large blue or red initial. The beginnings of new folios and columns of writing within them are indicated in the margins of the edition.

Significant variants from *B* and/or *T* are listed at the end. As MS *T* was partially destroyed in the Turin fire of 1904 and is now almost illegible, *T* readings from Löseth's edition are included on the assumption that the care with which he transcribed the other two manuscripts was also taken in this case. Where information about the *T* reading is absent, this is because the manuscript is illegible and Löseth does not include it in his variants. The present edition aims to correct Raynaud de Lage's many errors of transcription (see the review by van Emden and Pratt 1978) and to eliminate his frequently unnecessary correction of the base manuscript (see below). However, although it is less interventionist than its immediate predecessor, it supplies in the list of variants (which includes some readings from Meister Otte's Middle High German adaptation as a further early witness) a great deal of information to enable readers to reconstruct for themselves, as far as is currently possible, Gautier's original text and to analyse the *mouvance* (evolution over time) of its manuscript transmission.

In the Rejected Readings at the bottom of the page and the Variants & Textual Notes at the end of the edition the following sigla are used A = Paris, BNF, fr. 1444; B = Paris, BNF, fr. 24430; T = Turin, Biblioteca Nazionale, L. I. 13; AE = Eskénazi; H = Hayes; L = Löseth; M = Ménard; O = Meister Otte's *Eraclius*; R = Raynaud de Lage.

The Major Differences between Raynaud de Lage's Edition and the Present Text

In the present edition the numerous errors of transcription and punctuation noted by the reviewers of the CFMA edition have been corrected. My text also differs from my predecessor's in several ways:

(i) Many manuscript readings which Raynaud de Lage deemed unacceptable according to his view of Old French grammar have been retained.

(ii) Difficult lessons found in *A* have been preserved if they make reasonable sense.

(iii) Readings corrected in error by Raynaud de Lage have been restored.

(iv) Occasionally an alternative emendation has been made to the base manuscript.

(v) In rare cases further corrections have been made.

The following are selected examples of these types of divergence from the 1976 edition.

(i) Linguistic 'errors' corrected by Raynaud de Lage but retained in the present edition

316   R: *bien fait*; A: *biens fais* acceptable after *fors* (cf. 356, 6205: *fors Dius* and Roques 1981, 66).

832   R: *De lui*; A: *De li*; and 848 R: *celui*; A: *celi* acceptable forms for masculine pronouns (Roques 1981, 64-65).

1028   R: *fous*; AB: *sous* is an acceptable Picard rhyme with *vous*.

2045-46 no need to emend both MSS A and B as a plural verb is acceptable after *gens*.

2141   R: *eslite qu'une*; A: *eslit que une*; scribe omits feminine agreement also in the almost identical line 2206, therefore acceptable (cf. 2027-28, 3272 which I have correctd for ease of reading).

2838   R: *ses sires*; A: *se sires*; the masculine possessive adjective *se* is not always inflected by the scribe when there is no ambiguity of sense, cf. 4984.

3113	R: corrects *il* to *ele* when the former is acceptable in Picard as a feminine pronoun (Roques 1981, 65); cf. 4203, in which R suppresses *il*.
4754	R: *Trestuit*; A: *Trestout* is acceptable (cf. 5838 and Roques 1981, 66).
4955	R: *cui*; A: *coi* is acceptable (cf. 6131, 6351 and Roques 1981, 66).
5743	R: *cols*; A: *cals* is acceptable as a dialectal form (Roques 1981, 66).
5814	R: *test*; A: *tiés* is acceptable (Roques 1981, 66).
5958	R: *O lui*; A: *O soi* is acceptable (Roques 1981, 66).
6334	R: *S'orelle est tos jors ententive*; A: *S'orelle a* is acceptable (Roques 1981, 67).

(ii) Examples where the base manuscript does make sense

6	R: *cest fais*; A: *ces fais* = these tasks.
193	R: *non fera ja* (BT); A: *ce n'i ert ja* = makes sense if punctuated correctly.
467	R: *s'esmaie* (BT); A: *se maine* = she behaves.
1608	R: *vorra* (T); AB: *verra* makes sense and produces a better rhyme.
1789	R: *Del varlet et nïent d'autrui*; A: *Et del varlet et nïent d'autrui*; the line in A is not hypermetric as *nient* can be monosyllabic, cf. 802, 841, etc.
3093	R: *si harra l'eure que le vit* (BT); A: *Si harra l'eür qu'ele vit* fits in better with the idea that Athanaïs will resent her earlier good fortune.
3525	R: *Amors n'a cure de rentier* (T); A: *lanchier* = to fire an arrow.[87]
4545	R: *Qu'ele n'ait ensi desjuglé* (B); AT: *dessinglé* = tricked (literally thrown off a horse, appropriate in the circumstances).
5100	R: *chierement*; A *ricement* makes perfect sense.
6197	R: *Li soie cars n'est pas mortels*; A: *Li moie* is fine as an angel is speaking.
6243	A: *Quant il l'ot fait, se car derompre*; R corrects unnecessarily to *il ot fait*.

(iii) Restoration of readings corrected in error

1550	*De coi li piex Diex me desfende!* R follows the erroneous correction of a later hand, giving *fieus Dieus*, but cf. 1638.
3652-54	*Ne puet müer ne le confonde/Li empereres, s'il le set./– Il avra tort se il le het...* Here Athanaïs's conscience is mentioning the repercussions for Eracle (*cil* referred to in line 3649) if she commits adultery. R corrects erroneously (against all three manuscripts) to *ne te confonde* and *il me het*.
5017	*Tort ai, ne l'ai pas desservi...* Here Eracle is talking about criticisms levelled at himself for selecting Athanaïs as the emperor's wife. R corrects erroneously (with B against AT) to *ne l'a pas* as if Eracle were most concerned about injustice against the empress.

---

[87] R's emendation is controversial as it creates a link with Chrétien's *Cligés*; for further details, see pp. xiv-xv above.

The last two emendations undermine the role of Eracle and underestimate the importance Gautier places on his innocence.

(iv) Alternative emendations

2070   R emends to *desour le nue*, rejecting AB's *desous*, but *dessus* (cf. 5235) is preferable.

5237   R adopts the B reading *cavee*, but *cievee* suggested by Hayes is preferable, cf. 4400 and explains the error in A (*crevee*) much better.

(v) Additional corrections

255   R retains *aprent*; *reprent* (BT) is clearly preferable.

3072   R retains *volt*; *velt* (BT) is preferable.

3175   R retains *velt*; *volt* (BT) is preferable, followed by *fist*.

A Note on the Translation

This translation stays close to the Old French original, but aims to be readable. The usual mixture of past and present tenses found in medieval narrative poetry has been standardised into the past tense, but in order to reflect the sophisticated rhetoric of Gautier's work I have attempted to retain his repetition (even his elaborate examples of *annominatio*) rather than replacing it with variation, which would be more common in English. Having employed French punctuation in the edition – i.e. French inverted commas at the beginning and end of passages of speech, and en dashes to mark a change of speaker within them – I have copied this practice in the translation, in order to facilitate a comparison between the Old French text and the English rendering, although French inverted commas have been replaced by English ones.

Select Bibliography

Editions of Eracle
Eraclius, deutsches und französisches Gedicht des zwölften Jahrhunderts (jenes von Otte, dieses von Gautier d'Arras) zum ersten Mal herausgegeben von H. F. Massmann, edited by H. F. Massmann (Quedlinburg and Leipzig: G. Basse, 1842).
Oeuvres de Gautier d'Arras, edited by E. Löseth, 2 vols (Paris: Bouillon, 1890), I: *Eracle* [L].
Edition in unfinished doctoral thesis for the Sorbonne by Claude Hayes (Oxford, Taylorian Library, MS. Fol. F. 13-15, 15*, 1935-39) [H].
Gautier d'Arras, *Eracle*, edited by Guy Raynaud de Lage, CFMA 102 (Paris: Champion, 1976) [R].

Reviews of the CFMA Edition
Burgess, Glyn S., *Romance Philology*, 32 (1978), 254-55.
Ménard, Philippe, *Romania*, 99 (1978), 407-12.
Roques, Gilles, *Zeitschrift für romanische Philologie*, 95 (1979), 172-74.
van Emden, W. G., and K. E. Pratt, *French Studies*, 32 (1978), 436-38.

Translations
Eskénazi, André, *Gautier d'Arras, Éracle: traduit en français moderne d'après l'édition de G. Raynaud de Lage*, Traductions des classiques du Moyen Âge 54 (Paris: Champion, 2002) Introduction by Corinne Pierreville. [AE].
Gythiel, Anthony P., '*Ille et Galeron* and *Eracle*: Two Twelfth-Century French Romances, Translated with an Introduction', unpublished dissertation, University of Detroit, 1971.

Studies
Allinson, J. M., *A Literary Study of the* Roman d'Eracle *by Gautier d'Arras*, unpublished MA thesis, University of London, Westfield College, 1967.
Arzenton Valeri, Lorenza, 'Au nom de l'auteur: essai d'intervention auctoriale dans *Eracle*', *Bien dire et bien aprandre*, 8 (1990), 5-17.
Beckmann, Gustav Adolf, 'Der Tristandichter Thomas und Gautier d'Arras', *Romanistisches Jahrbuch*, 14 (1963), 87-104.
Benton, John F., 'The Court of Champagne as a Literary Center', *Speculum*, 36 (1961), 551-91.

Calin, William C., 'On the Chronology of Gautier d'Arras', *Modern Language Quarterly*, 20 (1959), 181-96.

Calin, William C., 'Structure and Meaning in the *Eracle* by Gautier d'Arras', *Symposium*, 16 (1962), 275-87.

Castellani, M.-M., 'La Cour et le pouvoir dans les romans de Gautier d'Arras', *Bien dire et bien aprandre*, 8 (1990), 19-34.

Cowper, F. A. G., 'Gautier d'Arras and Provins', *Romanic Review*, 22 (1931), 291-300.

Cowper, F. A. G., 'More Data on Gautier d'Arras', *PMLA*, 54 (1949), 302-16.

Cowper, F. A. G., 'Supplementary Material on Gautier d'Arras', *Bibliographical Bulletin of the International Arthurian Society*, 6 (1954), 110.

Delbouille, Maurice, 'A propos de rimes familières à Chrétien de Troyes et à Gautier d'Arras', *Etudes de langue et littérature du moyen âge: mélanges offerts à Félix Lecoy* (Paris: Champion, 1973), 55-65.

Eley, Penny, 'Patterns of Faith and Doubt: Gautier's *Eracle* and *Ille et Galeron*', *French Studies*, 43 (1989), 257-70.

Faral, Edmond, 'D'un "passionaire" latin à un roman français: quelques sources immédiates du roman d'*Eracle*', *Romania*, 46 (1920), 512-36.

Fourrier, Anthime, *Le Courant réaliste dans le roman courtois en France au Moyen-Âge* (Paris: Nizet, 1960), 2 vols, I, chapter 3.

Hayes, Claude, 'The Romance of Eracle by Gautier d'Arras: Its Sources, Composition and Place in Contemporary Literature', unpublished B. Litt. thesis, University of Oxford, 1934.

Heimer, Helge W., *Etude sur la langue de Gautier d'Arras* (Lund: Gleerupska Universitets-Bokhandeln, 1921).

Hüppe, W. *Der Sprachstil Gautiers von Arras*, unpublished dissertation, Münster, Bochum, 1937.

King, David S., 'Humor and Holy Crusade: *Eracle* and the *Pèlerinage de Charlemagne*', *Zeitschrift für französische Sprache und Literatur*, 109 (1999), 148-55.

Lacy, N. J., 'The Form of Gautier's *Eracle*', *Modern Philology*, 83 (1986), 227-32.

Love, Nathan, 'Polite Address and Characterization by Speech in Gautier's *Eracle*', *Romance Quarterly*, 25 (1988), 21-29.

Nykrog, Per, 'Two Creators of Narrative Form in Twelfth-Century France: Gautier d'Arras – Chrétien de Troyes', *Speculum*, 48 (1973), 258-76.

Pierreville, Corinne, *Gautier d'Arras, l'autre Chrétien* (Paris: Champion, 2001).

Pratt, Karen, *Meister Otte's Eraclius as an Adaptation of Eracle by Gautier d'Arras* (Göppingen: Kümmerle Verlag, 1987).

Pratt, Karen, 'The Rhetoric of Love in the Romances of Gautier d'Arras', in *Words of Love and Love of Words in the Middle Ages and the Renaissance*, edited by Albrecht Classen,

Medieval and Renaissance Texts and Studies (Tempe, AZ: Arizona Center for Medieval and Renaissance Studies at Arizona State University, 2007), 255-74.

Pratt, Karen, '*De vetula*: the Figure of the Old Woman in Medieval French Literature', in *Old Age in the Middle Ages and the Renaissance: Interdisciplinary Approaches to a Neglected Topic*, edited by Albrecht Classen, Fundamentals of Medieval and Early Modern Culture 2 (Berlin and New York: de Gruyter, 2007), 321-42.

Raynaud de Lage, Guy, 'De quelques images de Chrétien de Troyes chez Gautier d'Arras', *Studi di filologia romanza offerti a Silvio Pellegrini* (Padua: Liviana, 1971), 489-94.

Raynaud de Lage, Guy, 'La Religion d'*Eracle*', in *Mélanges de langue et de littérature médiévales offerts à Pierre Le Gentil* (Paris: SEDES, 1973), 707-13.

Rauhut, Franz, 'Das Psychologische in den Romanen Gautiers von Arras', in *Der altfranzösische höfische Roman*, edited by E. Köhler (Darmstadt: Wissenschaftliche Buchgesellschaft, 1978), 142-69.

Renzi, Lorenzo, *Tradizione cortese e realismo in Gautier d'Arras* (Florence: Leo S. Olschki, 1964).

Roques, Gilles, 'Remarques sur le texte d'*Eracle* de Gautier d'Arras', *Travaux de linguistique et de littérature*, 19:1 (1981), 63-67.

Schmitz, Silvia, '"Der vil wol erchennen chan": zu Gautiers und Ottes *Eraclius*', *Germanisch-romanische Monatsschrift*, 73 (1992), 129-50.

Warren, F. M., 'Some Features of Style in Early French Narrative Poetry (1150-1170)', *Modern Philology*, 3 (1905-1906), 179-209 and 513-39; 4 (1906-1907), 655-75.

Wolfzettel, Friedrich, 'Wahrheit der Geschichte und Wahrheit der Frau: *honor de feme* und weibliche *aventure* im altfranzösischen Roman', *Zeitschrift für romanische Philologie*, 104 (1988), 197-217.

Wolfzettel, Friedrich, 'La Découverte de la femme dans les romans de Gautier d'Arras', *Bien dire et bien aprandre*, 8 (1990), 35-54.

Wolfzettel, Friedrich, 'La Recherche de l'universel. Pour une nouvelle lecture des romans de Gautier d'Arras', *Cahiers de civilisation médiévale*, 33 (1990), 113-31.

Wolsey, Mary Lou Morris, *The 'Eracle' of Gautier d'Arras: A Critical Study*, unpublished dissertation, University of Minnesota, 1972.

Zumthor, Paul, 'L'Écriture et la voix: le *Roman d'Eracle*', in *The Craft of Fiction: Essays in Medieval Poetics*, edited by Leigh A. Arrathoon (Rochester, MI: Solaris Press, 1984), 161-209.

Other Primary Texts

Gautier d'Arras, *Ille et Galeron*, edited by Yves Lefèvre, CFMA 109 (Paris: Champion, 1988).

Gautier d'Arras, *Ille et Galeron*, edited and translated by Penny Eley, King's College London Medieval Studies XIII (London: King's College London Centre for Late Antique and Medieval Studies, 1996).

Meister Otte, *Eraclius, deutsches Gedicht des dreizehnten Jahrhunderts*, edited by Harald Graef (Strassburg: K. J. Trübner, 1883) [O].

Proverbes français antérieurs au XVe siècle, edited by Joseph Morawski, CFMA 47 (Paris: Champion, 1925).

Les Romans de Chrétien de Troyes: Erec et Enide, edited by Mario Roques, CFMA 80 (Paris: Champion, 1952).

Les Romans de Chrétien de Troyes: Cligés, edited by Alexandre Micha, CFMA 84 (Paris: Champion, 1957).

Les Romans de Chrétien de Troyes: Le Chevalier de la charrete, edited by Mario Roques, CFMA 86 (Paris: Champion, 1958).

Les Romans de Chrétien de Troyes: Le Chevalier au lion (Yvain), edited by Mario Roques, CFMA 89 (Paris: Champion, 1960).

Ch'est d'eracle l'empereour

127 a]
    Se Gautiers d'Arras fist ainc rien
    C'on atorner li doive a bien,
    Or li estuet tel traitié faire[1]
    Que sor tous autres doive plaire;
5   Car li princes est de tel pris
    Por cui il a ces fais empris
    Que li biens qui en lui habunde
    Enlumine trestout le monde.
    Je faiç de lui sanlance a l'eure
10   Qui aprés prime ne demeure,
    Car li jors vient lors et fait caut,
    Et tent li solaus plus en haut
    Et seut li jors en biauté croistre;
    Et cil qui tant fait a connoistre,
15   Dont je vous ai ichi conté,
    Croist et vient tous jors en bonté,
    Et tent en haut et plus est caus
    Et plus trençans que n'est li faus
    D'aquerre par molt grant prouece
20   Çou qu'il adiés met en larguece.
    Se n'ert Envie seulement,
    Çou c'on tesmoigne plainement[2]
    Tesmoigneroient roi et conte.
    Mais il desfait trestout lor conte
25   Et vient li de Saint Esperit
    Qu'il jue adiés et adiés rit.
    Li autre pleurent quant il donent,
    Et li pluisor un mot ne sonnent

---

[1] estuel]L.
[2] Et con]L.

This is about the Emperor Eracle

If Gautier d'Arras ever did anything to his credit, now is the time for him to produce a work that will give more pleasure than all others.[1] This is because the prince for whom he has undertaken these tasks is of such worth that the virtues which abound in him brighten up the whole world. I am minded to compare him to the hour which follows hard on prime,[2] for that is when daylight comes bringing its warmth and the sun climbs higher in the sky and the day always grows in beauty; and this man who does so many things worthy of note, the one I have just been telling you about, grows and increases each day in goodness, striving ever higher and warming to his task, keener than a scythe to acquire through extraordinary prowess what he then generously gives to others. If it were not for Envy, kings and counts would also bear witness to what is clear for all to witness; yet he gives the lie to all their accounts,[3] and, inspired by the Holy Spirit, he is always in joyful mood, always full of fun. **27** The others weep when they give and most do not utter a word

---

[1] Some critics read this line as evidence that Gautier had already composed other works, although he may simply be hoping to outdo rival poets.
[2] Prime is the first of the canonical hours, 6 a.m.
[3] Gautier plays on the narrative and financial meanings of 'accounts', cf. ll. 4913 and 5006.

As napes metre, et il me cante.
30 Il est faés, car il descante
Canques li autre vont faisant,
Qui lores sont mu et taisant:
Il tienent ordre et ont tel riule
Que il ne prisent une tiule
35 Cançon ne son ne rotruenge,
Car Covoitise les calenge.[3]
Il n'a el monde canteour,
Maistre estrument ne conteour
Qui un seul mot lor ost tentir, [b]
40 Car ne s'i voelent assentir
A oïr fable ne cançon,
Car aver sont li eschançon[4]
Et cil qui donent a laver,
Et il meïme sont aver;
45 S'on i velt joie entremeller,
Lors commencent d'el a parler.
Mais je demain trop longe lime;
Je vois trop alongant me rime,
Car on n'i puet nul bien pinchier;
50 Or voel me bouce recinchier.
Du plus vaillant dirai le some
Qui fust d'Illande dusc'a Rome,
Del bon conte Tibaut de Blois,
Del preu, del large, del cortois;
55 Que gré m'en sara tous li pire
Quant tous les biens m'en orra dire;
Mais tant dirai, comment qu'il aut,
Que riens del mont en lui ne faut
Que nus bons princes ait eü
60 C'on ait el siecle conneü.

Molt est li quens Tibaus preudon,
Bien a ataint dusques en son.
Il vient sovent u gens s'assemble,
Mais cuidiés vous que il s'en emble?
65 A l'endemain del parlement
S'en fuient tout conmunalment
A l'ajornee, je vous di,
Mais il atent jusc'a midi,
Con s'il estoit lor cambrelens.
70 Lors fait aporter ses berlens
Et les eskiekiers por nombrer[5]
L'avoir dont se velt descombrer.[6]
Cil ne li vont pas anoiant
U il le sien vait estuiant,
75 Qu'il done tous jors sans proumetre,
Ne velt en autre tresor metre.
Et tous li mons prise se vie,
Mais une riens, çou est Envie,
Qui talt le bien u que il soit; [c]
80 Si fait molt bien que faire doit,
Car tous jors mesdist del plus halt
Con de le cose qui mix vaut.[7]
Ja ne mesdira de nului
Se preu nel voit; si het cestui.
85 Mais mes cuers l'aime molt et prise,
Por lui ai jou ceste oevre emprise.
D'Eracle ichi endroit commence
Qui onques jor n'ot soig de tence;
Si l'acata li senescaus
90 Et povre et nu et tout descaus,
Et tout l'avoir qu'en prist le mere
Donna por l'ame son cier pere:

---

[3] le]B.
[4] enfancon]L.
[5] escuiers por iuer]B (T: Et ses echies quiert pour Iever).
[6] le v.]BT (T: desnuer).
[7] Qui d.]B.

while the tables are being laid, yet my lord sings. He has magic powers, for his song breaks whatever spells are being cast by the taciturnity and silence of the others: they keep their vows and obey such a strict rule[4] that they do not care a fig[5] for songs, tunes or love-songs,[6] for they are forbidden by Avarice to do so; in the whole world there is not a singer, master musician or storyteller who would dare to utter in their presence a single word, since they are unwilling to agree to hear stories or songs; their cupbearers are mean, and so are those who bring water to wash one's hands, because their lords are mean; if anyone tries to inject some fun into the proceedings, they immediately change the subject. But I am spending too long carping, and I am spinning out my verse too much, for one can derive no benefit from it; I prefer to rinse my mouth out now. **51** To put it in a nutshell, I shall describe the most valiant man you could possibly meet between Ireland and Rome: good count Thibaut of Blois,[7] the brave, the generous, the courtly. Even the very worst of men, when he has heard me tell of all his virtues, will be grateful to me;[8] but this much I shall say, whatever the consequences, that he lacks no quality whatsoever possessed by any good prince who ever lived on this earth. Count Thibaut is a very worthy man and has reached the very height of virtue. He often attends large gatherings, but do you think that he steals away from them? The day after the celebrations everyone with one accord rushes off at dawn, I can assure you, yet he waits until midday, as if he were their chamberlain. Then he calls for his gaming tables and his chessboards in order to count out the money he wishes to give away.[9] The people in whose safe-keeping he places his wealth do not need to keep pestering him, for he always makes gifts rather than promises, nor does he wish to place his money in any other kind of coffer. **77** And everyone would admire the way he lives if it were not for one thing – Envy, which refuses to acknowledge virtue wherever it may be. And it does its job very effectively because it always slanders the most noble of individuals since they are the most virtuous: it will never slander anyone unless it sees that he is worthy and then it hates him. But I love him dearly in my heart and admire him greatly, so I have undertaken this work for him. Here now begins the story of Eracle, who never set out to cause trouble. The seneschal bought him when he was poor, naked and completely barefoot, and all the money his mother received from his sale was given away to save his dear father's soul.

---

[4] The imagery here is monastic.
[5] An expression of minimal value; literally 'a tile', cf. ll. 783, 800, 802, 972, etc.
[6] A *rotruenge* is a love song with a refrain.
[7] Thibaut V of Blois (1152-91), seneschal of France, son of Thibaut IV (see l. 6524) and brother of Henri I of Champagne.
[8] If the more logical *BT* reading is authentic, then Gautier is saying that the most wicked man will hate his praise of Thibaut, but he will continue nevertheless.
[9] A chessboard could be used as an abacus for calculations.

　　　　Que bien connissoit li vassaus
　　　　Pierres et femmes et cevaus.
95　　Assés vous dirai el romans[8]
　　　　Les prouecces et les conmans
　　　　Que l'emperere fist de lui;
　　　　Et con il mescreï celui,
　　　　Cum des deus coses l'esprouva,
100　　Et quant le grant bien i trouva
　　　　Par lui se marïa li sire,
　　　　Si con m'orés el romans dire;[9]
　　　　A con grant tort il fu gabés
　　　　Et con il fu puis adoubés;
105　　Com il vint puis a tele honour
　　　　C'om fist de lui empereour
　　　　Et tint Coustantinoble quite;
　　　　Et si vous ert la cose dite
　　　　Con il le sainte Crois conquist
110　　Sur Cordroé, que il ocist;[10]
　　　　Con se gens fu reconfortee,
　　　　Et con le Crois en fu portee
　　　　La u on seut a Diu tenchier.
　　　　Humais voel m'oevre commenchier.
115　　　　En Rome ot ja un senator
　　　　Qui molt amoit son Creator;
　　　　Mirïados l'apieloit on,
　　　　Frans et prex ert et loiax hon.
　　　　Se feme avoit a non Cassine,　　[d]
120　　Li plus cortoise et li plus fine
　　　　Qui onques esteüst en Ronme.
　　　　En son mari ot molt preudome,
　　　　Et selonc tans et eure et leu
　　　　Estoient au siecle et a Deu.
125　　Biele ert li vie qu'il menoient
　　　　Et por Diu grant avoir donnoient.

　　　　A Diu, au siecle si s'aerdent
　　　　Que l'un por l'autre pas ne perdent.
　　　　Il orent bien ensanle esté
130　　Deus yvers plains et un esté
　　　　C'onques la dame enfant nen ot.
　　　　Grans ert li deus qu'ele en menot
　　　　Et grignor duel en ot li sire
　　　　Que nus ne pot conter ne dire.
135　　Diu en reclamoit doucement
　　　　Que il par son conmandement
　　　　Lor doigne tele engenreüre
　　　　Qu'il ait en lui sens et mesure.
　　　　Longues proient en tel maniere,
140　　Et Dix entendi lor proiere
　　　　Au cief de set ans, ce m'est vis,
　　　　Car a la dame fu avis
　　　　Par une nuit en son dormant
　　　　C'uns angles vint en son devant
145　　Et se li dist: «Esvelle toi!
　　　　Dix le te mande ci par moi,
　　　　Qui a te parole entendue.
　　　　Or n'i ait pas longe atendue,
　　　　Mais lieve sus isnielement,
150　　Si qu'il n'i ait demourement.
　　　　Cel rice tapi me prendras
　　　　Et en cele aire l'estendras;
　　　　Cel drap de soie esten desore.
　　　　Jhesus qui toute riens aoure
155　　Te mande que tu sempres dies
　　　　Ten mari, en cui tu t'afies,
　　　　Si voist desor le drap seoir
　　　　Ains qu'il puist riens del jor veoir;
　　　　Entor lui mece son mantiel　　[e]
160　　Tout le millor et le plus biel;

---

[8] es], cf. 102.
[9] remans]BT.
[10] Sous]T.

for the young boy was an excellent judge of stones and women and horses. I shall recount to you at some length in this romance[10] the great feats and tasks the emperor required of him and how his lord doubted him, how he put him to the test in two of these matters, and when his great gifts had been confirmed, his lord took a wife on his advice, as you will hear me relate in this romance. **103** Also how undeservedly he was ridiculed and how he was then dubbed a knight; how he then rose to a position of such honour that he was elected emperor and became the unchallenged ruler of Constantinople. And then you will be told the story of how he won back the Holy Cross from Chosroes, whom he killed; how his men's hearts were gladdened by this and how the Cross was borne away from the place where people often challenge the authority of God. Now I would like to begin my story.

In Rome there was once a senator who loved his Maker dearly; he was called Miriados and was a noble, virtuous and loyal man. His wife was called Cassine, the most courtly and most excellent lady who ever lived in Rome. She had in her husband a very worthy man and as time, opportunity and circumstances allowed they dedicated themselves to this world and to God. **125** The life they lived was virtuous and they gave away large sums of money for God. They were so attached both to God and to this world that they did not forfeit one for the sake of the other. They had been together for two full winters and one summer without the lady bearing a child. Great was the grief she felt over this, but her lord's grief was greater than anyone could describe or relate. He meekly prayed to God to give them on His authority a child who possessed good sense and moderation. They prayed in this manner for a long time and after seven years had elapsed, or so I believe, God heard their prayer, for it seemed to the lady one night as she slept that an angel appeared before her and said to her: 'Wake up! I have been sent to you with a message from God, who has heard your words. Now do not wait any longer, but get up quickly so that there is no delay. **151** You will take this splendid carpet from me and spread it out here on the floor; spread this silk cloth on top of it. Jesus, whom every creature worships, commands you immediately to tell your husband, in whom you trust, to go and sit on the silk cloth before he sees any trace of daylight, and to place his best and most beautiful cloak around him

---

10   The *BT* reading *en romans* means 'in the vernacular', and would suggest that Gautier had a Latin source. The *A* reading *es* is most likely to be a scribal error for *el* which would imply, as in l. 102, that Gautier was using *romans* as a generic label for his work. See my Introduction, p. xxiii.

A soi t'apelt isnielement
Et gise a toi delivrement.
Et si diras a ton mari
C'or se puet tenir a gari,
165 Car Dix le dist: en ceste nuit
Engendrera en toi tel fruit
Dont toute Rome joie ara;[11]
Çou ert uns fix, qui plus sara
Que nus hom qui el siecle soit.
170 Ne puet perir qui en Diu croit;
Il n'i a pas creü en vain.
Face messe canter demain
Del Saint Esprit, et se li proie
Que il ofre cel drap de soie,[12]
175 Par tel ententïon le face
Que il doinst a l'enfant se grasce.
Por Diu soit doné as mesiaus
Et li tapis et li mantiaus.»
Li angles Diu s'esvanuïst
180 Et li dame du lit s'en ist;
Le tapi et le drap estent[13]
L'un desor l'autre el pavement;
Dedens son lit se rest assise,
Si a pensé en mainte guise
185 De çou que li angles a dit.
«Aiue, Dius, Saint Esperit,
Se pense ele, con sera çou?
Mon mari conment dirai jou
Qu'il voist sifaitement en l'aire
190 Et qu'il m'apiaut por tel afaire?
Noter i pora legerie,
Cuidier i pora lecherie.
Mais se Diu plaist, ce n'i ert ja,
Car li angles le m'encarja,
195 Et cose u Dix ait rien a faire

Ne puet pas torner a contraire.»[14]
Atant se leva li preudom,
Que jou Mirïados vous nom.
Cele li moustre mot a mot [f]
200 Ce que li angles dit li ot:
Voist sor le tapi, si l'apiaut;
Tout li demoustre et li espiaut.
Cil n'est ne vilains ne leciere,
Se feme croit et tient molt ciere;
205 Saut sus et si l'apiele a lui,
Si engenra en li celui
Qui fist puis maint home esjoïr,
Et dont il fait bien a oïr –
De çou me puis je bien vanter.
210 L'endemain fist messe canter
Mirïados a molt grant joie,
Si a offert cel drap de soie;
Le bon mantiel as mesiax donne
Et le tapis lor abandone.
215 Tout depart a la povre gent,
Son blé, son or et son argent,
Que Dix, quil fist a se faiture,
Soit garde de s'engenreüre.
La dame, qui son fil conçut,
220 L'ot droit au jor c'avoir le dut,
Et saciés c'a tel eure l'ot
C'onques fors Diu nuls ne le sot,[15]
Et fu li plus tres biele riens
C'onques veïst hom terrïens.
225 Si l'apielerent Diudonné,
Por ce qu'issi l'ot Dix donné;
Puis fu nonmés el baptestire
Eracles, ensi l'oï dire.
Au tierç jor qu'il fu baptisiés
230 Li vint uns briés trestous ploiés;

---

[11] j. i ara]BT.
[12] oste c.]B.
[13] sor l. d.]BT.

[14] p. t. pas]R.
[15] C. sous D. plus n.].

and to beckon you quickly to his side and to lie with you straight away. And you will tell your husband that he can now rest assured, for this was God's command that on this night he will beget in you a fruit that will bring joy to the whole of Rome; this will be a son, who will know more than any man alive today. Whoever believes in God will be saved;[11] he has not believed in Him in vain. Let him arrange for a mass to be sung for the Holy Spirit tomorrow and ask him to offer up this silk cloth, and let him do it with the aim of procuring His grace for the child. **177** Let both the carpet and the cloak be given to the lepers for the Lord's sake.' The angel of the Lord disappeared and the lady got out of bed; she spread the carpet and the cloth one upon the other on the floor; then she got into bed again and sat turning over in her mind what the angel had said. 'Please help me God and the Holy Spirit,' she said to herself, 'how can this be done? How shall I tell my husband to go and lie on the floor in this manner and to beckon me to him for such an act? He may well detect frivolity in me and may well think me lewd. Yet if it pleases God, this will not be the case, for the angel instructed me to do this, and any matter which involves God cannot turn out badly.'

197 Then the worthy man, whose name, I told you, was Mirïados, got up, and she explained to him word for word what the angel had said to her: that he should go and lie on the carpet and beckon her to him; she described and explained everything to him. Being neither base nor lewd, he believed his wife and held her very dear; he leapt up, beckoned her to him and begot in her the boy who later made many a man rejoice and whose story is good to hear – of this I can confidently boast. The next day Miriados, with great joy in his heart, had a mass sung and made an offering of the silk cloth; he gave the fine cloak to the lepers and also handed over the carpet to them; he divided everything up amongst the poor: his wheat, his gold and his silver, so that God, who had made him in his likeness, would protect his offspring.

The lady who was carrying his son gave birth to him exactly on the appointed day and let me tell you that she had him at a time of day when nobody but God knew about it, and he was quite the most beautiful creature that any mortal had ever seen. **225** So they called him 'Gift of God',[12] because God had given him to them in this way; then later at his baptism he was called Eracle, or so I heard tell.[13] On the third day after he had been baptised a letter arrived for him, all folded up;[14]

---

11   See St Paul to the Romans, 9:33.
12   This was the name given at first to Philippe-Auguste (born 1165), the long-awaited son of Louis VII of France and nephew of Thibaut V of Blois.
13   Gautier seems to be implying an oral source here.
14   For the motif of the divine letter which falls from heaven, see Pierreville 2001, 24-25. Letters in the Middle Ages were written on parchment, folded and were then sealed with wax, hence *cire* in l. 244.

Dix nostre Sire li tramist
Par le saint angle qui le mist
Sor le berçuel u il gisoit.
Li letre par defors disoit
235 C'on mesist cel enfant a letre
Quant eure et tans seroit del metre.
Encor ot defors autre cose:
Que la dame ne fust tant ose
Que desploier laissast le
          brief,   128 a]
240 Mais, sor les deus ix de son cief
Fust bien gardés et en sauf mis,
Tant que l'enfes fust si apris
Qu'il le peüst espondre et lire,
Et lors li baillast on se cire.
245 La dame saut sus de son lit,
Les letres prent et si en list
Tant seulement que lire en doit:
Çou est çou que defors pendoit;
Le brief estoie maintenant;
250 Or voit que Dix a cier l'enfant.
Norir le fait molt ricement.
Quant il a cinc ans plainement,
Mis est as letres li petis,
Mais ainc ne fu teux aprentis:
255 Son maistre au cief de l'an reprent.[16]
Molt est senés, car il aprent
Plus en un an c'autres en quatre;
Ne se fait laidengier ne batre.
Li mere quel voit tant sené
260 L'a devant un autel mené,
Le brief li tent, cil le desploie,[17]
Et si le list; s'en a tel joie

Que nus ne puet grignor avoir,
Car Dix li a fait assavoir
265 Qu'il ert de femes connissieres
Et canque valt cevax ne pieres
Savra, tels sera se merite,
Par Diu et par saint Esperite.
Quant il ot tout le brief leü
270 De cief en cief et porveü,[18]
Toutes les pieres connissoit
De quel vertu cascune estoit;
De femes savoit ensement
Toute le vie et l'errement,
275 Et quels cascune estoit el point
Qu'il le veoit, n'en doutoit point;
Et des cevax resavoit il
Li quels valoit mix entre mil.
Mais ains qu'il par eüst dis ans, [b]
280 Morut ses peres, li vaillans
Mirïados, li gens, li biaus,
Si tint se mere les castiaus,
Les viles et les fremetés,
Les manoirs et les yretés.[19]
285 Mais trestout volt laisser encore
Por l'ame son pere secore.
Avant savrés con ele fist
Et con son fil a raison mist,
Con Eracles li respondi
290 Quant la parole en entendi.
    «Fix, dist li mere, je te voi
Desconforté, ce poise moi.
Mors est Mirïados li sages,
Çou est grans deus et grans damages,
295 Fix, et a toi meesmement,

---

[16] aprent]BT; O, 417: rihten *reflects* BT.
[17] se li]B.
[18] cies e. c.]. *The spelling with* k *adopted by* R *is that of* B *and of a later scribe who corrected this line in* A *against the practice of the original copyist, cf.* 4451 *and passim.*
[19] maneoirs les]B.

Our Lord God sent it to him by means of the holy angel who placed it on the cradle where he lay. The lettering on the outside said that the child should be taught to read when it was the right time and age for him to be taught. A further instruction on the outside was that the lady should not be so rash as to allow the letter to be unfolded, but, on pain of losing both the eyes in her head, it should be securely locked away and put in a safe place until the child was educated enough to decipher and read it, then he was to be given his wax-sealed letter. The lady jumped out of her bed, seized the letter and read only what she was supposed to read, namely what was attached to the outside. She immediately locked away the letter; now she could see that God dearly loved the child. **251** She gave him a splendid upbringing. When he reached the age of five the little lad was taught his letters, yet never was there such a gifted learner: by the end of the year he was correcting his teacher. He was very intelligent, for he learned more in a year than another child would learn in four; he did not need to be scolded or beaten. When she saw that he was so intelligent his mother led him before an altar and handed him the letter, which he unfolded and read. This gave him greater joy than anyone could possibly experience, for God informed him that he would be an expert judge of women, and he would know the value of horses and precious stones – this would be his talent, given him by God and the Holy Spirit. When he had read the whole letter from top to bottom and scrutinized it, he knew about all manner of stones and the qualities each possessed; likewise he knew all about every woman's life and conduct, and he was in no doubt what sort of person she was at the moment when he saw her;[15] and similarly he knew about horses, which one of a thousand was the best. **279** Yet before he was quite ten years old his father, worthy, noble, handsome Miriados, died and his mother took possession of their castles, towns and fortresses, their manors and all their inherited land. However, she wished to give everything away to save his father's soul. First though you will learn how she went about it and how she addressed her son, how Eracle replied when he heard her views on the matter.

'My son,' said the mother, 'I see you are disconsolate and this upsets me. Miriados the wise is dead, this is a cause of great sorrow and a great loss to me, my son, and especially to you,

---

[15] Since Eracle does not need to see the woman in order to know what she is doing, *veoit* is problematic (cf. ll. 549 and 4723ff.). I have, however, rejected Raynaud de Lage's reading of the passage, who claims a sexual connotation for 'el point' in l. 275 and whose use of brackets seems to suggest the translation 'when he saw her he was in no doubt' for l. 276. 'El point que' is a set expression which recurs in ll. 2662, 2721 and 4943 and means 'at the point/time when'.

Car il t'ama molt tenrement.
– Et jou si aim l'ame mon pere
Tant con le moie, douce mere.
– Fix, jel verrai dedens tierç jor
300 Se tu l'aimes de bone amor;
Je le verrai. – Vous? En quel guise?
– Fix, que m'en valra le devise?
– Si fera, mere, voirement,
Car je ferai vostre talent.
305 – Se le tenoies, fix, a bien,
Ten avoir donroie et le mien
Por amor Diu le Creator,
Qu'il mete l'ame mon signor,
Vostre bon pere, en paradis,
310 La u li bon mainent toudis.
Tu ses tant de devinement
Que tu te garras ricement
Et avras bien tes volentés.
Et poi de cose m'ert plentés:
315 Feme sui, poi me soufira;
Et tout fors biens fais tresira,[20]
Tout tresira fors seul bien fait;
Molt par est sages qui bien fait.
Faisomes bien, biens en venra   [c]
320 L'ame celui qui t'engenra.
– Douce mere, Dix le vous mire!
Grans loiautés le vous fait dire
Et jel devroie vous requerre;
Ne de l'avoir ne de la terre
325 Ne me quier je faire saisir;
Or en faites vostre plaisir.
Se l'ame a nul mestier d'aïe,
Si sera par itant garie
Et iert mais en repos tos jors,
330 Et s'el n'a mestier de secors,
Dix le vous sara bien merir,
Car nus biens fais ne puet perir.
Biens fais vient la u venir doit
Comment qu'il onques donés soit.»
335 Ne vous irai pas porlongant,
Mais tout vendirent maintenant,
Si font larges osteleries,
Et molt rices herbegeries
Et abeïes et moustiers;
340 Et selonc ce qu'il ert mestiers
Donent as povres soufraiteus,
As orfelins, as vergondeus:
Lor terres lor ont racatees
As useriers et aquitees.
345 Ains que li mois fust tos passés,
Se sont plus povre fait assés
De tous les plus caitis de Ronme;
Et on oublie tost povre home,
Car cose c'on veoir ne veut
350 Oublie on tost, avenir seut;
Et il sont si mis en oubli
C'on ne connoist ne lui ne li
Fors povre gent, u il estont,
En vielle Rome, sus amont
355 Del grant palais qui lor seut estre;[21]
Nus hom fors Dius ne set lor estre.
Sainte est li vie que il mainent;
Lor cors travaillent molt et painnent,
Et font tout içou entresait   [d]
360 Que povres por soi garir fait.
De se quenoulle vit Cassine,
Li plus cortoise et li plus fine
Et toute li miudre aumosniere

---

[20] tous]T.

[21] u il s. e.]B.

for he loved you most tenderly. – And I love my father's soul as much as my own, gentle mother. – My son, within the next three days I shall see whether your love for him is true. **301** I shall see. – Will you? In what way? – My son, is there any point in my revealing what I have in mind? – Yes, indeed, mother, because then I shall carry out your wishes. – If you considered it the right thing to do, son, I would give away your possessions and mine for the love of God our Maker, so that he might convey the soul of my lord, your good father, to paradise, where the virtuous dwell for ever. You have such powers of second sight that you will be able to provide for yourself splendidly and you will have everything you desire; little will be plenty for me: as I am a woman, little will be sufficient for me, and nothing apart from good deeds lasts, nothing at all lasts except for good deeds;[16] whoever performs good deeds is very wise indeed. Let us do good, for good will then come to the soul of the man who fathered you. – Gentle mother, may God give you the recognition you deserve for this! You say this out of great loyalty and I should be asking this of you; I do not wish to take possession of either the money or the land;[17] now do with it what you please. **327** If his soul is in need of any help, it will be saved by this and will be at rest for ever more, and if it does not need help, God will find a way to reward you well for this, since no good deed can go to waste. A good deed finds its way to where it is needed, regardless of the intention of the person who performs it.'[18] I shall not spin out my tale any longer, suffice it to say that they immediately sold everything and set up generous hospices, and well equipped alms-houses, and abbeys and churches; and they gave whatever was needed to the poor and destitute, to orphans, to those fallen on hard times: they redeemed their lands from usurers, paying off their debts. Before the month was out they had made themselves much poorer than the most wretched inhabitants of Rome; and a poor man is quickly forgotten, for it is commonly the case that one quickly forgets what is unpleasant to the eye; **351** and they were forgotten so completely that no one recognized either him or her except for the poor folk they lived with in the old quarter of Rome, above the great palace which used to belong to them; no one but God knew how they were living. The life they led was pious; they subjected themselves to physical hardship and toil, doing exactly what a poor man does in order to survive. Cassine, the most courtly and most perfect and most generous alms-giver

---

[16] Cassine is expressing the biblical idea of *vanitas vanitatum* – all that is worldly is transient.
[17] A distinction is being made here between *avoir* (moveable property/money) and land.
[18] Eracle is here expressing the belief that Christian charity and prayer will always be rewarded by God, either for the benefit of those whose souls need to be saved, or for those praying on their behalf; cf. ll. 6467-78.

Qui onques fust des le premiere ;
365 Eracle en paist, sen tres douç fil.
Mout suefrent por Diu grant escil
Et grant mesaise et jor et nuit,
Et si n'ont rien qui lor anuit
Fors de çou qu'il n'ont que donner
370 Por amor Diu quis doit sauver ;
Ne plaignent pas ce que rien n'ont,
Fors que por Diu nul bien ne font.
    Eracles ert de molt grant sens ;
Coustume estoit en icel tens
375 Qui enfant avoit, sel vendist ;
Ja li enfes nel desfendist
Por que il pleüst a son pere
U que il sesist a sa mere.
Voirs fu et celi en souvint,
380 En cuer et en pensé li vint
De vendre Eracle, son enfant
Et de donner l'avoir avant
Por Diu qui le forma et fist.
Son enfant baisa, se li dist
385 «Mes dous biax fix, nen aies ire
D'une cose que je voel dire.
– Biele mere, non arai jou,
Mais dites moi, que sera çou ?
– Eracle fix, je te voel vendre,
390 Car grant avoir en porai prendre,
Ne mais que nostre bons visnages[22]
Seüst que tu fusses tant sages,
Et conneüst ton grant savoir.
Et j'en prendrai cel grant avoir
395 Sel donrai a la povre gent,
Que Dix par son conmandement
Prenge l'ame Mirïados,
Et si le mece en son repos.

Biax fix, por Diu ne te desplaise, [e]
400 Car tu aras molt grignor aise
U que tu soies c'or n'en as.
Fai le de cuer, bon le feras ;
Garde que tu ne m'escondies.
En une de ces abeïes
405 Que faite avons me garirai,
Et Damediu i servirai,
Qui tous les biens prent a se part.
– Me douce mere, il m'est trop tart
Que l'aie fait, par Diu le voir ;
410 Je ne quier ja repos avoir
Devant que vos m'aiés vendu ;
N'i ait plus longes atendu,
Mais dusc'al marcié me menés
Et au vendre bien vous tenés.
415 Pensés de Rome bien cerkier ;
Qui que m'ait vil, tenés me cier ;
N'en laissiés riens de mil besans,
Qui qu'en soit haitiés ne dolans ;
Tant en arés, se Dix me vaille,
420 N'en ert a dire une maaille.
– Fix, bien ait tele engenreüre ! »
Li mere a prise sa çainture,
Entor le col li lace et lie.
Eracles forment s'umelie,
425 Ne fait sanlant qu'il le desvoelle ;
El toup devant a une fuelle
Con cevax que on maine vendre
Por faire le gent a entendre.
Onques aigniax plus simplement
430 N'ala u liu u on le vent
Con fait li tendre cars, li biele,
Le col estraint de le cordiele.
Se mere siut, qui buer fu nee,
Car d'amer Diu s'est molt penee.

---

[22] vignages]B.

who ever lived since the first of her sex, earned her living with her spinning wheel; she fed Eracle, her dearest son, on the proceeds. They suffered great privation for the Lord's sake and great discomfort day and night, and yet they were troubled by nothing except that they had nothing left to give for the love of God, who was their Saviour; they did not complain about having nothing except insofar as they were not able to do good works for God.

373 Eracle was full of good sense; it was the custom in those days for anyone who had a child to sell it; the child never refused, provided that it pleased his father or suited his mother to do so. This was indeed the case and Cassine remembered this. So she conceived in her heart the idea of selling Eracle, her child, and of giving away the proceeds for the sake of God, who created and made him. She kissed her child and said to him: 'Fair gentle son, do not be angry at what I am going to say to you. – Fair mother, I shall not be, but tell me what it is. – Eracle, my son, I want to sell you, because I shall be able to obtain a large sum of money for you, provided that our good neighbours know how clever you are and discover your great expertise. And I shall take the large sum of money from the sale and I shall give it to the poor, so that God will authorise the salvation of Miriados's soul and will grant it eternal peace. **399** Fair son, for the Lord's sake, do not be displeased, for you will have a much more comfortable life wherever you end up than you have at present; do it with a glad heart and you will do it well; make sure that you do not refuse me this. I shall take refuge in one of the abbeys we have founded and there I shall serve the Lord God, who claims all good deeds for his own purposes. – Sweet mother, I wish it were already done, by God the true; I shall not rest until you have sold me; let there be no more delay, but take me to the market and when selling me hold out for the best price. Make sure you scour the whole of Rome; whoever may consider me worthless, you must hold me dear; do not accept anything less than a thousand *besants*,[19] whoever may be pleased or angry about it; you will get that much for me, if God is on my side, and you will not have to accept a penny less. – My son, may such a child as you be blessed with good fortune!' The mother took her belt and looped and tied it around his neck. **424** Eracle submitted to great humiliation, not appearing to be at all unwilling. Attached to his forelock he had a leaf to let everyone know that he was for sale, just as with a horse being taken to market.[20] Never did a lamb go more innocently to the place where it would be sold than this fair, tender creature, around whose neck the cord was pulled tight.[21] He followed his mother, for whose life we should be grateful, since she went to great lengths to love God.

---

[19] A *besant* was a Byzantine gold coin of much greater value than the copper *maaille*.
[20] A leaf or sprig of leaves indicated that he was for sale; people were expected to ask the price.
[21] Eracle is here being compared to Christ as *agnus dei* (the lamb of God).

Quant sont eslongié de lor rue,
Tant con on une piere rue,
N'est hom qui tant les ait veüs
Ques ait de riens reconneüs,
Por le mesaise quis fait gaunes[23] [f]
Dont il ont eu a grans aunes;
Et il ont soufert plus d'un an
Cele mesaise et cel ahan,
Et povres hom, con je vous dis,
Est oublïés en quinze dis.
Li dame qui son marcié quiert
Fait canqu'a marceant afiert;
Le maistre rue en est venue
U molt d'onor avoit eüe,
Lassus el grant marcié de Rome.
Illuec l'arainnent plusor home,
Et dient li un: «Douce suer,
Di nous de cest enfant le fuer.
— Biau douç signor, cil l'en menra
Qui mil besans en paiera.
— Amie, font il, tu iés sote.
Se les as cousus en se cote,[24]
Donques les valt il plainement!
Fals est qui l'acate autrement.
Tant con il a sor lui, si valt.
— Signor, por Diu qui maint en halt,
Cui sanle trop, si laist ester;
Nos n'avons mestier de gaber.»
Icil s'en vont, autre revienent,
Qui del varlet en grant le tienent,
Ne que li premier riens n'i font:

Oent le fuer et puis en vont.
Cele se maine durement,
Eracles son penser entent:
«Mere, fait il, ne pensés rien,
Car vos me venderés tres bien;
G'iere encor hui si chier tenus,
Cil qui m'ara n'est pas venus.»
Lors ont esgardé tout un val
Et voient venir a ceval
Le senescal l'empereour,
Et si escuier, li pluisor,
Voient l'enfant qui est a vendre
Sel font lor signor a entendre.
Li senescaus i vient atant   [129 a]
Et dist: «Que fait on cest enfant?
— Sire, mil besans i donrés,
Se biel vos est, si l'en menrés,
Et si en ferés vostre afaire.
— Amie, suer, que set il faire?
A el en lui que je n'i voi,[25]
U a il nule rien en soi
Que je n'i voie, qui tant vaille?
Il les poise molt bien, sans faille,
Mais n'acatai ainc home a pois
Ne ne ferai, je croi, des mois.»
Et quant li vallés l'entendi
Molt sagement li respondi:
«Sire, nel tornés a barat,
Mais qui tant m'aime tant m'acat.
Se li marciés ne vous contece,
Laissieme ester, car pire tece

---
[23] Por les mesaises cont fait gandes/dont il ont eu a grans annes]B. *The 'corrections' of a later hand have simply added to the confusion in* A 439.
[24] Sil]. *My emendation is supported by the conditional construction in* O, 724, *and by the second person form* ir. *It also explains the variants in* B: Tu les as *and* T: Sil les a *(adopted by* R).
[25] A il en l.; T]B.

Once they had gone a stone's throw away from their street there was no one who would have recognised them in any way, however often he had seen them, because of the hardship which had sallowed their complexions and which they had experienced by the cartload;[22] and they had suffered this hardship and pain for more than a year, and a poor man, as I said before, is forgotten within a fortnight. The lady, who was intent on making a sale, did everything a merchant should do; she went along the main street, where she had enjoyed considerable honour, up to Rome's great market-place. **450** There several men spoke to her, some saying: 'Sweet sister, tell us the price of this child. – Fair gentle lords, he will be taken home by the man who pays a thousand *besants* for him. – My friend,' they said, 'you're mad! He's only worth that much if you have sewn them into his tunic. Anyone who buys him on a different basis is a fool. He's worth only as much as he has on him. – My lords, by God who dwells on high, if anyone finds the price too high, let him withdraw from the bargaining; we are not interested in banter.' Those men left and others approached who eagerly questioned her about the boy, yet they did no more than the first lot: having heard the price, they left. Cassine was very upset, but Eracle could read her thoughts. 'Mother,' he said, 'don't worry, for you will succeed in selling me; before the day is out I shall be considered worth the price, the man who will buy me hasn't come yet.' Then they looked downhill and saw the emperor's seneschal riding up, and his numerous squires saw the child who was for sale and drew their lord's attention to this. **479** The seneschal approached straight away and said: 'What's the asking price for this child? – My lord, if it pleases you, you will pay a thousand *besants* for him, and then you may take him away and do with him what you will. – My dear sister, what can he do? Is there more to him than meets the eye, or indeed is there something about him which I cannot see, but which is so valuable? There is no doubting that he easily weighs that much, but I have never yet bought a man by weight, nor shall I, if I can help it, for a long time to come.' And when the boy heard him, he replied to him very wisely: 'My lord, do not think this is a trick, but let anyone who wants me that much pay the price. If you are not happy with this deal, let's call it off, for there is no worse fault

---

[22] Literally by the ell, a medieval measure of length, somewhat further than a modern metre.

N'est que de povre ramproner.
N'en poriés pas trop donner:
Poi savés que j'ai sous le cape;
500 Se cis marciés vous en escape,[26]
Jamais n'arés millor ne tel.
Molt bien emploie son catel
Hom qui en bon liu le despent.
– Varlet, por Diu or m'en repent,
505 Mais ne t'en dois pas mervillier,
J'ai veü sovent consillier
De molt mains que de mil besans;
Mais en Rome, qui si est grans,
N'est qui t'acat plus tost de moi,
510 Mais que je sace le por coi.
Tant saces tu, que que on die,
D'acater cose est musardie
Se on ne set a qu'ele monte;
Mais fols hom torne tout a honte.
515 Biel me seroit d'avoir apris
Por coi tu iés de si grant pris.
– Biax sire ciers, tant avés dit
Vous le saverés sans respit:
Je sui li miudre connissiere [b]
520 Qui soit el mont de bone piere;
Onques mais nus hom tant n'en sot;
Ne se fait pas tenir por sot
Hom qui en moi met son avoir.
– Varlet, molt a ci grant savoir,
525 A çou que tu n'iés mie viex.
Se ce est voirs, dont vaus tu mix.
– Biax sire ciers, or m'entendés,
Se çou n'est voirs, si me pendés.
– Et ses tu plus? – Par Diu, sire, oie,
530 Car se je mil cevax veoie,
Si vous saroie lués a dire
Qui fust li miudre ne li pire.

– Amis varlés, bien le saciés,
Or amende nostre marciés.
535 Di moi verté, esce ta mere?
– Biax sire, oïl. – Certes, biau frere,
Se ce est voirs que tu me dis,
Dont iés tu de grant sens garnis.
– Sire, nel tenés mie a songe.
540 Se vous m'ataigniés a mençoigne,
Si me faites les ix crever;
Ja mar me ferés mains grever.[27]
– Et ses tu plus, se Dix te saut?
– Oie, une cose qui mix vaut
545 Que canques je vous ai conté:
De feme connois la bonté,
S'ele a en soi sens u folie,
Et canc'a fait toute sa vie;
Et s'ele est lonc ensus de moi,
550 Si sai jou se pensee et voi.
– Amis, or oi jou grans miracles.
Con as tu non? Biax sire, Eracles.
– Amis, molt iés por Diu senés,
Et je te di, buer fus ainc nés
555 Et buer veïs le jor entrer
Que je te poi hui encontrer,
Se çou est voirs que tu me contes.
– Sire, faites moi lais et hontes,
Se ce n'est voirs, et metre en feu; [c]
560 Ja mar me ferés autre preu.[28]
– Eracle, amis, et jel verrai
Et orendroit t'acaterai,
U face savoir u folie.»
Uns serjans u il plus se fie
565 Fait a la dame son creant.
Al departir firent duel grant;
Li mere crie et li fix pleure,
Cent fois se baisent en poi d'eure.

---

[26] The spelling markies seems to be that of a later scribe.
[27] ne f.]B.
[28] artre]BT.

than to poke fun at a poor man. You could never give too much for me, for you have little idea what I have up my sleeve. If you allow this deal to escape you, never again will you find a better or similar one. **502** Anyone who spends his money in a good cause, puts it to very good use. – Young man, by God, I am sorry, yet you should not be amazed, for I have often seen men deliberate over much less than a thousand *besants*; yet in the whole of Rome, which is such a great city, there is no one who would buy you more readily than I, provided that I know the reason why. Whatever people say, this much you should know, that it is stupid to buy a thing without knowing what it is worth. Yet a foolish man brings shame on whatever he does. I should be pleased to learn why your price is so high. – My dear lord, you have said enough for me to tell you without delay: I am the greatest expert in the world today on precious stones; never before has a man known so much about them; a man who invests his wealth in me will not be deemed a fool. – Young man, this is great knowledge indeed, considering that you are not at all old. **526** If it is true, then you are worth even more. – My dear lord, listen to me, if this is not true, then hang me. – And can you do anything else? – By God, my lord, yes, for if I were to see before me a thousand horses, I would be able to tell you immediately which was the best and which the worst. – Young friend, as well you know, our deal is now looking even more attractive. Tell me truly, is this your mother? – Fair lord, yes. – Indeed, fair brother, if what you tell me is true, then you are indeed blessed with great intelligence. – My lord, don't consider what I say to be pure fabrication. If you can prove me a liar, then have my eyes put out; it would be quite wrong for you to do me any less harm than that. – And can you do more, if the Lord is your Saviour? – Yes, I can do something more useful than anything I have told you about thus far: I can judge the virtue of a woman, whether she is wise or foolish, and know everything she has done throughout her life; even if she is a long way away from me, I know and can read her thoughts. – My friend, now I am hearing marvellous things. **552** What is your name? – Fair lord, Eracle. – My friend, you are, by God, very clever and I must say it is fortunate that you were ever born and fortunate that you saw this day dawn on which we were able to meet, if what you tell me is true. – My lord, if it is not true, have me tortured and dishonoured and burnt alive; it would be quite wrong for you to do me any other favour. – Eracle, my friend, we shall see, but now I shall purchase you, whether this be a wise or a foolish move.' A sergeant whom he trusted most of all gave the lady her payment. There was great lamenting when they parted; the mother cried and the son wept, within a short while they kissed each other a hundred times.

Grans est li dues qu'il vont faisant,
570 El li a dit tout en baisant:
«Dix, bien ait tele engenreüre![29]
Onques plus douce creature
Ne fist mais feme que j'ai faite,
Et ceste ert mais tos jors retraite,
575 C'ainc mais ne fu si dure mere
Con je par sui. E! Dix, biax pere,
Avint mais el siecle vivant
Que feme vendist son enfant?
Onques mais feme ne fu tex,
580 Ramembre toi, biax sire Dex!
Biax sire Dix, ramembre t'ent,
Maintien mon fil, garde son sens,
Aies ent pitié et de moi,
Car cest marcié fai je por toi.
585 Nus ne se prent a toi en vain:
Tuit s'en loent a l'endemain,
Et je m'en loerai, mien voel.
A poi mes cuers ne part de duel;
Ja fust partis, ne fusses tu;
590 Aiue, Dix, par ta vertu,
Car a toi est toute m'entente,
Et cil qui a si rice atente[30]
Ne doit riens contre Diu sosfrir;
A toi me voel del tot offrir,
595 Langirai mais si docement;
N'a mal qui si grant joie atent
Con est te joie, sire Dex,
Car onques nule ne fu tex.
Sire, nel tornés a desdaing [d]
600 D'Eracle, mon filg, que je plaing;
Mais or lairai le plainte ester.
Tu nel me fesis fors prester;
Prestas le moi, et jel te renç,

Car tout est tien ce que je pren.
605 Fix, je t'envoi ci en escil,
C'ainc mere ne fist mais de fil.
– Mere, fait il, laissiés cest plait,
Ne l'avés pas por mon mal fait,
Ne por sorfait qui en vous soit,
610 Ains est por Diu, qui molt cler voit
Canc'on por lui fait et despent;
Et nus hom fors Dix seulement
Ne done a home large don
Ne ne set rendre gueredon.
615 Riens n'est envers le soie grasce;
N'est hom el mont qui por lui face
Ke cent itant ne puist trouver,
Se ne li doit nus reprouver
Bien fais, almosnes ne biax dons,
620 Car mains en valt ses gueredons,
Et qui le plus pert por le mains
N'est mie de grant savoir plains.
Mere, soiés le Diu amie,
Gardés ne li reprouvés mie
625 Vostre bien fait ne vostre amor,
Mais merciés l'ent nuit et jor
Que il vous a si aspiree
Et tele entention donee,
Et moi ne plaigniés vous mais rien,
630 Car je me garirai tres bien.
Si ferés vous, se Dix me saut,
Car qui crient Diu, riens ne li faut.»
Li mere atant son fil rebaise,
C'a piece mais nen ara aise
635 De lui baisier, qu'il n'est pas siens;
Autres en ara mais les biens.
Grans pitiés prent le senescal
Et de la dame et du vassal;

---

[29] The initial letter of Dix has been corrected from f to d.
[30] entente; T]B.

Great was their lamenting, and Cassine said to Eracle as she kissed him: 'My Lord, may such a child be blessed with good fortune! **572** No woman ever bore a sweeter creature than I have borne, and I shall be forever remembered as the most hard-hearted mother who ever lived. Oh God, dear Father, has it ever happened before in this world that a mother sold her son? Never before has there been a woman like me; do not forget, dear Lord God! Dear Lord God, do not forget this, protect my son, preserve his intelligence, take pity on him and on me, for I am making this sale for you. No one who has dealings with you does so in vain, for later everyone congratulates themselves on it, and I shall congratulate myself, if I have my way. My heart is almost breaking with grief; it would already have broken if it were not for you; Lord, through your strength, help me, for in all my endeavours I have you in mind, and anyone who has such high aspirations should tolerate nothing which is against God's will; I wish to offer myself completely to you; then I shall languish so sweetly; anyone who aspires to a joy as great as your joy, my Lord God, knows no pain, for never was there a joy like yours. **599** My Lord, do not be annoyed at my lamenting over Eracle, my son; but now I shall cease to lament. You gave him to me only on loan; you loaned him to me and I am now returning him to you, for all that I have received is yours. My son, I am sending you off to fend for yourself; never did a mother treat her son so badly.'

'Mother,' he said, 'do not carry on in this vein, you have not done this to harm me nor because of any overweening fault in you, but for God, who sees very clearly everything that one does and sacrifices for him; and no one but God alone gives man such generous gifts or knows how to reward so justly. Nothing compares to His grace, and there is no one on this earth who is not compensated a hundredfold for what he does for Him; and nobody should begrudge Him a good deed, alms-giving or a generous gift, for the reward from God would then be smaller, and anyone who forfeits the greater on account of the lesser is not endowed with good sense. **622** Mother, love God and make sure you do not begrudge Him in any way your good deed or your love, but thank Him night and day for having inspired you so and given you such a purpose, and do not feel sorry for me any more, for I shall be absolutely fine. And so will you, if God is my Saviour, for whoever fears God will want for nothing.' Then the mother kissed her son again, for very soon she would no longer have the opportunity to kiss him, as he was no longer hers; from now on his talents would belong to another. The seneschal felt great pity for both the lady and the young man;

Nes eüst hui veüs, sien voel. [e]
640 Il ne puet mais soufrir le duel;
Le varlet prent, mener l'en fait.
Li mere plorant s'en revait;
Ses besans cange isnielement
Si en revest la povre gent,
645 Et quant faite a se departie,
Si se rent a une abeïe
Que faite avoit del sien demaine.
Sainte est li vie qu'ele maine;
Haire desous ses dras viestoit,
650 Mais nus ne set qui ele estoit.
Dix fist por li puis maint miracle.
Li senescax en maine Eracle,
Et ains qu'il beüst molt de vin
Se repenti de son devin,
655 Que il onques l'acatast mie.
Tuit li tornent a grant folie,
Trestuit en gabent et en rient:
«Ne set riens deviner», ce dient;
Et vienent dont li gabeour
660 Sel noncent a l'empereour;
Et l'emperere adonc le mande,
Le senescal, et lui conmande
Que le varlet face amener
Por savoir s'il set assener
665 A cose dont il s'est vantés.
«Il vos a, fait il, encantés.
Onques mais ne vous tinc pour sot[31]
N'ainc mais hom gaber ne vous pot,
Et uns gars qui ne set noient
670 Vous a gabé sifaitement!»
Li senescaus atant le mande
Et l'empereres li demande[32]
«Se çou est voirs que on m'a dit.
– Sire, ne sai, se Dix m'aït,

675 Ne sai s'on m'a sordit de rien;
Mais une cose sai je bien:
Se je ne sui de sens garnis,
Que me sire ert molt escarnis,
Et qu'il puet estre molt pesans [f]
680 Que il m'acata mil besans.
Mais nes a pas tos puer gietés.
Toutes les pieres me metés
Qui sont el mont ci en ceste aire,
Dirai que set cascune faire;
685 S'ensanle fussent en cel val
De toutes terres li ceval,
Si vous saroie dire lués
Li quels vous aroit grignor oeus;
De feme connois, biax dous sire,
690 Canques ses cuers sossiel desire
Et canque pense et canque velt
Et canques ele faire seut.
– Amis varlés, se ce est voirs,
Bien est emploiiés li avoirs;
695 Mais je sarai toute le fin
Encore anuit u le matin,
U dedens quint jor au plus tart,
Ains que jou aille nule part.
– Biax sire ciers, bien l'esprovés
700 Et se vous mençoigne i trovés,
Faites ent con d'un traïtor:
Si doit on baillir leceor.
– Amis, tele oevre me contece,
Car molt me sanle bone tece
705 D'arme qui fait sans grant proiere
Ce qu'ele set; plus en est ciere.»
Molt par s'en doute l'emperere
Et molt crient qu'il ne soit bordere.
Trestout le tienent a laron,
710 Li chevalier et li baron,

---

[31] tienc]H.
[32] conmande B]T.

he would have preferred not to have seen them that day. He could no longer stand their grief; he took the young man and had him led away. The mother went home weeping, quickly changed her *besants* into smaller denominations and donated the money to the poor. And when she had finished distributing everything, she took herself off to an abbey which she had founded with her own money. Pious was the life she led; she wore a hairshirt under her clothes, but no one knew who she was. **651** Later God performed many a miracle for her. The seneschal took Eracle away, but before he had drunk much wine he regretted ever having bought this youth claiming to have second sight. Everyone viewed it as great folly on his part, everyone ridiculed and made fun of him. 'He can't foresee anything,' they said, and the mockers came to the emperor and told him about it. The emperor immediately sent for the seneschal and ordered him to have the young man brought to him in order to ascertain whether he could live up to his boasts. 'He has,' he said, 'cast a spell on you! Never before did I consider you to be an idiot and never before was anyone able to make a fool of you, yet a young rascal who knows nothing has made a fool of you in this way!' The seneschal sent for him straight away and the emperor asked him if what he had been told was true.[23] **674** 'My Lord, I do not know, so help me God, for I do not know if I have been slandered in any way, but one thing I know for sure, if I am not blessed with great intelligence, then my lord will be a laughing-stock and will rightly be very upset that he paid a thousand *besants* for me. But he has not wasted all his money. Place all the stones in the world here on the floor in front of me and I shall say what each can do; if all the horses from every country on earth were herded together in this valley, I would be able to tell you at once which would be of greatest use to you; as for women, fair sweet lord, I know whatever a woman's heart desires in the whole world and whatever she is thinking and whatever she wants and whatever she is in the habit of doing. – My young friend, if this is true then the money has been well spent; but I shall need detailed proof of this by tonight or tomorrow morning or at the latest within five days, and I shan't leave until I get it. **699** – My dear lord, test my claim thoroughly and if you do find any falsehood in it, treat me as you would a traitor, for that's the way to treat a scoundrel. – My friend, this proposal suits me well, for I consider it to be a very good quality in a soul if he demonstrates his abilities without much persuasion, thereby gaining in esteem.'

    The emperor was racked with doubt and was very much afraid that Eracle was a hoaxer. All of the knights and barons thought he was a fraud,

---

[23]   In MS *A* Gautier mixes direct and indirect speech here; cf ll. 712-14.

Et dient qu'il a fait entendre
Qu'il est devins por soi mix vendre;
«Ce n'est pas li premiere fois;
Or i parra se fausse fois»,
715 Ce dient tout cil de le cort;
A fol le tienent et a lort
Por plaisir a l'empereour.
Al cuer a il molt grant paour
Qu'il ne soit tex c'on li
        tesmoigne.   [130 a]
720 Ne mais si est, ce li besoigne;
Dix li adite et amministre
Con son desciple et son ministre
Les trois savoirs que je vous dis.
Esprouvés ert ains quinze dis,
725 Car l'empereres le mescroit,
Ja nel kerra s'il çou ne voit.
    Il ne se valt plus demourer,
Ains a lués fait son ban crier:
Que il n'i ait en toute Rome
730 Ni environ si hardi home
N'aport ses prescïeuses pieres,
Et celes ains qu'il a plus cieres[33]
Venir les face, et s'il nel fait,
Il perdera tout entresait
735 Canc'on porra del sien aherdre,
Et son cors s'il n'a el que perdre.
Li jors fu mis droit au mardi,
Se n'i a un seul si hardi
S'il nule piere a qui riens vaille
740 Qu'il ne l'aport le jor sans faille.
Le mardi droit i vienent tuit,
Car autrement fussent destruit,[34]

Si font deus bieles establies
De rices pierres bien garnies.
745 Si sieent privé et estrange[35]
Tout autressi c'on fait au cange.
Li sire apiele Eracle a soi:
«Amis, fait il, entent a moi.
Je sarai ja, se Dix m'aït,
750 S'il est ensi con tu m'as dit.
Va moi la jus veoir ces pieres,
Et en trestoutes les plus cieres
Acate celi qui mix vaut;
De le coustance ne te caut,
755 Mais qu'ele soit de grant vertu.
Nus ne le connoist mix que tu.
Ensanle o toi iront me gent,
Qui en feront le paiement.
Je te ferai abandonner   [b]
760 Tout quanques oseras donner
Et paiier toute le droiture.
Mes avoirs est en aventure,
Je faiç que faus de l'envoiier,
C'a le fois doit on foloiier
765 Tant c'on soit batu du vergant.
Diva, fait il a un sergant,
Va o cestui, et si li livre
Tant marc d'argent et tante livre
Que il t'osera ja rouver;
770 Se bone piere puet trouver,
Livre li tant, jel voel tres bien.
Ja soit ce qu'il ne vaille rien:
Hui en cest jor le voel ataindre;
Quel qu'il me coust, ne puet
        remaindre.»

---

[33] il ont]T.
[34] f. trestuit]BT.

[35] Sieent il p.]B.

and said that he had claimed to have second sight in order to obtain a higher price for himself: 'and this is not the first time it has happened. His bad faith will now be revealed,' said all the courtiers; they made him out to be a fool and an idiot in order to please the emperor. In his heart the emperor was sore afraid that Eracle might turn out to be what they claimed he was. But not a bit of it; he could not possibly be, for God had conferred and bestowed on him, as his disciple and his servant, the three gifts I have told you about. **724** He would be put to the test before the fortnight had elapsed,[24] for the emperor did not believe him and would never believe him until he saw it with his own eyes.

He did not wish to delay any longer, but immediately issued a proclamation to the effect that no man in the whole of Rome or its surroundings should be so rash as to fail to bring his precious stones there and he should in particular have those brought which he valued most highly and if he did not do this, he would immediately lose all those possessions which could be confiscated, and even his life if he had nothing else to lose. The following Tuesday had been chosen as the appointed day and no one, if he owned a stone of any value whatsoever, should be so rash as to fail to bring it on that very day. On the appointed Tuesday everyone arrived, for otherwise they would have been put to death, and they set up two magnificent stalls piled up with precious stones. There sat Roman citizens and those from the surrounding area, just as if they were money-changers. The emperor called Eracle to him: 'Friend,' he said, 'listen to me. I shall soon know, so help me God, if what you have told me is true. **751** Go down there and inspect these stones for me and from amongst the most precious buy the one which is the most valuable; don't worry about the price provided that it has great powers.[25] No one can judge this better than you. My men will go along with you and will make the payment. I shall put at your disposal whatever you dare to give and shall honour the payment. My money is at stake here. I know I am acting foolishly in sending it, but one should occasionally behave like a fool until one is beaten with a stick.[26] 'Come on,' he said to a sergeant, 'go with this lad and give him as many silver marks and as many pounds as he dares to ask of you; if he can find a valuable stone, give him what he asks, for this is my earnest wish. It may well be that he is a good-for-nothing: I want to catch him out this very day; whatever the cost, it must be done soon.'

---

[24] There seems to be a contradiction here between the emperor's desire to resolve matters within five days (l. 697) and the narrator's deadline of a fortnight. The contradiction could be scribal, or Gautier may be implying the emperor's impatience when Laïs imposes such an impractical time-scale. See Eskénazi 2002, 43-45.

[25] In the Middle Ages precious stones were believed to have magic powers, many medicinal, as described in lapidaries.

[26] This expression seems to be proverbial, perhaps referring to the beating given to madmen in medieval theatre.

775	Eracles prise molt petit		U mais ne voit ciel ne terre.[41]
	Tout quanque l'empereres dist;		Li maistre serjans, qui le garde,
	Bien set qu'il ja atains nen iert,	810	Deproie Diu que max fus l'arde:
	Mais qu'il puist trover ce qu'il quiert.		«Diva, fait il, n'iés pas senés
	Icil a cui on l'a cargié		Qui por noient nos as penés;
780	L'en mainne droit dusqu'al marcié.[36]		Tu nous fais ci paiier le bee.
	Eracles voit les mons des pieres,		Por c'as tu ceste gent gabee
	Et celes c'on tient les plus cieres	815	Qui toute jor te vont sivant?
	Ne prise mie deus alies.		Mais tu t'en vas, je cuiç, juant.
	Cargies sont les establies,[37]		Se l'empereres me creoit
785	Il les regarde en trespassant;		Et s'il a son cuer li seoit,
	Entor lui se vont amassant		Sifaite justice en feroit
	Li home, et tienent a mervelle[38]	820	Que tout le mont en vengeroit!»
	Que l'emperere s'i conselle:		Molt tienent tuit Eracle a sot,
	«Ci a, font il, bon marceant,		Mais il ne daigne souner mot
790	Ne mais que vait il delaiant?[39]		Quant bien n'i feroit a respondre;
	Ci sont les pieres pressïeuses		Par bien taisir les velt confundre
	Del monde les plus glorïeuses,	825	Et desmentir, s'il veïst piere
	Et il ne prise riens qu'il voie.»		Qui prescïeuse fust et ciere.
	Grans est li pules quil convoie		Mais entre mil noires brebis
795	Por lui escarnir, non por el,		Troveroit on bien a envis
	Qu'iluec a tel piere venel		Une blanque s'ele n'i ert,
	C'om prise tout l'or de Toulouse.	830	Et nule piere illuec ne pert
	Trestous li mondes le goulouse.		Qu'il puist prisier ne tant ne quant.
	De teus i a, je ne sai quans [c]		De li se gabent li auquant,
800	Et il nes prise mie uns gans;		Tous les estaus as marceans
	N'i a nule qui li contece		A trespassés lor ix voians.
	Nient plus que feroit une flece;	835	Au cief des rens avoit un home[42]
	Outre s'en part, et cil en rient,		Qui vendoit povre merc en Rome.
	Et si a de teus qui en dient[40]		Une piere a, dont nus n'a cure,
805	Qu'il sera bons a metre en sauf;		Que il trova par aventure;
	N'i a ne cavelu ne cauf		Le ban avoit oï pieça, [d]
	Nel lot tres bien a metre en serre,	840	Ne valt trespasser ne n'osa;

---
36 len mainnent]BT.
37 Dont c. s. l. tablies]L, *cf.* 743 (B: Garnies sour les e.; T: Garnies sont les e.).
38 h. t.]B.
39 vont]B.
40 rient]BT.
41 Hu m.]B.
42 res]B.

Eracle attached little importance to all that the emperor had said; he knew that he would not be caught out, provided that he could find what he was looking for.

The man to whom he had been entrusted took him directly to the market. Eracle saw the piles of stones, yet those considered most valuable were not in his view worth two pins.[27] The stalls were piled high; he looked at them as he walked by. Men gathered around him, amazed that the emperor was relying on his judgement. They said: 'There is many a good merchant here, so what is he waiting for? Here are the most superb examples of precious stones in the whole world, yet he is not impressed by anything he sees.' The huge crowd accompanying him was there for no other reason than to deride him, for there were stones on sale in that market which were considered to be worth all the gold of Toulouse. Everyone wanted to own them. I do not know how many such stones there were there, yet in Eracle's view they were not worth a pair of gloves; not one of them pleased him any more than an arrow would. **803** He walked on by and they laughed at him, and there were even some who said that he was fit to be locked up; there was no one either hairy or bald who did not readily suggest that he should be thrown into prison, where he would no longer be able to see heaven or earth. The senior sergeant escorting him prayed to God that he should burn in hell. 'Well now,' he said, 'it wasn't very sensible of you to cause us all this trouble for nothing. You are wasting our time here. Why have you made fools of these people who have been following you around all day? But I think you're playing games. If the emperor were to believe me and if it were to suit his intentions, he would inflict such a dreadful punishment on you for this that the whole world would be avenged!' Everyone thought that Eracle was a complete fool, yet he did not design to say a word, for there would be no point in replying; by remaining silent he hoped to confound them and to prove them wrong, as long as he found a stone which was precious and valuable. **827** Yet amongst a thousand black sheep one would be hard pressed indeed to find a white one if it was not present, and there seemed to be no stone there that he could value in any way at all. Some people made fun of him, since before their very eyes he had walked by all the merchants' counters. At the end of the rows there was a man who sold low-priced wares in Rome. He had a stone which interested no one and which he had found by chance; he had heard the proclamation a while before, and did not wish nor dare to disobey it;

---

27 Literally two sorb apples, cf. ll. 34, 800, 802, 972, etc.

Nient por ice, ce saciés bien,
Qu'il cremist fors que sen cors rien,
Car il n'ot el que cele piere
Que il ne nus hom ne tient ciere,
845 Ne il ne nus hom n'en a soing.
Eracles le coisist de loing
Et de si loing que il le voit.
Traist soi vers celi qui l'avoit.
Et quant de pres l'a remiree:
850 «Or ai, fait il, ma desiree.
Or se taisent li recreant,
Li mençoignier, li mescreant.
Dix a sen home revidé;
Ne puet perir qui croit en Dé;
855 Molt par est caitis qui n'i croit,
Et cil qui sor sa mort acroit
N'est mie, certes, bien senés.
C'or sui a droit port assenés,
Or ne crien je fors Diu nului.
860 Diva, fait il dont a celui,
Est ce te piere? Vent le moi.
– Sire, ele est moie et je, par foi,
Le vous vendrai molt volentiers,
Et vostre soit por sis deniers.
865 Je sui molt povres entresait,
Si ai grant mestier de bien fait.
– As tu donques tel povreté?
– Oïl, biau varlet, par verté.
– Por ce que t'as mestier d'avoir
870 T'en ferai or vint mars avoir.
– Biax dous varlet, bien le saciés,
De gaber povre home est peciés;
Il en poise Diu de lassus.
– Amis, voir, or en aras plus;
875 Je t'en donrai, au plus escars,

Por toi garir, quarante mars.»
A un qui fait molt grouçanment
Faire li fait son paiement;
Mais il ne l'ose refuser. [e]
880 Molt le manace a encuser
Quant il tant doner li conmande
De çou dont il si poi demande.
Cil prent le piere et cil l'argent;
Assés en ont gabé le gent.
885 Eracle a son segnor le livre,
Et li sergans, quil tient por yvre,
Vient, se li dist: «Vous ne savés
De cest caitif que ci veés:
Por ceste piere c'ot veüe
890 Qu'eüst por sis deniers eüe,[43]
Me fist livrer quarante mars!
Bien eust desservi qu'il fust ars![44]
Onques des bones cure n'ot,
Ne nule bargignier n'en volt;
895 U nule bone n'en connut,
U le pïor de gré eslut.»
Li empereres s'en aïre,
Par maltalent li prist a dire:
«Por c'as tu la donné le mien
900 Por le piere qui ne valt rien?
Et quant malvaise l'acatas,
Quarante mars por qu'en dounas?
Faire me valsis paringal
A ton signor le senescal,
905 Qui por toi dona mil besans.
J'en sui, certes, grains et pesans!
– Ains devés estre liés, biax sire,
Car bien l'os tesmoignier et dire
Que ceste piere valt tout l'or
910 Que vous avés mis en tresor:

---

[43] deniers *omitted by* A.
[44] 892 *is hypermetric in all MSS if* eust *is disyllabic as in* 890, 914, *etc.*

not, I can assure you, because he was afraid of losing anything but his life, for he owned nothing apart from this stone, on which neither he nor anyone else placed any value, and which neither he nor anyone else cared about. Eracle spotted it from a long way off and from the distant spot where he first caught sight of it he made straight for the man who owned it. And when he had examined it closely, he said: 'Now I have found what I was looking for. **851** Now let the cowards, liars and disbelievers hold their tongues! God has acknowledged his servant; whoever believes in God will be saved and whoever does not believe in Him is a wretch indeed, and whoever gambles with his own death is certainly not wise at all. For now I have reached a safe harbour, and now I fear no one but God. Come tell me,' he then said to the man, 'Is this your stone? Sell it to me. – My lord, yes, it is mine and by my faith I shall very gladly sell it to you, and it can be yours for six *deniers*.[28] I am, however, very poor and in great need of a kindness. – Are you so very poor then? – Yes, fair youth, I am, truly. – Since you are in need of money I shall now see that you get twenty marks. **871** – Fair gentle youth, may I say that it is a sin to make fun of the poor; it displeases God who dwells on high. – My friend, indeed, now you shall have more, I shall give you at the very least forty marks so that you can live comfortably.' On Eracle's orders he was paid the agreed amount by a man who did so with a great deal of grumbling; but he dared not refuse him. He made numerous threats to denounce him for ordering him to pay out so much for something which could have cost so little. Eracle took the stone and the poor man took the money; and the bystanders had a good laugh over it. Eracle handed it over to his lord and the sergeant, who thought he was mad, came up and said: 'You do not know what this wretch, whom you see before you, has done: he made me hand over forty marks for this stone which he had spotted and which he could have had for six *deniers*! He deserved to be burnt alive! He was not a bit interested in the really precious stones and he did not wish to haggle over any of them; either he was incapable of identifying a good stone or he chose the worst on purpose.' **897** The emperor was furious, and began to speak angrily: 'Why did you pay out my money for this worthless stone, and why, when you bought this inferior one, did you give forty marks for it? You wanted to treat me the same way as you treated your lord the seneschal, who gave a thousand *besants* for you! I am angry, in fact, furious about this. – Well you should be happy instead, fair lord, for I would go as far as to attest and assert that this stone is worth all the gold you have stored in your treasury:

---

[28] *Deniers* were small denomination coins.

Qu'eve ne fu n'arme ne crient,
Ne ne puet cremoir, qui le tient.
Se li caitis, li deceüs,
N'eüst que sis deniers eüs,
915 Se vertu perdist. – Puet cë estre?
– Por ce en donai tant au mestre.
Biax sire, un seul petit m'oés:
Ardés m'en fu, se vous poés,
Mais sor moi l'aie, el ne demant; [f]
920 U m'assaiiés d'arme trencant,[45]
De toutes pars a moi lanciés,
Et en aige me balociés;
S'a pïeur vient, si soit sor moi.
– Eracle, voir, ensi l'otroi.»
925   Il ne se valt plus detrïer;
Une grant muele fist loier
Entor Eracle le varlet;
Se bone piere au col li met.
Toute se gent i fait aler,
930 Et si le fait adevaler
El Toivre, qui est molt parfons,
Et li muele le trait au fons.
Une corde i ont atacie[46]
A coi li muele ert sus sacie
935 Et li varlés, u mors ou vis.
Une grant liue, ce m'est vis,
I a Eracles si geü
Qu'il ne l'ont onques remeü;
Et je vous di que li pluisor
940 Deprient Diu le Creator
Par se merci qu'il le garisse,
Que il en l'eve ne perisse.
«Folie, font il, vos travaille.
Qui cuide que prïere vaille?
945 Noiés est pieça et estains.
Grans biens seroit qu'il fust atains,

Et c'on li fesist sepulture.
Mar fu si biele creature!
Il ne fu lere ne triciere
950 Ne baretere ne boisiere,
Mais por garir se mere, espoir,
Dist qu'il estoit de tel savoir.»
Molt en pleurent le gent menue;
Cil ont le corde fort tenue,
955 Si sont anuié del tenir
Et font il plus de gent venir
Por celui traire contremont,
Car li sire les en semont
Et reuve c'on le traie a fait, [131 a]
960 Por veoir con li cose vait
Et s'il est si con il a dit.
Trestout i vont sans contredit
Et traient fors a le polie.
Al signor tienent a folie
965 De ce qu'il cuide qu'il soit vis.
Pluisor valroient, ce m'est vis,
Que Dix l'eüst sauvé en vie;
Et li pluisour en ont envie[47]
Por ce qu'il est de jovene aage,
970 Et si s'est fais d'eus tos plus sage;
Et il ont dit que cele piere
Ne valt pas une fuelle d'iere,
Si l'ameroient mix estaint
Qu'il fussent de mençoigne ataint.
975 Mais d'autrui feront or lor gas,
Qu'il ne morra encore pas;
N'a encor talent de morir;
Dix le velt a son oeus norir:
S'oïr volés l'ovre et cerchier,
980 Oïr poés con Dix l'ot cier.
   A traire n'ont pas mis granment
Si le deslïent erranment;

---

45   U vous soiees d'a. trecant]B.
46   o. sus (*corrected to* sas) facie]B.

47   Et me dame sainte marie]BT.

for anyone who has it on his person need have no fear of water, fire nor the sword, nor can he be burnt. If the poor wretch had received only six *deniers* for it, it would have lost its power. – Can this be true? – This was the reason why I gave so much to its owner. Dear lord, listen to me for a moment: burn me in a fire if you can, just let me have the stone on me, I ask for nothing else; or attack me with a sharp sword, throw missiles at me from all sides and plunge me into water; if the worst occurs, on my head be it. – Eracle, truly, you have my permission.'

925 He did not wish to delay any longer; he ordered a huge millstone to be tied around the youth Eracle and hung his special stone around his neck.[29] He sent all his men along and had him lowered into the Tiber, which is very deep, and the stone dragged him down to the bottom. They had attached a rope to the millstone with which to pull it up along with the young lad, either dead or alive. I think Eracle lay there as long as it takes to walk a good league without their disturbing him at all, and I can tell you that most of them prayed to God our Maker to be merciful and to protect him from dying in the water. Yet they said to one another: 'You are mad. Who believes that praying is of any use? He's been dead for a while now, drowned. It would be a great kindness if he were to be fished out and given a decent burial. **948** What a pity such a handsome creature ever lived! He was neither thief nor trickster, neither liar nor conman, but perhaps he claimed to have such knowledge in order to provide comfortably for his mother.' The ordinary folk wept profusely over him; the emperor's men held on tightly to the rope, yet they tired of holding it and summoned more people to come and haul him to the surface, for their lord commanded and ordered them to pull him out completely to see how things were going and to see if what he had said had come about. They all went there without voicing any objection and pulled him out using a pulley. They thought their lord was mad to believe that he might still be alive. It seems to me that many would have preferred God to have saved his life; yet the majority were jealous of him because he was young and yet had claimed to be wiser than all of them; and they said that this stone was not worth an ivy leaf, and they would prefer him to be dead rather than that they should be proved liars. **975** But they would now have to make fun of others, for he was not going to die yet. He had no intention of dying yet; God wished to raise him for his own purposes: if you are willing to listen right to the end of this work, you will hear how God held him dear.

It did not take them long to pull him out and they quickly untied him;

---

[29] It is unclear whether the stone was hung or attached to his clothing at his neck.

Il saut en piés trestous delivres.
Or se tienent pluisor por yvres[48]
985 De çou qu'il ont mesdit de lui;
Et pluisor voelent son anui,
Et dient par lor legerie
Qu'il oeuvre tout par trecerie,
Par sorcerie et par enchant;
990 Molt le tienent a nonsaçant
Qu'il s'ose meller de tel giu,
Meïsmement en itel liu.
Molt l'ont sordit trestout le soir,
Mais al varlet n'estuet caloir.
995 Il est tous nus et tous descaus
Et moilliés, et li senescaus
Li giete au col un mantiel gris.
Or est Eracles de grant pris,
Nus ne puet mais trover son
                  maistre. [b]
1000 Bien ait li Sire quil fist naistre,
Qu'en tout le monde n'en a tel.
Bien a emploiié son catel
Li senescaus, si con il dist.
Li empereres s'en sorrist,
1005 Que il est molt de bon espoir
U cil l'a mis por dire voir;
Molt par est liés de l'esprouvance,[49]
Et cent tans plus de l'esperance
U cil l'a mis del tierç savoir:
1010 Qu'il voloit une feme avoir,
Le millor c'on peüst trouver;
Mais ains le velt mix esprover:[50]
S'il en deus coses siut le voire,
Si fera mix le tierce a croire.
1015   Eracles l'a veü sourrire,

Et dist: «Comment vous sanle, sire?
Ne sont mi dit bien veritable?
– Amis, s'il sont tuit si estable
Com a li premerains esté,
1020 Rices seras ains cest esté.
– Sire, ostés vous de mescreance;
Faites faire sans demorance
Un feu molt grant et molt plenier;
Je ne lairai por nul denier
1025 Que je n'i entre demanois.
Or saciés bien que je connois
Le piere mix que nus de vous,
U je sui molt caitis et sous;
Car folie est de soi embatre[51]
1030 La u vint home u trente et quatre
N'aroient pooir ne vertu,
S'il s'i estoient embatu;
Et folie est d'emprendre rien
Se on n'en voit le fin molt bien;
1035 Encor l'apialt on hardement,
Çou est folie, voirement.
Facent le feu!» Et cil le font,
Qui mervilleuse crieme en ont;
Molt ont grant pité del varlet. [c]
1040 Mais il se saigne et puis s'i met,[52]
Tres en mi liu del fu ardant.
Molt par le vont dont regardant
Icil d'entor por le mervelle;[53]
Nus n'i parole ne conselle,[54]
1045 Car il en sont tout esbaihi
Et tienent celui a traï:
«Hé las! caitis! n'istra pas si
De feu comme de l'aige issi,»
Ce dient tuit; mais si fera,

---

[48] yres]BT.
[49] Molt est l.]T
[50] M. ens]BT.

[51] foilie].
[52] il *inserted by later hand.*
[53] Il cil]BT.
[54] Il ni]BT.

he leapt to his feet, safe and sound. Now many thought they must have been mad to have slandered him, yet many wished him harm and said shamelessly that everything he did was the result of trickery, sorcery and magic; they thought he was very stupid to risk getting involved in such tomfoolery, especially in such high places. They spent the whole evening slandering him, yet the young man could not care less about it. He was completely naked, barefoot and wet through, and the seneschal threw a grey fur cloak around his shoulders. Now Eracle was held in great esteem, his better could never be found again. **1000** May the Lord, who created him, be blessed, for in the whole world there was no one like him. As the seneschal himself was quick to point out, he had used his money well. The emperor smiled at this, for he had high hopes inspired by Eracle's speaking the truth; he was very pleased with the way the test had gone and a hundred times more pleased because of the hope Eracle had inspired in him concerning his third gift: for he wished to take a wife, the best one could possibly find; yet first he wished to test him further: if he was sticking to the truth regarding the first two gifts, this would make his third gift more credible.

Eracle saw him smile and said: 'Well, my lord, what do you think? Aren't my claims true after all? – My friend, if they are all as reliable as the first one has been, you will be rich before this summer. – My lord, expel all doubt; have a huge, raging fire built without delay. No amount of money will prevent me from entering it straight away. **1026** I assure you that I know this stone better than any of you, and if not, I am a miserable wretch and a fool; for it is folly to rush into a situation in which twenty or thirty-four men would be powerless and helpless if they were to rush into it, and it is folly to undertake anything to which one cannot clearly envisage a successful outcome; although one might call such an act bravery, it is in fact sheer folly. Let them build the fire!' Those who built the fire found it extremely frightening; they felt very sorry for the young man. However, he crossed himself and then stepped right into the centre of the roaring fire. The crowd surrounded him, peering at him in total amazement; no one spoke aloud or in a whisper, for they were all aghast, thinking that he was lost: 'Alas, poor wretch, you will not survive the fire as easily as you did the water,' they all said; but he would do,

1050 Car ars ne blemis n'i sera.
Dix et li piere le soustient;
Tous sains et saus del fu s'en vient.
Ançois orent mervelle eüe,
Mais quant il ont cesti veüe,
1055 Si se prendent tuit a segnier,
C'or ont il plus a mervillier,
Car teus hom puet sor aige bien
Qu'encontre feu ne poroit rien.
   Or sont dolant et malbailli
1060 Li anemi, li cuer failli;
Envie lor fait grant contraire
Et grant angroisse lor fait traire,
Qu'Envie est tos jors en porcas
Des siens honir et prendre a las.
1065 Envïeus languist d'autrui aise;
Lors primes est il a malaise
Quant voit que on preudome alieve;
Riens nule el mont si ne li grieve.
Molt porte envïeus hom grant some;
1070 Quant voit a cort venir preudome,
Il voit bien qu'el non de celui
N'ara on ja cure de lui,
Et por ce dient cil glouton
Qu'Eracles ne valt un bouton
1075 Et cele piere n'a de force,
Ce dient bien, ne c'une escorce;
Par sorcerie est quanqu'il fait;
Mervelle est molt qu'il ne s'en vait[55]
Et c'a le voie ne se met.   [d]
1080 A grant tort jugent le varlet;
Eracles l'ot, si en sourist,
Et a l'empereor a dit:
«Sire, dist il, mervelles oi!
Mervelles dient ci de moi.
1085 Sire, il ont dit que c'est baras

Et max engiens quanque je fas;
Or me soiés por Diu garans,
Que li voirs soit plus apparans
Qu'encor ne soit, por aus desdire:
1090 Prendés le piere, biax dous sire,
Si vous metés el fu atout;
Mar douterés ne que g'i dout.
Se vous sentés ne tant ne quant,
Mar irés puis un pas avant;
1095 Et ja ne vous en sentirois,
Biax sire, et des que vous verrois
Que vous n'i arés se bien non,
Passés avant tout a bandon;
Si verront ceste male gent,
1100 Qui ont parlé vilainement,
Quel vertu a li piere en soi.
– Eracle, veus tu par ta foi
Que j'entre el fu en tel maniere?
– Oïl, se Dix me soit aidiere;
1105 Biax sire, se il vous plaisoit,
Si verront s'il ont tort u droit,[56]
Et plus en seront aseür.
– Varlet, se Dix me doinst eür,
Tu m'as tant dit que jel ferai;
1110 Mais une cose te dirai:
Se je me senç de rien blecié,
Par ton cors sera tout adrecié.[57]
– Si m'aït Dix, biax sire ciers,
Içou voel je molt volentiers.»
1115 La piere a prise del varlet
Li emperere, et puis s'i met
El fu ardant isnielement.
A premiers passe bielement;
Mais ainques coulor n'i mua,   [e]
1120 Ni ainc por calor n'i sua,
Ne que s'il fust une aune en sus;

---

[55] Mervel]BT.
[56] verroit sil ait t.]BT.
[57] tout *absent from* A.

for he would not be burnt or harmed. **1051** God and the stone protected him and he stepped out of the fire quite safe and sound. They had already witnessed one marvel, but when they saw this one, they all began to cross themselves, for now they had something greater to marvel at, because there are those capable of surviving water who would be incapable of protecting themselves against fire.

Now his enemies, who lacked faith in their hearts, were disconsolate and downcast. Envy caused them great distress and made them suffer great anguish, for Envy is always intent on shaming its supporters and trapping them in its snares. An envious person is upset by the happiness of others; he is particularly unhappy when he sees a worthy man raised in status; nothing in the world upsets him so. An envious man carries a huge burden around with him; when he sees a worthy man arrive at court, he realises that because of this man no one will take any notice of him. For this reason these knaves said that Eracle was not worth a button and they even said that the stone had no more power than a piece of bark; everything he did was the result of black magic and it was a great wonder that he did not leave and set off on his way. **1080** They judged the young man quite wrongly. Eracle heard what they were saying, but did not take it seriously, and spoke to the emperor thus: 'My lord,' he said, 'I'm hearing some extraordinary things! They are saying extraordinary things about me; they have said, my lord, that everything I do involves trickery and foul play; for the Lord's sake, may you supply further proof so that the truth can become even more manifest than it is now, thereby proving them wrong: take the stone, kind, gentle lord, and step right into the fire. Do not be afraid any more than I am. If you feel anything at all, do not advance a step further; but you will not feel a thing, kind lord, and as soon as you can see that you will come to no harm, go forward confidently; these evil people with their malicious tongues will see what power the stone possesses. **1102** – Eracle, do you truly wish me to enter the fire in this way? – Yes, so help me God, kind lord, if you were in agreement, and then they will see if they are right or wrong and they will be all the more convinced. – Young man, may God grant me good fortune. Your words have convinced me to do it, but I wish to say one thing: if I feel that I have been harmed in any way, you will pay for everything with your life. – So help me God, dear, kind lord, this I'm quite willing to agree to.' The emperor took the stone from the young man and then stepped quickly into the burning fire. Right from the start he fared well, not even his complexion changed colour, nor did he perspire from the heat any more than if he had been standing an ell away from it.

Si s'asseüre plus et plus;
Lors se conmande tout a Diu
Et puis s'en va dusqu'en mi liu.
1125 Tant i demoura et estut
Que on cuida, et cuidier dut,
Que il i fust tous ars en cendre;
Et quant il n'i volt plus atendre,
Si s'en ist for tous saus et sains.
1130 Al varlet tent andeus ses mains,[58]
Voiant trestous l'acole et baise
Tantost con ot et liu et aise.
    Eracles fu dont cier tenus,
Or est il cent tans mix venus,
1135 Or l'aime tant li empereres
Con s'il li fust cousins u freres.
Li senescaus l'aime autretant
En un endroit con son enfant.
Es deus vertus l'a si bien fait
1140 Que l'emperere ne tient plait
De le tierce vertu plus ciere
Qui estre doit en cele piere,
Ne li ose metre devant;
Et cil s'en vait apercevant,
1145 Et puis a dit, oiant trestous:
«Or viegne avant li plus estous,
Et qui grignor force a en soi;
De son branc nu fiere sor moi;
Se il mon cors puet entamer,
1150 Face moi gieter en la mer
Me sire, ou a cevax detraire,
Et tant de mal et de contraire
Con il soussiel faire porra,
Autre loiier mar me donra;
1155 Si doit on treceor baillir.»

Uns qui ne velt a cop faillir
Et qui ressanle mix gaiant
Qu'il ne fait nule rien vivant,[59]
S'est poroffers devant le roi: [f]
1160 «Biax sire, fait il, quel desroi,
Confait outrage et quel folie!
Mais j'otroi c'on me bat et lie,
Et c'on me giete en un fangnier
Se je n'abaç tout cest dangier
1165 Au trençant de m'espee nue.
– Ceste vous ert tres bien tenue,
Fait li varlés, endroit de moi.
Pres sui de faire cest otroi.
– Par les sains Diu, et je del prendre.
1170 Un noviel ju vous cuiç aprendre!
– Amis, en Diu soit me desfense;
De ce remaint molt que fax pense.
Fax ne tient mie bien covent
Et s'il le fait, nel fait sovent;
1175 Faus hom est molt d'estrange fuer;
Por seul itant m'avés sour cuer[60]
Que vous veés en moi raison;
Fax hom quiert plus tost ocoison
De haïr home que d'amer:
1180 Por ce le doit on fol clamer.
Fols n'aime mie volentiers,
N'il n'est amés ne tenus ciers.»[61]
L'empereres ot l'aatine,[62]
Le tieste tient un poi encline
1185 Et pense: «Dix! Con grans peciés
Se cis varlés est detrenciés
Et ocis par si grant folie!
Mais se cis fiert a la falie,
Par tous les sains c'on quiert et nonme,

---

58   Li varles]BT; *for* an .ii. *read* andeus.
59   Qui]T (Ke il ne).
60   i. cange son cuer]BT.
61   Nis]B.
62   Lempere]BT.

Hence he grew more and more confident, and having commended himself totally to God, he then advanced right into the midst of the flames. **1125** He remained standing there so long that everyone believed, and rightly so, that he would be completely burnt to ashes there. When he did not wish to stay there any longer, he emerged from it quite safe and sound. He held out both hands to the young man, and he embraced and kissed him in front of everyone as soon as he had the chance and opportunity to do so.

Eracle was now held in high esteem and was now treated a hundredfold better than before. The emperor loved him as much as if he were his cousin or brother. The seneschal loved him just as much and in the same way as he would his own child. Two of the stone's powers had been so successfully demonstrated that the emperor did not mention the third more important power it was supposed to possess, nor did he dare to broach the subject, but Eracle was aware of this and said in front of everyone: 'let the boldest and strongest of you come forward and let him strike me with his naked sword; if he manages to cut into my flesh, my lord ought to have me thrown into the sea, or drawn and quartered by horses, and should make me suffer as much pain and agony as he can possibly devise in this world; woe betide him if he rewards me any differently – this is how a trickster should be treated.' **1156** A man who wanted to miss no opportunity to fight, who looked more like a giant than like any living creature, came before the king to offer his services. 'Kind lord,' he said, 'what nonsense, what an outrageous claim and what sheer stupidity! But I agree to be beaten, bound and thrown in the mire if I do not put an end to all this presumption with the blade of my naked sword. – As far as I am concerned,' said the young man, 'you will be held to these conditions. I am ready to agree to this arrangement. – And I am ready to accept it, by God's saints. I expect to teach you a new trick or two. – My friend, may God be my protector. Thanks to Him a fool's plans often come to nought. A fool is not good at keeping promises, and if he does, he doesn't do it often. **1175** A foolish man is made of very strange stuff indeed; the only reason why you are antagonistic towards me is because you can detect good sense in me; a foolish man prefers to look for excuses to hate a man rather than to love him; this is why he deserves to be called foolish. A fool is very reluctant to love, nor is he loved or held in affection.' The emperor heard the spiteful challenge, bowed his head a little and thought: 'Oh God, what a terrible misfortune it will be if this young man is hacked to pieces and killed through such madness! But if this man's blow misses its mark, then by all the saints whom we invoke by name,

1190 Mar vit cestui entrer en Rome.
Mervelle est molt de cuer felon;
Con cis a male ententïon!
C'ainc mais ne vit en son vivant
Cestui, si le het por noiant;
1195 Mais por furnir se felonie
Le volroit or gieter de vie.⁶³
Quels prex seroit il s'il morust?⁶⁴
Ahi! se Dix te secourust⁶⁵
A cest besoig, Eracle amis.   [132 a]
1200 Si mar i vint vostre anemis!»
Cil voit bien de l'empereour
Qu'il a de lui crieme et paor:⁶⁶
«Sire, fait il, ne vous tamés!
Je voi molt bien que vous m'amés,
1205 Ce fait forment a mercïer;
Mais de petit m'i puis fïer
Se li vassaus n'a ce qu'il quiert.⁶⁷
Tex muet estrif qui pau conquiert⁶⁸
Et tex commence le mellee
1210 Qui puis emporte le collee;
Il n'est si caude ne refroide.⁶⁹
Bien sai, l'espee est fors et roide,
Mais Dix, qui mist vertus en pieres,
Qui prescïeuses sont et cieres,
1215 Est molt plus fors que il ne soit.⁷⁰
Il dist molt bien que dire doit.
Dix m'a bien aidié dusc'a ore,
Si me puet bien aidier encore.
– Amis Eracles, jel vaudroie;
1220 S'estre peüst, je li rendroie

Le convenant qu'il i a mis;
De droit noient s'est entremis.»
Et cil diables, cis maufés,
Qui de mal faire est escaufés,
1225 Hauce le branc, celui requiert
Et molt grandisme cop le fiert;
Fiert le de tort et d'entravers;
Uns autres en caïst envers.
Dis caus li done grans et fors,
1230 Del menor fust uns autres mors,
Mais en car ainc ne l'adesa.⁷¹
Çou li fu lait, si l'en pesa,
Et l'emperere en est molt liés
Et reuve dont qu'il soit loiiés.
1235 Bediax apiele dusc'a quatre
Et durement le fait dont batre.
Quant acointié li ont lor giu,⁷²
Si l'ont gieté en un ort liu.
Ensi gaaigne mainte fois   [b]
1240 Li hom malvais, et si est drois:
Çou qu'il engigne a oés autrui⁷³
Revient a daerains sor lui;
Ne puet muer que cascuns n'ait
Selonc ce qu'il manevre et fait.
1245   Or est Eracles bien de court,
Et sera mix ains qu'il s'en tourt.
Bien est esprouvés en poi d'eure.
Li senescaus l'aime et honeure,
Et l'emperere durement;
1250 Or l'aiment tout conmunalment,
Se ce n'est aucuns par envie;

---

63   on]T.
64   si m.]B.
65   le] BT.
66   Qui a]BT.
67   v. a]BT.
68   q. paut c.] (BT: poi).
69   ne si froide]BT.
70   Et]BT.

71   M. encor]BT.
72   a. lor o.]BT.
73   e. avoec]L.

he will live to regret the day he arrived in Rome. He has an amazingly cruel heart; how evil his intentions are! For he has never seen Eracle before in his life, yet hates him for no good reason. However, in order to satisfy his wickedness, he now wants to end his life. What good would come of it if he were to die? Oh, if only God would protect you in this time of need, Eracle, my friend! What a pity your enemy ever came here!'
1201 Eracle was very much aware that the emperor was afraid for him and feared for his life: 'My lord,' he said, 'do not be afraid. I can see quite clearly that you are fond of me, and I am very grateful for it, but that will not be much help to me if this knight does not get what he is asking for. People who start quarrels usually gain little and those who pick fights often receive the greater share of the blows; nothing gets so hot that it doesn't eventually cool down.[30] I know that the sword is strong and tough, but God, who endowed stones with special powers, making them precious and highly valued, is much stronger than this man. He says exactly what he is expected to say. In the past God has always come to my aid and can certainly come to my aid again. – Eracle, my friend, let's hope so; if it were to turn out that way, I would happily make him comply with the terms of his promise; he is on a hiding to nothing.' Then this devil, this demon, burning with a desire to do harm, raised his blade, made for Eracle and struck him a mighty blow; he rained blows down on him from all angles; anyone else would have fallen to the ground. **1229** He gave him ten huge vicious blows, the gentlest of which would have killed anyone else, but he was not able to inflict a wound on him at all. This annoyed and angered him, but the emperor was very pleased about this and ordered him to be bound. He summoned three or four beadles and then had him soundly beaten. When they had taught him a trick or two[31] they threw him into a filthy pit. This is how an evil man is often repaid for his efforts, and rightly so: the fate he has cunningly devised for someone else reverts to him in the end. It is an immutable fact that you reap what you sow.

Now Eracle was popular at court, and would become even more so before he left it. Within a short time he had been exonerated. The seneschal loved and respected him and so did the emperor, very much; everyone now loved him, except for those driven by envy,

---

[30] Eracle's speech is characterised by proverbial expressions; see *Proverbes français* 1379: 'N'est si chauz ne refroide'.

[31] Cf. l. 1170; Gautier humorously evokes the man's own words.

Mais nus ne maine bone vie
Qu'Envie ne li voele nuire.
Or prions trestout qu'ele muire!
1255 En envïous a mal voisin;
Cui caut? li biens vaint en le fin,
Car Dix en prent molt bon conroi.
Eracles est molt bien del roi,⁷⁴
Car en ce qu'il l'a esprouvé
1260 L'a molt por fin loial trouvé
Et par lui vaura feme prendre;
Mais il valra ançois aprendre
Se l'enfes, qui n'a que dis ans,
Ert es cevax si voir disans
1265 Et si loiaus con a la gemme.
Il se doute forment de feme,
Car feme prendre est molt grans cose:
Cil prent l'ortie et cil le rose;
A le fois cil qui pis i vaut
1270 Prent le millor, et li bons faut.
Çou fait douter l'empereour,
Sel met en crieme et en paour.
Son ban a fait crier itel
Qu'il atendra le cop mortel
1275 Qui a ceval, s'il ne l'amaine
Por vendre, a cief de la semaine.
Le jor ont ricement tenu,
De toutes pars i sont venu;
A une liue defors Rome   [c]
1280 Amaint lor cevax maint home;
Criee i fu illuec le foire,
Encor l'ont maint home en memoire.
Un ceval i ot l'empere̤re,⁷⁵
Qui bien valt, por vendre a son frere,
1285 Deus cens mars d'argent plainnement,
Ce m'a on dit certainement.
Biax ert et gens et si seoit

Toute le gent qui le veoit.
Autres avoit, ce vos plevis,
1290 Qu'il molt amoit mais, ce m'est vis,
Il n'amoit nul tant con celui.
Le senescal apiele a lui;
Por fausser celui qui ne faut
En grant se met, mais ne li valt.
1295 «Senescal, fait il, or oés:
J'envoierai, se vous loés,
Mon ceval aussi con por vendre;
Or poons nous Eracle atendre,
S'il fait de mon ceval acat,
1300 Qu'en lui nen a point de barat,
Que c'est li miudre et li plus biax,
De tout le mont li plus isniax.
– Sire, por Diu qui lassus maint,
Je lo molt bien c'on l'i amaint.»
1305 Mainent l'i dont isnielement
Trestout sans nul demorement;
Vait i Eracles li senés,
Li damoisiax qui buer fu nés.
Li senescax vait en le foire,
1310 Et maint o lui, ce poés croire;
Eracles vait partout et vient,
Et cerque molt, ce li convient,
Car cui on velt ensi prover,
A grant paine puet il trover⁷⁶
1315 Le millor de cent mil cevaus.
Cerque les mons, cerque les vaus,
En grant se met, et si a droit
Tant que il vient illuec endroit
U li cevax ert au signor.   [d]
1320 U mont n'ot plus biel ne grignor;
Al senescal sanla molt tart
Que venist torner cele part,
Por amor a l'empereor,

---

⁷⁴ Eeracles (s *in later hand*)]BT.
⁷⁵ empere]BT.

⁷⁶ p. on t.]B.

for Dame Envy likes to harm anyone who lives a virtuous life. Let us all pray for her death. **1255** An envious person makes an evil neighbour, but who cares? Virtue wins through in the end, for God makes quite sure of it. Eracle was on very good terms with the emperor, because in those areas in which he had been tested Eracle had proved to be perfectly truthful and so the emperor wanted his help in choosing a wife. But first he wanted to ascertain whether the boy, who was only ten years old, was as truthful and reliable a judge of horses as he was of precious stones. He was very nervous about choosing a wife, for getting married is a serious business: one man ends up with a nettle and another a rose. Sometimes the worst of men gets the best woman and the excellent man fails. This made the emperor worried, anxious and afraid. He issued a proclamation to the effect that anyone who owned a horse and did not bring it to market at the end of the week would be put to death. **1277** Everyone turned up on the appointed day, coming from every corner of the empire. Crowds of people brought their horses to a spot a league outside Rome. There the horse fair, which many people can still remember, was held. A horse owned by the emperor was there, which would easily have fetched two hundred silver marks, even if you were selling it to your brother; I was told this as a fact. It was handsome and fine, and everyone who saw it wanted it. I swear he had others too, to which he was very attached, but I don't think he valued any as highly as this one. He called the seneschal to him and did his utmost to trick the boy who never failed, but to no avail. 'Seneschal,' he said, 'now listen to me. If you think it's a good idea, I shall send my horse along too as if it were for sale; then, if Eracle buys my horse, we shall know that he is devoid of trickery, as this is the best, the finest and the swiftest horse in the whole world. **1303** –My lord, by God who dwells on high, I think it is a very good idea to bring it here.' They therefore quickly fetched it without any delay at all; Eracle, the clever young boy who was blessed at birth, went to the fair and so did the seneschal, along with many others, believe me. Eracle went back and forth, searching everywhere; and he needed to, for if you wish to test a person in this way, it is very difficult for him to find the best horse amongst a hundred thousand. He searched high and low, doing his utmost, and rightly so, until he came to the very spot where his lord's horse was. There was no finer nor taller horse in the world and it seemed to the seneschal that it was high time that Eracle should head in that direction, out of love for the emperor

Qu'il nel tenist a menteor.[77]
1325 Molt par est liés de grant maniere
Qu'il se prova bien en la piere,
Et molt ara le cuer pesant
S'il or nel treuve voir disant.[78]
Li senescaus forment l'esgarde,[79]
1330 Molt li anuie et molt li tarde
Que il acat itel ceval
Qui valt des autres plain un val,
Ce cuident il, ce dient il.
Quant il le voit, sel tient plus vil,
1335 C'onques por voir ne l'adaigna,
Ne tant ne quant ne bargigna;
En lui n'a rien de canqu'il velt.
Outre s'en vait; et cil s'en deut[80]
Qui mil besans l'a acaté;
1340 Or cuide qu'il l'ait bareté:
«Eracle, pense il, or est pis.
Or te lais je, or te guerpis,
Or n'ai je mais cure de toi;
Jamais n'aras amor de moi.
1345 Me sire or en fera ses gas,
Car d'autre rien ne m'est il pas.
Il cuida bien par toi savoir
Se il peüst ja feme avoir
Qui n'eüst tece en soi malvaise;
1350 Or n'i voi cose qui me plaise;
A fol te tieng et a vilain!»
Eracles coisist un poulain
Qui quatre dens encor tenoit,
Et avoit canqu'il convenoit
1355 A tel ceval con il demande.
Trespassoit toute cele lande,
Ainc ne fina, si vint a lui;

S'i a tel mil, estre cestui,
A contes et a castelains, [e]
1360 Quil prisent bien tels mil poulains
Trestout le pïor, a voir dire.
Li senescax molt s'en aïre,
Et cil d'entor li dient donques:
«Amis, por coi vous avint onques
1365 De vous aïrer? Viax, por honte!
Et d'un garçon a vous que monte?
Le piere avés de troveüre,
Qu'il acata par aventure;
Or est bien saus vostre cateus.
1370 Grans aventure est qu'ele est teus.
Ne l'en devés ja gré savoir,
Dignes seroit de honte avoir.»
Al signor torne a grant contraire
Ce que l'on dist; si doit il faire.[81]
1375 «Signor, fait il, ce n'i a rien.
Si m'aït Dix, or voi je bien
Que contre un home qui retrait
Prince de faire hontex plait,
Sont il mil qui a mal l'empaignent,[82]
1380 Et qui le honte li ensaignent.
Mais contre ce convient regart;[83]
Soit preudom qui le maison gart.
Mal dites, signor, par saint Piere;
N'est home el monde qui le piere
1385 Quesist, por voir, u il le quist;
Quant le trouva, cascuns le dist
Qu'il estoit fax et mal senés,
Et por noient les a penés;
De ce dont il s'est delivrés,[84]
1390 Vo voel a tous, fust encombrés.
Se vous le haés par envie,

---

[77] ne t.]B.
[78] noir u blanc]BT.
[79] lesgrarde]BT.
[80] v. e. puis]BT.

[81] on f.]BT.
[82] lemplaignent]B.
[83] c. ce con en r.]BT.
[84] molt penes]BT.

and so that he would not be considered a liar. He was really very pleased that Eracle had proved himself right regarding the stone, and he would be very upset if he were not to find him truthful now. **1329** The seneschal scrutinised him closely, very impatient and eager for him to buy this horse, which was worth a valley full of the other horses, as everyone thought and said. When Eracle looked at it, he did not value it so highly, indeed he did not consider it worthy of his attention at all and did not bother to haggle over it. It possessed nothing he was looking for, so he walked on by; and the man who had paid a thousand *besants* for Eracle was upset, for he now believed that he had been deceived: 'Eracle,' he thought to himself, 'now things are going badly. Now I'm going to drop you, now I'm going to abandon you; I shall no longer care about you; you will never again win my affection. My lord will now have a good laugh at my expense, for that's all I deserve. He really thought that he would learn from you whether he could ever have a wife with no bad qualities; now I can see nothing here to please me; I think you are a fool and a scoundrel.' **1352** Eracle noticed a colt, which still had four milk teeth and possessed all those qualities he was looking for in a horse. He walked right across the field and did not pause until he reached it. There were a thousand similar colts, apart from this one, belonging to counts and castellans, who considered it, to tell the truth, to be the very worst of the thousand of them. When the seneschal became very angry, those nearby said to him: 'My friend, why on earth have you allowed yourself to get angry, and just because you are ashamed of him? What's a mere boy to you? You still have the stone, a lucky find which he bought by chance; your money is thus well spent. It was pure luck that the stone is special. You do not owe him any thanks; he ought to be ashamed of himself.' Their lord was very angry at what they said, and rightly so. **1375** 'My lords,' he said, 'you are quite wrong. So help me God, I now realise that for every man who prevents a prince from embarking on a shameful course of action there are always a thousand who incite him to do evil and encourage shameful behaviour. However, we need to be on our guard against this; let whoever guards the house be an honourable man.[32] You slander him, my lords, by St Peter; to tell the truth there is no one alive who would have sought the stone where he sought it out; when he found it, everyone said that he was a fool and stupid, and that he had caused everyone a lot of needless trouble. If all of you had had your way, he would have been destroyed by the very thing that he escaped from with his life. If in your envy you hate him,

---

[32] This sounds proverbial; cf. *Proverbes français* 1180: 'Mal se garde du larron qui l'enclot en sa meson'.

Vous avés droit, car de se vie
Doivent li malvais avoir duel,
Car ja, si m'aït Dix, lor voel
1395 Ne vivroit bone cose en pais;
Mais ja, certes, por les malvais
N'iert mains li varlés mes amis;[85]
Jou ai sauf canque g'i ai mis.
Fax est qui croit malvaise rien   [f]
1400 De faire preudome el que bien;
Por çou le het que il est preus,
Et qu'il n'est mie ses pareus,
Et por ce vait il decevant.
Le catel m'avés mis devant
1405 Por lui honir, mais ne vos valt,
Car par cel Diu qui maint en haut,
S'aussi malvaise fust li piere
Con ele est prescïeuse et ciere,
N'aroit il ja por moi anui.
1410 A si rice home con je sui
Est sifais cateus poi de cose;
Je ne me plaig de nule cose.
Or ne remaint il en vous mie
Que li varlés ne pert le vie![86]
1415 Fols est qui croit faus consillier
De soi honir et avillier.»
    Eracles le preudome aresne
Qui le poulain tient par le resne
«Preudom, fait il, ça entendés;
1420 Cest vostre poulain me vendés.
– Varlet, par foi, molt volentiers,
Mais il vos est, espoirs, trop ciers.
– Trop ciers? fait il, fais le cent mars?

– Amis, nenil, mix fust il ars
1425 Que il vous fust sorapielés!
Jel vos vendrai, se vous volés,
Comme a voisin et a ami;
Deus mars en donés et demi,
S'avoir en volés le saisine,
1430 Mais jel vos vendrai en plevine.
– Preudom, j'oi bien a vostre dit[87]
Que vous le connissiés petit;
Ne que vous veés qui je sui[88]
Ne veés vous qu'il a en lui.
1435 – Tant sai je bien, fait li vilains,
Que quatre dens tient li poulains;
Mais n'i a un seul plus isniel
N'amont n'aval, tant par soit biel,
Del pris qu'il est, ce sai je
                    bien.[89]   [133a]
1440 Mais cis marciés ne monte rien;
Trop estes jones, ce m'est vis,
Por tant acater sans amis.
Onques encor ne vi enfant
Qui sans amis acatast tant.
1445 Mais se consel en aviés[90]
Et vous bon gré m'en saviés,
Le demi marc vous en lairoie,
Por les deus mars le vous donroie.
Si me garisse Dix mon cief,
1450 Que jou en faiç molt grant mescief,
Qu'il m'a molt durement cousté:
Bien a deus ans qu'il n'a gousté
Riens que n'acreïsse a usure,[91]
Et molt a petite mesure.

---

85 ses a.]BT.
86 parert]BT.
87 je voi bien v.]B.
88 v. que j. s.]BT.
89 Des p.]BT.
90 s. vous c.]R. Vous *omitted to allow for a trisyllabic* aviés *to rhyme with* saviés.
91 Biens]BT.

it is not surprising, since evil men are bound to be discomfited by his life, for, so help me God, they would never allow a good thing to live in peace. However, I am determined that this young boy will be no less of a friend of mine just because of what evil men say; all that I have invested in him is safe. A man is a fool if he believes the evil creatures who advise him to do anything but good to a worthy man; he is hated because he is worthy and not at all like them, that's why he frustrates them. **1404** You have brought up the question of my money to impugn his honour, but it has done you no good, for by God who dwells on high, if the stone had been as worthless as it is precious and valuable, he would still not have had any trouble from me. That sum of money is of little consequence to a person as rich as I am; I have no cause for complaint. And now it is no thanks to you that this young man is not going to lose his life. Anyone who, in following the advice of a treacherous counsellor, dishonours and degrades himself, is a fool indeed.'

Eracle addressed the honest fellow who was holding the colt by the rein: 'Good fellow,' he said, 'a word in your ear: do sell this colt of yours to me. – By my faith, young man, I would do so gladly, but it's probably too expensive for you. – Too expensive,' he said, 'are you asking a hundred marks for it? – No, my friend, it would be better if it were burnt than that you were overcharged for it. **1426** If you like, I shall sell it to you at the reduced price for neighbours and friends; give me two and a half marks, if you wish to own it, but I shall sell it to you at your word. – Good fellow, I can tell from what you are saying that you know very little about it; just as you don't realise who I am, so you can't see what qualities it possesses. – This much I do know for sure,' said the peasant, 'that this colt has four milk-teeth; but you will find none, in the valleys nor the mountains, however handsome it might be, that is swifter than him for the same price, that's for sure. But this deal is going nowhere; it seems to me that you are too young to buy something so expensive on your own. I have never yet seen a child buy such an expensive item on his own. But if you had someone to help you and were to thank me for it, I would knock off half a mark and let you have it for two marks. May God protect me though, for I am incurring a big loss, since it has cost me a great deal of money. **1452** For at least the last two years it has eaten nothing that hasn't been paid for on credit, albeit in very small quantities.

1455 Povretés m'a molt assailli;
Cil quil me douna m'a failli,[92]
Car il me dist par verité
Qu'il me gietroit de povreté.
– Et qui fu il? Savés le vous?
1460 – Nenil, par Diu qui maint sor nous,
Ne sai qui il est, nel connois,[93]
Mais il fu plus blans comme nois.
Por amor Diu le me dona,
Que onques plus mot n'i sonna;
1465 Et nouri l'ai en bon espoir,
Cuidai bien qu'il me desist voir;
Çou m'a fait outre m'aise atendre.
Or le me fait besoigne vendre,
Car plus sui povres que mendis.
1470 Prendés le ensi con je vous dis.
– Preudom, se Dix me doinst eür,
Or poés bien estre aseür;
Qui croit preudome, il fait que sages;
Ja ne vous ert dex ne damages
1475 Que vous avés cestui creü,
Ne sor sa parole acreü.[94]
Biens fais ne sera ja estains
Ne preudom de mençoigne atains.[95]
Vint mars vous donrai del poulain; [b]
1480 Ne l'avés pas nouri en vain.
– Biax dous varlet, gabés me vous
Por ce que povres sui trestous
Et que verté vous ai gehie?
– Nou faiç, se Dix me beneïe.[96]
1485 Au departir le verrés bien,
Que ne vous ai gabé de rien,
Car par cel Diu qui maint lassus,
Or en averés vint mars plus!»
Quarante mars li fait peser,
1490 Mais cil nes osa adeser.
En sus se trait, forment se tient,
Car povres hom tous jors se crient.
Mais cil qui plus n'i velt atendre
Li fait a force l'argent prendre.
1495 Encor se crient molt li vilains,
Si tient l'argent entre ses mains;
Muçant s'en va outre la gent,
Crient c'on li tolle son argent.
Or est dolans li senescaus;
1500 Nus vauroit estrë et descaus
Enmi le Toivre dusc'al col,
Par si c'on nel tenist por fol
Endroit del varlet acaté.
Tuit dient qu'il l'a bareté,
1505 Sel noncent a l'empereor,
Car pieç'a qu'il sont gaingleor,
N'est d'ui ne d'ier que il commencent.
Cil de le cort al vallet tencent[97]
Por lor signor servir a gré;
1510 Or est il molt em bas degré,
Mais Diex le metra en plus haut,
Car c'est li sire qui ne faut.
Ore est Eracles el desous,
Or est il molt sor cuer a tous,
1515 C'on trueve poi a cort amis
Puis que li sire est anemis.
Ore est Eracle molt par mal

---

92 qui]B.
93 Nessai]. *The double consonant is a feature of Scribe* 1, *cf.* 2088, 2198, 4342, etc.
94 le p.]BT.
95 parole a.] BT (*cf.* 974, 1572).
96 s. D. *repeated*].
97 1508-58 *Scribe* 2.

I have suffered greatly from poverty; the man who gave the foal to me let me down, for he assured me that it would save me from poverty. – And do you know who he was? – No, by God, who dwells in heaven above, I don't know who he is, nor am I acquainted with him, but he was whiter than snow. He gave me the colt for the love of God, without uttering another word, and I have fed it with high expectations, really believing that he was telling the truth; this has made me wait longer than was good for me. Now necessity is forcing me to sell it, for I am poorer than a beggar. Take it at the price I quoted. – Good fellow, as God may give me good fortune, you can now rest assured; whoever believes a worthy man is very wise to do so. It will never be to your disdavantage or detriment that you have believed this man or accumulated debts because of what he said. **1477** A good deed will never go to waste, nor can an honest man be proved a liar. I shall give you twenty marks for the colt; you have not reared it in vain. – Kind, gentle young man, are you making fun of me because I am extremely poor and because I have revealed the truth to you? – No, I am not, as God may give me His blessing. When it comes to handing over the money, it will become patently clear that I have not been making fun of you at all, for by God who dwells in heaven above, now you shall have an extra twenty marks.' He had forty marks weighed out for him, but the colt owner did not dare to touch them; he stepped backwards, restraining himself, for a poor man lives constantly in fear. But Eracle, who was in a hurry, forced him to take the money. The peasant was still very much afraid, even though he held the money in his grasp. He made his way discreetly through the crowd, fearing that someone would grab his money from him.

1499 Now the seneschal was really upset. He would have preferred to be up to his neck in the middle of the Tiber, naked and with no shoes on rather than be considered a fool on account of the young boy he had purchased. Everyone said that he had tricked him and they told the emperor, for they had been slanderers for a while now, they had not begun on that day or even the day before. The courtiers criticised the young man in order to please their lord with their service; now he had sunk very low, but God would raise him up again, for He is the Lord who does not fail us. Now Eracle had reached rock bottom, now everyone was against him, for one finds few friends at court when the lord is one's enemy. Now Eracle was on very bad terms

Al signor et al senescal.
Li empereres li a dit: [c]
1520 «Eracle, je vous aim petit.
– Sire, fait il, por Dieu merchi,
Por coi est çou? – Por le ronchi
Dont tu as erré folement,
Et fols est qui a toi s'atent.
1525 Achater deüs le millor,
Ore as achaté le pïor
De tous ciaus qui sont en le foire;
Se je mon cuer voloie croire,
Je te feroie ja anui,
1530 Mais il me sovient qui je sui.
Se tu eüsses asené
A tel cheval i ot mené,
Ja certes ne me peseroit[98]
A doner cent mars outre droit.
1535 – Bials sire ciers, ne faites plait;
Çou que je fis ai de gré fait.
A tort vous aïrés vers moi,
Car plus bonté a il en soi,
Cis poulains que vostre home ont vil,
1540 Que n'en aient li millor mil
Que il i aient hui veüs.
Et que dont s'il fust parcreüs![99]
Lors vauroit il molt grant catel,
Qu'en tot le monde n'aroit tel;
1545 Et s'il vous plaist, tes con il est,
Soient or troi li millor prest
Que vous trestot aiés a cois,
Et s'il nes vaint al cors tos trois,

J'otroi, biax sire, c'on me pende,
1550 De coi li piex Diex me desfende![100]
Esprovés se le cose est voire:
Il a chevals en ceste foire;
Soient eslit li millor troi,
Et s'il nes vaint, je vous otroi
1555 Me teste a prendre et a trenchier.
Metés ichi tot le plus chier;
Al cief del cors, la jus a val,
Faites metre l'autre ceval;
Le tierç metés al cors aprés[101] [d]
1560 Et li bousne soit al ciprés,[102]
U ele soit dusc'al pumier.
Le poulain courrai al premier;[103]
Si mouvrons droit de ceste plance.[104]
Se je nel tieg tout a estance[105]
1565 Ains que je viegne a l'autre enmi,
Si me faites trencier par mi;
Se je de l'autre autel ne fais,
Andoi li oel me soient trais!
– Puet ce estre voirs que m'as dit?
1570 – Biax sire, oïl, se Dix m'aït.
Je ne vois querant nule alonge,
Ja ne m'ataindrés de mençoigne.[106]
– Eracle, et je l'esprouverai;
Selonc ce que je troverai,
1575 S'en rendrai plus le gerredon.
– Biaux sire, a Diu beneïçon!
Ne mais, or soiiés bien certains,
Perdus en sera li poulains
Se il a fait ceste aramie.

---

[98] pesoroit]BT.
[99] fist]B.
[100] A *later hand corrects* piex *wrongly to* fiex, *which* R *adopts, but cf.* 1638.
[101] *Scribe* 1 *resumes briefly.*
[102] s. de ci pres]L.
[103] c. tout p.]L.
[104] mouvront]B.
[105] nes t.]B.
[106] m'ataindras]BT.

with his lord and with the seneschal. 'Eracle,' said the emperor, 'I don't like you very much. – My lord, by God's mercy,' he said, 'why is that so? – Because of the incident with the nag, during which you behaved foolishly. And anyone who relies on you is a fool. **1525** You ought to have bought the best horse, yet you have just bought the worst of all those at the fair; if I wished to follow my inclinations, I would immediately do you some harm, but I haven't forgotten who I am. If you had decided upon a certain horse that had been taken there I would definitely not mind paying a hundred marks over the odds. – My dear, kind lord, do not quarrel with me; I did this on purpose. You are wrong to get angry with me, for this colt, which your men consider a poor specimen, possesses more good qualities than a thousand of the best horses they have seen here today. Imagine then what it would be like if fully grown! Then it would be worth a great deal of money, for it would have no equal in the whole world. And even as it is now, if it pleases you, prepare the best three horses at your disposal and if it doesn't beat all three of them in a relay race, I agree, kind lord, to be hanged, though may merciful God protect me from this! Set up a test to ascertain the truth: there are plenty of horses in this fair; let the best three be chosen and if the colt does not beat them, take my head and cut it off. **1556** Place the very best horse here; have the second horse positioned down there in the valley at the beginning of its section of the relay course[33] and position the third at the beginning of the next section. The finishing line could be either at the cypress tree or as far as the apple tree. I shall race the colt against the first horse; we shall set off straight from this bridge.[34] If I have not winded the first horse before I catch up with the next one, have me cut in half; if I don't do the same with the next one, may both my eyes be gouged out! – Can what you have told me be true? – Kind lord, yes, so God help me. I am not seeking any delay; you will never prove me a liar. – And I shall put this to the test, Eracle. The reward I shall give will be commensurate with what I find. **1576** – Kind lord, blessed be God! However, you should know that the colt will be ruined once it has performed this incredible feat.

---

[33] 'Al cief del cors' could be at the beginning of the second horse's stretch or at the end of the first horse's; in a relay race this amounts to the same position.

[34] A 'plance' could be anything made out of wooden planks: a bridge, planks for crossing muddy ground, etc.

1580 — Eracle, amis, ce n'i a mie,
 Or me vas tu ci baretant.
 — Sire, nou faiç ne tant ne quant;
 Sans demorance l'esprouvés,
 Mais ja si bons n'ert mais trovés
1585 Come cil, qui gardé l'eüst[107]
 Un an entier qu'il ne courust.[108]
 — Eracle, voir, dist l'empere,
 Ci endroit iés tu baretere;
 Or n'iés tu mie sans engieng.[109]
1590 Mais par le main dont je te tieng,
 Ne monte rien, car il corra.
 — Non fera, voir, il ne porra,
 Font adonques li mençoignier,[110]
 Qui ne finent de losengier.
1595 Sire, font il, çou est noiens,
 Nel creés pas, ralés laiens.
 Espace i metroit volentiers
 Si s'enfuiroit endementiers,
 Mais il n'en ara nul loisir. [e]
1600 Se il vos vient, sire, a plaisir,
 Laisiés le nos, ralés vous ent,
 Si parlerons priveement;
 Le siecle en vengerons et vos
 Ralés vos ent, laissiés le nos!»
1605 Et quant li senescals l'entent,
 Si s'en aïre durement:
 «Signor, fait il, qui vos querra
 Honis soit il, et qui verra
 Que on li face se bien non.
1610 Tels gens honisent maint baron,
 Mais bien est menés a son droit
 Princes malvais qui tels gens croit.
 — Sire, por Dieu le fil Marie,
 Fait li vallés, nes creés mie![111]
1615 Nes creés mie, gentis hom,[112]
 Mais les cevals en amaint l'on;
 Si metés cascun d'els par soi
 Si con vos di, puis soit sor moi.
 — Molt volentiers, se Diex me salt,
1620 Mais por Dieu, tot ce rien ne valt.»
 Amener fait son bon ceval[113]
 Et un qui fu au senescal;
 Le tierç on giete de l'estable,
 Cil estoit a son conestable.
1625 Plus estoit prisiés tous li pire
 Que tous li miudres de l'empire.
 Si les fait mener erraument
 La u li varlés les atent.
 Eracles monte en son poulain,
1630 U ainc ançois n'ot eü frain,
 Et broce et point molt durement,
 Et li escuiers ensement.
 Li ceval keurent a esploit,
 Molt s'esmervellent, si ont droit,
1635 Con li poulains se tient une eure
 Al bon ceval, et molt demeure
 As envïeus que il recroie,
 Mais ja li pix Dix nes en croie!
 Biax est li tans et clers li jors; [f]
1640 Deus liues durent li troi cors.
 Ens el moien del cors premier
 Est l'empere, al mien cuidier;
 El autre après, le counestable.[114]
 Cil qui plus croit le cose estable,
1645 Ce est li senescaus, li sire,
 S'est mis al tiers, por le voir dire.
 Li grans cevax cort de randon,

---

[107] c. il]B.
[108] qui]BT.
[109] 1589-1620 *Scribe* 2.
[110] F. le donques]B.

[111] ne c.]T (B: nel).
[112] Ne]R (B: nel).
[113] 1621-1934 *Scribe* 1.
[114] Et l'autre]B.

– Eracle, my friend, that can't be right; now you are having me on. – No I'm not, my lord, not at all; put it to the test without delay, but you will never find a horse as excellent as this one would be if it were kept for a whole year without being raced. – Yes, indeed, Eracle,' said the emperor, 'now you are trying to trick me; now you are being crafty. But, by this hand which binds you to me, it is of no use, for it shall race! – No it won't, for in fact it won't be able to,' interjected the liars, who never tired of being two-faced. 'My lord,' they said, 'this is nonsense, don't believe him, go back inside. He is hoping to put distance between you and thereby to escape, but he won't get the chance to do so. **1600** If it is your wish, sire, leave him to us, go away and we shall discuss this privately together; we shall avenge you and the whole human race; go away and leave him to us!' And when the seneschal heard this, he became very angry. 'My lords,' he said, 'shame on him who believes you and who stands by and watches him treated in any way but well. Such people bring shame on many a powerful man, but an evil prince who believes such people really does get his just deserts. – My lord, by God, the son of Mary, do not believe them,' said the young boy. 'Do not believe them, noble lord, but let the horses be brought out, then position each one of them according to my instructions, and on my head be it. – As God is my Saviour, I am quite happy to agree, but, by God, all of this is to no avail.'

He ordered his excellent horse to be brought out and one which belonged to the seneschal; the third, which belonged to his constable, was taken out of its stable. **1625** The very worst of these was still valued more highly than the best in the empire. He had them brought quickly to where the young man was waiting for them. Eracle mounted his colt, which had not yet had the bit between its teeth, and spurred and urged it on vigorously, and the squire chosen as rider did likewise.[35] The horses set off at top speed and everyone rightly marvelled at how the colt kept up with the excellent horse for so long, and the envious could not wait for it to give up, but may merciful God take no notice of them! The weather was fine and the sun was shining; the three sections of the course covered two leagues: in the very middle of the first section stood the emperor, I think; in the next one the constable; and finally, the person who was most convinced by Eracle's claims, his lord the seneschal, took up his position, to tell the truth, in the third. The fully grown horse raced at top speed

---

[35] Although all three of Eracle's rivals must have mounted and gone to their respective positions, it seems that Gautier is here describing the race with the first horse. 'Li escuiers' (nom. sg.) is therefore translated as 'the squire' (pace Eskénazi 2002, 104).

Bien a les resnes a bandon;
Al signor a mervelle vient
1650 Que li poulains a lui se tient;
Son ceval aime et tient molt chier,
Mais par verté l'os aficier,[115]
Se li cevax valoit mil mars,
Si ameroit il qu'il fust ars,
1655 Par si que li poulains velus
Eüst les trois cors parvencus,[116]
Qu'il le tenroit a grant miracle,[117]
Et puis se tenroit a Eracle
Seürement de feme prendre,
1660 Car nel saroit de coi reprendre.[118]
Icil qui queurt le bon ceval[119]
Tient a desdaig et torne a mal
Que li poulains si longe dure;
Un poi engroisse s'aleüre
1665 Qu'il quide adosser le poulain;
Mais je vous di que c'est en vain,
Nel puet trespasser un seul pas.
Cil est sejornés et molt cras,
Se li angoisse molt l'alaine.
1670 Enmi le quarte quarentaine
Le col estent, li cors li grieve,
Li oins li font, li cuers li crieve,
A terre ciet, fait est de lui.
As envïeus torne a anui,
1675 Les cuers ont enflés et plains d'ire,
Mais ne sevent soussiel que dire,
Et li varlés, cui Dix en maine,
Molt grant joie en son cuer demaine.
Un poi rafrescist son poulain; [134 a]
1680 Regnes sierees vait sor frain

Tres c'al relais de l'autre aprés.[120]
Tant a alé qu'il i est prés;
Quant li cevax le poulain sent,
Si se desroie durement;
1685 De lonc sejor iert envoisiés,[121]
Hennist et soufle et fiert des piés.
Bien dient toute gent por voir
Qu'el mont ne puet millor avoir.
Li escuiers qui sus estoit,
1690 Qui largement gardé l'avoit,
Coumence a poindre et a brocier
Quant le poulain voit aprocier.
Encoste Eracle le varlet
Isnielement el cours se met,
1695 Delivrement s'aroute a lui.
Bien ceurent li ceval andui.
Deus arpens vont sieré et joint
Que l'uns l'autre ne passe point;
Mais il fu sempres autrement
1700 Quant fu venu au tierç arpent:
Li poulains passe, et cil remaint,
N'a mestier mais c'on plus l'amaint,
Ses quatre piés met tout ensanle,
Trestous li cors li sue et tranle,
1705 Recreans est et tous atains;
Petit en faut qu'il n'est estains.[122]
N'a mais mestier, autant se vaut,
N'a mais mester c'on le travaut.
Et dient lor li malvais home:
1710 «Par tous les sains c'on quiert a Rome,
Molt par nous a cis encantés.
Diables est en lui entrés.
Mais ne cauroit, ne moi, ne moi,

---

115 los bien a.] *hypermetric line in* A.
116 parveus]B.
117 Qui]B.
118 savoit]B.
119 quiert]T (B: tient).

120 T. ca]B.
121 envoies]BT.
122 atains]BT.

and was given full rein; his owner was amazed that the colt was keeping up with it; **1651** he loved his horse and was very fond of it, but I can assure you truly that even if the horse had been worth a thousand marks, he would have preferred it to be burnt, if it meant that the shaggy colt successfully completed the three sections of the course. For he would have considered this to be a great miracle, and would therefore have trusted Eracle completely in the matter of taking a wife, for he would have been able to find no fault in him. The man who was riding the excellent horse was unconcerned and dismissive of the fact that the colt was keeping up for so long; he increased his speed a little, expecting to shake off the colt; but I can tell you that it was to no avail, for he could not put even a single stride between them. His horse was well rested and rather heavy, and its breathing became very painful. In the fourth *quarantaine*[36] it stretched its neck forward, its body was racked with pain, its fat melted and its heart gave out; it fell to the ground – that was the end of it. **1674** This upset the envious, whose hearts were full to bursting with anger, but they did not know what on earth to say, and the young boy, may God be with him, felt very great joy in his heart. He gave his colt the chance to recover a little, holding it back on a tight rein until they reached the next part of the relay course. He rode until he got quite close; when the horse sensed the colt approaching, it became very unsettled; being fully rested it was raring to go, it neighed and panted and stamped its hoofs. Indeed, everyone said quite truthfully that you could not find a better horse on earth. The squire seated on it, who had been restraining it for some time, began to spur and urge it on when he saw the colt approach. As the young man Eracle came alongside, he quickly joined the race, swiftly making for him; the two horses ran well together. They ran neck and neck over two *arpents*,[37] neither overtaking the other at all; **1699** but things soon changed when they reached the third arpent: the colt overtook and the other horse remained behind. There was no point in goading it on any longer; it drew its four legs together, stopping dead in its tracks, its whole body was sweating and shaking – it was beaten and totally exhausted; it was very close to death. There was no longer any point, it was of no use, there was no point in making it suffer any further. Then the evil men said: 'By all the saints we seek in Rome, this lad really has bewitched us. He is possessed by the devil. But I am not upset for myself, nor I for myself,'

---

[36] A *quarantaine* was forty perches long; a perch could measure about six metres, but varied from region to region.
[37] An *arpent* measured one hundred perches.

Fait soi cascuns, mais por le roi,
1715 Qui se metoit en nos conseus.
Cis est si vertueus et preus
Qu'il nous metra del tout defors.
Malëois soit hui li siens cors!»
Molt desirent que il perisse, [b]
1720 Mais Damedix l'en escremisse!
N'est hom soussiel cui voelle mal.[123]
Sor frain vait trusc'au tierç ceval,[124]
Qui molt demainne grant desroi
Quant voit le poulain prés de soi.
1725 Cil qui sus iert plus n'i demeure,
El cours se met donques en l'eure.
Plus est isniax cis daerains
C'orains ne fu li premerains,
Et li poulains se rafrescist
1730 Et ceurt or mix c'umais ne fist.
Li senescaus, qui est au cors,
Prie que Dix li doinst secours,
Et que ses bons cevax recroie;
Ice requiert molt Diu et proie,
1735 Mix vauroit qu'il fust recreüs
Que li varlés fust mescreüs.
Li poulains court molt ricement,
Et li cevax court ensement.
Si rices cours ne fu ainc mais
1740 Com est cis tiers, ne n'ert jamais.
Ensanle se sont tant tenu
Qu'il sont enmi le cors venu.
Li varlés au cuer debonaire
Set del poulain canqu'il puet faire;
1745 Un poi le broce et esperonne
Et les renes li abandonne.
Le ceval passe illuec endroit,

Grant joie maine, si ot droit;
Et li cevax atant se laske;
1750 Cil qui le cors ot pris en taske,
Qui sus estoit, le broce et fiert,
Mais sempres venra qu'il en iert:
Au brocier qu'il a fait le tue,
Car li cevax s'en esvertue
1755 Outre pooir, et si enfont.
Cil qui le broce le confont,
Car cose trop desmesuree
Ne puet avoir longe duree.
Li cevax va par tel angousse[125] [c]
1760 Que li espaule li eslousse;
Ne puet mais endurer le paine,
Et cil en va, cui Dix en maine;
Ses regnes serre et garde arriere,[126]
Et voit gesir lonc le quariere
1765 Le tierç ceval; atant retorne.
Or est il liés et cil sont morne
Qui l'ont sordit de felounie,
Or connoit on lor vilounie.[127]
Por ce sont fol, ce truis lisant,
1770 Li mal parlier, li mesdisant,
Car s'il mesdient de nului,
Et on voit puis le bien en lui,
Por menteor tenir se font;
Çou est li prex que il en ont.
1775 Et la rencargent il grant fais
U il mesdient del malvais,
Qu'en mesdisant avilenissent
Et de lor bones teces issent.
Grans vilounie est de mesdire,
1780 De nului blasmer et desdire;
Assés se blasme et juge l'euvre

---

[123] soussies]T.
[124] Sou f.]B.

[125] broce]B (T: chiet).
[126] garde et serre a.]L.
[127] l. felounie]T.

they all claimed, 'but for the king, who was relying on our advice; this fellow is so talented and brave that he is going to usurp our positions. May his body be damned today!' They really wanted him to die, but may God protect him from them. Eracle wished no harm to anyone under the sun. Reining back the colt he proceeded to the third horse, which champed at the bit when it saw the colt approach. **1725** Its rider did not delay, but immediately set off down the course. The last horse was even swifter than the first had been earlier, yet the colt, having regained its strength, now raced better than it had ever done. The seneschal, who was standing at the final section of the course, prayed to God to come to Eracle's aid, asking for his fine horse to be defeated; he besought and entreated God fervently, preferring his horse to be defeated rather than that the young boy's word be doubted. The colt galloped quite splendidly and the horse ran equally well. Never was there nor shall there ever be such a splendid race as this third one. They stayed together so long that they reached the middle of the last stretch. The young boy with a noble heart knew what the colt was capable of; he spurred it and urged it on a little and gave it full rein. He immediately overtook the horse, and deservedly felt elated; and the horse then grew weary; **1750** the rider who had undertaken to race against Eracle spurred it on and whipped it, but he was soon to see what would come of this: from spurring it on he killed it, for the horse overreached itself and collapsed. The man who spurred it on killed it, for anything excessive cannot last for long. The horse continued in such agony that it dislocated its shoulder; it could not stand the pain any longer, and Eracle, God's protégé, went on ahead; he pulled in the reins and looked behind him and saw the third horse lying beside the track; he returned immediately. Now he was joyful and those who had accused him wrongly of treachery were dejected, now their wickedness was clear for all to see. This is why slanderers and malicious gossips are fools, as the books I have read show, for if they slander someone and he later proves to be virtuous, they gain a reputation as liars; this is the profit they get from it. **1775** And they take on an equally great burden when they slander an evil man, for in the very act of slandering they degrade themselves and negate even their good qualities. To slander, criticise or wrongfully accuse someone is a terribly wicked thing to do. The action brings its own criticism and judgement with it,

A çou que nus fais ne se cuevre;[128]
Couvrir se puet, mais a la fin
Se descuevre li faus del fin.[129]
1785 Eracles a les plains tenus
Par ou il iert ançois venus;
Trait soi envers le senescal,
Qui se desresne au marissal
Et del varlet et nient d'autrui;
1790 Voit le, si vait encontre lui;
Ansdeus ses bras au col li met,
Et puis si baise le varlet:
«Amis, fait il, se je vous bais,
Cuidiés por çou i soit li pais
1795 De mon ceval que m'avés mort?
Se je vous bais, çou est a tort!
– Biax sire, sauve vostre grasce,
Ne l'ai pas mort; ja Diu ne place
Que je tant vive desor terre   [d]
1800 Que vous tant me pussiés requerre
Al mien tort ne a vostre droit.
Mes cors por honnis se tenroit
Se jou avoie retraçon.
– Eracle, amis, biele façon,
1805 Cuidiés vous que je die a certes?
Aussi me destourt Dix de pertes,
Que j'onques mais si liés ne fui
Que jou de cest damage sui!
Eracles, certes, biax dous frere,
1810 Or vous tenra cier l'emperere;
Or vous metés tost a la voie,
Car molt li tarde qu'il vous voie;
Ce est li riens qu'il plus couvoite.
De Diu soit l'eure beneoite
1815 Que je vous vi n'i encontrai,
Et le jor que a Rome alai!»[130]
Baise le dont ameement,
Et quant li sire ot et entent,
Et il a tout le voir seü,[131]
1820 Que li ceval sont recreü,
Encontre le varlet en vait.
Quant il le voit, grant joie en fait;
Molt bonement l'acole et baise,
Tantost com ot et liu et aise.
1825 «Amis, fait il, bien viegnes tu!
Petit en faut que jou ne tu
Ne faiç morir de male mort[132]
Tous ceus qui t'ont blamé a tort.
Voirs est que jengleor glouton
1830 Ne blament s'eus meïme non;
Ja preudom n'ert par eus blamés
Ne n'iert mains ciers ne mains amés
Ne mains octorisiés au long.
Preudom porte o lui son tesmoig;
1835 Nel puet empirier male bouce,[133]
Ne malvais hom a lui ne touce,[134]
Ne ja preudom n'ert por lui pire,
Por canqu'il onques set mesdire,
Car li mauvais, il s'en confont.   [e]
1840 Car li plons art et l'argens font,
Et si s'afine par le plom,[135]
Qui s'art por lui; li mauvais hom[136]
Art enfin por le proude gent,[137]

---

[128] f. se descuevre]B.
[129] de f.]BT.
[130] Et que le jor]T.
[131] Que il]B.
[132] f. morr]BT.
[133] Ne]B.
[134] mais h.]BT.
[135] l'afine]BT.
[136] Qui]T.
[137] Arr]R.

since no deed can be concealed for ever; it can be covered up for a while, but eventually the false distinguishes itself from the true.

Eracle rode back along the flat course, making for the seneschal, who was talking to the marshal about none other than the young lad; when he saw the boy he went up to him and flung both his arms around his neck, then he kissed him, saying: 'My friend, if I kiss you, do you think it is to show that I have forgiven you for killing my horse? If I kiss you, you don't deserve it! – Kind lord, saving your grace, I didn't kill it; may it not please God that I should live on this earth long enough for you to accuse me of anything regarding which I am in the wrong and you are in the right. **1802** I would consider myself shamed if the reproach were justified. – Eracle, my friend, charming creature, did you think I was being serious? May God preserve me henceforth from such losses, if it is not the case that I was never before so happy as I am at this loss. Eracle, fair gentle brother, now the emperor will certainly treat you well; now off you go, for he is very impatient to see you; it's the thing he most wants in the world. May God bless the hour when I first saw and met you and the day when I went to Rome.' Then he kissed him fondly and when his lord heard, was told and learned the whole truth, namely that the horses had been defeated, he went to meet the young man. When he saw him, he made a great fuss of him; he embraced and kissed him very fondly, as soon as circumstances and opportunity allowed. **1825** 'My friend,' he said, 'you are welcome! I am a hair's breadth away from killing all those who have accused you wrongfully, or from making them suffer a terrible death. It is true that two-faced rogues accuse everyone but themselves; but just because a worthy man is accused by them, this does not mean that he will be less appreciated or loved or less respected in the long run. A worthy man brings with him his own testimonial; an evil tongue cannot ruin him, nor can an evil man affect him, nor will a worthy man's reputation suffer because of him, whatever slanders he manages to devise, for the evil man destroys himself in the process. Lead burns so that silver can melt and purify itself using the lead, which burns for it; so the evil man eventually burns for the worthy man,

Si con li plons fait por l'argent.
1845 Eracle, Diex porgart te vie!
Ja ne remanra por envie
Que del tout ne me mete en toi.
De mes conseus conselle moi;
Mes consilliers vels que tu soies,[138]
1850 Ne ferai rien que tu ne voies.
Ja ne m'i ert tant a talent
C'on ne me truist de faire lent,
Por qu'il te soit encontre cuer.
Ja nel vauroie a nesun fuer
1855 Que tu ne m'eüsses voir dit
Del poulain que j'euç en despit;
Or est il bons, ce voi je bien.
– Sire, non est, il ne valt rien.
Hui fu li miudres qui i fust,
1860 Or ne valt pas un pouri fust.
a   Se il est bons, sire emperere,[139]
b   Donkes sui jou enfin menteres,
c   Car je disc k'il afoleroit
d   Enfin, ki coure le feroit;
e   Il a couru, si est perdus.
f   Li cuirs des gambes soit fendus.
Or nel tenés pas a escar,
Vous venrés entre cuir et car
Que le mooule i est trestoute.
Ce vous di jou sans nule doute,
1865 Car issir toute l'en couvient,
Si tost con il a travail vient;
Des os est toute fors issue;
Ne c'une toile cler tissue,[140]
Ne le poroit tenir li os.
1870 Trusc'a un an desor son dos

Ne deüst nus estre montés;
Perdue en est se grans bontés.
– Puet estre, bons biax dous amis?
– Sire, li biens qui m'est promis
1875 Me soit tolus, se ce n'est voirs.
– Frere, bien ait li tiens savoirs!
Boinairement le me desis
Et a croire le me fesis
Que il afoleroit por courre, [f]
1880 Et, si me puisse Dix secourre,
Ja n'amerai mais menteor
Ne losengier ne gangleor
Tout por l'amor de cest afaire.»
Li varlés au cuer debonaire
1885 A fait le poulain jus abatre
Et fait les gambes toutes quatre
Fendre et le moule jus espandre
Et as varlés si l'a fait prandre.
Aprés si ont les os troués
1890 Et si les ont tous vuis trouvés,
Si qu'il n'i a grant ne petit
Ne voie ensi con il ot dit.
    Or est Eracles par raison
Bien de tous cex de la maison;
1895 Il n'i a ame si hardie[141]
Qui nule rien li escondie;
Toute li cors, qui molt est ample,
Prent a l'empereor example
De lui amer et conjoïr;
1900 De lui servir, de lui joïr;
Car puis que sire assaut son cien,
Tout li autre le sivent bien;
Tant que li sire a cier celui,

---
[138] toi s.]BT.
[139] *These 6 lines absent from* A *after* 1860 (*a likely* saut du même au même *on* Or) *are found in* BT *and quoted from* B, *cf.* 1879-87.
[140] t. fort t.]BT.
[141] feme]BT.

just as lead does for silver. Eracle, may God preserve you! I shall not, out of envy, fail to rely on you in every matter. Please advise me whenever I need advice; I wish you to be my adviser and I shall do nothing without your knowledge. **1851** However keen I am to do something, if it is against your wishes, you will find me slow to carry it out. I would never have wished, at any price, for you to have lied to me regarding the colt that I underestimated; now it is obvious to me that it is a fine horse. – Oh no it isn't, my lord, it's worthless. Earlier today it was the best one here, now it's not worth a bit of rotten wood. If it is a fine specimen, my imperial lord, then I am in fact a liar, for I told you that eventually it would be ruined if someone were to race it; it did race and it is ruined. I am not joking; have the skin on its legs slit open and you will see that all the marrow has spread into the gap between the hide and the flesh. I am in no doubt about what I am saying: it can't help but all seep out as soon as the colt exerts itself; there is no marrow left in its bones; the bone would not have been able to keep it in any more than loosely spun cloth could have done. No one should have ridden on its back for another year; its excellent qualities have all been lost. **1873** – Can this be so, good, kind, sweet friend? – My lord, may the rich rewards I am promised be taken away from me if it is not true. – Brother, blessed be your knowledge! You kindly told me and tried to convince me that it would be ruined if it were to race, and in recognition of this incident, I shall never again be well disposed towards liars, flatterers or slanderers, so help me God.' The young boy with the noble heart had the colt killed, all four legs split open and the marrow poured out; he then gave it to the emperor's servants to take away. They then bored holes into the bones and found that they were all empty. Thus there was no one, tall or short, who did not see with his own eyes what Eracle had predicted.

Now Eracle was rightly on good terms with everyone of the household; there was no soul rash enough to refuse him anything; all of the courtiers, and there were many of them, followed the emperor's example in loving him and making him feel welcome, in serving him and making him happy; **1901** for when a master beats his dog, everyone else follows suit; but if its master is fond of it,

Tant le cierist n'i a celui.
1905 Et il l'a cier et aime autant
Con fait li pere son enfant;
Par tout conmande plainement
C'on face son comandement.
En lui se croit, en lui se met,
1910 De lui alever s'entremet;
Quil velt de rien esleecier[142]
N'a oeus del varlet courechier;
Qui faire velt c'a gré li viegne
Face quanqu'al varlet coviegne.
1915 Bien li conmande l'emperere
Qu'il soit et sire et comandere,
Et ne li soit nus a contraire
De quanques onques valra faire.
  Or est si alé que li sire [135 a]
1920 Croit quanque Eracle valra dire.
Bacelers est et feme veut,
Mais molt se crient, si con il seut;
Il est li plus haus hom qui soit,
Por ce dist, et si a grant droit,
1925 Qu'il doit le millor feme avoir.
Au varlet le fait assavoir,
Dist lui: «Par toi m'estuet aprendre
En quel liu puisse feme prendre;
Consel te quier, conselle moi,
1930 Car tous mes consaus est en toi.
– Grés et mercis, biax tres dos sire,
De ce qu'il le vous loist a dire.
Biax sire ciers, or n'aiés soig,
Aidier vos cuiç a cest besoig
1935 Tot a vostre devisement;[143]
Mais or n'i ait alongement:
Faites metre vos briés en chire,
Si tramétes a vostre empire;
Mandés que vostre gentil home

1940 Soient a jor nomé a Rome;
Od vos remanront une pieche,
Et cascuns i amaint se nieche
U sa seror, u sa parente,
U fille, s'il l'a bele et gente.
1945 Escrit avra en cascun brief
Que cele avra corone el cief
Qui miels vos plaira del conmun;[144]
Çou ert escrit, sire, en cascun.
Tout i venront sans contredit
1950 Dés qu'il veront icest escrit,
Car cascuns ert en esperance
Qu'a le siue soit la cevanche.
De bon cuer cascune i venra
Qui ceste novelle entendra,
1955 Car cascune iert en bon espoir
Que doie le corone avoir.
– Eracle amis, che lo je bien;
Ichi ne voi je nule rien
Qui face a blamer n'a reprendre. [b]
1960 Li brief sont fait sans plus atendre,
Si les envoient largement,
As gentils homes solement
U il les doivent envoier.
Ne se font mie trop proier
1965 Ne cil ne cil qui oent lire;
Lor filles prendent a eslire
Et lor nieces et lor parentes,
Lor beles suers et les plus gentes;
De les atorner s'entremetent
1970 Et toute lor entente i metent.
Muevent et lor jornees vont,
Al jor nomé a Rome sont.
Ce fu par un bel jor d'esté;
Nus hom ki ait el siecle esté,
1975 Ne qui veües ait puceles,

---
[142] vel]T.
[143] 1935-2016 Scribe 2.

[144] de c.]T.

there is no one who can love it enough.³⁸ And the emperor was fond of him and loved him as much as a father does his child; he issued strict orders to everyone without exception that Eracle's orders should be obeyed. He placed his trust in him, relied on him and began to promote him at court. If anyone wanted to please the emperor in any way, it was not in his interests to antagonise the young man; whoever wished to win the emperor's approval, had to do whatever suited the young man. Indeed, the emperor commanded that Eracle should be treated as lord and master, and that no one should stand in the way of whatever he wished to do.

It had got to the point where the emperor believed whatever Eracle chose to say. He was unmarried and wished to wed, but as always he was fearful of the step. He was the most powerful man alive, which is why he was justified in saying that he deserved to have the best woman as his wife. **1926** He informed the youth, saying: 'I need to learn from you where I can find a wife; I am seeking your advice, advise me, for you are my one and only adviser. – I am grateful and thankful to you, fair most gentle lord, that you have found it possible to speak to me about this. Dear lord, don't worry, for I think I can help you find an entirely satisfactory solution to this problem, but you must not delay: have your letters sealed in wax³⁹ and sent throughout the empire; order your noble barons to come to Rome on the appointed day, so that they can stay awhile with you; let each bring with him his niece, sister, daughter, or other female relative, provided that she is beautiful and accomplished. Let it be written in every letter that the girl whom you find most pleasing of all shall wear the crown on her head; this will be written, my lord, in each one. **1949** They will all come willingly when they see this message, for every one of them will hope that his relative will win the highest prize.⁴⁰ Every young woman who hears the news will come eagerly, for each of them will have high hopes of being awarded the crown. – Eracle, my friend, I approve your plan wholeheartedly, for I see nothing in it to provoke blame or criticism.' The letters were prepared without delay and sent to all corners of the empire, but only to the nobility, as was right and proper. They did not need much persuading, nor did those who heard the proclamation read out to them; they began to select their daughters, their nieces, their beautiful sisters and their most accomplished female relatives; they began to prepare them, devoting all their effort to their adornment. Then they set out and travelled until they arrived in Rome on the appointed day. **1973** It was a beautiful summer's day. No one who has lived on this earth and has seen young maidens

---

38   Gautier here alludes to the proverb 'Qui m'aime, si aime mon chien', *Proverbes français* 88.
39   The wax may refer to wax seals on twelfth-century letters, or may refer to wax tablets, if Gautier is attempting historical accuracy. See note 14 above.
40   Literally 'subsistence living', but an example of litotes.

N'en vit onques tant de si beles;
Nus ne vit mais si bele gent.
Li chevalier sont bel et gent
Qui les guient par grant douçor;
1980 Cascuns se fille u se serour
U se nieche tient par le resne;
Et cascuns d'els le soie aresne,[145]
Et si li dist: «Me bele nee,
Se ceste honors vos est donee,
1985 N'oublïés pas vostre parage
Ne ne soiés vers nos salvage.
Oï avés, espoir, qu'onours
Mue sovent corage et mors,
Mais qui çou n'aime k'amer doit
1990 Sovent en vient a mains d'esploit,
Et s'en abaisse molt son pris.»[146]
Celes, qui n'ont encore pris,[147]
Respondent toutes a talent;
C'est prés coustume a tote gent
1995 Qu'il sont de service gringnor
Entrués qu'il beent a honor,
Et quant il ont l'onor eüe,
Si cornent lués le recreüe.
Nus ne set home que il valt   [c]
2000 Ançois qu'il soit montés en halt;
Quant il est montés dusqu'en som,
Lors primers pert s'il est prodom.
Les puceles et cil quis guient
Parolent de ceste oevre et dient
2005 Que molt a povre gentelisse
Qui pour avoir pert se francise;
Tant que li hom est en pooir,
Si doit il plus franc cuer avoir.
       Defors le vile en une plaigne
2010 S'est descendue le conpaigne;

La tendent pavilons et trés
Et a grant joie i sont remés.
Les puceles sont descendues,
Et grans ententes ont eües
2015 A elles vestir et lachier.
Qui tot le mont volroit trachier,
Ne trouveroit, mien ensïent,[148]
Tant bon drap ne bon garniment
Con a illuec en cele place,
2020 Et je vous di qu'en peu d'espace
I vienent tel mil citouain,
Qui perent estre castelain.
Oï avoient les nouvieles
Et des barons et des pucieles,
2025 Et je vous di plus de mil sont
Qui maintenant veoir les vont,
Qu'el mont n'a tant de si senees.[149]
Cil qui les orent assenees,[150]
Tout li plus haut et li millor,
2030 En vont veoir l'empereour.
       Molt par est courtois l'emperere,
Qu'il ne forligne pas son pere.
Dés que li voirs li est contés,
Si est il maintenant montés,
2035 Car les pucieles velt veoir
Dont il espoire l'une avoir.
Tant con il est li plus hals hom
C'on sace et de plus halt renon,
De tant est il tous li plus biax   [d]
2040 C'on sace, et tous li plus loiaus.
Molt est bien fais, molt a grant cors.
A molt grant gent s'en ist la fors;
Li gens que l'emperere amaine,
Qui n'est pas laide ne vilaine,
2045 Ont cele voie tant tenue

---

[145] A *omits* Et.
[146] sin a.]BT.
[147] e. pis]B.
[148] 2017-276 *Scribe* 1.
[149] senes; BT].
[150] assenes] (BT: amenees).

ever saw so many beautiful ones; no one has ever seen such a collection of beauties since. The knights who were so gently escorting them were handsome and courtly; each was leading his daughter, sister, or niece by the rein; and each was addressing his relative as follows: 'My fair one, if this honour is bestowed upon you, do not forget your family and do not treat us harshly. Perhaps you have heard that worldly success often changes a person's nature and behaviour, but those who fail to love what they should are often less successful in the end than they hoped to be and their reputation suffers greatly.' Those girls, who had not yet obtained anything, all gave the desired reply; it is almost universally the case that we are of greater service to others while we are striving for success, but once we have achieved success, we soon sound the retreat. No one knows what a person is worth until he has risen in fortune; **2001** only when he has reached the top can we tell if he is an honest man. The maidens and those escorting them discussed this matter and said that whoever sacrificed their noble behaviour in the pursuit of a fortune was not truly noble, and that when a man reached a position of power, his heart should be all the nobler.

The whole company dismounted outside the town, in an area of level ground. There they erected tents and pavilions, and remained there in joyful anticipation. Having dismounted, the maidens took a great deal of care over dressing and lacing themselves. If you were to travel the whole world over you would not find, in my view, such splendid clothes or fabulous accessories as were found there in that place. And I can tell you that in a short space of time at least a thousand townsfolk turned up looking as rich as powerful lords. They had heard the news about the barons and the young maidens, and believe me, more than a thousand of them rushed at once to see them, for you could not find elsewhere in the world so many girls with such accomplishements. **2028** The great and the good from amongst those who had escorted them there went off to see the emperor.

The emperor was very courtly and in no way disgraced his father's line. As soon as he had been told the facts of the matter he mounted his horse immediately, for he wished to see the girls from whom he hoped to select a wife. Just as he was the most powerful man alive and of the greatest repute, so he was the most handsome and most loyal man one could ever meet. He was very well-built and very tall. He set out with a huge retinue; the emperor and his escorts, who were neither ugly nor uncouth, continued on their way

C'a le grant porte sont venue.
La ont les barons encontrés,
Ains que nus d'eus i fust entrés.
Quant il voient lor avoué,
2050 Molt gentement l'ont salué.
Il lor respont molt doucement,[151]
Puis si les baise bielement,
Si les mercie de l'enhan,
Et des pucieles et del ban
2055 Qu'il ont si ricement tenu.
Tant vont parlant qu'il sont venu.
Quant il sont venu prés des tentes,
Si voient les pucieles gentes;
Les tentes sont a or tissues,
2060 Dont les pucieles sont issues,
Et sont a la reonde entor;
Mais molt par sont de rice ator:
Mix sont vestues les mescines
Ou aussi bien comme roïnes.
2065   Biele est li place et biax li rens,
Et les pucieles en tout sens
Sont tout entor a la reonde.
Li plus haus hom de tout le monde,
C'est l'emperere, il les salue
2070 De Diu qui est dessus le nue;[152]
Celes de prés salus li rendent,
Celes de lonc, qui ne l'entendent,
Qui sont de boin entendement,
L'enclinent toutes humlement.
2075 Li sire un baron i envoie
Qui les mercie de lor voie,
Et mande lor que de matin
Fera eslire a son devin[153]
Une a son oeus sans plus atendre, [e]
2080 Car par lui valra feme prendre.
Cil a tost furni son message,
A fuer de cortois et de sage.
Signor, feme a grant couvoitise
D'avoir honor et doëlisse.
2085 Ains riens mais tant ne covoita[154]
Et malement en esploita
La premeraine, tout por voir,
Qui couvoita plus assavoir
Que Cil qui l'ot de noient faite;
2090 Molt nos a en grant paine traite!
Cestes covoitent molt l'onor,
Et voient de l'empereor
Qu'il n'a el monde creature
De se biauté, de se figure;
2095 Lor covoitise en est doublee.
N'i a celi ne soit troublee[155]
En son corage et molt pensive,
Et l'une en est vers l'autre eschive,
Et porte li si grant envie
2100 Con s'eüst ja esté plevie
Se por li non; ce n'est pas une
Tant seulement, ains est cascune
Qui ceste pensee a en soi.
Eracles est moustrés al doi,
2105 Car le vertés est entendue
Et li noviele est espandue
Qu'il set tout canque feme velt
Et canque pense et faire seut.
Or ont paour les damoisieles,
2110 Celes qui ne sont pas pucieles.
Or se crient molt n'i a celi
Por tant qu'il ait pleü sor li:
Teus i a qui tout ont seü

---

[151] doucemt].
[152] desous; B] (T: De damredieu qui fist la nue).
[153] lor]BT.
[154] A. r. tant ne le c.]T.
[155] *Line omitted by* A]B.

until they reached the main gate. There they met the barons before any of them had entered the city. When they saw their liege-lord they greeted him very politely. **2051** He responded in a very courtly fashion, then kissed them affectionately, thanking them for their assiduity over his proclamation regarding the young ladies, which they had so unstintingly obeyed. They went along chatting until they arrived. As they approached the tents they saw the comely maidens; the tents from which the girls emerged were made of gold cloth and arranged in a circle, but the girls were very splendidly equipped indeed – these maidens were better dressed than, or at least as well dressed as queens.

The location was pleasant and the rows impressive, and in every direction one looked there were young ladies standing in a complete circle. The most powerful man in the world was the emperor, and he greeted them in the name of God, who is in heaven above. The young women nearby responded to his greeting; those further away, who did not hear him, but were well-mannered, all humbly bowed to him. **2075** Their lord sent a baron to them to thank them for making the journey and to tell them that he would ask his seer to choose next morning, without further delay, a girl for him to marry, since he wished to take a wife on his advice. The baron quickly delivered his message in a courtly and prudent fashion. My lords, women covet greatly high status and the fortune they might acquire on marrying. Never did the first woman covet anything as much, and for this reason behaved so badly, she who, if the truth be told, desired to know more than Him who had made her from nought; great was the suffering she brought upon us as a result.[41] These girls really coveted high status and when they saw that there was no creature in the world more handsome, more impressive than the emperor, their covetousness doubled in strength. There was not one of them who was not troubled in her heart and very anxious, and each was hostile towards her fellow and resented her hugely, thinking that she would already have been betrothed to him had it not been for her rival. And this was not the view of just one of them, but each of them harboured such thoughts. **2104** Eracle was frequently pointed out, for the truth was known and the news had spread that he knew exactly what each woman wanted, what she was thinking and what she was in the habit of doing. Now those young noblewomen who were not virgins were afraid. Each of them was sore afraid, depending on how much she had been out in the rain.[42] There were some who had seen

---

[41] A reference to Eve and her role in the Fall. The bride-show episode contains much traditional medieval misogyny, tempered though by humour.
[42] A euphemism for sexual experience.

Le ju, que tout n'ont pas veü;
2115 Et tels qui ont mains esploitié,
Qui n'ont seü lor amistié;
Et teus qui ont defors apris;
Toutes n'ont pas ingaument pris,[156]
C'on estaint fu en mainte gise [f]
2120 Dés que li maisons est esprise;
Ce sevent cestes, les pluisors,
Si lor en prent molt grans paors
Que cil ne die lor covingne,
Si li portent molt grant corine.[157]
2125 Cascune crient d'estre acusee,
U que por ce soit refusee.
Trestoutes si dolantes sont
Que n'est mervelles s'eles ont
Le nuit devant molt grief songié.
2130 Li empereres prent congié;
Bas vespres est, por ce s'en vait;
A cele fois n'i ot plus fait,
Dusc'au demain qu'il i tramet
Et ses barons et le varlet.
2135 Il fu proiiés de vint et deus
Qu'il i alast ensanle o eus,
Mais por proiier, por enhorter,
N'i valt onques ses piés porter:[158]
«N'i irai pas, fait il, signor,
2140 Car mil covoitent ceste honor
Et n'i ara eslit que une;
Et esperance i a cascune,
Si s'est cascune tant penee[159]
Con cele ki iert assenee,

2145 Et si n'i ara nule, espoir,[160]
Qui ne cuit bien autant valoir[161]
Con cele qui ert courounee,
Cui ceste honors sera donee;
Et saciés que grant duel merront
2150 Trestoutes celes qui verront
L'une prendre tout a veüe
Ce por coi cascune est venue.
Mainte parole mal seant
I ara dite vostre oiant,
2155 Car feme set assés que dire
Pour qu'ele ait au cuer duel et ire,[162]
Et feme enfantiument se
                    deut [136 a]
Quant autre prent çou qu'ele velt.
Feme n'esgarde pas raison,
2160 Se il puet estre ensi ou non;
Çou que li plaist li sanle bien,
N'i puet on trouver autre rien.»
Li baron a itant s'en vont,
Ne targent gaires que la sont.
2165 Les pucieles sont acesmees
Et sont bien dusc'a mil esmees;
N'i a vilaine ne borgoise,
Li mains aprise est molt cortoise,
Sans vilounie et sans anui.
2170 Ja nes uns hom si con je sui
N'i saroit ja que calengier.
Molt les ont fait bien arengier
A le reonde entor le place;
D'el ont paor que de manace;[163]

---

[156] This line is written over 2 lines in A to compensate for the omission of 2096.
[157] lor]B.
[158] Line repeated in A.
[159] A second hand has corrected the initial letters of s'est in 2143 and cele in 2144, leaving some ambiguity between c and s in both cases.
[160] nul]R.
[161] Ne cui ie b.]L.
[162] 2156 written over 2 lines to compensate for the repetition of line 2138.
[163] d. damanace]BT.

the game through to the end, but had not foreseen all the consequences; and those who had done less and had not gone the whole way; and those who had learned the game only superficially; they had not all partaken in equal measure, for a fire can be put out in different ways once the house has been set alight. The majority of them knew this and were therefore very worried indeed that Eracle might reveal their secret; which is why they resented him so much. **2125** Each girl was afraid of being accused and consequently of being rejected. They were all so upset that it is not surprising if they had had horrible dreams the night before. The emperor took his leave of them; it was late evening, so he had to go home. He did nothing more on that occasion, until the following morning, when he sent his barons and the young man to them. He was entreated by twenty-two men to accompany them, but neither prayers nor entreaties could persuade him to take himself there. 'My lords,' he said, 'I shall not go, for a thousand girls covet this honour and only one will be selected. Every one of them is hopeful and each has made such a great effort to be the chosen one, and I don't expect there will be any who does not believe that she is as worthy as the one who is crowned and receives this honour. And I can assure you that all those women who witness with their own eyes one young lady actually obtaining what they have all come for will be mightily aggrieved. **2153** Many an unseemly word will be spoken in your presence, for woman never lacks eloquence when she has grief and anger in her heart, and woman throws a childish tantrum when another gets what she wants. Woman is not interested in reason, whether what she wants is feasible or not; what she wants seems fine to her, and no other outcome will do.'[43]

At this the barons left, delaying their arrival there no longer. The young women, whose number was estimated at a good thousand, were in all their finery. There was no peasant or bourgoise amongst them, for the least accomplished was very courtly, with no hint of base or boorish behaviour. Not even a man like myself could find anything in them to criticise. They had been carefully arranged in a circle with a space in the centre. Their fear was not of being threatened,

---

[43] In this speech the emperor employs many antifeminist commonplaces found in contemporary didactic literature.

2175 Molt ont souvent coulors muees.
Eracles les a saluees,
Eles respondent simplement,[164]
Car feme est au commencement
Cortoise, sage et coie et simple;
2180 Ne pert pas quanqu'a sos le guimple.
Eracles les a fait seoir,
Car en seant les velt veoir.
El cerne tout a pié se met.
Al cief des rens, tout en soumet,
2185 Esgarde et voit une puciele;
En un roiaume n'a plus biele,
En se biauté n'a que reprendre,
Mais il, qui velt a el entendre,
Note se ciere et son samblant.[165]
2190 Toutes les autres vont tramblant
De le paor qu'eles n'i faillent,
Et que faillies ne s'en aillent,
Et vont pensant en lor corage
Que li puciele fist que sage
2195 Quant ele el cief des rens s'assist,
Et quant en si bon liu se mist.
Cascune pense qui voit çou:[166] [b]
«Hé Dix! C'or i seïsse jou![167]
Molt par est cil de povre sens,
2200 Qui deüst cerchier tous les rens.
De molt plus bieles en i a.
Cil Damedius qui tout crïa
Confonde nostre empereour
Par cui nous somes en paour.
2205 Cui caut, ce pense dont cascune,
Quant n'en ara eslit que une?

Je ne sui pas si Diu amie
Que jou avant le fusse mie.»
Eles pensent molt grant enfance,
2210 Car n'avenroit por toute France
Que cil cel tresor eslëust,
Qui bien set canqu'estre i deüst,
Car il set tout, et ens et hors,
Et voit le ceuvre desous l'or,
2215 Et le plont paroir sos l'argent.
Ensi est vis a toute gent
Que Dix ne fist ainc creature
Si preu, si large ne si pure,
Et le ciere a aperte et clere;
2220 Mais el siecle n'a plus avere;
Si n'a en feme pïour visse
Ne pïor tece c'avarisse,
Qu'il n'a el siecle avere espeuse
Qui ne soit povre et soufraiteuse;
2225 Encore ait ele en son tresor
Mil mars d'argent et mil mars d'or,
Si est povre n'i a celi
Por qu'ele ait avarisse en li,
Et s'ele a tel fais encargié,[168]
2230 Si fait de canqu'ele a marcié,
Por qu'ele soit souvent requise:
Qu'il a grief fais en covoitise:
Qu'il n'a el siecle nule rien
U paire avoir autant de bien
2235 Con en cesti, mais bien vil laine[169]
Voit on sovent bien tainte en graine.
Eracles set toute le fin; [c]
Bien set son estre et son traïn,

---

[164] E eles]BT.
[165] Toute; B]T.
[166] q. soit c.]H (B: p. ensi sour cou; 2197-98 T: p. et dist encore/Hé dieus et car i fuisse ore).
[167] c. isseisse j.] *Note the double consonant.*

[168] fait]BT.
[169] vilaine]B.

but their faces often changed colour. **2176** Eracle greeted them and they responded modestly, for to begin with women are courtly, wise, discrete and modest, not revealing what they have up their sleeves.[44] Eracle asked them to sit down, for he wished to inspect them seated. He got off his horse in the centre of the circle. He looked at those in the front row, in a very prominent position, and saw a maiden: there was none more beautiful in the whole kingdom and one could find no fault with her beauty. However, Eracle, whose priorities were different, took note of her expression and her demeanour. All the other girls trembled, fearing that they were going to fail and have to depart as failures. And they privately thought to themselves that the maiden had been clever when she had sat down in the front row and had chosen such a favourable spot. On seeing this, each one said to herself: 'Oh God, if only I had sat there myself! This man is extremely stupid, for he should have searched systematically through all the rows. **2201** There are some far more beautiful girls here. May Our Lord God, who created everything, confound our emperor because of the trepidation he is placing us in.' Then each of them thought: 'what does it matter, since only one of us will be chosen? I am not favoured enough by God to be ranked above her.' Their thoughts were very childish, for he would not have chosen this 'treasure' even if he had been offered the whole of France. He knew what had to be, since he knew everything, inside and out, and could see the brass underneath the gold and the lead showing through the silver. Thus it seemed to everyone that God had never before created such a virtuous, generous and pure soul; and she had an open and innocent face; yet there was no one more avaricious under the sun than she was, and there is no worse vice nor worse blemish in a woman than avarice; for here on earth an avaricious wife always lives in poverty and want. **2225** Even if she has in her coffers a thousand marks of silver and a thousand marks of gold, there is no one as poor as she is on account of her avarice; and once she has agreed to carry such a burden, she is willing to sell everything she has, provided she is asked frequently enough. For covetousness is a heavy burden indeed: there was no creature in the whole world in whom as much virtue seemed to reside as in this maiden, but one often finds cheap cloth dyed royal scarlet. Eracle knew the whole story; he was familiar with her character and her behaviour,

---

[44] Literally 'under their wimples'.

Le goupil qui tapist en l'ombre,
2240 Qui durement se cose encombre.
Il n'i a nule creature
Fors seulement la doreüre;[170]
N'a home el mont qui plus i truist,
Car n'est pas ors tout canqu'il luist.
2245 Ele est puciele, mais cui caut
Quant Avarisse adiés l'assaut
Et reuve qu'ele prenge aniaus
Et aumosnieres et joiaus,
Bones çaintures et afices,
2250 De tous, de povres et de rices.
Eracles l'a por ce laissie,[171]
Par s'avarisse est abaissie;
Molt en abaissent les pluisors
Et si en perdent grans honors.
2255 Ceste en a perdue grant masse.
Eracles soissante en trespasse
C'onques a une n'i areste,
Qu'il n'i voit une n'ait arieste.
 Une en i vient isnielement,
2260 Qui se contient molt simplement;
Caste se fait a tous sambler,[172]
Mais lui ne puet on riens embler.
Eracle l'esgarde a mervelle,[173]
Car nule a li ne s'aparelle
2265 De ciere ne de contenance.
Eracles voit le mesestance,
Mais or cuident li plus sené
Qu'Eracles ait bien asséné,
Et dient tuit sans contredit
2270 Qu'il a bonismement eslit:
«Ceste ara la beneïçon,
Ne nous en venra se bien non;

Et Dix li puist s'ounor doubler!
Ne pert que sace eve troubler.»
2275 Cele meïme cuide et croit
Qu'Eracles l'eslise orendroit
Por ce que tant l'a avisee,[174] [d]
Et cil en fait une risee
De çou qu'ele a pensé tel rage;
2280 Car il voit bien tot son corage;
Et cele atent que cil li die:
«Tu serras coronee, amie»
Et pense donc: «Ahi! bels frere,
Con est mal sages l'emperere,
2285 Quant il si grant sens cuide en toi;
Molt ses petit qu'il a en moi;
Molt ses petit con je me duel
De mon ami que j'aim et voel.
Je l'aim et amerai tous jors,
2290 Qu'il a eües mes amors;
Molt iert dolans quant il sara
Que l'emperere ensi m'ara.
Amis, ne laisiés por lui mie
Que vos ne voiés vostre amie.
2295 Non ferés vos, si con je pens;
Malade me ferai par tens,
Vos i venrés en liu de mire.
Tel fois ostoiera mesire
Que vos me donrés medecine
2300 En me cambre, sos ma cortine;
Tote pais avron del devin,
Ançois qu'il boive un mui de vin.»
Eracles emprent a sourire,
Et pense dont: «Ne sai que dire;
2305 Je me sui ensi cha tornés,
Qu'a mal le tenroit li barnés

---

[170] F. seulemt (cf. 2051) le closeure]BT.
[171] par]B.
[172] Ceste; B]T.
[173] esgarda]BT.

[174] 2277-2674 Scribe 2.

he could see the fox hiding in the shadows, which greatly compromised her chances. She was an empty shell with nothing to her apart from her gilded exterior; no man alive would have been able to find more to her, for all that glitters is not gold. She was a virgin, but what good was that, since she was constantly under attack from Avarice, urging her to accept rings, purses and jewels, good quality belts and brooches from all-comers, poor and rich?[45] **2251** For this reason Eracle rejected her, for her avarice devalued her. Many people are devalued because of it and thereby miss out on high honours. This young lady's loss was huge. Eracle walked on past sixty of them without stopping to consider any girl, for he could not find a single one without some defect or other.

Suddenly he came upon one who was behaving very discreetly; she pretended to everyone that she was chaste, but you could not pull the wool over Eracle's eyes. He looked at her with amazement, for none equalled her in appearance or manner. Eracle could see the disadvantage in her, but the wisest amongst them now thought that Eracle had landed on the right one, and they agreed unanimously that he had chosen perfectly: 'This girl will receive the ultimate blessing and nothing but good will come of it for us; may God increase her honour twofold. It doesn't seem as if she is capable of muddying the waters.'[46] **2275** She herself was convinced that Eracle was about to select her, since he had spent so long contemplating her. Yet he laughed scornfully at her for harbouring such an outrageous thought, for he could read her mind. She expected him to say to her: 'You will be crowned, my friend,' and thought to herself: 'Ah, my lad, the emperor is a fool indeed for believing you to be so wise. You barely know what I'm like, you hardly know how upset I am about my lover, whom I adore and desire. I love him and shall always love him, for he has enjoyed the fruits of my love. He will be very upset when he learns that the emperor is going to have me in this way. Beloved, do not give up seeing your mistress just because of him. I don't think you will; I shall pretend to be ill from time to time and you will visit me in the guise of a doctor. When my lord goes on campaign you will administer medication to me in my bedroom, behind the bed-curtains. Before he has the chance to drink a quart of wine, the emperor's seer will not be in a position to disturb us at all.'[47] **2303** Eracle began to smile and then thought: 'I don't know what to say. I came over to her because the assembled barons would have taken it amiss

---

[45] These objects are all traditional presents from lovers, often mentioned in antifeminist discourse to stress the venality of women; cf. *Le Roman de la Rose*.
[46] This seems to be a metaphor for sexual infidelity; cf. the bride test in *Floire et Blancheflor*, edited by Jean-Luc Leclanche, CFMA (Paris: Champion, 1980), 2068-72.
[47] *Mui* is a measurement of volume used for grain and liquids.

Se je trespassés fuisse en haste,
Qu'en tot le mont ne pert si caste
Con ceste fait (si n'i a rien),
2310 Que il i cuident molt grant bien.
Se je di a le gent se vie,
Il le tenront a vilonnie,
Et se je ne les fas entendre[175]
Quels cose me fait chi atendre,
2315 Si m'iert torné a musardie;
Dont m'estuet il que je lor die,[176]
U que jel fache li gehir. [e]
Ensi me puisse Diex tehir
Que je le cose atorneroie[177]
2320 Molt volentiers, se je pooie,
Salve s'onor et me parole;
Mais j'aim miex c'on le tiengne a fole
Et a vilaine, mal que mal,
Que on me tiengne a desloial.»[178]
2325 Dedens le cerne a achenés
Quatre barons des miex senés;
Venir i fait le damoisiele,
Et si li dist: «Amie bele,
Ichi n'a fors nos cinc et vous;
2330 Tous soit uns consels entre nous.
Vos cuidiés molt bien, al voir dire,
Que j'orendroit vos doie eslire,
Mais je vos di que ne puet estre;
Ains dirai orendroit vostre estre,
2335 U vos dites vostre pensé,
Par icel Dieu qui m'a tensé.»
Ele se taist, sel tient por sot.
«Je dirai, fait il, le mal mot
Del mire et de le medecine.
2340 – Ha! non ferés, fait la mescine,

Por l'amor Dieu, et je dirai.
– Dont dites. – Vallet, je cuidai
Que vos ne me conneüssiés
Et que por çou m'esleüssiés;
2345 Si le vos tornai a folie.
Estuet me il que plus vos die?
– Oïl, par Dieu! Je voel c'on oie
Le geredon que jo aroie,
Se je eslite vos eüsse.
2350 – Amis vallet, se je peüsse,
Itels fust vostre destinee:
Le vie eüssiés tost finee.
– Suer, chi aroit mal geredon!
Mais n'atent el qui sert felon.
2355 Or alés en vo liu seoir,
Et nos irons aillors veoir,[179]
Savoir mon se ja loialtés [f]
Et fine simplece et bialtés[180]
Peüssent en un cors durer,
2360 Que on peüst por voir jurer:
«Iceste est boine et bele et caste»;
Mais je cuiç ains avoir grant laste.»
Cele qui volroit estre aillors
Se rest assise, et les plusors
2365 En sont molt lies, jel vous di;
Ele ert vengie ains miedi,
Car d'autretels i avoit tante.
Cil en trespasse bien soissante
C'onques a nule ne se tarde,
2370 Mais en trespassant les esgarde,
Qu'il voit cascune u fole u fiere
U orgilleuse u trop parliere;
Por çou les met en noncaloir.
A une qui pert molt valoir

---
[175] se jel ne]BT.
[176] li d.]B.
[177] Con]BT.
[178] Quele m.]BT.

[179] 2355-56 *inverted in* A.
[180] sigplece]BT.

if I had walked by hastily, for in the whole world there is none who appears to be so chaste as this woman (although she really isn't at all), and they think she possesses great virtue. If I reveal her true lifestyle to everyone, they will think I am being malicious, but if I do not tell them why I am hesitating over her, I shall be considered a fool. So I shall be obliged to tell them or make her confess. Thus, may God increase my good fortune by enabling me to settle the matter, as I would willingly do if I could, in such a way as to protect her honour and my veracity. But I prefer people to think she is lewd and immoral, whatever the consequences, than that they should think me untrustworthy.' **2325** He beckoned four of the wisest barons to come into the centre of the circle, then asked the girl to join them, saying: 'fair friend, here there are just the five of us and you; let us decide the matter between us. Frankly speaking, you clearly believe that I should choose you at once, but I can tell you that this cannot happen; either I shall reveal at once your true nature or you can tell us what you have in mind, by God my protector.' She remained silent, thinking he was a fool. 'I'll tell them about your evil plan concerning the doctor and his medication,' he said. 'Oh no, for the love of God, don't,' said the girl, 'and I shall tell you everything. – Well then, speak. – Young sir, I thought that you did not know me well, and that consequently you would choose me. I put it down to your stupidity. Do I need to say more? – Yes, by God! I want them to hear the reward you would have given me if I had chosen you. **2350** – Young friend, if I could have brought it about, your fate would have been to have a short life. – Sister, this would have been a terrible reward indeed! Yet anyone who helps a scoundrel can expect nothing else. Now go and sit down in your place and we shall look elsewhere to see if loyalty, complete innocence and beauty can reside in one body, such that one might swear truthfully that "this woman is virtuous, beautiful and chaste". But I think I'll have my work cut out to find her.' She who would have preferred to be elsewhere sat down again, and I can assure you that most of the others were very pleased indeed. Yet she would have her revenge before midday, for there were so many present who were just as bad. Eracle walked by a good sixty without pausing next to any of them, but as he passed he looked at them, noticing that each one was either foolish, proud, arrogant or too talkative; that is why they were of no interest to him. **2374** To please the crowd

2375 S'areste Eracles por le gent,
Car molt fu bele estrangement;
Ele est pucele encor, por voir,
Si l'en doit on bon gré savoir,
Con cele qui n'est pas conquise
2380 Por çou que n'a esté requise.
Je ne vi onques nule tor
Rendre sans plait et sans estor.
Eracles voit bien que le rose[181]
N'est pas de tel palis enclose
2385 Qu'il se fust ja un mois tenus,
Tes i peüst estre venus.
Ceste est encore et nete et pure,[182]
Ne mais Eracles n'en a cure,
Qu'il est bien certains et seürs
2390 C'ainc que li formens soit meürs,
I venra tant de gargerie
Que li messons sera perie.
Eracles s'en trespasse atant,
Cent en trepasse, u il n'a tant
2395 Por qu'il se voelle delaier,
Car nule ne se puet paier
Por tele qu'il demande et
           voelt;[183]   [137 a]
Ce poise lui et molt s'en doelt.
Ne perent estre ne ne sont
2400 De bonté, ne bon samblant n'ont;
Ne s'i doit hals hom marïer,
N'il nes velt toutes tarïer,
Car il n'en venroit ja a cief.[184]
Tot lor estre voit en son brief;
2405 Eles n'ont nule rien seü
Qu'il en trespassant n'ait veü.
    A une en vient qui est pucele,
Et est forment bien faite et bele;
Caste est encore, bien le sai,
2410 C'onques ne vint a cel asai[185]
Que les puceles tant resoignent[186]
Et dont plus a envis s'eslongent.
Ceste ne fu onques en lieu
U eüst cure de tel gieu,
2415 Mais tant a qu'ele est trop parliere.[187]
Dame qui est de tel maniere
Ne oevre mie par savoir,[188]
Car ne puet pïor teche avoir.
Un fol escoute on qui parole,
2420 Si fait on une feme fole.
Mais qui le roveroit taisir?
Tot l'escoutent a son plaisir,
Mais tel s'en rient en devant
Qui en deriere en vont gabant.
2425 Fols est qui en çou a delit
Que tous li mons a en despit;
Plusor le font tot lor eage[189]
U pour delit u pour usage.
Iceste est preus en casteé
2430 Et estre puet tot son aé;
Casteé aime estrangement,
Mais une vertus solement
A nule dame ne soufist;
Une teche le desconfist
2435 Et bien tresperce dis escus.
Jo di que quarante vertus
Ne pueent pas si halt ataindre   [b]

---

[181] rome *or* roine]BT.
[182] nete pure]B.
[183] Fors]BT.
[184] veroit]B.
[185] vit]B; 2409-10 *are inverted in all 3 MSS.*
[186] Et les; B]L.
[187] A *omits* a]H.
[188] savor]BT.
[189] A *omits* tot] BT.

Eracle stopped in front of one woman who seemed very worthy because she was incredibly beautiful; it is true that she was still a virgin, yet she deserved to be congratulated on this only as much as any woman who has not been conquered because she has never been pursued. I have never seen a tower fall without being attacked and stormed. Eracle noted that the rose was not surrounded by such a sturdy palisade that it would have resisted for a month had a suitor come to win it.[48] This woman was still untainted and pure, yet Eracle was not interested in her, for he was absolutely certain that before the wheat was fully ripe, so many tares would mingle with it that the crop would be ruined.[49] Eracle moved swiftly on and walked past a hundred girls, who possessed nothing to delay him, for none was able to demonstrate that she was what he required and was seeking. This upset and distressed him. They neither seemed to be nor actually were virtuous, not even in appearance; **2401** they were not suitable to be married to a powerful man. Eracle did not wish to single out each of them individually, for he would never have accomplished his task. He could read their whole life-stories at a glance; they had experienced nothing that he did not glimpse as he walked by.

He paused for a moment at one girl who was a virgin and who was very shapely and beautiful. I know that she was still chaste, for she had not yet had the testing experience which maidens so fear and yet they avoid it even more reluctantly! She had never been in a position to interest herself in that game, but it was enough that she was too talkative. A lady who is of that disposition does not behave wisely, for she cannot have a worse defect. We listen to a foolish man talk and likewise with a foolish woman. Yet who would ask her to be quiet? All humour her by listening, yet there are those who laugh along with her who make fun of her behind her back. **2425** A person is a fool if he takes pleasure in what everyone else scorns. Many do this throughout their lives, whether out of pleasure or habit. She was perfectly chaste and could have remained so throughout her life. Her love of chastity was extraordinary; yet one virtue alone is not enough for a lady; she is defeated by one vice, which can easily pierce ten shields. In my view, forty virtues cannot reach such heights of perfection

---

[48] *Eracle* offers early examples of the erotic metaphors of castle storming and rose plucking made famous by the thirteenth-century *Roman de la Rose*.
[49] The metaphor is biblical; see the parable of the tares, Matthew 13: 24ff.

C'une teche ne puist estaindre,
Et vint vertus, non vint et quatre,[190]
2440 Ne pueent une teche abatre.
De plain poing d'eve estaint on bien[191]
Dis cierges tot sans autre rien;
Qui vint et quatre en l'eve empaint,
Li fus s'en va, l'eve remaint.[192]
2445 Molt fait a haïr dont vils teche,
Qui tels vertus estaint et seche.
Vils teche est molt de trop parler,
Si em puet on bien fol sambler;
Qui trop parole, il s'en abaisse.
2450 Eracles le pucele laisse,
Cent en trespasse en un randon;
Li pire n'est mie a bandon.
Çou nen iert pas, je cuit, li pire
Qui dame sera de l'empire.
2455 Oï avés que il s'en torne
Et laise celi triste et morne;
Tous en est hontels et destrois,
Cent en trespasse a celi fois,
Et je le cuiç assés par foi,
2460 Cascune en a assés en soi
Por qu'il les doie refuser;
Mais il nes velt mie encuser,
Ne dire trestout lor afaire,[193]
Qu'il en crimbroit avoir contraire.
2465   Lors vint a une damoisiele
Qui molt est avenans et bele;
Casteé aime et molt l'ot ciere,
Mais ele est molt estoute et fiere.
Mervelles est de caste vie,
2470 Mais ele velt par estoutie;
Çou qu'ele est caste est grans chiertés,[194]
Mais trop par couste se fiertés.
Amere douchor a en miel
U il a mellé suie et fiel,
2475 Et dame por coi fait tel cose
Dont cascuns le reprent et cose,
Et dont ses pris baisse et descent?[195] [c]
Eracles en trespasse cent.
A une bele qu'il i voit,
2480 Qui pert li miudre qui i soit,
S'areste atant li damoisials;[196]
C'est de sen cors li plus loials
Qui onques mais alast a messe,
Ne mais qu'ele est trop felenesse.
2485 Molt li couvenroit a tracier
Et molt aroit a porchacier
Qui plus loial volroit trover;
En li n'aroit que reprover,
Se ne fust cele felenie,
2490 Qui onques n'est sans vilenie,
Car fel ne puet estre cortois,
Ne que fols hom sages des lois.
Eracles plaint son cors loial,
Car molt le voit caste et roial,
2495 Mais que l'ortie est o le rose,
Qui molt va empirant le cose;
N'afert pas a l'empereor
Qu'il ait ortie entor se flor,
Ne nule rien qui sace amer.
2500 Cil qui ne puet vil teche amer

---

190 Et .m.]BT.
191 De plaing d.]BT.
192 se v.]T.
193 Ne faire]BT.
194 quele caste e. g. fertes]L.
195 A *omits* dont]BT.
196 tant]T (B: adont).

that they cannot be cancelled out by one vice, and twenty virtues, or even twenty-four, cannot overcome a single vice. Ten candles can be extinguished easily by a handful of water and nothing else; if you plunge twenty-four in the water, the flames go out and the water remains. Thus a horrible vice should be much feared, since it extinguishes and consumes such virtues. Loquaciousness is a horrible vice indeed and it can make one seem very foolish; he who talks too much demeans himself. **2450** Eracle left the girl behind and walked past a hundred in one go, even the worst of them was not free to leave. But I do not think it will be the worst of them who will be first lady of the empire. As I told you, he walked away and left this girl sad and downcast; he was very ashamed and distressed about it. This time he walked past another hundred girls, but I have complete confidence in him that there were plenty of reasons for rejecting each one of them. He did not, however, wish to accuse them or reveal all their secrets, for he feared this might cause trouble for him.

Then he came to a girl who was very attractive and beautiful. She loved chastity and it was very important to her, but she was very arrogant and proud. She led a wonderously chaste life, but chose it out of arrogance; it was a very precious thing that she was chaste, but her pride cost her dearly. Honey which is mixed with soot and bile has a bitter sweetness, so why does a lady do something for which everyone criticises and blames her, lowering and debasing her worth? **2478** Eracle walked by a hundred of them. Then the young man stopped in front of a beauty he saw there and who seemed to be the best of them all. She had the chastest body of any woman who ever went to mass; if only she were not so nasty. You would have to travel a long way and search high and low to find a more faithful person. There would have been nothing in her to criticise had it not been for that nastiness which is incompatible with courtliness. For a nasty person cannot be courtly, any more than a fool can become knowledgeable in the law. Eracle regretted rejecting her virginal body, for he could see it was very chaste and regal. However, there was a nettle next to the rose which was spoiling her chances. It was not fitting for the emperor to have nettles around his flower, or anything else that produced a bitter taste. **2500** Eracle, who could not approve of any base vice,

Prie molt Dieu qu'il trover puist
Une a plaisir; ains qu'il le truist
Ara les gambes bien lassees;[197]
Trois vins en a bien trespassees.
2505 A le plus bele creature
C'onques el mont fesist Nature
S'aresta tant li damoisiaus
Qu'il voit qu'ele est caste et loiaus;
De mainte cose est ensignie,
2510 Mais d'une seule est engiengnie[198]
Dont ele est adés coustumiere.[199]
A tot le monde fust lumiere
Et mireoirs, mais mençoigniers
Et gangleors et losengiers
2515 Croit molt et aime et fait lor bon.
Ja bone gent n'aront del son
Qu'il ne li soit encontre cuer. [d]
Veés con est d'estrange fuer![200]
Miels velt ensi perdre son pris
2520 Que laisier çou qu'ele a empris.
Vils us fait maint home abaissier
Et riens n'est plus griés a laissier;
De tot se puet on faire sage
Fors sol de laier vil usage;
2525 Por çou est fols qui l'acoustume,
Qui plus s'i tient, plus s'en alume.
Mal fait dame qui plus a cier
Un gangleor c'un bel parlier;
Dame qui aime gengleor
2530 Fait de chevalier gougleor,
Car cascuns hom pener se soelt[201]
Qu'il soit tels con sa dame voelt.

Eracles n'a de ceste cure
Por cest usage, qui li dure
2535 Et li duëra son aé.
El li estuet que casteé
A estre tel con il demande
Et con li sires li conmande.
Eracle cerke tos les rens,
2540 Ne trueve pucele en nul sens[202]
Qui ait trestotes les bontés.
En son ceval en est montés,[203]
Parole dont et dist en haut:
«Puceles, Damediex vos saut.[204]
2545 Vos remanrés, je m'en irai,
Que nule de vos n'eslirai;
Non por içou, par saint Vincent,
Que chi n'en ait bien plus d'un cent
Dont li mains vaillans et li pire
2550 Ne fust bien digne d'un empire,
Et bien i saroie asener.[205]
Mais je crembroie avilener
S'une en faisoie esleecier
Por le remanant courecier.»
2555 Vait s'en, iceles a orer[206]
Que malfés le puist devorer,
Et assés fu qui dit li a:[207] [e]
«Ahi! Confait devin chi a!
Con l'emperere est mal senés
2560 Qui tant barons a chi penés,
Et dont por un tel connissor
Cui Diex doinst honte et deshonor!»
Molt lor fust bel, s'estre peüst,
Que li vallés eslit eüst,

---
[197] Ore a l. g.]B (T: Ensi a les dames outrees).
[198] Mains]BT.
[199] D. ele ades]BT.
[200] c. ele est; T]B. *Hypermetric line in* AT.
[201] voelt; B]T.
[202] tos s.]BT.
[203] castel]BT.
[204] *Later hand corrects* haut *to* saut, *hence* R's *incorrect reading of* i saut.
[205] sairoie]B.
[206] Voit]T.
[207] a. plus que d.]BT.

prayed earnestly to God that he might find a woman to his liking; but before he could find her his legs would be worn out; he had already walked past a good three score.

The young man lingered so long near the most beautiful creature that Nature had ever created on this earth that he could see that she was chaste and faithful; she was accomplished in many things, but she was let down by one habit, to which she had become accustomed. She would have been a beacon and mirror for everyone if she had not loved, supported and put too much trust in liars, slanderers and flatterers. Only reluctantly did she pay any attention to good people. See what a strange person she was! She preferred to lose her good name rather than to abandon her old ways. Bad habits degrade many a man and nothing is more difficult to give up. One can behave wisely in every respect yet still be unable to abandon bad habits. **2525** It is therefore unwise to acquire them in the first place, for the more you persist, the more you become addicted. A lady who prefers a slanderer to an honest speaker does wrong; a lady who loves slanderers turns knights into deceivers, for it is normal for each man to strive to conform to his lady's wishes. Eracle was not interested in this woman because of this habit, which she maintained and would maintain for the rest of her life. She needed more than chastity to comply with his requirements and with his lord's command. Eracle searched up and down the rows, but in whichever direction he looked, he could not find a maid who had all the virtues. Having mounted his horse, he addressed the women, speaking in a loud voice: 'Maidens, may God save you! You will stay here and I shall leave, for I shall not be choosing any of you. Not, by St Vincent, because there is none here present who merits an empire, for here are at least a hundred ladies of whom even the least worthy and the worst would deserve it, thus enabling me to arrive at a good decision. **2552** Yet I would be afraid of acting discourteously if I made one of you very happy and thereby angered the rest of you.' He went away, and the women began to pray that the devil might swallow him up, and there were many who said: 'Alas! What sort of seer is this? How unwise the emperor has been to put so many barons to such trouble and all on account of this so-called expert, whom, let us hope, God will shame and dishonour!' It would have pleased them greatly had it been possible for the young man to make a choice,

2565 Mais bien saciés n'i a celi
Quil volsist d'autre que de li.
Molt sont dolantes les puceles,
Oïes ont dures noveles.
Quant li baron ont congié pris,
2570 Si s'en revont en lor païs;
Les puceles ont ramenees,
Qui se tienent por enganees.
Eracles s'en revint honteus
Et tous pensis et corouceus;[208]
2575 Ains Diex ne fist si dolant home.
Si con il entre en ville Rome,
Une mescine i a veüe
Qui d'un viés bliaut iert vestue.
Un signator ot ja a pere,
2580 Mors estoit et morte sa mere;
S'ante l'avoit en mainbrunie.
Li meschinete iert embarnie
Aussi con enfes de dis ans,
Et quant le voit li voirdisans,
2585 Molt par li plait, molt li conteche,[209]
Car n'i voit nule male teche,
N'onques ne vit en son eage
Pucele de plus bel corsage,
Ne nule u eüst mains d'orguel.
2590 Bel sont si crin, bel sont si oel,
Bele bouce, bel nés, bel vis;[210]
Bele fu toute, ce m'est vis,
En li n'a riens mesavenant.
Cil broce vers li maintenant,
2595 Et cele fu jovenete et tendre,
Tel paor a, lui n'ose atendre;
Ne cuide a tans avoir secors:[211] [f]
Le rue trespasse a un cors,

Tost s'est lancie ciés celi
2600 Qui duel et joie avra de li.
Le mescinete va tramblant,
Car il pert bien a son samblant
Qu'ele a la fors tel cose oïe
Dont gaires ne s'est esjoïe;
2605 A grant esfroi en le cambre entre,
Molt li tresalt li cuers el ventre.
La soie ante, qui la estoit,
Qui le paisoit, qui le vestoit,
S'escrie: «Nieche, qui te chace?
2610 Grant pecié fait qui te manache!
Se tes bons pere fust en vie,
Juree fuisses et plevie;
Or t'estuet souffrir maint dangier,
Or te puet on molt laidengier
2615 Et dire honte et faire anui.»
Atant es vos poignant celui;
Le dame troeve solement,
Qui grant duel mainne por noient.
«Dame, fait il, Diex soit od vos!
2620 – Vallés, cil Diex qui maint sor nos
Vos salt et gart et beneïe.
– Dame, se Diex vos face aïe,
Qui est le mescine au bliaut?
– Biaus dous amis, se Diex me salt,
2625 Ce fu la fille au plus rice home
Qui onques esteüst en Rome;
Mais il est mors il a grant piece;
Mes freres fu, ceste est me niece,
Si l'ai norie grant pieche a.
2630 – Dame, faites le venir cha.
– Por Dieu, vallés, vos pri merchi;
Vostre deduis n'est mie chi,

---

[208] pensis corouceus]BT.
[209] p. li c.]BT.
[210] Bele bouce et bel le vis]BT. *Line hypometric in* A.
[211] avoirs]BT.

but I can tell you that not one of them wished another girl to be chosen rather than herself. The girls were very distressed, for they had heard harsh news. Having taken their leave, the barons returned to their lands, taking with them the young girls who thought they had been made fools of. Eracle came away shame-faced, worried and upset; never before had one of God's creatures been so distressed. **2576** As he entered the ancient quarter of Rome, he saw a young girl there dressed in an old tunic. Her father had once been a senator, but he was now dead, and so was her mother. She was under the guardianship of her aunt. This slip of a girl was built like a ten-year-old child and when the youth with second sight saw her, she was much to his liking and pleased him greatly. For he could see no moral blemish in her; nor had he ever seen in his whole life a virgin with a more beautiful figure, nor one who possessed less pride. Her hair was beautiful; she had beautiful eyes, a beautiful mouth, nose and face; in fact, it seems to me she was beautiful all over, and there was nothing unseemly about her at all. Immediately, he spurred his horse towards her, and being such a tender young girl, she was too afraid to wait for him. Thinking that no one would rescue her in time, she dashed across the road and rushed into the house of the woman who was to have joy and sorrow on her account. **2601** The young girl was trembling, and it was obvious from her demeanour that she had heard something outside that had hardly filled her with joy. She entered the room in a fright, her heart pounding in her breast. Her aunt, who was there at that moment, the one who fed and clothed her, cried out: 'Niece, who is pursuing you? Whoever is threatening you is committing a great wrong! If your good father were alive, you would be promised and betrothed. As it is, you have to suffer many a danger; now people can insult you horribly, say shameful things and harrass you.' At that moment Eracle arrived at top speed; he found the lady alone, lamenting loudly, but unnecessarily. 'My lady,' he said, 'God be with you. – Young man, may the God who dwells above save, protect and bless you. – My lady, as God is your aid, who is the young girl wearing the tunic? – Fair gentle friend, if God be my Saviour, she was the daughter of the most powerful man who ever lived in Rome. **2627** But he died a while ago now; he was my brother and she is my niece. I have been looking after her for a long time now. – My lady, have her come here. – For God's sake, young man, pray have mercy on her; your pleasure is not to be found here.

Çou n'est pas çou que vos querrés.
Je ne sai que vos esperés,
2635 Nos le lairiesmes ains detraire
Que de son cors folie faire,
Car ce seroit mals et peciés, [138 a]
N'ele n'a cure, che saciés;
Onques encor ne fu en vie
2640 Qui l'oïst parler de folie;
Nes li oïrs itant li grieve,
S'ele en ot parler, si s'en lieve.[212]
Trop fu ses pere a çou prodom,
Se mere fu de boin renon;
2645 Ceste n'est pas des noaillors.
Querrés vostre deduit aillors,
Ci n'a a vostre oés nule riens.[213]
– Dame, se Diex me face bien,
N'i ving por nule vilenie,
2650 Car ce seroit molt grans folie.»
La dame atant sa nieche apele
Et ele i vint, bien faite et bele.
Molt a grant honte de celui.
Cil le salue, et ele lui;
2655 Molt crient qu'ele ne soit traïe,
Forment requiert sainte Marie.
Cil le fait aler pas por pas,
Esgarde en haut, esgarde en bas;
Molt par li plait bien s'aleüre,
2660 Se chiere et se regardeüre.
Or est il asenés a droit:
En icel point que or le voit[214]
S'ele se tient qu'ele n'empirt,
Plene sera del saint Espirt.[215]
2665 Eracles voit qu'il n'a plus fine

Desci la u li terre fine.
«Dame, dist il, entendés moi.
Je vos conmanç et ruis et proi
Que vos ma dame me gardés,
2670 Et molt sovent le regardés;
Je vos di bien qu'assés avra
Anuit qui servir le savra,
Car li plus haut et li millor
De cest empire et de l'honor
2675 Seront a son service enclin[216]
Ains que solaus tourt a declin,
Et par cel Diu qui maint sor nous, [b]
Nous devons bien et jou et vous[217]
Faire son bon et son plaisir,[218]
2680 C'ains tierç jor le verrés saisir[219]
De ceste honor et de l'empire.
– Par Diu, varlet, il n'ert ja pire
Por canques vous l'avés gabee,
Et vous alés querant le bee.
2685 Laissiés le mescinete ester;
Encor li puet bien Dix douner
Le bien que il li a servé.
Vous n'avés pas bien entervé,
Vous n'estes pas bien assenés,
2690 U cis n'est mie bien senés
Qui chi vous a ensi tramis.
Alés vous ent, biax dos amis,
Por Diu, pour l'ame vostre pere.
Vous savés bien que l'emperere
2695 A ajornees les pucieles
De son roiaume les plus bieles,
Si i tramist un sien devin;

---

[212] Si le en o.]R.
[213] *No correction as both scribes of* A (*and MS T*) *tolerate such rhymes, cf.* 2859.
[214] que il lor v.]B.
[215] esprirt].

[216] 2675-2740 *Scribe* 1.
[217] n. s devons]B.
[218] plaisire]BT.
[219] saillir]BT.

This is not what you are seeking; I do not know what you are hoping for, but we would prefer her to be pulled to pieces rather than dishonour her body; for it would be an evil sin, and be assured, she has no interest in it whatsoever. Nor is there anyone alive who has heard her speak of immodest acts; even hearing such things pains her so much that if she hears people speak of them, she leaves their company. Her father was a very worthy man and her mother was of good repute. This girl is not of base stock. Seek your pleasure elsewhere, here is nothing to your purpose. – My lady, I swear by God's favour that I did not come here with any vile intent, for it would be a very great crime.' **2651** Then the lady summoned her niece and the shapely, beautiful girl joined them. She was very shy in his presence. He greeted her and she responded. She was very much afraid that she had been betrayed and she prayed fervently to Holy Mary. Eracle asked her to walk to and fro and examined her up and down. He was absolutely delighted with her demeanour, facial expression and the look in her eyes. Now he had found what he was seeking. If she remained, without deteriorating, at the level of perfection he was now witnessing in her, she would be filled with the Holy Spirit. Eracle saw that there was no more perfect woman from there to the end of the earth. 'My lady, listen to me,' he said, 'I command, ask and beseech you to look after my lady for me and keep an eye on her all the time. I assure you that by this evening she will have plenty of people to serve her; for before the sun begins to set the most important and best men in the empire and in this land will be eager to serve her. **2677** And by the God who dwells above, both you and I must do what she wants and what pleases her. For within three days you will see her become mistress of this land and empire. – By God, young man, the situation can't get any worse however much you have made fun of her and are wasting our time with your stories. Leave the girl alone; there is still time for God to grant her the good fortune he has reserved for her. Either you have failed to find the right path or to come to the right place, or the man who sent you here is not very bright. Fair gentle friend, away with you, by God and by your father's soul. You know full well that the emperor has summoned the most beautiful maidens in his kingdom and has sent one of his seers to them;

Ce savons nos des hui matin;
Eslire doit le bielissor
2700 Et le plus fine et le millor.
– Dame, je sui cil qui devine;
Ne puis trover la fors si fine
Con je vauroie; or l'ai trovee;
Por ce vos ai cesti rovee.
2705 Je l'ai demandee et demant
Et comandee et recoumant
A Diu tant que je le revoie.»
Atant se met tost a la voie;
A son signor vient erraument
2710 Et se li conte l'errement.
 «Sire, fait il, je fui la fors,
Mais, si garisse Dix mon cors,[220]
N'i peuç riens trover a vostre oels.
Hontex et pris m'en tornai lués.
2715 Si con en vielle Rome entrai,
Une puciele i encontrai;
Fille fu a un signator.   [c]
Merciés ent le Creator,
Car c'est li flors et c'est li gemme
2720 De tout cest siecle, et passe feme.
S'ele se tient en point c'or est,
Dont n'a c'un arbre en le forest,
Et une rose ens el vergié,
Et un seul clerc ens el clergié,
2725 Qu'en tout le mont nen a son per.
Or ne le laissons escaper.
Ja n'ert mais feme de son pris
S'ensi le fait con l'a empris.»
Or est molt liés li emperere:
2730 «Eracle, fait il, biax dous frere,
Faites li riches dras baillier,
Se li faites coudre et taillier

Tex comme empereïs couvient.
Bien me ramembre et me sovient
2735 Que vos m'avés servi en foi;
Buer vos vi onques et vos moi.
N'i a atente ne sojor,
Feme prendrai dedens tierç jor.»
Et cil n'i valt plus arester;
2740 Ses dras fait faire et aprester
Al miex qu'il set et que il puet,[221]
Et tels con a tel dame estuet.
Baignier la fait deus jors entiers,
Si fait semonre endementiers
2745 Ces castelains, ces dus, ces contes.
Huimais commencera li contes.
 Li ante, qui Dieu aime et croit,
En est molt lie, et estre doit,
Et dist: «Aïe, Diex, biax sire,
2750 Or n'ai je mais ne duel ne ire,
Or ne me calt il quant je muire,
Or ne me puet mais li mors nuire.
Norir cuidai une orfenine,
Et j'ai nori une roïne.
2755 Nieche, se l'ame a ton bon pere
Le seüst ore, et a te mere,
Jamais n'aroient se bien non.   [d]
Cil qui fist ceste election
Soit beneois de Dieu lasus.
2760 Nieche, ne pués or monter plus.
Onques encor, se Diex me salt,
Ne fist nule si riche salt.
Il n'ot plus povre en ceste honor,[222]
Or aras un empereor;
2765 Or as tu, nieche, tot esté.
Selonc çou que Diex t'a presté
Doit estre le reconnissance.

---
[220] diu]B.
[221] 2741-2830 *Scribe* 2.
[222] Il ot]BT.

we have known this since this morning. He is supposed to select the most beautiful, the most perfect and the best of them. **2701** – My lady, I am the man possessed of second sight; I can't find a young lady out there who is as perfect as I would wish; but now I have found her; that is why I have asked you for this girl. I have requested her and request again, commended her to God and commend her once more until I see her again.' He immediately set off on his way, went straight to his lord and told him the whole story.

'My lord,' he said, 'I have been out there, but, may God protect my person, I could find no creature suitable for you. Shame-faced and crestfallen I started to come back. As I entered the ancient quarter of Rome I came upon a maid; she was the daughter of a senator. Give thanks to our Creator, for she is the flower, the jewel of this whole world, surpassing all other women. If she remains as she is now, then there is only one tree in the forest, and only one rose in the walled garden and only one cleric in the clergy, for she has no equal in all the world. **2726** Now we must not let her get away. There will never again be a woman of such worth if she continues as she has begun.' Now the emperor was overjoyed: 'Eracle,' he said, 'fair sweet friend, procure for her some precious cloth and have it sewn and fashioned into garments fit for an empress. I am very mindful and cognizant of the fact that you have served me faithfully; happy was the day I first saw you and you me. There will be no waiting period or delay, I shall marry within three days.' Eracle did not wish to wait any longer; to the best of his knowledge and ability he arranged for her garments to be fashioned and made ready as was fitting for such a lady. He had her bathed for two whole days and meanwhile summoned the castellans, dukes and counts. Now our story will really begin.

The aunt, who loved and believed in God, was very happy and rightly so. **2749** She said: 'So help me God, my fair Lord, now I no longer have any worries or concerns; now I no longer care when I die, for now death can no longer harm me. I thought I was bringing up an orphan and I have brought up a queen. Niece, if your good father's and mother's souls knew the truth, they would have nothing but bliss from now on. May the man who selected you be blessed by God above. Niece, you cannot now rise any further; if God is my Saviour, never was any woman granted such a leap in fortune. There was no one poorer in this land and now you will have an emperor as your husband. Now, niece, you have been totally fulfilled. Your gratitude should be commensurate with God's generosity towards you.

Cui Diex done grignor poissance,
Plus doit doner et departir;
2770 Ensi fisent li saint martir:
Cil qui plus ot et plus dona,
Et qui miex sot miex sermona.
– Ante, se Diex me face aïe,
Ja ne serai trop esbahie
2775 Ne trop por riqueche avulee;
Forment seroie desjuglee
Se a Dieu ne savoie rendre
Çou qu'il m'a doné por despendre.
S'il ne m'eüst riens conmandé,
2780 Riens ne me seroit demandé,
Mais il m'a doné tot mon bien,
Sel servirai de es le sien[223]
A son plaisir plenierement,
Car je sai bien certainement[224]
2785 Que cascun home faire estuet
Tous jors al miex que faire puet.»
L'empereres ot non Laïs,
Et li pucele Athanaïs;
Al tierç jor que li flors d'esté
2790 Ot ciés s'antain a aise esté,
Et qu'ele ot bien son cors vestu,
Ne prisissiés pas un festu
Belté de feme envers celi
Que Athanaïs ot en li.
2795 Or le baisierent li voisin,
Or l'apellerent si cousin,
Car cascuns a grant parenté   [e]
Quant il a riqueche et plenté.
Al grant mostier c'on dist Saint Pere
2800 L'espousa Laïs l'emperere

Al tierç jor de l'election[225]
Et met en se subjection
Tote l'onor et tot l'empire,
Et fait tes noces comme sire.
2805 Le nuit se coucent en lor lis,
Et cele i est a tels delis
Con jovene dame a son signor.
Li sire i est a molt grignor,
Qu'il se set miex de li avoir
2810 Qu'ele ne puist encor savoir.[226]
Et cele est bele estrangement,
Si est de bel contenement;
N'est mie fole ne eschive,[227]
Si li plaist plus que riens qui vive.
2815 Le dame croist molt en biauté,
Si aime honor et loiauté.[228]
Je vos di bien et dire l'os,
Tot a conquis, et pris et los;
Ains que li tiers ans soit passés,
2820 Vos di bien qu'ele en a assés.[229]
Cascun jor tehist en corsage,
Si le tient on a le plus sage
Qui onques jor alast a messe;
Onques ne fist fausse promesse,
2825 Mais s'ele est de rien malhaitie,
Si est de tot si afaitie
Que plus li valt ses bialparlers
Que face a plusors lor doners.
Al doner fait si boine ciere
2830 C'on l'en set gré et tient plus ciere
C'une autre s'ele dounast plus.[230]
Molt l'a bons cuers mis au dessus,
Car ne fait mie par degrés;

---
[223] Ses]BT.
[224] plenierement]BT.
[225] delection]L.
[226] Ne quele]BT.
[227] chaitive]T.
[228] fausete]BT.
[229] q. en asses].
[230] 2831-5537 *Scribe* 1.

The more power a person is granted by God, the more he should give away and share out his fortune, just as the holy martyrs did: whichever of them had the most, gave away the most and whichever knew more, preached better. – Aunt, so help me God, I shall never be so carried away or so blinded by wealth. **2776** I would be horribly deceived if I did not know how to render unto God what He has given me to spend.[50] If He had placed nothing in my care, nothing would be asked of me, but he has given me all that I possess and I shall use his own goods to serve him and fulfil his every wish. For I know for certain that every man should always do the best he can.' The emperor's name was Laïs and the young girl was called Athanaïs. Once the flower of summer had spent a couple of days resting at her aunt's house and had adorned herself beautifully, you would not have given a straw for the beauty of any other woman in comparison with that of Athanaïs. Now her neighbours started to make a fuss of her and now her cousins acknowledged her, for when people have an abundance of wealth they acquire lots of relatives. **2799** On the third day after she had been chosen, Laïs the emperor married her in the great church called St Peter's and he placed under her authority all of his land and the whole empire, and his wedding celebrations were fit for a king. That night they went to bed and she experienced the rapture any young woman has with her lord. Her husband had far greater pleasure still, for he knew better than she could yet know how to derive pleasure from her. And she was amazingly beautiful and behaved perfectly. She was neither immodest nor too reticent and she pleased him more than any creature alive. The lady grew greatly in beauty, loved honour and fidelity. I can assure you and venture to say that she won for herself great esteem and praise. Before the end of the third year I can assure you that she was greatly esteemed. Every day she grew in stature and she was considered to be the wisest person who ever attended mass. **2824** She never made a false promise, but if she needed to deny a request, she was so polite about it that her courtly words were worth more than the gifts of many others. She gave with such good grace that people thanked her and held her in greater affection than any other woman, even if the latter had given more. Her good heart made her superior to all, for she did nothing by halves

---

[50] Gautier is here invoking the parable of the talents.

Bien set conquerre doubles grés:[231]
2835 Povres retient par biel doner,
Riches par biel araisouner.
Justice ne va pas en destre[232] [f]
La ou se sires ne puet estre:[233]
Por coi il soit, la d'estre enquiert
2840 Et fait canqu'a justice affiert
D'alever droit, d'abaissier tort;
Le foible aiue envers le fort.
Molt l'en loeent tout li Romain.
Nus ne parole a li en vain,
2845 Nus ne s'en va desconsilliés;
Al departir les fait tous liés.
  Or est Eracle et ert toudis
En molt bon point, ce m'est avis;
Car s'il par Diu est en avant,
2850 Bien est drois que tous jors s'en vant
Et qu'il voist par amendement,
Selonc le mien entendement;
Ainc n'oï parler de grant bien
Qui se peüst celer por rien:
2855 Ce avons nos tous jors veü.
Or est d'Eracle tout seü:
Com l'angles en fist demostrance,
Ançois qu'il venist a naissance;
Or set on bien qui fu ses peres,[234]
2860 Or connoist on qui fu se mere,
Com ele mist arriere dos,
Aprés le mort Mirïados,
Son blé, son or et son argent,
Sel dona tout a povre gent;
2865 Quant doné ot si grant riquece,

Si fist aprés grignor larghece,
Car ele vendi son cier fil,
Si l'en envoia en eschil;
Por Diu dona canqu'ele en prist,
2870 Et por Diu dure vie aprist.
D'Eracle est seü en maint liu
Que çou qu'il set li vient de Diu;
Or est li voirs par tout retrais
Qu'il est de bones gens estrais.
2875 Devant ce qu'il fust esprovés,
Et que li polains fust trovés,
Et que li dame eslite fust, [139 a]
Ne sot nus hom qui vie eüst
Qui fu Eracles, ne li mere
2880 Qui le vendi, ne qui ses pere;
Or le set on et sara mils,
Ains que il soit gaire plus vieus.
Or n'a li sire nule honte
De ce qu'Eracles a lui monte,
2885 Si est li plais a tant venus
Qu'il en est aussi cier tenus[235]
En toutes cors, mais por celui,
Com il, de çou qu'il monte a lui.
Tout vienent consel a lui querre;
2890 Il sanle princes de la terre.
Armes demande, et on li quiert
Molt hautement quanqu'i affiert.
Li sire l'aime estrainement,
Por çou l'adoube hautement,
2895 Et trente por le siue amor;
Et puis revit on bien le jor[236]
Car le siue chevalerie

---

[231] double]L.
[232] Juistice].
[233] *No need to correct to* ses sires *as there is no ambiguity of sense, cf.* 4984.
[234] *No need to correct to* pere, *as such rhymes are tolerated elsewhere, cf.* 2647.
[235] 2885-86 *Couplet inverted in* A.
[236] revint]B.

and knew how to earn double the thanks: she kept the loyalty of the poor through her cheerful generosity and the rich through her courtly speech. Justice was not given a rest[51] when her husband could not be present: whatever the case, she asked to be there, and did whatever justice required in order to promote right and demote wrong. She helped the weak against the strong. The whole of Rome was full of praise for her. No one spoke to her in vain, no one left her presence downhearted, for as they took their leave she made everyone feel good.

Now Eracle was and would always be in a very advantageous position, it seems to me, for if his success was thanks to God, then it was only right, in my view, that he should boast of this every day and that he should continue to improve himself. **2853** I have never heard of great virtue that could be concealed in any way; every day we find evidence of this fact. Now Eracle's whole story became common knowledge: how the angel announced everything even before he was born. Now everyone knew who his father was and they knew who his mother was too; how after the death of Miriados she cared nothing for his wheat, gold and silver, and gave it all to the poor. Once she had given away such great wealth, she made an even more generous gift, for she sold her dear son and sent him away to fend for himself. She gave away all the proceeds in the name of God and became accustomed to hardship for God's sake. Throughout the land it was made known that all Eracle's knowledge came from God, and now the truth was told everywhere that he was descended from a good family. **2875** Before he had been put to the test and had found the colt and selected the lady, no man alive knew who Eracle was, nor who his mother was, who sold him, nor who his father was. Yet now it was common knowledge and it would become even more widely known before he grew much older. Now his lord was not at all ashamed to be so fond of Eracle. The situation was such that at every court Eracle was held in as much affection as the emperor, but on the latter's account, since Eracle meant so much to him. Everyone came to seek his advice; he seemed just like the country's ruler. He asked to be dubbed and high quality equipment was procured for him. His lord's love for him was exceptional; therefore he was knighted magnificently and thirty others were dubbed in his honour. This day was later looked upon positively, for his chivalry

---

51 The image Gautier employs is of the *destrier* being led riderless – a spare horse with no job to do.

Ne torna pas a jouglerie:
Ja de si haute n'orrés mais.
2900 Ichis mist sainte Glise en pais
Si li conquist si grant anour[237]
Com de le crois Nostre Signor.
Ne voel pas ci entrelacier[238]
L'ahan qu'il ot au porcacier,
2905 Qu'ensi ne vait pas le matyre;[239]
Ains dirai l'uevre tote entire
De nostre empereor Laïs
Et de se feme Atanaïs,
Et de l'honor vous dirai puis
2910 Qu'Eracles ot, et se jou puis,
Aprés dirai de cele crois
U Nostre Sire fu destrois,
Con fu perdue par foiblece
Et reconquise par proueche.
2915 Eracles est bons chevaliers,
Preus et loiaus et droituriers;
Por voir os dire et aficier   [b]
Que l'emperere l'a si cier
Con s'il fust mil fois de se car.[240]
2920 N'est mie torné a escar
Çou qu'il conmande par le terre;
Ne vait pas autre signor querre
Qui de grant cose velt plaidier,
Il puet trestous nuire et aidier.
2925 Chevaliers est teus de se main
Con vous orrés, mais aparmain
Vous dirai de l'empereïs,
Con oevre en li sains Esperis,
Car loiauté aime et droiture,
2930 Et Diu sour toute creature.
Quanqu'ele emprent velt acomplir,

Ce vous voel je por voir plevir,
Mais n'emprent onques nule rien
U il nen ait raison et bien.
2935 Dame a esté set ans de Rome,
Si c'onques Dix ne fist cel home
Qui en puist dire vilenie,
S'il ne le sordist par envie.
Onques mais nule ne fu tels:
2940 Recuevre tous auteus,
Messes fait canter et matines,
Et fait nourir ces orphenines
Por l'amor Diu et por Marie,
Et por l'amor Diu les marie;
2945 De soi meïsme li souvient,
Si fait molt bien ce qui covient;[241]
Et quant ce vient c'on doit juner,
Ces povres prent a gouvrener
De quanques onques ont mestier:
2950 Qu'ele set bien, contre un sestier
Qu'ele i met, cent en prendera,
Que Dix meïme li rendra.
Ele establit mainte abeïe
U Nostre Dame est obeïe.
2955 Molt est ameë et proisie,
Car el siecle est si envoisie
O ce qu'ele aime Diu et sert, [c]
Que l'un por l'autre pas ne pert.
Li empereres l'a si ciere
2960 Qu'il ne puet savoir le mainiere
Con il le puist assés oïr,
Assés veoir et conjoïr;
Onques ne cuida riens veoir
Qui li peüst tant bien seoir;
2965 Il ne le puet veoir assés,

---

[237] A *omits* si grant.
[238] entrelaissier; BT]L, *an error common to all 3 MSS.*
[239] martyre]BT.
[240] si f.]BT.

[241] ce li c.]BT.

was never the cause of derision; you will never again hear of such excellent chivalry. **2900** He brought peace to Holy Church and won great honour for it by capturing the Cross of Our Lord. I do not wish to tell the story here of his strenuous efforts to win it back, for I shall be ordering my material differently; I prefer first to relate in full the story of our emperor Laïs and his wife Athanaïs, and then I shall tell you about the honour won by Eracle, and, if I can, I shall then talk about the Cross on which Our Lord was killed, how it was lost through weakness and recovered through prowess.

Eracle was a good knight, brave, loyal and just; I am happy to state for a fact and to assure you that he meant as much to the emperor as if he had been a thousand times his flesh and blood. People did not underestimate his power to command throughout the land. If anyone had an important legal case to argue they would not seek out any other lord for judgement; he had the power to ruin or help anyone. **2925** His feats of arms you will hear about later, but for the moment I shall tell you about the empress, and how the Holy Spirit worked in her, for she loved loyalty and rectitude and God above all of his creatures. Whatever she undertook to do she strove to accomplish, I can tell you that for a fact, yet she never undertook anything that was not sensible and good. She had been empress of Rome for seven years, yet no man created by God could speak ill of her, unless he slandered her out of envy. There has never been such a woman since. She provided coverings for all altars, had masses and matins sung, and arranged the upbringing of female orphans for the love of God and Holy Mary, and also for the love of God she found them suitable husbands. And she did not forget her own salvation, doing happily whatever was appropriate, and on fast-days she occupied herself looking after the poor, giving them whatever they needed: for she knew that one pound invested in this way would earn her a hundred, repaid by God himself.[52] **2953** She founded many an abbey where Our Lady was served. She was much loved and esteemed, for she was fun-loving in her secular life while at the same time loving and serving God, not sacrificing one for the other. The emperor loved her so much that he did not know how he would be able to hear, see or enjoy her company enough; he did not believe that he would ever meet anyone who suited him so well; he still could not manage to see enough of her,

---

[52] Again the parable of the talents. A *sestier* was usually a measure of volume: of liquid, grain, salt or land.

Et si a bien set ans passés
Qu'il l'a plainement conneüe;
Cascun jor si li vient veüe.
    Il avint si que gent faillie[242]
2970 Orent requise et asaillie
Une cité l'empereour;
Or se li torne a deshonor,
Molt par s'en fait et tristre et morne.
S'ost fait semonre, si s'atorne.
2975 Or ne se set il consillier,
A envis part de se moullier;
Mais je vos di, rien ne li valt,
Ne puet muer que il n'i aut,
Et del mener est il noians,
2980 Car çou est tant parfont laians,
En une terre molt lontaine,
Que del mener est si grans paine.
Or a li sire grant anui
Que mener ne le puet o lui,
2985 Ne consirer preu ne s'en puet;
Mais si fera; faire l'estuet.
Quant voit que faire li convient,
De mainte cose li sovient,
Car je vos di tout plainement,
2990 Faire le vauroit sainement;
Mais ne li vaut rien entresait.
Tos jors estuet que crieme i ait,
Que fins amans tos jors se crient
De perdre ce c'a ses mains tient,
2995 Qu'il a tos jors crieme en amor:
Qui ne mescroit, ainc n'ama jor!
Et sages hom meïmement   [d]
Se crient tous jors molt durement,
Mais ja nus hom sages nen iert
3000 S'il fait tout ce c'Amors requiert.

Mais se folie n'est pas teus
Com est folie natureus,
Car teus est de molt sage ator
Qui molt est faus en fine amor,
3005 Et tel folie et tel savoir
Font en amor paour avoir.[243]
Çou pert a nostre empereor,
Qui en amor a grant paour;
Amors le fait sovent villier.
3010 D'une part trait son consillier:[244]
«Eracle, dist il, biaus amis,
En vostre consel me sui mis,
Et si m'en est venus tous biens.
Ostoiier irai o les miens
3015 Si remanra l'empereïs,
Dont je sui molt grains et maris.
Vous en venrés ensanle o moi.
Ensi me consilliés par foi
Con je le puisse mix garder.
3020 – Sire, faites moi vif larder
Se nule garde estuet en li;
Trop m'aroit Dix mis en oubli
S'un poi i eüst de folie.
– Amis, je ne le mescroi mie,
3025 Mais je l'aim si de tout mon cuer
Que nel puis laissier a nul fuer
Que garder ne le face entreus
Si ricement con a mon oeus,
Car n'en voel pas estre engigniés.
3030 – Sire, se vos le destraigniés
N'en fremetés n'en siereüre,
Loiiens de fer ne fremeüre[245]
Ne le poroit jamais tenir.
Se vous laissiés çou couvenir,
3035 Si bone feme n'ert jamais.

---

[242] gen].
[243] folie a.]BT.
[244] soi c.]BT.
[245] loiies]BT.

even after a good seven years of complete familiarity; so he came to see her every day.

It so happened that a group of rebels had attacked and besieged one of the emperor's cities; this redounded to his dishonour and made him very sad and depressed. He summoned his army and made preparations. **2975** He did not know what to do, for he was reluctant to leave his wife; but I can tell you, there was nothing for it, he could not avoid going there himself. And to take her with him was out of the question, for it was such a long journey to such a distant, remote area, that taking her with him would have been too arduous. So now the emperor was very distressed, for he could not take her with him, nor could he easily do without her. Yet he would, for he would have to. When he realised what he had to do, he was mindful of many things, for, to tell you the truth, he wished to act wisely; yet none of this did him any good. He would be forced to live in constant fear, for a true lover always fears to lose what he holds in his hands, for he is always afraid when in love: anyone who has never been suspicious has never loved! And even a wise man is beset every day with great fear, but no man will ever be wise if he does all that Love requires of him. **3001** But a lover's madness is not the same as natural madness, for one can be very wise by nature, yet very foolish when it comes to true love, and such a combination of madness and wisdom makes lovers fearful. This phenomenon was apparent in our emperor, for he was very fearful in love. Love often kept him awake at night. He drew his counsellor to one side and said: 'Eracle, dear friend, I have relied on your advice and it has brought me untold benefit. I shall be going on campaign with my troops and the empress will remain here. This makes me very worried and upset. You will be coming with me. So please advise me faithfully how I might best keep an eye on her. – My lord, burn me alive if you ever find it necessary to place her under guard. God would have forgotten me altogether if there were the slightest hint of indiscretion in her. **3024** – My friend, I do not mistrust her at all, but I love her so wholeheartedly that I cannot refrain at any price from placing her under guard during my absence. She will receive the usual comforts, but I do not wish to be deceived by her. – My lord, if you restrain her either in fortresses or behind locked doors, neither iron shackles nor bars would ever manage to hold her. If you allow her to do what she wants, there will never be such a good wife.

Laissiés le, sire, tout em pais
Si arés tous jors bone amie. [e]
Biax sire, vos ne savés mie
Tous les afaires qui i gisent,
3040 Trestoutes coses se devisent:
Il a tel feme voirement,
S'ele n'eüst encajement,
Tost aroit un fol plait basti,
Et tele c'on pert par casti:
3045 Car cil l'embat en le folie
Qui por noient le bat et lie.
Laissiés ma dame a sa devise;
Si ne faura en nule ghise
Que ce ne soit li miudre riens
3050 C'onques veïst hom terriens.
– Eracle amis, vos veés bien
Le sien corage, mais le mien
Ne poés pas ensi veoir.
Une cité vois asseoir;
3055 Li sieges ert molt lonc, je croi,
Et je lais chi arriere moi
Le cose el mont que g'ai plus ciere:
Si vauroie estre mix en biere
Que il m'en fust mesavenu.
3060 Mais or n'i ait lonc plait tenu,
Consilliés moi que jou ferai.
– Sire, por Diu, ne vous dirai
Riens mie avant que je vous dis;
Se vous nel faites, il ert pis.
3065 Il ert tels hom qui consel quiert,
Ja li conseus si bons nen iert
Que tous jors ne se tiegne al suen.
Hom qui velt faire adiés son buen,
Si doit avoir son loëmer
3070 Qui ce li lot qu'il puist amer,[246]
U voelle folie u savoir.

Qui velt signor mal sage avoir[247]
Adiés se tiegne a son signor,
U face honte u face honor;
3075 Ja autrement n'ara son gré.
Mais Dix me mece a mal degré
Se ja vos siu de nule rien [f]
Se jou n'i voi raison et bien;
Et il m'est vis que c'est raisons
3080 Que me dame aut par ses maisons,
Par ses viles, par ses castiaus,
Par ses manoirs qu'ele a molt biaus;
Verra les terres et le gent,
Verra son or et son argent,
3085 Si pensera en son corage
Qu'amer doit bien le signorage
Dont tele honors li est venue;
Et s'ele est en destroit tenue,
Anuis li sera del sejor,
3090 Si maudira cent fois le jor
Le haute honor et le riquece
Por qu'ele est mise en tel destrece,
Si harra l'eür qu'ele vit.
Et feme qui s'a en despit
3095 Porcace engien en mainte gise[248]
Por qu'ele soit a honte mise.
Feme se het estraignement
Quant on le maine malement.
Quant on le sert a bone ciere,
3100 Ne se tient ele pas si ciere
Com li seroit oeus et mestiers?
Si m'aït Dix, biax sire ciers,
Quant feme fait mal, molt folie,
Se li grieve il s'on le castie;
3105 Et ceste qui a sormonté
Trestoutes femes de bonté,
Cuidiés vos qu'il ne li anuit

---

[246] Que]BT.
[247] volt]BT.
[248] maint *hypometric line*]BT.

Leave her in peace, my lord, and you will always have a perfect beloved. Fair lord, you have no idea how complicated all of this is; there are all kinds of possible consequences: true, there are women who, if they were not locked up, would soon hatch a foolish plan. But there are also those whom one loses through being too harsh; for the man who beats and restrains his wife for no good reason pushes her onto the path of folly. Leave my lady to her own devices and she will not fail in any way to be the best creature ever seen by mortal man. **3051** – Eracle, my friend, you can see clearly into her heart, but you do not have such insights into mine. I am going to besiege a city; I expect the siege to be very long and I am going to leave behind the thing most dear to me in the world: I'd rather be in my coffin than suffer some misfortune because of her. But let's not talk about it any longer, advise me on what I should do. – My lord, by God, I shall tell you nothing that I have not already told you; if you don't follow my advice, all the worse for you. There will always be some men who seek advice, yet however good that advice might be, they still follow their own. A man who always wants to do exactly what he likes ought to choose a counsellor whose advice suits him, whether it is foolish or wise. Anyone who wishes to have a foolish lord should always agree with his master, whether his actions are shameful or honourable; otherwise he won't win his favour. **3076** Yet may God cast me down should I ever follow your will in any matter unless I find it reasonable and good; and I think that it is reasonable to allow my lady to visit freely her properties, her towns, her castles and her very fine manor houses; she will see her land and her subjects, she will see her gold and her silver, and she will think to herself that she should dearly love the husband's authority which has brought her such honours. Yet if she is held in prison, her time there will anger her and she will curse a hundred times a day the high status and wealth which cause her to suffer such restrictions; and she will hate the good fortune she enjoyed. And a woman who holds herself in contempt hatches various plots which will lead to her dishonour. Women experience a strange self-loathing when they are mistreated. When they are treated kindly doesn't their self-respect rise to the appropriate and desired level? **3102** So help me God, fair dear lord, a woman who strays from the path of virtue commits an act of great folly;[53] even so, she will react badly to being disciplined, so do you imagine that this woman, whose virtue has surpassed all other women's, will not resent

---

53   It is quite likely that Gautier originally wrote 'Qui feme fait mal' in l. 3103, in which case he would be criticising here the *man* who harms a woman, as he does again in l. 3116.

S'on li taut se joie et deduit?
Itant vos os je bien gehir,[249]
3110 Se on li fait or espanir
C'ainc ne li vint n'en sens n'en pens,
Ele querra engien par tens,
S'il onques puet, come le face.
Cil mostre a feme bien le trace
3115 De folïer et de mesfaire
Qui por noient li fait contraire,[250]
Et cil empire plus le plait   [140a]
Qui le destraint por son bien fait,
Car on l'asert tout son aé[251]
3120 Por bien sauver se caasté.
Si di encor que Dix le tient
Quant de folie se retient.
Sire, ne malmetés le rose,
Car s'ele est quatre mois enclose,
3125 Tant en venrés au repentir,
Itant vous di jou sans mentir,
Se Damedix n'en fait miracle.
– Coument? Biax dous amis Eracle,
N'orrai autre consel par vous?
3130 – Nenil, par Diu qui maint sor nous.
– Et je le metrai en tel leu,
Par cele foi que je doi Deu,
Qu'al mix i ert de tot le monde,
Qu'en cele tor fort et reonde
3135 L'enfremerai, biax amis chiers,
A vint et quatre chevaliers
Qui a me volenté seront.
Cist vint et quatre le verront
Et au lever et au couchier,
3140 Que riens ne puisse a li touchier
De nule part que il nel voient;

Que je voel que les couces soient[252]
A le reonde tout entor,
Et ses lis ert enmi le tor;
3145 Lor lit seront si establi
Que tout aront lor ix sor li;
Lor cavés ert en tel maniere
Que il joindra a le maisiere.
Cascuns se moullier i ara
3150 Si que nus parler n'i porra
Que sa feme del tout ne l'oie,
U au mains si que tout ne voie.
C'iert fait ains demain miedi.
Li chevalier dont je vous di
3155 Seront de tous les plus meürs,[253]
Les plus senés, les plus seürs.
Ja hom ne feme n'i metra   [b]
Le pié fors cil qui servira.
– Biax sire, a vostre plaisir soit,
3160 Ne mais, par foi, s'il vous plaisoit,
Il seroit molt mix autrement.
– Eracle, or ert sifaitement.»
Li emperere est molt en grant
Des barons querre a son creant,
3165 Qu'en le folie est enlaciés.
Les chevaliers a aprociés,
Et toute l'oevre lor devise.
Cascuns d'eus a se moullier mise
En cele tor ensanle o soi.
3170 L'empereïs de bone foi
I ert enclose et ensieree,
Et mainte huissure bien ferree
A en le tor; max fus les arde!
A cascun huis a double garde.
3175 Quanque li sire volt, si fist[254]

---

[249] v. oc je bien gesir]B.
[250] font]BT.
[251] le sert; BT]R.

[252] le c.].
[253] creus]BT.
[254] velt]BT.

having her joy and pleasure taken away from her? Thus, I venture to say to you in no uncertain terms that if we now make her expiate a sin before the idea even enters her head to do wrong, she will soon work out a strategy to do it, if she can. Whoever mistreats a woman for no good reason points her clearly in the direction of foolish and sinful behaviour, and he makes matters worse if he locks her up to preserve her virtue, for one would have to restrict her freedom for the rest of her life in order to protect her chastity. So I repeat that God supports her when she refrains from committing folly. My lord, do not damage the rose, for if she is incarcerated for four months I can tell you truthfully that you will come to regret it, unless God performs a miracle. **3128** – What are you saying, Eracle, fair sweet friend, shall I hear no other advice from you? – No, by God who dwells on high. – Well, by the faith I owe God, I shall put her in the best place for her in the whole world, for I shall lock her in this heavily fortified round tower, dear fair friend, with twenty-four knights all obeying my instructions. These twenty-four men will observe her when she gets up and when she goes to bed, so that she can have no contact with anyone whatsoever without their seeing it. For I want their beds to be arranged in a circle around her and her bed will be placed in the middle of the tower; their beds will be positioned in such a way that they will all be looking at her; their bed-heads will be so disposed that they will be up against the wall. Each will have his wife with him so that none will be able to speak to the empress without his wife hearing everything or at least seeing everything. **3153** These arrangements will be carried out before midday tomorrow. The knights I am talking about will be the oldest, wisest and most loyal of all my men. No man or woman will set foot in the tower except for her servant. – My lord, let it be as you please; however, I swear, if it pleased you it would be much better otherwise. – Eracle, this is exactly how it's going to be.'

The emperor was very eager to find barons he could rely on, for he had been ensnared by folly. He approached the knights and explained the whole plan to them. Each one of them took his wife with him into the tower. The loyal empress was imprisoned and incarcerated there, and there was many a securely locked door in the tower; may they burn in hell! At each door there were two guards. **3175** All the emperor's wishes were carried out

Et de la dame congié prist;
Tous coreciés et tous maris
Se part dont de l'empereïs.
La vient delivrement et tost
3180 U il ot fait ajouster s'ost;
Ses gens sont molt bien atornees
Et il les maine a grans jornees,
Que par cemins, que par sentiers.
Tost est passés li mois entiers
3185 Ançois qu'il soient la venu
U cil se sont contre eus tenu,
Qui ont fait a l'empereour
Et honte et lait et deshonor.
    Al cief del mois a quel que paine[255]
3190 I vint li sire et cil qu'il maine;
A une chité bone et rice
Vient l'emperere, bien s'afice
N'en tornera si l'ara prise,
U de fu grigois toute esprise.
3195 Les loges tendent environ
Li chevalier et li baron.
Li emperere est descendus;   [c]
Ses trés demaine i est tendus[256]
Jouste un rocier d'antiquité
3200 Dont il sorvoit bien le cité.[257]
Les engiens vont aparillier
Por faire ceus dedens villier
Et por els prendre et malbaillir;
Mais il i poront assaillir,[258]
3205 Mien ensiant, toute lor vie
Ains qu'il lor toillent le navie
Qui lor amaine le viande
Et quanque cascuns i demande[259]

De pain, de vin, de car, de blé,
3210 Trestout sans venir en emblé;
Ja par famine conquis n'ierent.
Et cil defors molt les requierent,
Assés i a trait et lanchié
As murs, et petit avanchié;
3215 Mais ce n'est mie grans depors
A dire es quels a plus d'esfors,
U en iceus qui sont assis,
U en icex quis ont requis,
U es maisnés u es plus viex,
3220 Je vous cuiç assés dire mix.
Aprés vous dirai, se je puis,
L'esploit que il i fisent puis,
Mais de la dame orrés avant
Coument ses cuers li met devant
3225 Le tort, le honte, le destrece,
Que on li fait por se prouece,[260]
Et pense: «Dix, confaite cose,
C'on m'a por noient chi enclose!
Se je savoie le forfait
3230 Por c'on m'a fait et honte et lait,
Je souferroie me pesance
A mains d'anui et d'esmaiance;
Car qui dessert qu'il ait damage,
Se conscience l'assouage,
3235 S'ele li dist et fait savoir
Que tout ce doit on bien avoir;
Mais le moie ne m'en dist rien   [d]
Que j'ainc desservisse el que bien:
Por ce me grieve il assés plus.
3240 Aussi m'aït Dix de lassus,
Que ci a trop grant mesproison

---

[255] a que que]T.
[256] iestendus]B.
[257] servoit]BT.
[258] poroit]BT.
[259] cascune d.]BT.

[260] par; B]T.

and then he took his leave of his lady; very upset and very downhearted he then parted from the empress. He went quickly and speedily to the place where he had assembled his army; his troops were very well equipped and he led them on forced marches along highroads and by-roads. A whole month quickly elapsed before they arrived at the spot where the rebels had risen up against them, those men who had brought shame, harm and dishonour upon the emperor.

After considerable effort the emperor and his followers arrived there at the end of the month; the emperor came to a splendid, prosperous city, and he promised himself that he would not leave until he had captured it or burnt it down with Greek fire.[54] His knights and barons set up camp all around it. The emperor dismounted; his personal tent was erected next to an ancient rock from which he could survey the whole city. **3201** They went about preparing their siege engines to give the inhabitants sleepless nights, and to capture and do violence to them; but in my opinion, they could have spent their whole lives attacking them to no avail. For without intercepting the ships which were coming and going quite openly, bringing them food and all they needed in the way of bread, wine, meat and wheat, they would never have starved the enemy into submission. Those outside attacked them frequently; many a missile was catapulted and hurled at the walls, yet they gained little advantage. It is not very entertaining for me to tell you which side had the greater strength, those besieged or those attacking them, the youngest or the most experienced, for I think I have more interesting things to tell you about. **3221** If I can, I shall tell you later about the exploits they subsequently performed, but first you will hear about the lady, how her heart set out for her the injustice, shame and distress she was suffering in return for her virtue; so she thought to herself: 'Oh my God, how on earth have I come to be imprisoned here for no good reason! If only I knew the crime for which I have been shamed and punished, I would endure my cares with less anguish and dismay. For if we deserve to suffer, we are consoled by our conscience, if it instructs and informs us that it is right for us to experience all this. However, my conscience tells me that I never merited anything but good, that is why it pains me so much more. So may God above help me, for the fact that they are

---

[54] Greek fire was a burning liquid which the Byzantines used on missiles hurled during siege warfare.

Quant il me tienent en prison;
Et si ne sai por coi m'afolent,
Fors por tant que les nues volent,
3245 U por ce que li lune luist
Mains del solel. U ce me nuist[261]
Que le lune croist et descroist.
Si fera, mais que bien me poist;[262]
Por me desserte n'est çou pas,
3250 Car por eschiver le mal pas
Ai vilenie refusee.
Envie, espoir, m'a encusee,[263]
Et si me porte por ce faide
Que je ne sui pas li plus laide.[264]
3255 Lasse! Con sui mal eüree,
Con je sui por nient ensieree!
Cil qui m'a mis en cest anui
A honte fait et moi et lui,[265]
Car il cuide molt bien par foi[266]
3260 Qu'il i ait veü le pourquoi,
Mais nel fist onques, Dix le set,
Et por ce quit je qu'il me het.
Se il ne m'eüst esprouvee
Et s'il ne m'eüst tel trouvee,
3265 Il m'alast molt mix qu'il ne vait.
Biax sire Dix, quel pecié fait
Qui rent a home mal por bien,
Qui le honist sor toute rien!
Car ce le fait de bien retraire
3270 C'on li fait por son bien contraire.
Hé! Dix, con sont felon et dur
Qui m'ont ensieree en cest mur![267]
Mais ce n'est mie lor durtés,

Ains est ma grans maleürtés,[268]
3275 Car jou ai veü maint felon
Qui ne fet tos jors se mal non,[269]
Qui mix a por se cuivertise   [e]
C'uns preudom por son biel servise.
Bien puet cascuns estre asseür
3280 C'a biel service esteut eür,
Mais il ne croient mie bien
Qui dient qu'eürs monte a rien.
Je di bien que c'est nule cose;[270]
Ains est Maufés, s'on dire l'ose,
3285 Qui a les pluisors desjouglés.
Peciés les a si aveulés
Qu'il ne puent le mix eslire,
U il ne voelent, car li pire
I a mix fait de le moitié
3290 Que cil qui a tous jors coitié[271]
De bien faire et de bien ouvrer.
Preudom ne puet rien recovrer.
N'est pas mes cuers seürs de lui,
Ains est li peciés de cestui
3295 Qui devoit veoir et aprendre
U il devoit ses mains estendre.[272]
Se tant ai fait vers mon signor
Que il me doive faire honor,
Et il n'est teus que il le face,[273]
3300 Illuec pert il de Diu le grasse;
Et qui çou pert, il pert grant perte,
Et je n'i pert fors me desserte.
Mais se li deus m'est de cuer pres,[274]
Autres s'en daura ci aprés,
3305 Si m'aït Dix, qu'il n'en set mot.

---

[261] Mais; BT]L; nuit]BT.
[262] ferai]BT.
[263] escusee]B.
[264] p. por ce l.]BT.
[265] Et]T.
[266] C. ele c. b.]B.
[267] m. ensiere

[268] lor g.]B.
[269] set t.]B.
[270] Si bien]BT.
[271] jor].
[272] mevers e.]M, *cf.* 6414.
[273] il nel f.]B.
[274] n'est]B.

keeping me in prison is a great miscarriage of justice, and I don't even know why they are punishing me, except perhaps because clouds flit across the sky or the moon shines less brightly than the sun. Or I'm being wronged because the moon waxes and wanes. **3248** It will continue to do so, even if it grieves me; yet I have not merited this, for in order to avoid the path of evil I have shunned all vile behaviour. Perhaps Envy has accused me and is pursuing a vendetta against me because I am not the most ugly woman in the world. Alas, how unlucky I am to be locked up for no reason. The man who has inflicted this pain on me has brought shame upon me and himself, for although he sincerely believed that he had good reason for acting in this way, God knows he did not. That's why I think he hates me. If he had not put me to the test and if he had not found me to be as I am, things would be much better for me than they are now. Fair Lord God, what an awful sin a man commits when he rewards another's goodness with evil, which shames him above all else! For when a person's goodness is greeted with malevolence this makes him shy away from doing good. Oh, God, how treacherous and cruel are those who have imprisoned me within these walls. **3273** But it is not their cruelty that upsets me most, but rather my great misfortune, for I have seen many a traitor who does nothing but ill, who receives greater rewards for his wickedness than a good man does for his loyal service. It is all very well for people to be sure that loyal service should be rewarded with worldly fortune, but they are wrong to say that the gifts of fortune are valuable in themselves. I can tell you, good fortune is worthless, or rather it is the devil, if I may say so, who has deceived most people in this respect. Sin has so blinded them that they can't discern which course of action is best, or they don't wish to, for the worst man fares better by half than the man who has always striven to do good and behave virtuously. A good person can never get anywhere in life. My heart has no confidence in him, but what I am confident of is that the sin lies with him who should have seen and discovered where to extend his generosity. If I have done enough for my lord to expect to be treated honourably in return, yet his nature is such that he fails to do so, then he will forfeit God's grace; **3301** and whoever forfeits that, forfeits a great deal, while all I lose is the reward I deserve. But if at present grief consumes my heart, another will grieve in the future, so help me God, yet he suspects nothing yet.

Au pis a fait qu'il onques pot
Ciex qui en ceste tor m'a mise;
Miax ameroie en me cemise
Estre a honor et a delivre
3310 Qu'enpereïs a honte vivre!
A honte sui je voirement,
Qu'on cuide qu'il soit autrement;
Autrement seroit il, mon voel!
Bien cacent mainte feme a duel,
3315 Por lor folie mainte gent,
Dont puis sont al cuer molt dolent.
Je ne voi onques nule cose[275]   [f]
Qui ne me griet; mes cuers me cose[276]
Que je por Diu et por honor[277]
3320 Ai foi gardee mon signor;[278]
Car je ne sui aperceüe
De cose que jou aie eüe
Fors de grant honte c'on m'alieve.
Forment m'anuie et molt me grieve
3325 Que je ai pis por mon bien fait
Que se j'eüsse autrement fait;
Je ne sai home amont n'aval,
S'on por son bien li faisoit mal,
Qui n'en fust molt destalentés.
3330 Quant li formens est esventés,[279]
Plus en amende et plus en valt;
Si fait prodom, se Dix me salt;
Quant on tient plait de se proece,
Plus s'en amende et s'en adrece,
3335 Et plus s'efforce de bien faire,
Car por ce fait on qu'il i paire.[280]

A moi ne pert il onques mie
Que ainc menaisse bone vie:
Je sui en buies et en fierges.
3340 Molt par iert bien espris mes cierges,
Et bien me candoile alumee,
Quant cil le torna en fumee
Qui l'aluma premierement.
Molt a ci mal amendement.
3345 Lasse! Con male amende a chi
Et con ci a male merci.
Cil bien fais ait beneïçon[281]
Dont on atent le guerredon.[282]
Por ce sert on au roi celestre
3350 Que mix en doit a cascun estre;
Ja une fois nel serviroie
Ne de cuer ne l'apieleroie,
Se a lonc por mon bien ovrer
Ne cuidoie bien recovrer.
3355 Et lasse! tant ai bien servi
Et ainc si mal prouver ne vi.
Son tans et son service pert   [141 a]
Icil qui al diable sert;[283]
Je ne cuidoie en nule ghise
3360 Avoir esté en son servise.»
Si se demente mainte fois
La dame, car se bone fois
Qu'ele a tant longes maintenue
Li est sovent devant venue;
3365 Si est plus tormentee en soi
Quant li ramembre de se foi.
    Signor, oés: on vos devise
Qu'en Rome ot jadis mainte assise
Qui puis est tornee a noient;
3370 Usages cange molt sovent.
Encor le sevent bien maint home

---
[275] nuele c.].
[276] c. et c.]BT.
[277] Et j.]BT.
[278] Ai sorgardee]B (T: Ai je meffait viers mon s.).
[279] si forment]BT.
[280] i faire]B (B *inverts* 3335-36; T: Car por ce le fait qu'il apaire).
[281] et b.]B.
[282] De mains a.]B.
[283] as diables]BT.

The man who locked me in this tower has done the worst thing he could possibly do; I would rather live honourably and freely, dressed only in my slip, rather than live dishonourably as an empress! I am indeed living dishonourably, even if others think it is otherwise; however, if I have my way it will be otherwise. Many people in their madness force many a woman into despair, but they live to regret it. I can see nothing now that does not pain me; my heart criticises me for being loyal to my husband out of love of God and honour; for I am not aware of anything that I have gained from it, apart from having shame heaped upon me. **3324** I am very angry and upset that I have been treated worse for my virtue than if I had behaved differently. I know of no man, high or low who, if rewarded with mistreatment for his good deeds, would not have been very discouraged by it. When wheat is exposed to the air it improves and gains in value; a good man does the same, so help me God. If others comment on his virtue, he improves all the more, shows greater commitment and puts more effort into doing good, for they do this so that his virtue will be obvious. There is no obvious sign in me at all that I have ever led a good life: I am bound and in fetters. My torch was burning brightly and my candle was well aflame when the man who first kindled it reduced it to smoke. This is poor reward indeed! Alas, what poor reward we have here and what poor gratitude! Blessed be the good works for which we expect to be rewarded. We serve our Heavenly King so that each of us gains from it. **3351** I would never serve Him at all nor call on Him from the bottom of my heart if I did not think that my good deeds would be well rewarded in the long run. Oh woe is me! I have served so well and yet never have I seen myself so sorely tested. Anyone who serves the devil wastes his time and service, yet I didn't think for a moment that I was in his service.' Thus the lady lamented time and again, for her faithfulness, which she had maintained for so long, kept crossing her mind; and so she became even more tormented when she recalled her faithfulness.

Listen, my lords, we are told that in times gone by there was many a practice which has since fallen into disuse – traditions change very frequently. It is still common knowledge amongst many people

C'une feste ot jadis en Rome,[284]
Dont li Romain grant plait tenoient;
Et huit jors tos plains i venoient
3375 Et li forfait et li bani,
Fors seul li larron espani.
Venoient i les damoisieles,
Et les dames et les pucieles.
L'empereïs demainement
3380 I venoit huit jors plainement
Por plus esbaudir cele feste,
Et li varlés de haute geste
Soloient devant li harper;
Car li baron et li haut per
3385 Metoient lore lor enfans
As estrumens les premiers ans
Por plus estruire de simplece;
Car je vos di que grant prouece
N'ert encor preus en jogleor,
3390 Ni en chevalier jengleour.
Le feste font grant et pleniere;
Or s'esjoïst de grant maniere
Li dame qui est en le tour.
De trestout le plus rice ator
3395 Qu'ele pot onques porcachier
Se fait bien vestir et cauchier;
Quant fu vestue et bien paree,   [b]
Ne sanla pas feme dervee.
Li emperere, s'il le pert,
3400 Damage i ara trop apert.
Cil de le tor, li sejorné,
Se sont erraument atorné
Por aler o l'empereïs;
Et si le font molt a envis,

3405 Mais n'i a nul qui tant soit sire
Qui ost le dame contredire
Qu'ele n'i aut des qu'ele vuelt,
Car par coustume aler i seut,
Et vos savés c'on claime droit
3410 En ce que li coustume doit,
Car je vos di bien sans doutance
Que grant cose est d'acoustumance.
Li chevalier sont biel et gent
Et moevent a molt biele gent.
3415 Lor dame a cele feste mainent
Et de li garder molt se painent,
Qu'il en sont bien apris et duit;
Nus n'i parole sans conduit,
Et qu'il n'i ait trois d'iaus au mains;
3420 Molt est keüe en dures mains.
Il pueent bien son cors tenser,
Mais son corage et son penser
Ne pueent il destraindre mie
Que ne deviegne bien amie
3425 A cui qu'ele onques veut de mil;
Ja nel sara ne cil ne chil.
Bien les porra ensi deçoivre,[285]
Amer, haïr, sans aperçoivre;
A ce ne valent rien casti.[286]
3430 A le feste a maint ju basti,
Que varlet vestu de samit
I ont tant maint ju arramit:[287]
Salent, tymbrent, harpent et rotent,[288]
Balent, treskent, cantent et notent;[289]
3435 Cis calemiele et cis estive;
Ne vos puet dire riens qui vive
Le joie que il vont menant;   [c]

---

[284] feme]BT (O, 2814: spiles *reflects* A).

[285] le p.]B.
[286] cesti]BT.
[287] I i ont]B.
[288] tymbres, harpes].
[289] t. salent et n.]BT; O, 2836: singen *reflects* BT.

that there used to be a festival held in Rome which the Romans made much of and which they all attended, including crooks and exiles, for a full eight days; **3376** only hardened criminals were excluded. Young noblewomen, ladies and maidens all attended. The empress would appear in person on all eight days to enhance the festivities and the young men from the best families would play their harps for her. For in those days barons and members of the aristocracy would arrange for their children to study musical instruments when they were very young in order to encourage innocent simplicity in them, for I can tell you that great sophistication was not yet considered an advantage in an entertainer nor in a smooth-talking knight. The celebrations were impressive and sumptuous. Now the lady in the tower cheered up considerably. She clad her body and legs in the most precious finery she could manage to acquire. Once dressed and beautifully attired she did not look like a woman going out of her mind. If the emperor loses her, his loss will be all too obvious. **3401** Her guards from the tower, who were hardly overworked, quickly got ready to accompany the empress. And yet they did this very reluctantly, but there was none who had the authority to risk gainsaying the lady and stop her from going, since she wished to. For it was her custom to attend, and as you know, what custom demands is often called law, for I can tell you without hesitation that custom is a very weighty matter. The knights were handsome and noble, and set off with a very impressive retinue. They took their lady to the festivities and tried very hard to guard her, for they were experienced and were accustomed to do this; no one spoke to her without a chaperone, and without at least three of them at any given time. She had indeed fallen into cruel hands! They were able to guard her body effectively, but they could not in any way prevent her heart and mind from falling in love with any one of a thousand men she might choose, without a single one of her guards realising. **3427** She would thus be able to deceive them, to love or hate without being detected; in this respect their admonishments were of no use. Lots of games had been planned for the celebrations; the young men dressed in satin had arranged numerous competitions: they leapt in the air, played drums, harps and fiddles, performed *tresches* and other dances, sang and played music; some played the flute, others the pipes,[55] no man alive would be capable of describing for you the fun they were having.

---

55   It is difficult to identify the exact dances, mouvements and musical performances involved here. Gautier may not be using terms such as *treskent* technically.

Biel sont li ju et avenant.
Li plus legier n'ont soing de note,
3440 Ançois juent a le pelote;
Qui mix i cort, s'en a le pris,
Car si est li afaires pris;
Et quant il oent le noviele
C'Athanaïs i vient, li biele,[290]
3445 A estrumens encontre vont;
Biele est li joie qu'il li font.
L'empereïs ont encontree
Ains qu'en le rue soit entree
U li grant ju sont establi;
3450 Grans est li noise environ li;
Avironee est de tel gent
N'i a celi n'ait estrument
Se n'i a un seul si frarin
Qui ne soit frans et de halt lin;
3455 Et selonc ce que cascuns valt
S'en trait plus prés et tresque et salt.
Tos li mix fais et li plus biax
De tos les autres damoisiaus
I a harpé le jor adés;
3460 Icil a non Pariadés;
Fix a un sinator estoit.
Ce fu cil qui mix se viestoit,
Et qui se savoit mix avoir.
Cil ert garnis de grant savoir;
3465 El mont n'estuet plus sage querre
Si n'a si biel en nule terre.
Devant le dame a fait le jor
Mainte estampie et maint trestor;[291]
Il vait avant et puis retorne.
3470 L'empereïs voit un poi morne,
Tout autrement veoir le seut;
Pitié en a et si s'en deut;
Pense, se Dix garist son cors,

Qu'il le metra del pensé fors.
3475 Si fera il ains qu'il anuite;
Mais il le metra en tel luite,
Et lui et li proçainement, [d]
Dont il seront andoi dolent.
Paridés est de grant vaillance,
3480 Et bien pert a se contenance
Qu'il est de rice liu issus;
D'uns dras de soie a or tissus
S'estoit molt bien vestus a las;
Gent a le cors, bien fais les bras,
3485 Les ix a biax, le vis traitis,
Canqu'a sor lui a bien faitis:
Caveus a biax, recercelés,
Bien fais est molt et bien molés.
Paridés est molt avenans,
3490 De biauté rice et bien seans.
Devant le dame vait et vient
Et canqu'il fait molt li avient.
La dame esgarde et ele lui,
En un pensé cïent andui:
3495 Il pense que bons nés seroit
Qui cele dame adiés aroit,
Et quant entre ses dens l'a dit,
Si se deut molt que ainc le vit.
Pense: «Ci aroit mal couvent
3500 Se je estoie prés souvent,
Quant por li veïr une fois
En sui si durement destrois.
Mais quel destrece i doit avoir?
Folie ai dit et non savoir.
3505 Onques n'amai, ce sai je bien,
Mais de cesti ne m'est il rien;
Je sui ci venus por danchier,
Non por folie commencier!
Par ceus qui sont d'amor soupris

[290] Cathais].
[291] mant t.].

These competitions were impressive and entertaining. The most agile amongst the young men were not interested in making music, preferring to play ball games. Whoever ran fastest won the prize, for such were the rules of the game. And when they heard the news that the beautiful empress Athanaïs was coming, they went to greet her with their instruments, welcoming her joyfully. They met the empress just before she entered the street in which the great games were taking place. **3450** The commotion around her was deafening; she was surrounded by people all carrying instruments, and not a single one of them was so lowly as not to be from a noble, aristocratic family. The higher their status the closer they approached the empress, dancing and leaping as they went. The very best looking and handsomest of all the young noblemen had been playing his harp there throughout the day. His name was Paridés and he was a senator's son. He was the best dressed of them all and the one who behaved most courteously. He was blessed with great ability; there was no need to look any further on earth for a cleverer man, nor was there a more handsome one in any country. That day he performed in front of the lady many a vigorous dance and many a complicated move. He went back and forth. He noticed that the empress was a little subdued, yet he was used to seeing her otherwise; he pitied her and was upset for her, thinking to himself that with God's protection, he would make her forget what was preoccupying her; **3475** and indeed he did do so before nightfall, but subsequently created for her and himself a huge crisis, which made them both suffer. Paridés was very impressive and it was obvious from his appearance that he was of noble stock. He had laced himself into garments of silk cloth woven with gold. His body was handsome, his arms shapely, his eyes beautiful, his face was finely chiselled,[56] everything about him was attractive: he had beautiful, curly hair; he was very well-built and good-looking. Paridés was very handsome, rich in beauty and well-mannered. He went back and forth in front of the lady and whatever he did pleased her greatly. He looked at the lady and she looked at him, and they both arrived at the same conclusion: he thought that whoever were to possess this lady for ever would be fortunate indeed, and having admitted this quietly to himself, he deeply regretted ever seeing her, thinking: 'this would be a really bad situation for me if I were often in her presence, since seeing her just once has distressed me so deeply. **3503** But why should I be distressed? I have spoken foolishly not wisely. As I am well aware, I have never been in love, but this woman means nothing to me. I came here to dance, not to embark on an act of folly! I have often seen and learnt from those who have fallen madly in love

---

[56] Roques (1979, 174) suggests oval for *traitis* (l. 3485).

3510 Ai je bien veü et apris,
Qui aime, il est en male lime.»
Il dist molt bien a soi meïme
– Que ainques de mot n'i menti,
Ce saciés vos trestot de fi –
3515 Qu'il n'en a soing, mais ne li valt;
Dont tresque et bale et harpe et salt;
Il a les mains a l'estrument,   [e]
Ne mais li cuers n'i est nïent;
N'i a del cuer ne tant ne quant;
3520 Et se le dient li auquant²⁹²
Qu'on depart bien sen cuer en deus
Si l'envoie on en divers leus,
A ce c'on tient et a s'amie;
Mais qui çou fait, il n'aime mie.
3525 Amors n'a cure de lanchier
S'ele n'a tout le cuer entier,
Ne de cuer malvais a parchon,
C'Amors n'a cure de garçon.
Je sai c'on pense bien sor jor
3530 Souvent en el que en amor,
Une heure plus, une heure mains,
Qu'Amors alasque bien ses mains;
Car ele est france et debonaire,
Et amans a tel cose a faire²⁹³
3535 Qu'il ne poroit faire a nul fuer
S'il n'i avoit un poi del cuer,
Se ce n'estoit par grant usage.
Trestout son cuer et son corage²⁹⁴
A cil aillors qu'a l'estrument,
3540 Si harpe molt bien nequedent.
    Li dame durement se deut
Por le varlet, cui aime et velt,

Et pense: «Dix, quel creature!
Molt aroit millor aventure
3545 Qui de cestui seroit amee,
Que je, qui dame sui clamee
De ceste honor et de l'empire,
Qui vif en dolor et en ire.
Mais n'est pas vivres que je fas!
3550 Je m'ai sor cuer et si me has.
Je sui issi trop longement;
Oster m'en voel isnielement
S'il estre puet, et Dix m'en oie.
Mix valt un poi de bien a joie
3555 Que tous li mons et vivre en duel.
Il seroit autrement, mon voel.
Poi valt honors, poi valt riquece   [f]
Qui l'use a duel et a tristece;
Bien ait honeste povretés!
3560 Li vilains dist, s'est verités,
Que bien s'abaisse qui s'aaise;
Qui tous jors trait paine et mesaise,
Petit li valt se grans honors.
Cil qui aliege les dolours
3565 Me puist alegier hui me voie!
Quels max seroit se jou amoie
Cel biel varlet que je la voi?
– Nus, s'il t'amoit! – J'espoir, je croi,
Qu'il m'amera se il le set;
3570 Pechié fera se il me het.
– On n'aime pas, suer, bele amie,
De cuer tot ce c'on ne het mie;
Tel cose ne het on de rien
Cui on ne velt gaires de bien.
3575 Ne mais comment le saroit il

---

²⁹² li d.]BT.
²⁹³ E. amor]L (B: al mains; T: a maus).
²⁹⁴ Cascuns s. c.] BT.

that a lover finds himself in dire straits.' Then he told himself – and rest assured, he never lied[57] – that he was not interested in love, but all to no avail; so he performed various dances, played his harp and leapt in the air. His hands were on his instrument but his heart was not in it at all; not even a tiny part of his heart was in it. Yet some say that one can easily split one's heart into two and send each part off to different places, to what one is concentrating on at the time and to one's beloved, but whoever does this is not really in love! **3525** Love is not interested in shooting her arrow if she does not have the whole heart;[58] nor does she take any part of a vile heart, since Love is not interested in those who are inconstant. I know that during the day one often thinks of things other than love, because Love loosens her grip for long or short periods. For she is noble and generous, and lovers have things to do that they would not be able to accomplish in any way if they did not have a small part of their heart in it, unless they were functioning out of pure habit. Paridés's whole heart and mind were focused on matters other than his instrument, but he nevertheless played very well.

The lady was deeply distressed on account of the young man, whom she loved and desired. She thought to herself: 'Goodness me, what a creature! If a woman were loved by this man, she would be much more fortunate than I am, even though I am called mistress of this land[59] and empire. For I am living in pain and sorrow. But what I am doing is not living! **3550** I am annoyed with myself and hate myself. I have put up with this life for too long and I want to escape from it forthwith, if it is possible and God hears my prayer. It is better to have a few possessions and be happy than to possess the whole world and live unhappily; if I had my way, things would be different. Land and riches are worth little if they are accompanied by distress and sadness; honest poverty is far preferable! There is much truth in the rustic proverb that says that a life of luxury only leads to misfortune.[60] High status is worth little to the person who endures constant suffering and wretchedness. May He who relieves all suffering make my path easier today. What harm would it do if I were to love this handsome youth whom I see here? – None, if he returned your love.[61] – I hope, indeed I believe that he will love me once he knows. He will commit a sin if he hates me. – Sister, dear friend, we do not necessarily love wholeheartedly everything that we do not hate; nor do we have an ounce of hatred for something just because we barely wish it well. **3575** Yet, how would he know

---

[57] Although Gautier is probably stresssing Paridés's probity here, he may be making a veracity claim for himself, hence: 'I have not spoken a single untruth about this'.
[58] See my Introduction, pp. xiv-xv for a discussion of this passage and the variants to l. 3525.
[59] In ll. 3547 and 3557 *honor* can mean both land and the honour attached to it.
[60] See the variant of *Proverbes français* 2118 'Qui s'abesse sesaise'.
[61] Here and elsewhere in the lovers' monologues the speaker appears to split in two, Gautier employing this internal dialogue to convey the conflict within the protagonists between desire and reason or conscience.

Quant tu l'esgardes entre mil?
Nel pués esgarder si ne si[295]
Que tu n'esgardes autressi[296]
Trestos les autres qui i sont.
3580 Ti oeul vienent a lui et vont,
Et as autres tout ensement;
De cel meïme entendement
Que il i avra par esgart,[297]
Aront li autre tuit lor part,
3585 Si cuidera n'i a celui[298]
Que li esgars soit fais por lui.
– Si le ferai je voirement,
Ensi que le verront la gent,[299]
Si n'i penseront el que bien
3590 Ne ne les douterai de rien.
– Se tu l'esgardes tant ne quant
Plus que les autres, li auquant
S'en apercevront, puet cel estre.[300]
– Bien me covient garder mon estre.[301]
3595 – L'apercevront, ne puet müer,[302]
Chi ne fait mie bon jüer!
– Lasse! or ne sai dont que je
 face.   [142 a]
S'il, ains qu'il tort de ceste place,
Ne s'en aperçoit, morte sui.
3600 Et Dix me giet de cest anui!
Mais ce m'aliege me dolor
Qu'il n'i a nul de se valor,
N'i a nul fors lui seulement
Qui ait an lui tel hardement
3605 Qu'il une fois pensast a moi.

Il a molt plus de bien en soi
Que nus de canque jou en voie,
Si ert plus tost mis en le voie
C'uns hom de bas cuer ne seroit[303]
3610 Qui a çou penser n'oseroit;
Car cascuns pense tant en haut
Selonc içou qu'il set et valt.[304]
A! Paridés, biele faiture,
Je cuiç vous veés m'aventure;
3615 Vous le savés, si est bien drois,
Con mes cuers est por vous destrois,
Con il va por vos tressaillant.
Nos dui somes li plus vaillant
De tous, de petis et de grans.
3620 Ja ot on parler deus enfans
Que nus n'i entent fors jenglois
Ne que s'il estoit en englois,
Et li enfant ne dient rien
Que l'uns n'entende l'autre bien[305]
3625 Por ce qu'il sont d'une maniere;
Dont doit bien connoistre a ma ciere
Mes dous amis con il m'estait.
S'il ne me giete de cest plait,
Jamais n'arai force n'aïe;
3630 Amors m'a griement envaïe.
– Ma biele suer, car te castie!
Tel cose i puet avoir bastie
Dont tu aprés aras contraire;
Entreusque tu t'en pués retraire,
3635 Car t'en retrai, ma douce suer.
– Je ne poroie por nul fuer.

---
[295] puet]BT.
[296] m'e.]BT.
[297] Que se il laura]B.
[298] ait c.]BT.
[299] Si]H.
[300] aperceveront pue c.]R.
[301] B. ne c.]R.
[302] Il l.]T.

[303] feroit]BT.
[304] sert]L (B: pense; *couplet absent from* T).
[305] Q. nus]B.

since you look at him along with a thousand others? You cannot look at him however much you try without looking at all the others who are present at the same time. Your gaze lands on him and then wanders off just as it does with the others. All the others will place the very same interpretation on your gaze as he will and there will not be anyone who does not think that your eyes are for him only. – I assure you, I shall do it in such a way that everyone will see it, and yet they will not consider it to be anything but innocent, and I shall have nothing to fear from them. – If you look at him even slightly more than at the others, it is possible that some will notice. – I'll have to take great care then. – They cannot help but notice; this is not a game you should be playing. – Woe is me, then I don't know what to do. If he does not notice before he leaves here, I shall die. **3600** May God deliver me from this suffering. But the fact that none equals him in worth alleviates my pain; none apart from him possesses the courage to give me a single thought. He possesses more virtue than any of those I can see here and will be quicker to embark on this adventure than a man with an ignoble heart would be, who would not dare to contemplate this; for the more ability and worth a man has, the higher he aspires. Oh Paridés, beautiful creature, I think you can see what is happening to me; you know (and it is only right) how my heart is suffering because of you, how it keeps on missing a beat on account of you. We two are the most worthy of all, of the humble and the powerful. Two children have been known to talk together, whose babble is incomprehensible to everyone else, just as if they were speaking English, yet the children say nothing which cannot be perfectly understood by the other, for they are from the same mould. **3626** So my sweet friend should be able to tell easily from the expression on my face how I am faring. If he does not deliver me from this predicament, I shall never find the strength nor any help elsewhere. Love has violently invaded my heart. – My dear sister, restrain yourself. You could get yourself into a situation here which you will later have cause to regret. While you still have time to retreat, retreat, sweet sister. – I could not for any price.

– Damage i poras dont avoir! [b]
– U face folie u savoir,
Si voel je qu'il soit mes amis,
3640 Car c'est li miudres du païs.
– Et toi qu'en caut, se il est bons?
Ja ne puet il pas estre tons.[306]
– Ce poise moi qu'il ne puet estre.
– Suer, douce amie, par me destre,
3645 Tu vels tel cose commenchier
Dont tu feras a toi tenchier.
Athanaïs, c'or te porpense
Con estoit povre te despense
Quant cil t'esliut a tele honor
3650 Qui te tenoit a le millor
Qui lores fust en tout le monde;
Ne puet müer ne le confonde
Li emperere, s'il le set.
– Il avra tort se il le het,
3655 Car li miudre ere en cel termine[307]
Qui onques jor usast hermine,
Et fusse encor s'il me leüst,
Se il enclose ne m'eüst.
– Atanaïs, bontés que vaut
3660 Qui ains jor et ains heure faut?
Encor n'est pas li lune plaine.
Qui bien fait toute le semaine,
Por coi le pert il por une heure?
– Si m'aït Amors et seceure,
3665 Grans prouece est d'amor cachier,
De li aquerre et pourcachier;
Grans cose est molt del i venir
Et molt plus grans del retenir.
– Dame qui a fol u felon
3670 Se garde prent a son baron,
S'onnor pert toute et s'onnesté.
Se tu as preudefeme esté...
– Je pert m'onor, mais n'en puis mais.
– Si pués. – Comment? – Esta em pais.
3675 – Je nel puis trover en mon cuer.
– Dont ne puet remaindre a nul fuer
Que tu ne faces mesproison. [c]
Qui ne tient son cuer en prison,
Son cors aville et son parage.
3680 Ne croire pas ton fol corage,
Destrain ton cuer et bat et lie.
– Et comment? Se je faiç folie,
Je ne sui pas li premeraine,[308]
Ne ne serai li daeraine;
3685 Mainte a pis fait. – Et toi qu'en calt?
Autrui malisces que te valt?
Por ce n'est pas dols li aisius[309]
Que li fix est amers et vieus,
Ne por ce bons uns petis maus
3690 Que li graindre est si desloiaus;
Ja autrui peciés n'ert tant grans
Que au tien petit soit garans;
Ja t'ame n'en ert alaskie.[310]
– M'ame en aroit a tort haschie,[311]
3695 Car assés en traira li cors
Ains que mes cuers en soit desmors
De ce dont je cuiç estre morte
Se fine amors ne me conforte;
M'ame en aroit a tort contraire,
3700 C'assés en convient le cors traire.
– Seur, tes n'a onques se mal non
Dont l'ame est a perdission;

---

[306] Ja ne pas e. t.; A *hypometric, omits* puet il] B.
[307] ert; B]T.
[308] fui]BT.
[309] dels si]B.
[310] t. enen e.].
[311] haistie]BT.

– Then you may well suffer for it! – Whether this is foolish or sensible, I want him to be my beloved, for he is the best man in the country. – And if he is a good man, what is it to you? He can never be yours. – I am very upset that he cannot be mine. – Sister, sweet friend, by my right hand, you are intent on starting something which will only win you reproach. Athanaïs, reflect carefully on how poor your resources were when the man who considered you to be the best woman in the world at that time chose you for such an honour; **3652** it would not be possible to stop the emperor from ruining him if he knew.[62] – He will do wrong if he hates him, for at that time I was the best woman who had ever worn ermine and I would still be the best if I had been allowed to be and he had not locked me up. – Athanaïs, what good is virtue if it fails for as much as a day or even an hour? The moon is not yet full. Why on earth should a person who behaves well throughout the week risk everything for a single hour? – May Love help and protect me, it is a very brave thing to pursue love and to strive to win it; it is an impressive thing to obtain love and even more so to retain it. – A lady who, even if she is married to a fool or a traitor, refuses the protection of her husband loses all honour and respectability. If you have been a good wife... – I am going to lose my honour, but I cannot do otherwise. – Yes you can – How? – Calm down. – **3675** I can find no calm in my heart. – Then you cannot avoid making a big mistake, whatever the cost. Whoever cannot control their heart dishonours their body and their whole family. Do not heed your foolish inclinations, restrain, admonish and fetter your heart. – But how? If I act in madness I shall not be the first woman nor the last to do so; many have done worse. – And what's that to you? What difference does another's wrong-doing make to you? Just because bile is bitter and vile it does not make vinegar sweet, nor does a small misdemeanour become a good deed because a greater crime is so heinous. Never will another's crime be great enough to redeem your small fault; your soul will not gain relief from it. – My soul would not deserve to suffer torment for it, since my body will endure a great deal before my heart stops being tortured by the thing that I believe will cause my death if true love doesn't console me; my soul would not deserve to suffer, for my body will need to endure a great deal. **3701** – Sister, a person whose soul is damned never experiences anything but suffering;

---

[62] The man in question is, of course, Eracle.

Ne vois tu l'userier aver,
Qui au couchier et au lever,
3705 Est en dolor et en torment?
S'ame est perdue nekedent.
– De lui est drois, car Avarisse
Le hurte tost jus et anthice
Qu'il soit vilains, qu'il soit engrés;
3710 Mais cui Amors tient asés prés,
Orguel li taut et felounie[312]
Et fausseté et vilonie,[313]
Et si l'estruit de grant largece,
De cortoisie et de prouece;
3715 Et s'en amor a un mesfait,
Ces coses font vers Diu bon plait,
Qu'il aime honor et cortoisie[314]   [d]
Et fine Larguece est s'amie.
Or amerai, si serai large,
3720 Car Amors fine le m'encarge
Que je le soie, et jel serai,
Et sor içou si aquerrai.»
    La dame se demente issi,
Et Paridés tout autressi;
3725 Atanaïs se deut forment,
Et Paridés tout ensement;
D'un mal se sentent ambedui.
Il la regarde et ele lui;[315]
Le jor i font maint douç regart
3730 Et il et ele d'autre part;
Bien s'en fussent apercëu,
Mais ne s'erent entrevëu
Quatre ans devant, mien ensïent.
Il set tres bien et si entent
3735 Qu'ele l'esgarde en maint endroit;

Il pense puis : «Et s'a grant droit
S'ele m'esgarde en tel maniere,
Que devant tous port le baniere
De bien saillir, de bien harper.[316]
3740 En ceste place n'a son per
Me harpe, si est bone, eslite;
Ele l'entent, se s'i delite.
Onques selonc m'entention
Ne m'esgarda se por ce non.
3745 – Si est, espoir, por tes biaus iex.
– Or esce folie et orgiex
Quant tu cuides ne ne cuidas
Que fust por toi! – Je ne cuiç pas;
Ainc ne cuidai que fust por moi.[317]
3750 – Esta en toi! – Que dis «en toi»?[318]
Las! je ne puis en moi ester;
Mes cuers ne se velt arester,
Ains m'a relenqui des hui main,
Et si m'a mis en autrui main;
3755 En si haut liu s'est adonés[319]
Que ja n'en ert guerredonés,
Car qui n'a soig de povre don   [e]
N'en rent merci ne guerredon.
Las! je ne puis nul bien atendre.
3760 S'ele pooit neïs entendre[320]
Que l'amasse, ele m'ociroit;
Voir, mais ocirre me feroit:
Ele ne me tient pas si cier
Qu'ele daignast a moi touchier.
3765 Ice me seroit grans confors
Se je por li estoie mors;
Molt le vauroie bonement,
Fors por son pecié seulement.

---

[312] orgues]BT.
[313] faussetes]BT.
[314] aine]BT.
[315] regarda]BT.
[316] Ne]BT.
[317] A. en cuida]L.
[318] E. ent dont]BT.
[319] haus]BT.
[320] nul bien e.]BT.

have you not seen the avaricious money-lender, who is in pain and torment both on going to bed and getting up? His soul is nevertheless damned. – He deserves it, for Avarice soon casts him down[63] and incites him to be vile and wicked; but when Love chooses someone as her companion she removes from him all pride, treachery, dishonesty and wickedness, and teaches him great generosity, courtesy and nobility; and if under the influence of love one makes a mistake, God easily forgives such things, for He loves honour and courtesy, and pure generosity is His beloved. So I shall love and I shall be generous, for true love obliges me to be so, and so I shall be, and on this basis I shall reap my reward.'

The lady lamented thus and Paridés did likewise. **3725** Athanaïs suffered great distress and so did Paridés; they both experienced the same malady. He looked at her and she looked at him; that day both of them exchanged many a sweet glance. They would have noticed each other earlier, but they had not seen each other for the past four years, from what I can gather. He became well aware and realised that she was watching him wherever he went; then he thought to himself: 'It is quite right that she should watch me in this way, for I am the champion when it comes to jumping and playing the harp. In this competition my harp knows no equal, for it is excellent and of superior quality. She takes great pleasure in listening to it. As far as I can tell, this is the only reason why she was watching me. – Perhaps it's because of your good looks? – What folly and pride if you think or thought that it was because of you! – I do not think, nor did I ever think that it was because of me. – **3750** Calm down! – What do you mean, calm down? Alas, I cannot calm down, my heart will not stay put. In fact, it abandoned me this morning and placed me in another's hands; it has taken itself off to such a high place that it will never receive its desired reward; for whoever scorns a poor gift never gives thanks or a reward for it. Alas, I can expect no good to come from this. Even if she could be made to realise that I love her, she would kill me; or to tell the truth, she would have me killed. She does not consider me worthy enough to deign even to touch me. It would be a great comfort to me if I were to die because of her; I would eagerly wish for this, if it did not make a sinner of her.[64]

---

63   This may be a reference to those cast down by the wheel of fortune.
64   As Athanaïs would have killed Paridés, she would be a sinner.

Bien sai que morir me couvient;
3770 Ne va pas vuis qui ce soustient
Que j'ai tres orains encargié;
Molt par a chi greveus marchié.
Con sui malbaillis en poi d'eure!
Le nuis me tardë et demeure
3775 Comme je puisse men duel plaindre
Et en plaignant mon cuer refraindre;
Car cil s'aliege et assouage
Qui ose plaindre son malage,
Et cil molt plus qui l'ose dire.
3780 Mais je me lairoie ains ocire
Que li dessisse me destrece.[321]
Mar vi onques si grant riquece,[322]
Mar vi onques si grant honor.
Con des pluisors font li pluisor,
3785 S'ele savoit ce con je pens,
Jel comperroie, al mien porpens;
Car feme est orgilleuse et fiere
Neïs vers cose qu'ele a ciere,
Et feme rice ensorquetout[323]
3790 A molt le cuer fier et estout;
N'a riens el mont mains puist soufrir,
Ne plus tost viegne a mesofrir,[324]
Ne plus tost die a home lait
Por assés petit de mesfait;
3795 Et s'ele fait a un folie,
A un autre dist estoutie,
Voiant gens, canses «Tels sui jou». [f]
Tout finement le fait por çou

a Qu'ele veut couvrir par cestui
b Tout canqu'ele fait por celui.»[325]
 Li feste est biele et molt plentive;
3800 Li ju sont biel, de mainte guise.
Li dame molt biel se contient,
Et tels en jue qui n'en tient:
C'est Paridés, li dous, li biaus,
Li flors des autres damoisiax.
3805 Molt par se tient a malbailli,
Et quant li ju sont tout failli,
Si s'en depart l'empereïs,
Et Paridés tous esmaris.[326]
Nus ne vos puet conter ne dire
3810 Con il sont dolant et plain d'ire
Que li solaus ne se demeure,
Et d'autre part si targe l'eure
Qu'il peüssent celeement
Plaindre lor duel et lor torment,
3815 Qui molt lor est pesme et mortex.
Molt tost en vienent as ostex,[327]
Mais ains n'i orent cele nuit
Bien ne repos ne nul deduit,
Ne ja ne cuident liu avoir[328]
3820 Qu'il peüssent faire savoir
L'uns d'eus a l'autre son voloir;
Ce est qui plus les fait doloir.
Les deus d'amors et les desirs,
Les consirers et les soupirs[329]
3825 Vous puet on largement estendre,
Mais nus hom ne puet plus entendre[330]

---

[321] desfisse]BT.
[322] destrece]BT.
[323] r. en ce que tout]BT.
[324] N p.].

[325] 3798a-b *absent from* A]B, except 3798a por]T.
[326] P. tout autressi]BT.
[327] ortex]BT; O, 3097: herberge *reflects* BT.
[328] Ne c., A *omits* ja ne]BT.
[329] Des desiriers]B.
[330] atendre]R (B: aprendre; T *omits* 3825-38).

3769 I know that I must to die. Anyone who carries the burden I took up not long ago does not carry a light load; this is a very onerous business indeed. What a mess I have got myself into in such a short time! In my impatience I cannot wait for nightfall when I shall be able to give vent to my grief and to calm down my heart with lamenting, for whoever dares to lament his malady soothes and alleviates his pain, and even more so if he dares to speak to his lady about it. But I would rather be killed than speak to her about my distress. What a pity I ever laid eyes on a woman of such power; what a pity I ever laid eyes on a woman of such status. Just as many people behave towards many others, so if she could read my thoughts, I think I would pay for it, for woman is proud and arrogant, even towards someone who is dear to her, and above all a powerful woman's heart is very proud and arrogant. There is no creature in the world who is less indulgent or more likely to resort to insults, or quick to say nasty things to a man who has committed a very small mistake indeed. And if she commits an indiscretion with one man, to another she will speak haughtily in public, saying: "that's the way I am". Thus she behaves very cleverly, because she uses one man to hide what she is doing for another.'

3799 The festivities were impressive and extensive; there was a wide variety of entertaining games. The lady behaved very courteously, but there was one participant who did not care much for the games: this was sweet fair Paridés, the flower of all the young men. He considered himself to be in a very sorry state, and when the games were over, the empress left and so did Paridés, all upset. It would be impossible for anyone to tell you or describe for you just how upset and angry they were that the sun did not linger, and yet they longed for the hour when they could secretly lament their suffering and torment, which was terrible and left them in mortal danger. They soon came to their lodgings, but that night they did not obtain any benefit, rest, or solace, nor did either of them expect ever to have the opportunity to inform the other of their desire – this is what upset them the most. **3823** The pangs, the desire, the thoughts and the sighs induced by love can be described at length, but, to tell the truth, no one can understand better

Que cil qui aime, al bien voir dit,[331]
Ne que li ciex qui ainc ne vit[332]
Puet bien entendre et aperçoivre
3830 Que li vermeus del vert dessoivre;[333]
Ne qu'il puet veoir ces colors,
Ne puet il veoir ces dolors[334]
Que fins amans trait nuit et jor
Tant que cascuns se deut d'amor;
3835 Car par oïr conter en conte
N'entent nus hom a qu'ele monte,
Et s'il l'entent, nel croit il mie, [143 a]
Se il n'est amis ou amie,
U s'il ançois ne l'a esté.
3840 En tout le plus lonc jor d'esté
Ne poroit on conter ne dire
De ces deus amans le martire.
      Atanaïs se plaint adés.[335]
Grant dolor maine Paridés;
3845 Se joie est tornee en decors;
Se il nen a proçain secors
Tout i morra, n'i a c'un tor,
Et cil et cele de le tor.
Grans est li deus, grans est li max;
3850 Assés est partis par ingaus;
Assés est partis ingaument
Fors d'une cose seulement:
Que Paridés adiés se plaint,[336]
Et en plaignant son duel refraint;
3855 De la dame est l'angosse graindre,
Qui tant ne quant ne s'ose plaindre,
Car entre tex gens est enclose
Qui en diroient tost tel cose
Qui molt li seroit a contraire

3860 De ce qu'enpensé a a faire;
Car as octaves velt aler,
Mais ce n'est mie por baler,
Ne por juer ne por treschier:
Le varlet qu'ele aime et tient chier
3865 I espoire molt bien veoir,
Por son grant duel faire asseoir;
Et puis dist: «Lasse! Mar le vi!
A il dont juré et plevi
Qu'il m'ocirra? – Oïl, espoir.
3870 – Et qu'en puet il? – Si puet, por voir;
Car il est biax et clers et gens,
Et si est flors de toutes gens.
Enfrains tu dont te loiauté
Por se valor, por se biauté?
3875 – Nenil, par Diu qui tout adrece,[337]
Ne por biauté ne por proece.
Ceste aventure n'avenist   [b]
S'on en destroit ne me tenist;
Se je fuisse ensi con je suel,
3880 Je me laissasse ains traire l'uel
Que je fesisse tel desroi.
Li oisillons qui ist del broi
Quant il est pris a le campaigne,
As autres oisiaus s'acompaigne
3885 Et quant il est entr'ex assis,
Si en conjot tels set ou sis,
Qu'en son vivant ne congorroit
Se pour cele ocoisons n'estoit[338]
Qu'il en a tant esté en sus;
3890 Si les en congot plus et plus.
Grans est li joie qu'il en fait;
Aussi fis jou tout entresait

---
[331] a. al voir a dit]BT.
[332] liex]R (B: hon).
[333] dessoiuere]B.
[334] docors]L (Line absent from B).
[335] Atanias].
[336] Et P.]BT.
[337] Ne il]B.
[338] Se cele o.]BT.

than those who love, no more than a blind man who has never seen can understand and perceive the difference between scarlet and green. Just as he cannot see these colours, so he cannot see the suffering endured by true lovers day and night for as long as each of them suffers for love; for no one can understand what it is like from hearing about it in a story, and if one hears about it, one does not believe it at all, unless one is a man or woman in love, or unless one has been one. Even the longest summer's day would not be long enough to describe and relate the suffering of these two martyrs to love.[65]

Athanaïs lamented all the time and Paridés suffered terribly. His joy was rapidly on the wane; if he did not receive help forthwith, he would give up the ghost completely, there was no other way out either for him or for the lady of the tower. Their distress was great; great was their pain; it was shared quite equally between them; **3851** it was shared quite equally except for one thing: that Paridés lamented constantly and the lamenting eased his pain, but the anguish of the lady was greater as she dared not lament in any way, for she was surrounded by people who would soon say something which would prevent her from doing what she had decided to do; for she wanted to return a week later, not to dance, to play nor to dance a *tresche*,[66] but she hoped very much to see the young man whom she loved and held in great affection, in order to relieve her deep distress. And then she said: 'Alas, what a pity I ever laid eyes on him. Has he sworn and pledged to kill me? – Yes, perhaps. – And is he capable of it? – He is, indeed, for he is handsome, bright and noble, and he is the flower of all humankind. Are you going to break your conjugal vows because of his worth and beauty? – **3875** No, by God who is the ultimate judge, neither because of his beauty nor his worth. This situation would not have arisen if I had not been kept locked up; if I had been allowed to continue as before, I would rather have had my eye put out than commit such a crime. The little bird which escapes from a limed trap after being caught with the aid of a bell rushes to join the other birds, and when it is sitting amongst them, it makes a fuss of six or seven of them, over which it would normally not have fussed at all had it not been for the fact that it had been separated from them for so long; therefore it makes more and more of a fuss of them. Their reunion is very joyful. I behaved in a similar manner

---

[65] According to the medieval measurement of time the length of a day was dependent on the season; cf. l. 5162.
[66] A *tresche* was a type of dance; cf. l. 3434.

Quant j'escapai de le prison.
3895 Nel tieng a nule mesproison
Se je regardai les dansiaus
Dont li regars me fu molt biax:
Je fui por ex en prison mise,
Onques por el n'i fui tramise.
Esté i ai sis mois entiers,
3900 Si esgardai molt volentiers;
Car feme et enfes font sovent
Le cose c'on plus lor desfent;
Le cose el mont qui lor valt pis[339]
Ce voelent faire et font toudis.
3905 Ce puis je bien dire por moi,
Et por mainte autre que je voi:
Je voel celui qui ne me velt;
Por ce me duel que ne se deut,[340]
Por ce me duel que il nel set[341]
3910 Se mes cuers l'aime u il le het.
Caitive, lasse en fin me clain
Quant il ne set comment je l'aim!
Molt par en ai le cuer amer
Qu'il ne set con jel puis amer;
3915 Il nel puet savoir par nul fuer,
Por ce ai molt amer le cuer.
Certes, a gré molt me venroit   [c]
Por ce qu'il seüst orendroit
La dolor que je senç por lui.»
3920 La dame set poi de celui:
Con se demaine por s'amor,
Com ert atains tant nuit et jor.
Il n'entendra a home né;
Molt l'a Amors griement pené,
3925 Ne dort ne boit ne ne mangüe;

Tressaut, seglout et si tressue.
«E! las! fait il, con mar i mui
En le feste anvel u je fui.
Tant mainte fois i ai alé,
3930 Tant mainte fois i ai balé
Et maintes fois i ai sailli
C'onques li cuers ne m'en failli
Sifaitement con il fist ore;
Et se li jus durast encore,
3935 Ne m'iroit pas si malement,
Que quant vient au departement,
Departir m'estuet de mon cuer.[342]
Ahi! ma biele douce suer,
Amors deüst avoir soupris
3940 Un vaillant home de haut pris,
Tel qui se peüst travillier
Et soi et autre consillier,
Consel doner et consel querre.
Qui al plus foible de le terre
3945 Estrive et tence, poi li vaut.[343]
Force et Pooirs doit tendre halt;
Qui un foible home abat et vaint,
Se honte acroist, s'onor estaint,[344]
Et mains en est cremus de tous,
3950 C'on pense, se cist fust estous
a   Et preus et de vaillance plains,
b   Que il n'i mesist ja les mains.[345]
Amors, n'iés pas bien porveüe,
Tu meïsmes t'iés deceüe.
Tu as et toi et moi traï,
Qu'il n'a el mont si esbaihi
3955 Ne voie en moi tot ton esfors.
Jamais nus hom poissans ne fors

---
[339] Le cole]BT.
[340] qui]BT.
[341] Por me d.]BT.
[342] a m. c.]BT.
[343] tente]B.
[344] h. abat]BT.
[345] 3950a-b *absent from* A]L *based on* BT, *but* B, 3950a: de valances; 3950b: il ne m.; T, 3950b: Et a telz gens mesist ses m.

when I escaped from my prison. I do not consider it a fault in me if I looked at the young men and derived great pleasure from the sight; it was because of them that I was incarcerated; I was sent here for no other reason. I have been here for a full six months, so I happily feasted my eyes on them; **3901** for women and children often do the thing which they are most forbidden to do. They are keen to do and always do the very thing which most harms their reputation.[67] This is certainly true of me and of many another woman whom I know: I want the man who does not want me; I am distressed because he is not distressed, I am distressed because he does not know if my heart loves him or hates him. In sum, I call myself a pitiable wretch since he does not know how much I love him. My heart is very bitter indeed, for he does not know how much I am capable of loving him.[68] There is no way of letting him know, this is why my heart is so bitter. I would certainly be very pleased indeed if he could be informed immediately of the pain I am suffering because of him.' The lady knew little about Paridés's situation: how he was faring because of his love for her, how he was afflicted both night and day. He would soon take no notice of any living creature. Love had made him suffer so grievously that he could not sleep, drink or eat; instead he shook, sobbed and was bathed in perspiration.

3927 'Alas,' he said, 'what a pity I ever went to the annual festival I have just attended. I have been there many a time, I have danced there many a time, and many a time I have leapt in the air there without my heart ever giving way as it did this time. And if the games were still continuing, I would not be faring as badly as I did when it came to leaving, for I had to leave my heart behind. Oh, my fair sweet sister, Love ought to have ambushed a worthy man of high renown, one who could endure suffering while looking after himself and others, offering and seeking advice and support. By attacking and picking a fight with the weakest man in the country one hardly improves one's reputation. Strength and power should aim high; whoever casts down and overpowers a weak man increases his own shame and extinguishes his honour, and he is less feared by everyone, for they think that if his victim had been bold, brave and full of courage, he would never have laid hands on him. **3953** Love, you are not very clever, you have deceived yourself. You have betrayed yourself and me, for no one alive is so troubled in his mind that he cannot see that you have attacked me with all your might. Never again will a powerful or strong man

---

[67] Here Gautier has Athanaïs herself express a commonplace of medieval misogyny.
[68] In this rhetorically sophisticated passage, Gautier puns on *amer* meaning 'to love' and 'bitter', see Pratt 2007a

Ne te cremra, nou doit il faire.³⁴⁶ [d]
Se tu fusses de haut afaire
Et tels con tu jadis estoies,
3960 Autrui que moi le mousterroies.
Tu me devroies bien laissier,
Et les cuers orgilleus plaissier
Qui toi ne daignent obeïr.
Se Damedix me puist tehir,
3965 Je ne voi dame ne princhier
De cui tu puisses riens pinchier;
N'en voi nul gesir contre lit;
Nus n'aime fors por son delit,
Nus n'aime mais fors quant il velt,
3970 Et s'en part quant un poi se deut;
Nus n'aime mais contre voloir.
Je n'en voi mais nului doloir
Fors seulement cest las caitif.
Amors, tu prens a moi estrif,
3975 A moi te prens con cil qui passe
Le soif illuec u plus est basse,
Qui par aillors passer ne puet.
Cest las caitif qui ne se muet
As en trois jors fait gaune et pale.
3980 Amors, ainc mais ne fus si male,
Mais molt est gaune te tainture;
Amors, tu ses molt de painture,
Tu en as si mon cuer vestu
Que je ne pris mais un festu
3985 Force n'aïe ne savoir
Que je par toi peüsse avoir,³⁴⁷
Trestout seroit contre mon pois;
Uns autres m'aidera ançois,
Qui toutes gens tormente et grieve,
3990 Et qui toutes dolors achieve,³⁴⁸

Çou est li mors, qui metra terme
A me dolor, a mainte lerme
Que j'ai plouree des tierç jor.
Par toi n'atent je nul sejor³⁴⁹
3995 Que tu me puisses aplaidier,
Car tels nuist qui ne puet aidier.»
  Paridés est pales et tains [e]
Et iert ains tierç jor si atains
C'on n'i atent se l'eure non.
4000 Mar vit le dame del doignon.
Grans est li deus qu'en fait se mere,
Et regrete souvent son pere,
Qui est avoec l'empereor.
De lui ont tout molt grant paor;³⁵⁰
4005 Pleurent cousines et cousin,
Pleurent voisines et voisin,
Que il ne fu ainc cose nee
Si biele el mont ne tant senee,
N'onques encor ne fu en vie
4010 Riens nule de se cortoisie.
  Pres del palais son pere avoit³⁵¹
Une vielle qui molt savoit
De molt de riens dont mainte gent
Ont oeus et mestier molt sovent.
4015 Li vielle durement l'amot;
Se li fu conté mot a mot
Qu'il n'i a d'el que metre en l'aire
Le biel varlet, le debonaire.³⁵²
Li vielle vient a lui en haste,
4020 Son bras saisist, son pous portaste,
Ne sent rien qui mort li pormete,
Ne qui en nul esfroi le mete.
Li vielle est molt voiseuse et sage;
Regarde celui el visage,

---

346 Ne tenra n.]B.
347 A *omits* je]BT.
348 dolor].
349 nus]BT.
350 paror].
351 pais]BT; O, 3181: palas *reflects* BT.
352 debonaine].

fear you, nor should he. If you were at the height of your powers, as you used to be, you would prove it on someone other than myself. You ought to leave me alone and force into submission arrogant hearts, who refuse to obey you. If God is my strength, I cannot see any lady or prince whom you could force into giving you anything; nor can I see a single one of them taking to their beds; no one loves except for their own pleasure; no one loves nowadays except when they choose to and they abandon love when they start to suffer. No longer does anyone love against their will. I can no longer see anyone suffering, except for this weary wretch. **3974** Love, in picking a fight with me and attacking me you are behaving just like a man who jumps over a hedge at its lowest point, because he cannot get over it anywhere else. You have made this weary wretch, who cannot move, turn yellow and pale within three days. Love, never before were you so cruel, your paint is very yellow indeed. Love, you are an expert in painting, for you have coated my heart[69] in such a way that I care not a jot for any support or knowledge I might obtain through you; this would all be against my wishes. Someone else will help me instead, someone who torments and hurts everyone, and puts an end to all pain – I mean death, who will put an end to my pain, to many a tear that I have shed in the last three days. I don't expect your intercession to obtain any respite for me, for whatever harms a person cannot then help them.'

Paridés was pale and wan, and had been so sick for the preceding three days that everyone expected his final hour to be nigh. **4000** What a pity he ever saw the lady in the castle keep. His mother was deeply upset by the situation and often regretted his father's absence, for he was with the emperor. Everyone feared for him greatly; his male and female cousins wept, his neighbours, male and female, also wept, for there had never before been such a beautiful and intelligent creature born into the world, nor was there anyone still alive who equalled him in courtesy.

Near his father's palace there lived an old woman who knew a lot about a whole range of things which many people often wanted and needed to know. The old woman loved him dearly, and she was told in no uncertain terms that there was nothing for it but to bury the handsome, well-born young man in the ground. The old woman rushed to see him, grabbed his arm and tested his pulse. She could not feel anything that indicated that his death was imminent or that should cause her any alarm. The old woman was very clever and wise; she looked at his face

---

[69] The *B* reading *pointure* may be a graphy for *peinture* or may mean 'stitching', in which case the metaphor in *B* would refer to the dyeing and sewing of garments rather than to painting. A similar metaphor is used in *Ille et Galeron*, 6262-73, in which the tunic stitched by love is described: 'Fist les coustures et les pointes' (6268).

4025 Et sel voit molt descoulouré;
Bien s'aperçoit qu'il a plouré,
Et cil qui de le mort est prés
N'est pas de plourer molt engrés,
C'assés li livre on autre entente;
4030 Et cil pleure et se demente[353]
Qui ne puet faire tant n'ovrer
Que il son bon puist recouvrer.[354]
Par juner et par travillier,
Et par sifaitement villier,
4035 Et par plourer de tel dolour
Mue on souventes fois coulour,[355]
Tel come cil ou autretel.[356] [f]
Li vielle set molt d'un et d'el;
Voit de celui et aperçoit
4040 Que ses corages le deçoit;
Si l'aparole cointement,
Entr'eus deus, molt priveement:
«Amis, fait ele, j'aim et voeul
Vostre grant bien, et faire suel,
4045 Car li vostre m'ont maint bien fait;
Ne mais je voel tout entresait
Que ceste me soit amendee,
Que ne m'avés pieça mandee,
Por vostre preu, non por le mien.
4050 Se c'estoit neïs por mon bien.[357]
Mais a envis aliege autrui
Cil qui de gré se fait anui;
Ja d'autrui preu n'ert covoitex
Qui du sien faire est pereceus.
4055 Qui a nului ne se conselle,
Se il i pert, n'est pas mervelle;
Et certes, qui ne croit nului

N'est mie drois c'on croie lui.
Mais vos estes de jovene eage;
4060 Itel devroient estre sage
Qui ne font pas que faire doivent,
Ains se honissent et deçoivent.
De riens nule ne m'esmervel
Se jovenes hom ne quiert consel;
4065 Se seulement il bien le croit,
Bon guerredon avoir en doit;
Mais c'est folie plus k'enfance
Se il ne dist se mescaance
C'on li demande por son bien;
4070 Car teus ne feroit por lui rien[358]
Qui fait par autrui sa besongne,
Et fos est qui del bien s'eslonge,[359]
Et teus hom n'est gaires apers;
S'uns consaus li est descouvers
4075 Dont grans biens porroit avenir,
Si ne se doit nus trop tenir
De ce dont ses amis li quiert, [144a]
Que ja nus consilliés nen iert
Se on ne connoist se destrece.
4080 Folie, enfance et grans perece[360]
Est del celer, et sens del dire.
Bons amis est en liu de mire,
Qui nul malage n'assouage
S'il ains ne connoist son damage.
4085 Qui a son ami se descuevre,
U il par son consel recuevre,
U ses amis viax le castie,
S'il voit qu'il entende a folie.
Qui amis a, molt en valt plus;
4090 Par amis vient on au dessus.

---

[353] Et cil est pres qui se dementente]T (B: Ne mais il plaint et se d.).
[354] so b.].
[355] Mu on; BT]L.
[356] T. con cil a ou a.; T]B.
[357] S ce estoit].
[358] *Scribal confusion over* por/par.
[359] 4071-72 Qui par autrui besoigne bien/ Ice sa ge sans fausser rien]B (T's *reading is similar to* B).
[360] prouece]BT.

and noticed that he was very pale; **4026** it was obvious to her that he had been weeping, yet a man close to death is not inclined to weep, for he is given plenty of other things to worry about; and it is the man who, despite his best efforts, fails to obtain his heart's desire who weeps and goes mad with grief. One often produces changes in one's complexion by fasting, getting upset, not being able to sleep and by weeping over a painful subject, as in the case of Paridés and others like him. The old woman knew a thing or two, and in his case she saw and noticed that he was losing heart, so she spoke to him tactfully and privately, when they were alone together: 'My friend,' she said, 'as usual I have your best interests at heart, for your family has done a lot for me. Nevertheless, I insist that you compensate me for the fact that you have not called on me for a long time, to your benefit, not mine. **4050** Even though I might have benefited too. But whoever willingly harms himself is reluctant to comfort another; he will never be eager to benefit another if he is slow to obtain his own. It is no wonder that whoever refuses to ask for help loses out, and indeed whoever cannot trust anyone else deserves not to be trusted himself. But you are young in years; those who do not do what they should and instead shame and delude themselves ought to be wiser. I am not at all surprised if a young man does not seek advice; if he by himself considers a course of action to be right, he should reap the benefits from it. However, it is a sign of folly more than inexperience if he does not reveal his misfortune to whoever enquires about it in his interests. For such a man would not be able to do anything to help himself, yet he would get the job done by someone else; so he is a fool if he shies away from his own good, and such a man is not clever. If someone reveals to him a course of action which could solve his problems, then no one should hold back too long from doing what his friend asks of him, for no one can ever be helped if the cause of his distress is not made known. **4080** It is foolish, childish and very cowardly to remain silent and wise to speak out. A good friend is like a doctor who cannot cure an illness until he knows what the symptoms are. Whoever opens up to his friend will either be helped by his advice, or at the very least his friend will admonish him if he sees that he is intent on folly. If someone has a friend, he is so much the richer; success is guaranteed with the help of friends.

En bon ami a bon tresor;
Bons amis valt bien son pois d'or;
Et se je sui vo bone amie,
Si ne me devés celer mie
4095 Riens nule dont je vos enquier.
Mais dites moi, je vos requier,
Dont vient cis max premierement;
Dites moi le commencement.
Vostre santés n'est mie loing,
4100 Enclose l'ai ci en mon poing.
– Dont avés vos me mort enclose,
Car me santés n'est autre cose.
Le mort demant, morir m'estuet,[361]
Riens nule autre aidier ne me puet.
4105 – Biax dous amis, se Dix me voie,
Ne morrés pas a ceste voie.
A vos paroles, par verté,
Qui ne connoit vostre enferté?[362]
Et je seroie en fin traïe,
4110 Se por soufraite de m'aïe
Moriés issi faitierement.
Soiiés de bon afaitement,
Si vivés encore avoec nous,
Et uns vilains muire por vous,
4115 U doi u troi, s'il est mestiers,
Que por quarante et deus sestiers
De bons deniers, al voir jehir,   [b]
Ne me lairoie je morir,
Qui sui mais vielle piaucelue.
4120 Mais Desperance vos salue
Et Malvaistiés fine et Perece,
Car eles cuident que Prouece
Ne soit mais par vos regardee.[363]

Je vauroie estre mix lardee
4125 Que teus viutés en fust creüe!
Trop avés grant cose acreüe
Por estre mais en lor dangier.[364]
Vous deüssiés un poi mangier,
Por vostre mere rehaitier;
4130 Vous li meüstes tel plait ier,
Dont anemis vos dut deçoivre,
Que ele en dut le mort reçoivre;
Pres ne s'en fu desgeünee.
De gent i ot grant aünee,
4135 N'i ot celi n'i acourust
C'on cuida bien qu'ele morust.
Ocirre volés deus ensanle?
Est ce savoirs? Que vos en sanle?
Il nen a tant vil garce en Rome,
4140 S'ele veoit un bien haut home[365]
Languir por li en tel maniere,
Ne devenist estoute et fiere;
Feme est tos jors de tel tesmoing
Que mix li vient plus en est loing,
4145 Por qu'il n'i soit bien acointiés;
Et teus i est bien empointiés
Qui s'en reboute bien arriere[366]
Por dolouser en tel maniere.
A feme n'est pas de grant pris
4150 Hom, puis que trop en est soupris,
Mais celui aime, celui prise
Qui l'assouplist, qui l'a souprise.[367]
Jel di por moi, qui feme sui;
Ja ai je fait maint home anui
4155 Quant je estoie jovene touse;
Je n'amaisse home por Toulouse,

---

361 mor d.].
362 Quil n. c. v. fierte]R (B: Molt bien counois v. enfrete; T: Connois bien v. enfermete).
363 por v.]BT.

364 P. e. preus e.]B.
365 veot].
366 Q. de se bouce bee a.]T (B: Qui se deboute b. a.).
367 Q. las soupris] (B: Ki la sousduit; T: Qui l'a souspies; H: Qui la souprist).

A good friend is a real treasure; a good friend is worth his weight in gold; and if I am your good friend, then you should not conceal from me anything I might ask you about. But pray, tell me how this illness began. Describe its origins to me. Your recovery is not far off, for I have it here within my grasp. **4101** – Then you are holding my death in your hands, for my recovery is synonymous with it. I insist on death, I must die, nothing else can help me. – Fair sweet friend, as God is my witness, you will not die on this occasion. To tell the truth, who would not be able to diagnose your illness from what you say? And I would come to a sticky end if you were to die in this way for want of my help. Behave as your noble status requires by continuing to live with us, and let a low-born ruffian die instead of you, or two or three if necessary, for, to tell the truth, I would not allow myself to die for forty-two pounds weight of good coins and I am just an old bag of bones. But Despair has come out to greet you, and pure Cowardice and Lassitude too, for they think that Nobility is no longer respected by you. **4124** I would prefer to be burned alive than allow such vile things to be believed! You have built up too impressive a reputation to be in their power any longer. You ought to eat a little to cheer up your mother; you must have been possessed by the devil yesterday when you gave her such a fright that she nearly met her death; she almost breakfasted on it. Large crowds of people gathered, everyone came rushing in because they really thought she would die. Are you trying to kill both of you? Is that sensible? What do you think? Even the most lowly-born girl in Rome would become haughty and proud if she saw a man of very high rank languishing for her in such a way. Woman is always reputed to be more interested in a man who keeps his distance, thus preventing great familiarity; and there are those men who, having enjoyed initial success with her, suffer a considerable setback if they pine in this way. **4149** Men who are too besotted are not respected by women; women love and esteem those who, having made them fall in love, have the upper hand. I know because I am a woman; I have in the past caused many men pain, when I was a young wench; I would not have loved a man for all the wealth of Toulouse

Por qu'il m'amast, ains l'amusoie, [c]
Ne mais du sien tos jors prendoie;
A ceus le donoie a droiture
4160 Qui de m'amor n'avoient cure;
Si ne valoie pas granment.
Cele vaut mix que mil et cent
U vostre cuers tent si et tire,
Et s'ele savoit cest martire,
4165 Orguel demenroit et fierté.
Feme velt c'on l'ait en cierté,
Mais par mesure l'encierisse
Cil qui l'aime, qu'il n'en perisse.
Or vos esforciés un petit,
4170 Car, par cel Diu qui tos jors vit,
Il n'a en Rome damoisiele
Ne nule dame tant soit biele
Dont je n'abate bien l'orguel.
Il n'i a nule, se je voel,
4175 Que je ne face en mon diu croire;
Je parol bien d'el que d'estoire,
De patre nostre et d'evangile;
Tant sai de barat et de gile
Que vostres bons ert acomplis,
4180 Se c'ert nes li empereïs.»
Li varlés a cest mot se pame.
Lors cuide bien la vielle et asme
Que tant ait l'oevre demenee
Que le verté ait assenee.
4185 Mis a le varlet a raison,[368]
Quant il revint de pamison,
Et dist li: «Bien vos savés faindre!
Et je vous ferai la ataindre
U nus ne pot mais avenir.
4190 Mais or me laissiés covenir.

Je vos tienç molt a deceü
Que vos le m'avés tant teü.»
Cil voit celi de grans esfors,
Et pense qu'ensi est il mors,
4195 Et dist il: «Biele, il est ensi
Que morir m'estuet por celi
Que vos m'avés ici nomee. [d]
– Si soie je de Diu amee,
Biax dols amis, n'en morrés mie,
4200 S'aidier vos puet sifaite amie.
Mais or mangiés un petitet.»
Li vielle a tant dit au varlet
Qu'il li fait user un caudiel;
Ce met le mere en grant baudiel.[369]
4205 Celi aporte un mantiel bon,
Et se li done tant del son
Que rice en ert tout son vivant.
Or en pense d'ore en avant[370]
C'a ceste fois a bon loiier;
4210 Ce parra bien a son foiier.
Li vielle prent a souhaidier
Qu'ele puist celui bien aidier.
Aidier li puet boniement
Et en cest point meïmement:
4215 C'un cerisier ot fait enter,[371]
Dont ele soloit presenter
La dame un present cascun an,
Devant le feste Saint Jehan.
Or est li cherisiers meürs;
4220 Ce est, je cuiç, bien ses eürs.
Li vielle n'a pas cuer lanier;
L'endemain prent un biel panier;
Al plus bel qu'ele puet l'atorne,
Del fruit noviel i met a orne.

---

[368] Mis ai].
[369] Ce me].
[370] Or penst li viele d. *hypermetric*]B (T: Or penst la vielle de ma vie; L: Or penst ele).
[371] cerisie].

just because he loved me; instead I strung him along. However, I always took his money, and I gave it straight away to those who were not interested in my love; and yet I counted for little. The woman who so attracts your heart and draws it to her is worth more than eleven hundred of my kind and if she were aware of your suffering, she would treat you with pride and arrogance. A woman wants to be cherished, but whoever loves her must cherish her with moderation, so that she does not cause his ruin. Come on now, make a little effort, for by God the Everlasting, there is no maiden nor lady in Rome, however beautiful she may be, whose pride I cannot tame. **4174** If I put my mind to it, there is no woman whom I cannot persuade to believe in my god: and I am not talking about the God of Holy Scripture, the Lord's Prayer and the Gospels – I am such an expert in trickery and deception that you will have your heart's desire, even if it is the empress herself.'

The young man fainted when he heard these words. The old woman then realised and was convinced that she had gone about things in such a way that she had hit upon the truth. Once the young man had recovered from his swoon she spoke to him, saying: 'You are very good at dissimulation! I shall arrange for you to achieve what no one has ever managed before. But now leave it to me. I think you have been very ill-advised to keep this secret from me for so long.' He had great difficulty seeing her and thought that he was about to die, and he said: 'Fair lady, the situation is such that I must die for the lady whom you have just named. – For the love of God, fair sweet friend, you will not die at all if a friend such as myself can come to your aid. **4201** But for the time being, eat a little.' The old woman continued to speak to the young man until she convinced him to take some soup; this made his mother very happy. She fetched a good-quality cloak and gave the old woman enough money to make her very comfortable for the rest of her life. From that moment on she was of the opinion that she had been well paid on this occasion and it would make a visible difference to her home.

The old woman began to hope that she might be able to help Paridés. In fact, she could be of great help to him and in this particular that annually, just before the feast of St John, she always presented the empress with a gift of cherries from a grafted cherry tree she had planted. The cherry tree's fruit was now ripe, which was, in my view, lucky for her. The old woman was not faint-hearted; the next day she took a fine basket, decorated it as best she could and arranged the fresh fruit carefully in it.

4225 Quant ele ot fait tout son ator,
Si vait al postis de la tor;
Durement huce: «Laissiés me ens!»
Et li portiers n'est mie lens;
Le postiç a molt tost ouvert,
4230 Des fuelles voit le fruit covert.
Le vielle a molt bien conneüe,
Que maintes fois l'ot ains veüe;
Clost son postis, monte en l'estage,
La dame conte son message,
4235 Et li baron qui o li sont
Font venir cele vielle amont.
Tout ce li vient molt bien a gré;   [e]
Li vielle amonte maint degré
Ains qu'ele truist l'empereïs.
4240 La dame sist sor un tapis,
En sus des autres, auques loing;
De lor soc̈ïeté n'a soing,
Il ne li torne a nul delit.
Un livre tient et si i list.
4245 Li vielle vient molt tost amont
Et dist: «Cil Dix qui maint amont
Il saut ma dame et beneïe,
Et ceste siue compaignie!»
Devant la dame estant se met
4250 A genillons, si s'entremet
De parler d'el que de present.
Le fu atise durement,
Et si esgarde en sus del feu.
Por traire mix le cose a preu
4255 Mostre ses bras, mostre ses piés,
Qu'ele a mal vestus et cauchiés;
Oiant tos parole en tramblant;
Le voir cuevre de faus samblant.

Souavet dist: «Biele faiture,
4260 Me vie est ore en aventure
C'un message vos ai a dire,
Si crien que vos n'en aiiés ire;
Mais messagiers, al voir gehir,
Ne doit mal avoir ne oïr.[372]
4265 – Suer, di trestout, ce voel je bien,
Ja por ce n'aras mains del mien.
– Ha! fine biautés, flors de rose,
Ja vos plain ge sor toute cose,
Et tos li mondes ensement.
4270 Nos cuidames beninement,[373]
Quant on vos mist en cele honor,[374]
C'on vos mesist hors de dolor,
Et cil qui en l'onor vos mist
Duel et contraire vos tramist.
4275 Onques por vostre loiauté
N'i espargna vostre biauté,
N'onques por ce nen ot merci;   [f]
Vostre honor a enclose chi
Et fors tramise vostre honte.
4280 Molt vos plaignent et roi et conte,
C'on ne vos voit a ju n'a festes.
Se je fusse ensi con vos estes,
Mix ameroie o un bas home
Estre a honor que toute Rome
4285 Avoir ensi en ma baillie.
Mais si tres viex, si tres falie[375]
N'estes vos pas, je cuiç et croi,
Que n'en prendés aucun conroi
D'alegier vostre grant anui,
4290 De penser viax a aucunnui.
– Amie, et que dont se je pens?
Ne seroit pas raisons ne sens.

---
[372] ni o.]BT.
[373] cuidame].
[374] Q. vos m.]BT.
[375] tre falie]H.

4225 When she had completed her preparations, she went to the postern of the tower and shouted loudly: 'Let me in!' And the porter was not a laggard; he quickly opened the door and saw the fruit covered with leaves. He recognised the old woman quite easily, for he had seen her many times before. He closed the door, went up to the first floor, delivered his message to the lady, and the barons who were with her summoned the old woman upstairs. All of this suited her very well; the old woman had to climb a lot of steps before she reached the empress. Her lady was sitting on a carpet at a certain distance from the others; she was not interested in their company, for it gave her no pleasure. She was holding a book and reading it. The old woman went straight up to her and said: 'May God who dwells on high protect my lady and bless her and all her companions!' **4249** Then she immediately knelt before the lady and began to talk about other things than her present. She poked the fire vigorously, yet looked beyond the fire. To gain greater personal advantage from the situation she displayed her arms and displayed her feet, which were poorly clad and shod; in everyone's hearing she spoke with a tremble in her voice, covering the truth with false seeming. She said quietly: 'Fair creature, I am risking my life here, for I have a message to deliver to you, but I am afraid it might anger you, yet to speak frankly, a messenger should not suffer or hear any ill. – Sister, it is my wish that you tell me everything; you will not have less of a reward from me because of it. – Ah, perfect beauty, bloom of the rose,[70] for a while now I have felt more sorry for you than for any other creature, and so does everyone else. We sincerely believed when you were elevated to such a high rank that you would be exempt from pain, yet the man who bestowed this high rank on you also caused you distress and suffering. **4275** Not once did he take account of your loyalty and spare your beauty, not once did he ever take pity on you for that reason. He has locked away your honour here and broadcast your shame in the outside world. Both kings and counts deplore the fact that you are not seen at games or festivities. If I were to find myself in your situation, I would prefer to live honourably with a man of low estate than to hold the whole of Rome in my sway in these circumstances. But I believe and am convinced that you are not so weak and cowardly that you would not take measures to alleviate your great distress, and to at least consider someone else. – And what if I did consider someone else, friend? It would not be a sensible or wise thing to do.

---

[70] In referring to Athanaïs as a rose and in associating the old woman with false seeming, Gautier anticipates the thirteenth-century *Roman de la Rose*, see Pratt 2007b.

A tel puis je baer et tendre
Que rien li fesisse a entendre
4295 S'ains ne m'eüst mise a raison,
U aucuns viax de se maison.
A lui m'otroi, je sui s'amie;
Lasse! caitive! il nel set mie,
Ne ja nel sara, jel sai bien;
4300 Ne tos li mons n'en feroit rien
Ne mais icil u mes cuers tent,
Qui nuit et jor a lui s'atent.
– Dame, trop par l'asseürés.
Mais qui est si bons eürés
4305 Qu'il est dignes de vostre amor?
Dix meïmes, des icel jor
Qu'il primes fist et forma home,
N'en fist qu'un seul, qui est en Rome,[376]
Qui devroit seulement oser
4310 Entre vos deus bras reposer.[377]
Cil dont je di par est si bons
Qu'il est molt plus que rois, que coins.
Par aucun grant pecié de gent
L'a Dix fait si biel et si gent
4315 Que tos li mons, s'il ert ensanle,
Por se grant biauté lais resanle;
Tout home sont lait envers lui, [145a]
Et fin vilain et plain d'anui.
Por aucun pecié del coumun
4320 A Dix si grant bien mis en un;
Et par cel Diu qui maint sor nos,[378]
Por itant l'aim qu'il aime vous;
Ses cuers i pense et tent adés.
– Et qui est il? – C'est Paridés.
4325 – Caitive riens, cuers deceüs!
Por qu'est par toi ramenteüs

Li hom el mont qui pis me fait?
– Dame, merci! ce comment vait?
Cil dont je di morroitançois
4330 Qu'il fesist rien sor vostre pois,
Et qui li feroit felounie,
N'i penseroit il vilenie
Por vie perdre, ains i morroit;
N'engageroit ne ne donroit
4335 Se cortoisie por tout l'or
Qui est el mont mis en tresor.[379]
Qui vilenie ne feroit[380]
Por nule riens, comment seroit
Vilains vers vos qu'il aime tant?
4340 Mais or laissiés le cose atant.
– Mere, mal sens i avés mis.
Ne sai s'il est mes anemis,[381]
Mais tant sai bien, je sui s'amie.
Se je ne l'ai, je ne prois mie
4345 Un bouton canque g'ai vescu[382]
Ne ne demanç Diu autre escu,
Autre garant de mon contraire;
Il seus me puet de mort retraire.
Laissons le a tans por ces barons;
4350 On adevance bien larrons
Par contrepenser lor voloir;
Faus consaus fait musart doloir.
Va t'ent; demain devant midi
Aras mon present, je te di;
4355 Tout le recevras a ton oeus,
Mais le sorplus me porte lués
A mon ami, sel me salue, [b]
Et se li di de par sa drue
Qu'il obeïsse a mon escrit,
4360 S'il m'aime ensi con tu m'as dit.»

---
[376] Ne mais un seul; B]T.
[377] Entre vos bras et r.]T (B: En vostres b.).
[378] ces D.]BT.
[379] Q. est mont]BT.
[380] Qui]B.
[381] Nessai].
[382] veu]BT.

It's all very well for me to long and yearn for someone, but he would be unaware of anything unless he were to address me on the subject, or at least someone from his household. I have granted my heart to him, I am his beloved. Alas, woe is me, he knows nothing about this, and I am convinced he shall never know. And no one would be able to do anything about it, except for him whom my heart yearns for and longs for night and day. **4303** – My lady, you are too convinced of this. But who is so fortunate as to merit your love? God himself, since the day He first created and fashioned man, made only one man, who is here in Rome, who should even dare to lie in your arms. The man I am talking about is so very good that he is far worthier than a king or a count. Because of some major sin committed by the masses God has made him so handsome and attractive that if everyone in the world were gathered together, they would look ugly next to his amazing beauty; in comparison with him all men are ugly, extremely coarse and repulsive. To compensate for some sin in the population as a whole God has placed such excellent qualities in one man; and by the Lord who dwells on high, I love him for the very reason that he loves you; his heart thinks only of you and yearns for you constantly. – And who is he? – It's Paridés. **4325** – Oh wretched creature, oh treacherous heart! Why am I reminded by you of the one man in the world who does me the most harm? – My lady, for pity's sake, how can this be? The man I mentioned would rather die than do anything against your will. And even if he were betrayed, he would not contemplate a vile deed even to save his life, but would rather die. He would not compromise or abandon his courtesy for all the gold stored in treasure-chests throughout the world. A man who would not commit a vile deed under any circumstances, how could he possibly be vile towards you whom he loves so much? But now drop the matter immediately. – Mother, you have misunderstood me. I do not know if he is my enemy, but all I know is that I love him. If I can't have him, I shall not consider my life thus far to be worth a button, nor do I ask God for any other shield or protection against my misfortune; he alone can rescue me from death. Let's drop the matter immediately because of the presence of these barons; **4350** one can beat scoundrels at their own game by anticipating their every move; rash advice can make even a fool suffer. Go, and I promise you that tomorrow before midday you will receive a present from me. All that you receive will be for you, but take the extra item[71] immediately to my beloved, give him my greetings and tell him on behalf of his beloved to obey what I have written if he loves me as much as you have said he does.'

---

71   In l. 4356 *li sorplus* may also have sexual connotations, anticipating the consummation of the affair.

Cele prent congié, si s'en vait.
Ce qu'ele quiert a molt bien fait,
Bien a son present cier vendu.
N'i a pas longes atendu:
4365 Al varlet vient et conte li
Canqu'ele a trouvé vers celi;
Et Paridés, li afaitiés,
Saut sus tos sains et tos haitiés.
Tant en caoit de se pesance
4370 Con puet alegier Esperance,
Et c'est molt plus en haute amor
Que retorner al premier jor
En une basse, canc'on velt;
Amors n'est riens s'on ne se deut.
4375   A l'endemain del parlement
Que fist li vielle od son present,
Saut sus li dame par matin,
Prent enque, pene et parkemin
Jouste l'autel de se capiele;
4380 Nul autre escrivain n'i apiele
Ne mais son cors tant seulement;
Si escrit son conmandement,
Ploie le brief et si le lie;
Avant orrés qu'il senefie.
4385 Li dame a molt les keus hastés;
Conmande lor que ait pastés;
Mangier en velt, ce dist, a tierce.
Li rois ert matés par se fierce,
Mais ce n'ert mie par l'aufin:
4390 Par autrë ert li jus a fin.
Li dame velt molt c'on manguist,
Et k'eure soit que mangier puist;
L'eure vient tost c'assis se sont,
Tant que des pastés servir font.

4395 La dame pense canque puet;
Saciés que penser li estuet.
Le brief tient ploié en son doi,   [c]
Si a deus pastés devant soi;
De l'un le croste un poi solieve;
4400 Tant l'escroustë et tant le cieve
Que metre i puet le brief escrit;
Se l'i met petit et petit
Si c'onques riens n'i decovrut,
N'ainc ovreture n'i parut,[383]
4405 N'onques nel virent cele gent.
Une escuiele ataint d'argent,[384]
Le mes atout le brief i met[385]
Et a la viele le tramet;
Dist que servie bien l'avoit,
4410 Si est bien drois que mix l'en soit.
N'i a celui n'en die bien;
Mais je vos dirai une rien:
S'on seüst le farsisseüre,
Ja n'avenist cele aventure
4415 Qui avint puis. Li mes s'en vait;
A la vielle sen present fait,
Et puis s'en vait; et cele saut,
Qui riens n'i pert, comment qu'il aut;
Porpense soi et si s'esta
4420 Que d'une cose se douta:
Set que l'empereïs li dist,[386]
Quant ele son present li fist,
C'un present aroit de lassus
Qui siens seroit, mais li sorplus
4425 Portast au varlet sans delai.
Or est li vielle en grant esmai,
Et dist: «Ci n'a autre present
Ne mais cest pasté seulement,

---
[383] covreture]BT.
[384] atant]BT.
[385] briés]BT.
[386] L'emperis].

The old woman took her leave and went away; she had successfully achieved what she had set out to do, and had sold her present for a very good price. She did not wait long before she went to the young man and told him what she had found out about the empress; and noble Paridés jumped out of bed, all hale and hearty. As much of his distress fell away from him as could be dispelled by Hope, but one's distress is much greater if one aims at true love with a high-born lady rather than resorting early on to a lowly love, whatever one might wish. Love is nothing without suffering.

4375 On the day after the meeting engineered by the old woman with her present of cherries the lady leapt out of bed in the morning, took up ink, pen and parchment from next to the altar in her chapel; she summoned no other scribe there apart from her own person alone. She wrote her instructions, folded the letter and tied it. You will hear a little later what was in the letter. She chivvied her cooks constantly, instructing them to make pies. She said she wanted to eat them at terce.[72] The king was going to be check-mated by his queen, but not by a move involving the bishop – another piece would finish off the game. The lady was eager to eat and could not wait until it was time to eat. The time soon came for them to be seated, and the pies served. The lady thought carefully about what she would be able to do; and I can tell you that she needed to think carefully. She held the folded letter between her fingers and had two pies in front of her. She lifted up the crust of one a little; **4400** she raised the crust sufficiently and made a hole big enough to place the written letter in the pie. She introduced it gradually so that she left nothing uncovered, no opening was visible, nor did her guards observe this. She reached out for a silver dish and in it she placed the pie with the letter and sent it to the old woman, saying that she had served her well and that it was only right that she should benefit from it. There was no one who expressed disapproval at this. Yet I'll tell you one thing: if they had known what the filling was, the adventure which followed would never have occurred. The messenger set off and gave the present to the old woman and then he left. She who had nothing to lose whatever happened, leapt up, thought for a moment and stood still, for she was not sure about something: she knew that the empress had said, when she had handed over her present to her, that she would have a present in return, which would be for her, but that she should take the extra item to the young man straight away. **4426** Now the old woman was very disappointed, saying: 'There is no other present here apart from this pie,

---

[72] The third canonical hour: 9 am.

Et li sorplus est li argens;
4430 Que male goute ait en ses dens,
Que ça m'envoia cest pasté!
Ci a present de grant lasté.
Qui vit ainc mais tel druerie
Venir de si tres noble amie
4435 A varlet de si haut afaire?
C'a il de son argent a faire?
Il en a autretant con ele. [d]
Tramise m'eüst s'escuiele,
Et le çainture et l'aumoniere!
4440 Molt par me duel de grant maniere.»
Par maltalent le pasté brise;
Le chartre voit, et si l'a prise;
Dont dist : «Biax sire Dix, merci!
C'est li sorplus que je voi chi,
4445 C'est li sorplus que il i a.
Cil Damedix qui tout cria
Doinst a l'empereïs grans biens!
Je prent cest argent, qui est miens.»
Porte au varlet le brief en oirre
4450 Cil est molt liés, ce poés croire.
Tout l'a leü de cief en cief.
Ce li mande li dame el brief,
Qu'ele n'a fïance en nului
Sous Diu, fors seulement en lui;
4455 Sire ert de s'amor, qui qu'en poist.
A l'ostel a le vielle voist,
Un sousterin i face faire
Trestout de nuit, si qu'il n'i paire;[387]
Çou a el brief que tel le truist
4460 Qu'ensanle lui entrer i puist,
Et c'on puist l'uisset bien ouvrir
Et bien reclorre et bien covrir,
Qu'il n'i paire nule ovreture
Se nus i vient par aventure.

4465 Tres devant l'uis un flos avoit
Que li dame bien i savoit;
Al varlet mande par le letre
Qu'il i face de l'eve metre,[388]
Et mande el brief que Paridés
4470 L'atende en l'ovreor adés,
As octaves del jor passé,
Et que li vielle ait amassé
Tant de le busse en se maison
Qu'il i ait bon fu par raison;
4475 Des qu'oltre none bien le tiegne,
Et gart le jor que nus n'i viegne,
Car femes sevent molt plaidier, [e]
Parler adiés et souhaidier;
Le jor se gart bien de plait faire,
4480 C'on puet sovent tel home atraire
Dont li delivres est molt griés.
Or vos ai dit quels fu li briés.
Je ne cuiç pas que nus hom oie
D'ome qui fesist si grant joie
4485 Con cis fait de son mandement;
Or a il son coumandement,
De nule riens mais ne se delt,
Car bien cuide avoir quanqu'il velt.
A l'ostel a le vielle vait,
4490 Trestout de nuit, et faire fait
Quanque li letre li devise.[389]
N'ai soig de faire lonc devise,
Mais li jors est molt desirés
Dont il s'est griement consirés,
4495 Et cele griement consiree.
Tost vient li feste desiree
Et cil se met el sousterin.
La dame el doignon marberin
S'est auques matin atornee,
4500 Por bien esploitier se jornee;

---

[387] nuit si quil i p.]BT.
[388] de levee]BT.
[389] Line repeated in A.

and the extra item is the silver. May the person who sent me this pie have terrible toothache! This is a poor present indeed. Who ever saw such a love token sent by such a genteel lady to a nobleman of such high degree? What does he want with her silver? He has as much of it as she has. She ought to have sent me her dish, and her belt and purse too! I am extremely annoyed about this.' In anger she broke the pie, saw the letter and picked it up. Then she said: 'Thanks be to our fair Lord God! What I can see here is the extra item, here's the extra item meant for him. May the Lord God, Creator of everything, give the empress great good fortune. I shall take this silver, which is mine.' She quickly took the letter to the young man. **4450** As you can imagine, he was very happy. He read it all from beginning to end. In the letter the lady told him that she had faith in no one but himself, apart from God; whoever might be upset by this, he was lord of her heart. He should go to the old woman's lodgings and have an underground chamber built there, all this to be done at night so as not to be discovered. In the letter it was stated that the chamber should be designed so that she could enter it with him and that the trap door could easily be opened and closed, and covered up so that no opening was visible to a chance passer-by. Right in front of the door was a water-filled hole which the lady knew was there; she told the young man in writing to fill it up with water and she asked Paridés in the letter to wait patiently for her in the room in one week's time. The old woman was to store in her house as much firewood as was necessary for a suitably good fire; **4475** she should keep it going until after noon and make sure that no one came visiting on that day, for women are expert at gossiping, talking constantly and sharing their hopes; that day she should avoid entering into conversation, for in that way one often attracts people who are difficult to get rid of. Now I have told you what was in the letter. I do not think that anyone has ever heard of such a joyful man as Paridés was when he received her message. Now that he had her instructions he was no longer unhappy, for he really believed that he would get whatever he wished for. He went to the old woman's lodgings by night and had the work done that was described in the letter. I do not wish to spin out my tale, but the day for which he could hardly wait could not come quickly enough, and she could hardly wait either. Soon the longed-for final day's festivities arrived and he entered the underground chamber. The lady in the marble tower got ready fairly early in the morning to make the most of her day,

Si ne valroit pas estre en son.
Et cil que je Paridés vos non,³⁹⁰
Le verra, s'ele puet, ançois,
Et lor fera un tor françois
4505 Ains que n'i paraut a larron;
Deçoivre cuide maint baron
S'ele puet onques par nul fuer.
Feme com a si hardi cuer
Qu'ele ose engignier tantes gens?
4510 Esce folie ou hardemens?
Si con je puis par moi aprendre,
Folie est de folie enprendre,
N'i puet nul hardement avoir
S'on n'emprent l'ueuvre par savoir;³⁹¹
4515 Et ceste dame dont je di   [f]
A en folie cuer hardi:³⁹²
Hardiement en prent conroi
D'enprendre folie et desroi,³⁹³
Et de torner sen bien en mal.
4520 Li emperere ot un ceval,³⁹⁴
De lonc sejor molt envoisié;
En le tor n'ot nul tant proisié.
Sor cele beste mal dontee
Est li dame de gré montee;
4525 Montent li baron de la tor,
N'i a celui n'ait rice ator.
Lor dame en mainent liement
La dont il seront tuit dolent.
Tant vont parlant et d'un et d'el
4530 Qu'il sont venu pres de l'ostel
Le vielle qui le plait savoit.
En le maison bon fu avoit,
Et li flos ert illuec devant.

Li dame quis va decevant
4535 Fiert le ceval et il i saut;
Li dame ciet et crie haut:
«Sainte veraie Crois, aïe!
Con cis cevax m'a hui traïe,
Et engignie et deceüe!»
4540 Par son le flos est hui kaüe
Qu'ele a trestos ses dras molliés
Des les genous dusques as piés;
Et cil a terre mix que mieus!
N'i a nul, jovenes u vix³⁹⁵
4545 Qu'ele n'ait ensi dessinglé
Et engingnié et aveulé,
Et dist lor: «Signor, mal me vait!
Une goute ai, qui mal me fait;
Je l'ai molt longement celee;³⁹⁶
4550 Orendroit m'est renouvelee
Al caoir que je fis a terre;³⁹⁷
L'os de me gambe me desserre.³⁹⁸
Mais ne vos en desconfortés;
En cele maison me portés:
4555 Un fu i voi, caufer m'i voel;   [146a]
Sifaitement garir me suel.
Si m'aporç on uns autres dras.»
Cil, qui l'engien ne sevent pas,
L'i ont porté isnielement;
4560 Le vielle treuvent seulement,³⁹⁹
N'i voient nule creature
Dont venir puist mesaventure.
Il nen ont sos ciel nul regart
Qu'entrer i puist de nule part
4565 Riens nule el monde fors par l'uis;
N'i a feniestre ne pertruis.

---

³⁹⁰ P. ot n.]B, *cf.* 198 (T: Et chilz qui P. ot nom).
³⁹¹ memprent]BT.
³⁹² foli].
³⁹³ Denpre].
³⁹⁴ Li empere]T (B: L'empereïs).
³⁹⁵ n. soit j.] (B: Ni a nul ne govenes ne vious; T: Ni a celui ione ne vieuz).
³⁹⁶ Je l'a m.]B.
³⁹⁷ A c.]BT.
³⁹⁸ L'ol]BT.
³⁹⁹ treuve]BT.

which she would not want to be at an end. **4502** And if she could manage it, she would see the man whom I have called Paridés before nightfall, and was prepared to lead her guards a merry dance rather than not talk secretly with him; she planned to deceive many a baron if it was at all possible and whatever the cost. How can a woman's heart grow so bold that she dares to trick so many people? Is this folly or bravery? As far as I can tell it is folly to undertake a foolish deed; there can be no bravery if one does not embark on the deed wisely. And the lady of whom I am speaking has a brave heart in her folly; she bravely makes her preparations to embark on folly and madness, and to transform her good fortune into misfortune. The emperor owned a horse which was very frisky after being well rested; none of the horses in the tower was so highly valued. The lady deliberately chose to mount this unruly animal; **4525** the barons of the tower mounted their steeds, each one finely equipped. They led their lady joyfully to the place where they would all come to grief. They continued on their way chatting about this and that until they approached the lodgings of the old woman who was party to the plan; there was a good fire burning in the house and the large puddle was in front of it. The lady who was out to deceive them struck her horse and it bucked; the lady fell off and cried out in a loud voice: 'By the True and Holy Cross, help me! How this horse has let me down today, betrayed and disappointed me!' She had fallen right into the puddle so that her clothes were soaked from her knees down to her feet. And her escorts leapt to the ground as quickly as they could. There was not one of them, young or old, whom she had not tricked,[73] deceived and pulled the wool over their eyes in this way, and she said to them: 'My lords, I am in a bad way. I have a rheumatic condition, which is painful and which I have concealed for a long time; **4550** in falling to the ground I have triggered it off again; I have jarred the bone in my leg. But do not be dismayed; carry me into this house. I can see a fire burning there and I would like to warm myself at it; this is how I normally treat myself. Send someone to fetch me a change of clothing.' Those who were not privy to her ruse quickly carried her in. They found the old woman alone and could see no other person whose presence might lead to disaster. They had no suspicion whatsoever that anyone in the whole world might enter the house by any other route apart from the door, for there were no windows or other openings.

---

[73] *Dessinglé* in l. 4545 literally means 'thrown off balance when a horse is ungirthed'. The metaphor is very appropriate in this context.

«Signor, dist ele, alés vos ent.
Caufer me voel priveement,
Savoir mon ja se ceste goute,
4570 Qui si m'angoisse et me deboute,
Me tresiroit con ele seut,
Que caufer et froiier se veut.»
Icil s'en vont, li vielle saut,
L'uis a fermé; petit lor vaut
4575 Le gaite longe qu'il ont faite;
Ne set qu'il fait qui feme gaite,
Car folie est de soi grever
En ce c'on ne puet aciever.
Li vielle vient et si descuevre
4580 L'uis de l'escriene et puis li l'oevre.
Le dame par le main i maine,
D'autres deus fust l'escriene plaine.
Li uns de l'autre molt se claime,
Cascuns amans a ce qu'il aime;
4585 Molt a de bien en poi de liu,
Et en amor a si douç giu
Que riens el mont si bon ne set;
Noient plus que li hom qui het
Set bien amer ses anemis,
4590 Ne set nus hom qui n'est amis
Com par est doce l'assamblee
De deus amans si en emblee.
Cil n'ont de parler nul loisir,
Et fine amors les fait taisir
4595 Ce c'orent empensé a dire. [b]
Il n'i a noient d'escondire
Riens nule que requise soit,
Cascuns en prent en son endroit.[400]
Or sont li amant molt a aise;
4600 Or n'ont il rien qui lor desplaise,

Se de ce non que loisir n'ont
De faire longes ce qu'il font;
Il ont paor que nes deçoive
Peciés, c'aucuns les aperçoive.
4605 «Ahi! fait ele, dous amis,
En con grande nos somes mis
Por faire nostre volenté!
La defors a gent a plenté
Que g'ai par engien deceüe;
4610 Gieté serïens hors de mue,
Autrement c'on ne fait ostoir,
Sil savoient cest ouvreoir![401]
Diu et le siecle perç por vous;
Li face Diu est desor nous!
4615 Dix qui les malfaisans manace[402]
A sor nous gietee se face
Tos jors, non por doner se gloire,
Mais por destruire lor memoire.
Dix voit bien tout nostre errement.
4620 Eracles, li preus, qui ne ment,
Set ja molt bien con j'ai vescu,
S'en ai le cuer molt irascu
Que l'emperere nel creï.
Ore est l'eure qu'il a gehi[403]
4625 A mon signor con g'ai ovré.
Cui caut, quant je ai recouvré
Ce que m'est bon, ce que me plaist?»
Dont ne puet laissier que nel baist,
Car tant con plus coste le cose,
4630 Le joïst plus qui faire l'ose.
«Dame, fait il, vostre merchi
De quanque vos m'avés fait chi;
Mon cors et m'ame vos en doing
Par ces deus mains que je chi joing.

---

[400] en soit en droit]BT.

[401] Si saroient se cest ouuoir (*corrected from* outtoir)]BT.
[402] manage]BT.
[403] lueure]BT.

'My lords,' she said, 'leave me alone. I would like some privacy to warm myself up and to see if this rheumatism, which causes me so much pain and distress, will go away as it usually does, for it requires heat and rubbing.' The men went away and the old woman leapt up and closed the door. It did them little good that they had guarded the empress closely for so long. **4576** The man who keeps watch over a woman knows not what he does, for it is foolish to put all one's effort into a goal one cannot achieve. The old woman came and uncovered the door of the underground chamber and opened it for her. She led the lady in by the hand. Two more people and the chamber would have been really overcrowded. Athanaïs and Paridés frequently declared their love for each other; the lovers both had what they desired; in a short space of time they enjoyed great pleasure and found love to be such a sweet game that nothing in the world tasted so good to them. No more than a man full of hatred can truly love his enemies, so no one who has not experienced love can know how sweet such a secret meeting is between two lovers. They had no time to talk and true love prevented them from saying what they had planned to say. What each lover asked for was in no way denied by the other; they each took what was their due.

4599 Now the lovers were very happy. Nothing displeased them except for the fact that they did not have the opportunity to prolong what they were doing. They were afraid that bad luck would betray them in that someone would see them. 'Alas, sweet love,' she said, 'what great risks we have taken so that we can fulfil our desire. Outside there are a good many people whom I have tricked with my ruse; if they knew that this secret chamber existed, we would be thrown out of our hiding place rather differently from the way one releases a hawk after moulting. I am sacrificing God and this world for you. The face of the Lord is against us.[74] God, who threatens to punish those who commit evil, not so as to bestow his glory on them, but to destroy the memory of them, has for ever turned his face against us. God can see all that we do. Worthy Eracle, who never lies, already knows how I have been behaving, and I am very angry in my heart that the emperor did not believe him. This very moment he has revealed to my husband what I have done. **4626** Yet who cares, since I have obtained what I want and what pleases me.' Then she could not stop kissing him, for the more costly a thing, the more it is enjoyed by those who dare to indulge in it. 'My lady,' he said, 'thank you for all you have done for me here; in joining my two hands together I hereby grant you my body and my soul.[75]

---

[74] Psalms 34: 16; the *BT* variant mentions David the psalmist.
[75] Here Paridés uses a feudal gesture of allegiance to convey his love.

4635 Molt en renç povre gerredon, [c]
Dame, de si tres rice don,
Mais coi que nus ait receü,
Ne n'ait güé, ne n'ait eü,[404]
N'en puet merir fors son pooir.
4640 — Amis, ce sai je bien, por voir,
Mais del pooir remaint assés,
Puis que li termes est passés,
Al malvais home qui l'a pris;
Puis que il tient, ne bee a pris,
4645 Ja ne regardera bien fait
De nule rien c'on fait li ait.
Amis, por Diu, ne soiiés tex!
— Ma dame, tex confonge Deus!»
Lors s'entrebaisent docement
4650 Et prendent congié bonement;
Cil remaint et cele s'en ist.
Li vielle qui le plait porquist
Reclost et cuevre le bouchiel,
Qu'il n'i pert nule riens soussiel
4655 Fors seulement le terre et l'aire.
Cele qui molt sot de l'afaire
Revient au fu, si le ratise,
Et li dame se rest assise.
La vielle a tost son huis overt,
4660 Si c'on le voit a descouvert
Qu'il n'a riens laiens s'eles non;
Mais nen ont nule soupeçon.
L'empereïs s'en est levee,
Issi malade, issi grevee
4665 Con ele fu, et a l'entree[405]
A se grant maisnie encontree;

En l'uis estoit, que nus n'i entre.[406]
Molt li tressaut li cuers el ventre.
Se gent l'ont molt reconfortee;
4670 Une gupe orent aportee
Molt rice et bone, de samis;[407]
Vestue l'a l'empereïs,
S'affuble mantiel de meïme.
La vielle ara le bone disme,
4675 Et rique loiier de son feu;[408] [d]
Ele i ara bien fait son preu.[409]
L'autre mantiel doner li fait
L'empereïs, et puis s'en vait;
Montee est sor un palefroi.
4680 Humais ist fors de grant effroi,
Si est li varlés ensement.
Ist s'ent d'illuec isnielement,[410]
Vient a le feste, se s'i met,
Et de bien harper s'entremet.
4685 Or ne se deut il pas d'amor
Si durement con l'autre jor;[411]
Nequedent n'aime il se mix non.
Mix ardent assés li tison
Quant li busse est bien alumee
4690 Que quant le sorvaint le fumee;
Li fus n'a mie mains de force
Por le fumee de l'escorce,
Mais plus oscurs en est li fus
Et plus en est torbles li lix.[412]
4695 Si est amors par trop doloir:
Ele n'en pert pas son voloir,
Mais plus oscurement en velt
Quant trop s'en sent et trop s'en deut.

---

[404] n'ait veu]BT, *but cf.* 4787.
[405] a l'entree *partly illegible in* A]BT.

[406] q. nos n'i e.]BT.
[407] rice bone].
[408] Rique]BT.
[409] Ele a.]BT.
[410] Isent d.; B]L (T: D'illueques ist i.).
[411] durent].
[412] lux]BT.

I am rewarding your rich generosity with a very meagre gift, my lady, yet whatever one has received, enjoyed and obtained, one cannot pay for beyond one's means. – Beloved, I know this to be true, but when an evil man has taken a gift, he still retains a large proportion of what he can afford after the deadline for repayment has passed. Once he has gained possession of it he does not strive to enhance his reputation and has no regard for any good deed that one might have done for him. My love, by God, do not be such a man. – My lady, may God confound such people!' **4649** Then they sweetly kissed each other and tenderly took their leave. He remained and she left. The old woman who had organised the meeting closed and covered up the opening so that nothing at all was visible except the ground and the floor. She who knew all about the affair returned to the fire and poked it, and the lady sat down in front of it again. Then the old woman quickly opened her front door so that people could clearly see that there was no one else in the house except for the two women. However, they suspected nothing at all. The empress stood up, just as unwell and in pain as she had been before and she went to meet her great retinue at the entrance; she stood in the doorway so that no one could enter. Her heart was beating rapidly in her breast. Her guards tried hard to comfort her. They had brought with them a gown of very rich, costly satin. The empress put it on and donned a cloak in the same material. **4674** The old woman was about to receive a good tithe and a rich reward for her fire; she had managed to turn things greatly to her advantage. The empress gave the other cloak to her and then left. Once mounted on a palfrey, she was no longer terrified, and nor was the young man. He left there quickly, went to the games and joined in; he began to play the harp very well. Now he was not suffering from love pangs as much as he had been the other day; yet he was now even more deeply in love. Firewood burns a lot better when the logs are aflame rather than when they are covered in smoke.[76] The fire is not weaker because of the smoke from the bark, but the fire is less bright and the room fills with smoke. Love is like this if too much suffering is involved. Lovers do not lose their desire, but they desire it less brightly if they feel too deeply and suffer too deeply from love.

---

[76] This passage has been compared by Pierreville (2001, 53-54) to Chrétien's *Cligés*, 593-600 (Micha edition) and by Raynaud de Lage (1971, 493-94) to *Yvain*, 1779-82 (Roques edition). In neither case though has Gautier's debt to Chrétien been proved conclusively.

　　　　Fumee talt les oels defors;
4700　Les oels del cuer qui est el cors[413]
　　　　Talt le dolor, et si empire,
　　　　Car ele met le cuer en ire,
　　　　Et cuers irés n'a point de sens,
　　　　Car ire est plaine de forsens,
4705　Et forsenés ne doit plaisir,
　　　　Ne c'on doit parler ne taisir;
　　　　Et qui en amor trop se taist,
　　　　U trop parole, il li desplaist.
　　　　Icis se deut si a mesure
4710　Qu'en lui n'a nule mespresure,
　　　　Ne n'avoit en l'empereïs,[414]
　　　　Mais auques ont les cuers maris,
　　　　Qu'il ne cuident mais assanler;
　　　　Car tel chiet ore bien d'embler
4715　Qui molt fort le compere aprés.　[e]
　　　　Les gens les gardent mais de prés
　　　　Si s'en covient contregarder.
　　　　Cil se lairoient ains larder
　　　　Qu'il se mesissent mais en plait
4720　N'en tel destroit que il ont fait.
　　　　Li vespres vient et li baron
　　　　En mainent la dame en maison.
　　　　　　Eracles, qui est loing en l'ost,
　　　　Le dist l'empereour molt tost
4725　Que la dame pense a folie,
　　　　Et il ne le mescreï mie.
　　　　Angoisseus fu, ce poés croire,
　　　　Et si destrava tot son oirre;
　　　　Repaira s'ent delivrement,
4730　C'onques n'i fist porlongement.
　　　　Mais trop tart est li cose emprise,
　　　　Car li maisons est trop esprise,
　　　　Et vous savés, n'est mie jus

　　　　Des qu'en tous sens i est li fus.
4735　　Que que li sire s'en revint,
　　　　De ce tient plait dont plus li tint;
　　　　Enquiert d'Eracle se il set
　　　　De le cose el mont qu'il plus het
　　　　S'ele est encore traite a fin.
4740　«Sire, fait il, des hui matin
　　　　Fu le cose par assoumee
　　　　Dont j'arai male renomee,
　　　　Et a grant tort, mais mençoignier
　　　　Et gengleor et losengier
4745　Heent adiés ceus qui bien font;
　　　　Ja des malvais ne mesdiront,
　　　　Ançois lor tienent por ce pais
　　　　Que il meïsme sont malvais.»
　　　　D'un et d'el vont tant devisant
4750　Qu'il vont ja Rome ravisant,
　　　　Et vienent ains que il anuite.
　　　　Or est la dame en male luite
　　　　Qu'ele a sifaitement erré.
　　　　Trestout li huis sont desserré,
4755　Entrer i puënt cil et cil;　　　　[f]
　　　　Tost i entrerent plus de mil,
　　　　C'on voit molt volentiers por voir
　　　　Cose desfendue a veoir.
　　　　Tous li palais est portendus;[415]
4760　Li empereres est descendus.
　　　　Cele s'est vestue et paree,
　　　　Qui durement est esgaree;
　　　　Molt crient, et cremir li estuet.
　　　　Vient a son signor con ains puet,
4765　Dist lui: «Bien soiés vos venus,
　　　　Si con drois est, et retenus!
　　　　– Et vos si soiiés si trovee
　　　　Con vos vos estes puis prouvee

---

[413]　Les del c.]BT.
[414]　Ne le voit]R (B: Non avoit a l'.; T: Non avoir al e.).
[415]　palai].

4699 Smoke blinds our external eyes, while suffering blinds the eyes of the heart, which are deep within us; and it makes things worse, for it distresses the heart and a distressed heart knows no moderation; for distress leads to excess and a man who lacks moderation cannot possibly please, whether required to speak or remain silent; and the lover who is either dumb-struck or too talkative displeases his lady-love. Paridés suffered in such a moderate manner that he could not be faulted; nor could the empress. Yet their hearts were somewhat heavy, as they did not expect to meet again; for whoever succeeds in stealing one moment now will pay dearly for a second. They were being watched closely from then on and the lovers had to be vigilant; they would have preferred to be burned alive than to risk another meeting or place themselves in danger as they had done before. Evening fell and the barons escorted the lady home.

4723 Eracle, who was a long way away with the army, told the emperor straight away that his lady was contemplating folly, and the emperor did not disbelieve him. You can imagine how upset he was and he abandoned the whole campaign; he returned home quickly without delaying at all. But these measures came too late, for the house was completely consumed by flames and as you know, it is a serious matter when fire is already raging in all directions.

While the emperor was on the return journey he broached the subject which was most preoccupying him. He asked Eracle if he knew anything about the matter he most feared in the world and if it had come to pass yet. 'My lord,' he said, 'this very morning the affair was consummated. As a result my reputation will be ruined, though most undeservedly, but liars, gossips and slanderers always hate those who are virtuous. They will never slander evil people, preferring to hold their tongues because they themselves are evil.' They continued to talk privately about this and that until Rome came into view and they arrived there before nightfall. **4752** Now the lady was in dire straits as a result of her behaviour. The doors were all unbolted and everyone who wished to could enter. Soon more than a thousand people had flocked in, for it is true that we are always very keen to see whatever we were previously not allowed to see. The whole palace was decked out with wall hangings; the emperor dismounted. The empress, who was distraught, had dressed and adorned herself; she was sore afraid and rightly so. She approached her lord as quickly as she could and said: 'May you receive the welcome and hospitality that befits you! – And may you be treated as befits your behaviour

        Que je ne parlai mais a vous!
4770 Partie est mais l'amors de nous.[416]
        L'onors qui vos estoit juree
        Vos ara mais corte duree;
        Car or d'une feme meüre,
        Puis qu'est eslite s'asseüre
4775 Et se delite en foloiier;
        Legiere estroit a forvoiier
        Une autre qui ne fust eslite,
        Quant lors en se car se delite,
        Dont on faisoit sifait dangier.
4780 Trop sevent malement cangier
        Qui laissent riquece et honor
        Por vivre povre a deshonor;
        Mais faus u fole, s'il ont bien,
        Ne lor sovient de nule rien,
4785 De nule painne ne s'esmaient
        Desci adont que perdu aient;
        Lors primes sevent c'ont eü[417]
        Quant en povreté ont geü.
        Mar fu li vostres cors roiaus
4790 Qui fu ja povres et loiaus,
        Et quant ce vint a le grant aise,
        Si devenistes vos malvaise.
        A mal cief puist venir riquece
        Qui son signor met a destrece!
4795 Vos fustes en le povreté   [147 a]
        Et biele et plaine de verté,
        Et quant vos fustes rice et biele,
        Au fil a le virge puciele
        En deüssiés les grasses rendre;
4800 Car tant vos ferai a entendre:
        De lui vient toute loiautés
        Et tous biens et toute biautés;
        Se je sui biax, n'est pas de moi,

        Ne nus n'est biax ne bons de soi;
4805 Ne se doit nus enorgillir
        N'el enformer n'el envillir;
        S'il voit ses bons jors ajorner,
        A Diu le doit guerredoner.
        Caitive riens, bontés faillie,
4810 Dites, qui vos a si baillie?
        Quels hom est ce, qui est ses pere?
        – Merci, por Diu, sire emperere!
        – Quel merci volés vos avoir?
        Mais tost me faites assavoir,
4815 Qui est icil que je demanç.
        Només le moi, je le conmanç.
        – Merci, por Diu le roi celestre!
        Biax sire ciers, s'il pooit estre
        Que il venist a delivrance
4820 Et c'on presist de moi vengance.
        Faites moi ardoir ou ocire,
        Se li vengance puet soufire
        Que je seule muire por nos.
        Il n'i a riens mesfait vers vos
4825 Se par moi non, ce me doit nuire;
        Lui laissiés, por Diu, a destruire.
        Se li plons art, que l'argens fonde,
        N'est mie drois c'on le confonde.
        Nus ne doit por ce blasmer l'or
4830 Que l'archaus solle le tresor;
        Que puet li rose de l'ortie
        S'ele est vix erbe et amortie?
        Que puet li lune s'ele luist[418]
        Sor mainte cose qui molt nuist?
4835 Biax sire ciers, que puet il mais   [b]
        De ce que g'ai le cuer malvais?[419]
        Tant dis que je me ting en bien,
        Trestous li mons n'en fesist rien,

---

[416] vous]BT.
[417] veu]BT.
[418] nuist]BT.
[419] De ce quil gai de (*corrected to* le) c. m.]T (B: ke j'oc le c.).

since I last spoke to you! The love between us is now at an end. Your enjoyment of the high position pledged to you will be of short duration. For we have here the case of an excellent woman who, once chosen for high office, becomes too confident and takes pleasure in immoral behaviour.[77] **4776** It would be easy to seduce any other woman, who was not chosen, when the woman whose virtue used to be so closely guarded now gives herself up to the pleasures of the flesh. Those who abandon riches and an honourable estate to live in poverty and dishonour make a very poor exchange. Yet foolish men and women, if they have wealth, take it all for granted. They are troubled by no discomfiture until they lose everything; only when they have experienced poverty do they realise for the first time what they once had. What a pity you ever became queen, for you were poor yet loyal, and when you acquired great material comforts you became evil. May wealth be cursed if it causes so much distress to its owner. In poverty you were beautiful and full of integrity, and when you became rich and beautiful, you should have given thanks to the Son of the Virgin Maid. **4800** For this much I must tell you: all loyalty, fortune and beauty comes from Him. If I am handsome, I cannot take the credit for it, nor can anyone who is handsome or good; no one should congratulate himself on reaching maturity or old age; if he sees each new day bring good luck, he should thank God for it. Wretched creature, goodness which did not last, tell me who used you thus? Who is he? Who is his father? – For God's sake have mercy on me, your imperial majesty. – What sort of mercy do you want from me? Tell me quickly who the man is I have asked you about. I order you to give me his name. – In the name of God, our Heavenly King, have mercy on me. Fair dear lord, if only he could be saved and revenge could be taken on me alone. Have me burned or slain if my death alone can be vengeance enough on both of us. He has done you no wrong other than through me; I should pay for it. **4826** For God's sake, don't kill him. If lead burns so that silver can be smelted, it is not fair to destroy the silver too. No one should blame the gold if the presence of brass coins tarnishes the treasure-chest. What can the rose do about the fact that the nettle is a base and lifeless weed? Or the moon if it shines on many a harmful thing? Fair dear lord, what's it to do with him if I have an evil heart? During the period when I was behaving well, the whole world could not have done anything about it

---

77 For the translation of l. 4773, see Roques 1979, 173. An alternative translation would be 'this is how things develop with women' if the verb *meurer* is taken in its medical sense.

Et quant malvaistiés me prouva,
4840 Se cil en prist qui me trouva,
Que mesprist il vers si halt home
Comme l'empereor de Rome?
Biax sire, assés vos talt noient
Qui moi vos talt, mon ensïent;
4845 Ne vos plaigniés de si vil perte,
Mais a moi rendés me desserte:
Faites moi ardoir u noiier,[420]
U sus de vos lonc envoiier,
Car puis que fausse est li monoie,
4850 A gieter fait li coins en voie.
Sire, de ce dont perte est vostre
Doit estre li damage nostre
Et miens li max et li tormens.
Des que pouris est li formens,
4855 Se nus en a sans congié pris,[421]
Il n'a gaires vers vos mespris;
Car des que bles pourist et oelt,
Assés l'acate qui le quelt;
Mains rices hom que vos nen estes
4860 Le fait sovent gieter as bestes.
Ja li formens n'amenderoit
Se nus afolés en estoit;
Et seroit hontes et peciés,
Car des que bles est enteciés,
4865 Ja puis ne gietra malvais mors:
Faite le gieter, sire, as pors,
Por l'amor Diu, et cil s'en aut.
– Laissiés ester, car ne vos valt;
Nomer le vos convient adés.
4870 – Biax sire ciers, c'est Paridés.
Jel nome et aim et se li nuis,
Et il me nuira se je puis;
Que s'il est ars ou decolés
U de ses membres afolés,

4875 Ceste mains destre me manace, [c]
Se il n'est autres qui le face.»
Grans pitiés prent a cex d'entor,
Et maldient de Diu le tor
Par coi li dame est si malmise,
4880 Par cui enclose i fu et mise.
Duel ont de li et del signor,
Ne mais li sire en a grignor.
Il a tout quis et porcachié,
Le varlet ont tant portrachié
4885 Que il i ont droit asséné,
Et au signor l'ont amené.
Li varlés est molt angosseus,
Et angossant va li espeus,
Et molt angossant vait l'espeuse;
4890 Gens ne fu mais si angosseuse.
Li varlés crient, li sire plaint
Et li dame palit et taint.
Li uns se plaint molt durement,
Li doi ont paor de torment,
4895 Que gerredons lor soit rendus:
Qu'ele soit arse et il pendus.
Del varlet crient que il ne muire,[422]
Et cil, c'on face li destruire;
Espeneïr valroit tos seus
4900 En fin le mesfait d'ambedeus.
«Di moi, vassal, fait l'emperere,
Comment osa li fix ton pere
Me honte querre et porcachier?
Cuidoies tu faute d'acier,
4905 U qu'il ne fust mais point de fer
Ne tormens aillors qu'en infer?
Assés te sarai tormenter,
Et as tiens faire dementer.
Vels tu hardiement morir
4910 Por celi que g'ai fait nourir,

---

[420] F. moir a.]BT.
[421] congiei]BT.

[422] que ele m.]BT.

and when evil put me to the test, if the man who came into contact with me was infected by it, what crime did he commit against a man as powerful as the Emperor of Rome? Fair lord, in my opinion, a man who robs you of me is robbing you of nothing at all. Do not deplore the loss of such a tawdry thing, but give me my just deserts: have me burned or drowned, or banished far away from you, for when coinage has been debased one should throw the coin away. **4851** My lord, we should bear the consequences for what you have lost, but I should be punished and suffer for it. Once wheat has become rotten, even if a person has taken some without permission, he has hardly committed a crime against you; for once the wheat is rotten and smelly, whoever makes the effort to harvest it has already paid too high a price. Far less wealthy men than you would often feed it to their animals. The wheat would never improve even if someone were killed for taking it. And this would be a shameful and sinful deed, for once wheat is ruined, it will never get rid of its horrible taste. For the love of God, have it thrown to your pigs, my lord, and let this man go free. – Say no more, for it will do you no good; you must name him at once. – My dear fair lord, it's Paridés. In naming him, I express my love for him, yet I am causing his downfall, and he will cause mine if I have my way; for if he is burned or decapitated, or physically harmed, this my right hand will threaten to take my life, if there is no one else to do it.' **4877** Those present were overcome by great pity and they cursed in the name of God the tower which had caused the lady so much distress and in which she had been placed under lock and key. They grieved for her and for her lord, but her husband's grief was greater. He had his men search everywhere and follow up all leads. They tracked the young man down, went straight to him and brought him to their lord. The youth was very distressed, and so was the husband, and the wife was very distressed too. Never has such distress been experienced since. The young man was afraid, the husband lamented and the lady went pale and wan. The emperor complained bitterly while the other two feared that they would suffer and that they would receive their just deserts: that she would be burned and he hanged. She feared that the young man would die and he feared that she would be killed; he wanted to pay for once and for all for the crime committed by both of them. **4901** 'Tell me, young man,' said the emperor, 'how did your father's son have the temerity to seek and bring about my shame? Did you think that we lacked the steel to punish you or that there would be no irons or other instruments of torture apart from those in hell? I shall be able to devise horrible torments for you and make your family wail in grief. Do you wish to die bravely for the sake of the woman whom I nurtured

Qui por toi perdra tant honor?
Vels ent morir a deshonor?
– Sire, trop desfaites mon conte.
Ne quit pas que cil muire a honte
4915 Qui muert por fine amor veraie; [d]
Mix aim tel mort que vil mort aie,
Mix aim morir sifaitement
Que longues vivre por noient.
   – Or me di, feme fausse et vaine,
4920 Qui tant avoies en demaine,
Con osas tu cestui atraire?[423]
   – Biax sire, Amors le me fist faire.[424]
   – Comment? aimes le tu encore?[425]
   – Biax sire, comment seroit ore,
4925 Se je onques l'amai nul jor,
Que je ne voelle encor s'amor?
Saciés que finement l'amai,
Quant vos por siue amor faussai;
Icil qui aime finement
4930 N'en puet partir legierement;
Ne s'en part mie quant il veut
Cil qui de fine amor se deut.
   – E, feme, con iés mal senee!
Al point que Dix t'ot assenee,[426]
4935 C'on fist de toi empereïs,
Molt me perdisses a envis.
   – Sire, ne vos perdisse donques
Por trestot l'or que Dix fist onques,
Se il fust tos en une masse;
4940 Mais se je tant cestui amasse
Que je faiç ore, si fesisse;
De tot le mont me demesisse

Se je l'eüsse en mon demaine,
Por estre od lui une semaine.
4945 – E! feme, con iés maleoite!
Molt par est fax qui te covoite![427]
Tant durement te peuç amer[428]
Que je te fis dame clamer
De canc'on m'a signor clamé,
4950 Et or as autrui enamé!
Molt as fait grant desloiauté.
Fui je soufratos de biauté,
U eüs tu besoig d'avoir?
Mains fiance i puet or avoir[429]
4955 Cil por coi j'ai a toi tencié, [e]
Quant tu a moi l'as commencié
Qui te gietai de povreté;
Or puet il savoir par verté[430]
Que par usage le feras,
4960 Quant tu a moi le commenças.»
Eracles li a dit «Biax sire,
Se vos avés et duel et ire,
Ne s'en doit nus hom mervillier;
Mais s'on vos pooit consillier,
4965 Par bone foi vos loeroie,
(Et je meïme le feroie
Se il m'estoit si avenant):
N'alés mais, sire, demenant
La dame si vilainnement;
4970 Car je vos dis bien plainement[431]
N'i doit avoir honte ne lait,
Que c'est par vos canqu'ele a fait.
Ele ert et caste et fine et monde,
Ele ert li miudre riens del monde;
4975 Quant le mesistes en prison,

---
[423] cestu].
[424] honors le mist f.]BT.
[425] aime].
[426] D. tolt]BT.

[427] Molt est f.]T (B: Con est caitis q.).
[428] pouc? *word unclear and surmounted by circumflex in* A]H.
[429] p. on a.]H.
[430] pues].
[431] plainenement].

and who is going to lose such an honourable position because of you? Do you wish to die dishonourably? – My lord, your account of my situation is too unjust.[78] I do not believe that a man who dies for pure true love dies in shame. I prefer to die this way than to have a dishonourable death; I prefer to die in this manner than to have a long but meaningless life. – Now tell me, you weak and treacherous woman, you who had so much in your power, why did you dare to seduce this man? – Fair lord, Love made me do it. – What, do you still love him? – Fair lord, how could I no longer wish for his love if I once loved him? **4927** You should know that I loved him truly when I betrayed you on account of his love. Whoever loves truly cannot give love up lightly; he cannot give it up whenever he wishes, the man who suffers from true love.[79] – Oh woman, how foolish you are. At the time when God chose you to be empress you would have foresaken me very reluctantly. – My lord, I would not have foresaken you for all the gold that God had ever made, even if it had all been piled up in a heap before me; but if I had loved this man as much then as I love him now, then I would have done so. I would have given up the whole world, if I had possessed it, to spend just one week with him. – Oh woman, how cursed you are. He who covets you is a real fool. I came to love you so ardently that I made you empress over all that I ruled as lord and now you have fallen in love with someone else. **4951** You have been very disloyal indeed. Was I lacking in good looks or did you need money? The man who has caused this quarrel between us will not be able to trust you as much in future, since you have begun this behaviour with me, the man who rescued you from poverty. He can now know for sure that what you began with me will become a habit of yours.' Then Eracle said to him: 'Fair lord, that you are upset and angry should come as no surprise to anyone. But if one were allowed to give you some advice, I would advise you in good faith (and I would do this myself if it were appropriate for me) not to continue to treat the lady so discourteously. For I can tell you quite frankly that she should not be shamed or abused, for it is your fault that she has behaved in this way. She used to be chaste, true and pure, and was the best creature in the world. **4975** When you imprisoned her

---

[78] See l. 24 for an earlier pun on *conte*.
[79] The translation attempts to retain the poetic chiasmus of the original here.

Si fesistes grant mesproison,
Que je vos dis tout en oiant
Que vos le perderiés par tant;
Et on ot tant en moi veü
4980 Que s'on m'eüst donques creü,
Il ne fust mie de mervelle.[432]
Je voi maint home qui conselle
Son signor tos jors el que bien,
Sel croit se sire plus que rien;[433]
4985 Et je, selonc m'entention,
Ne vos dis onques se bien non,
Et loai tos jors vostre honor;
Ce sevent bien grant et menor
C'ainc ne vos loai rien a faire
4990 Que a vostre honor fust contraire,
Ne c'onques cose ne vos dis
Dont m'ame perdist paradis.
Ja mar soit nus hom qui ce die
C'onques fesistes felonnie,
4995 U que je sossiel le seüsse, [f]
Por que torner vos en peüsse;
De cesti vos voil destorner,[434]
Ne mais ne vos poi je torner.
Sont vos les colpes, ce saciés;
5000 Ce est grans dels et grans peciés
Que vos le dame en laidengiés;
Malvaisement vos en vengiés,
Que vos ensi le demenés;
Que se vos avant le tenés,
5005 Que plus li aleverés honte
Plus en desferés vostre conte.
Se vos nel volés mais tenir,

Toute le laissiés convenir,[435]
Se vos en partés bielement,
5010 Par l'apostole loiaument.
Dites li tant: «Je vos guerpis»;
Que li volés vos faire pis?
Assés a grant duel a mairier
Qui n'a laissor de repairier
5015 A tele honor con ele pert;
Laissiés li ce qu'ele dessert.[436]
Tort ai, ne l'ai pas desservi,
Mais vostre cors que je mar vi,
C'on dira cent ans ci après:
5020 «Cil qui se feme tint si pres
Faussa Eracle, son devin;
La dame prist malvaise fin.»
Ne diront pas que je vos dis
Que bone eüst esté toudis
5025 S'ele ne fust emprisonee;
Car toute gens s'est adonee
Et a mal dire et a mal faire,
Ja nes orrés un bien retraire;
Mix volent mal dire et mentir
5030 Que nule rien bien consentir
Que on le die de nului;
Cascuns se sent si plains d'anui
Ne velt pas c'on des autres die
Ce qu'il en soi ne cuide mie.
5035 Puet estre uns peciés les deçoit, [148a]
Que nus son mehaing n'aperçoit,
Et voient es preudomes l'ombre
De cele riens qui les encombre;
Ne voient pas dont l'ombre vient,

---
[432] fu].
[433] *No need to correct to* ses sire *as there is no ambiguity of sense, cf.* 2838.
[434] voel], *cf.* 5048, 5346, 5963, *confusion between present and past tense forms* (B: voç).
[435] laissi].
[436] Laisse].

you made a great error of judgement, for I told you publicly that you would thereby lose her. And enough had been discovered about me by then that no one would have been surprised if you had believed me. I have seen many a man who always advises his lord badly, yet his lord believes him above all others. And I, as far as I can tell, only ever said what was good for you and always gave you honourable counsel. Both the powerful and humble men of the empire are in no doubt that I never advised you to do anything in conflict with your honour. Nor did I ever say anything to you which might have prevented my soul from entering paradise. Let no man ever say that you committed a crime or that I somehow or other knew about it and could have dissuaded you from it. I wanted to dissuade you from this one, but I could not dissuade you. It is your fault, be in no doubt. **5000** It is a great pity and a great sin that you are insulting this lady because of it. You are avenging yourself wickedly by abusing her in this way; and if you continue to keep her, the more you increase her shame the more you will undermine your own reputation.[80] If you do not wish to keep her any longer, let her do whatever she wants and arrange an amicable separation in accordance with the law of the Church.[81] Just say to her "I am letting you go". Do you really want to do any worse to her? A person who has no opportunity to return to such an honourable position as she is now losing will suffer from plenty of regrets. Let her have what she deserves. I am being blamed, yet I have not deserved it, but what a pity I ever set eyes on you, for people will say in a hundred years' time: "he who kept his wife under such close guard was betrayed by Eracle,[82] his seer, and the lady came to a sticky end". They will not say that I told you that she would have remained virtuous to the end of her days had she not been imprisoned. **5026** For everyone is intent on speaking evil and doing evil. You will never hear people talk about anything good. They prefer to slander and tell lies rather than allow anything positive to be said about anyone. Every individual feels that he is so full of faults that he does not want people to attribute virtues to others that he does not feel he possesses at all. Perhaps these people are deceived by sin, for none is aware of his own fault, yet they see in the virtuous the shadow of the very vice that afflicts them. They do not see what is casting this shadow,

---

[80] Cf. ll. 24 and 4913 for more punning on conte.
[81] Gautier may be referring erroneously to the Pauline privilege (Corinthians I, 7: 15) on the dissolution of marriage between a Christian and non-Christian, or may be confusing Paul's teaching with Matthew 19: 8-9 on separation after adultery. The events in *Eracle* may reflect the Greek Church's less strict views on divorce and remarriage (see Raynaud de Lage's note to l. 5010). Since *l'apostole* is likely to refer to the pope, a reading supported by O: 4365, Gautier may be implying divorce by papal decree/authorisation.
[82] Although the nouns in l. 5021 seem to be in the object case, logically Eracle has to be the subject of *faussa*.

5040 Qui si tres pres des cuers lor tient.
Ne mais que calt? Li biens vaintra,
Et aucuns preudom le dira:
« Certes s'Eracles fust creüs,[437]
Laïs ne fust ja decheüs. »
5045 – Eracle, amis, ne puet autre estre.
Je pris cesti par main de prestre,
Si m'en voel loiaument partir.
Faire voil un nouviel martyr[438]
De cel varlet, mais nel ferai;
5050 La dame a mari le donrai,
Et s'ele a ce que tant desire,
Del sorplus qu'ele se consire;
Bien le metrai el biel deport;
Et g'iere arivés a mal port
5055 Qu'a paines m'en deporterai.
Ne mais de tant me vengerai:
N'ara mais mie de l'empere,
Mais le terre qui fu son pere
Li otroi toute cuitement,
5060 Et cent mars l'an d'acroissement.[439]
Chist a a pere molt rice home,
N'a plus manant en toute Rome;
Rices hom est, rice seront,
Et ricement se demenront. »
5065 Chil l'encline parfondement,
Et la dame tout ensement.
Tous coreciés et tous maris
Se depart de l'empereïs
Li emperere, et cil le prent,
5070 Qui por s'amor de joie esprent.
Je ne cuiç pas qu'il soit mains liés
Que l'emperere est coureciés;
Il en est tristres et dolens
De çou, au los de toutes gens,

5075 Que perdu a par se folie [b]
La dame de le millor vie,
Le plus vaillant, le plus senee
Qui onques fust de Rome nee,[440]
Dont tant maint felon sont estrait;
5080 Souvent a on dit et retrait
Qu'en nule cité n'a pïors;
Mais de femes esce la flors,
Et se n'i ot si bone puis
Con ceste fu, si con je truis;
5085 Proisie fu sor toute rien.
U fust a mal, u fust a bien,
Se consira puis l'emperere.
Il n'afiert pas a ma matere
Que je plus die de Laïs,
5090 De Pariden, d'Athanaïs;[441]
Iceus vos lairons ore em pais,
Si vos dirons d'Eracle humais.
Bien saciés qu'il est chevaliers,
Preus et loiaus et droituriers,
5095 Larges et dous a ses amis
Et crueus a ses anemis;
Et si ert molt amés en Rome.
En l'empire n'ot si haut home
Qui envers lui se main tendist
5100 Que ricement ne li vendist.
Trestous les orgillous plaissoit,
Et durement les abaissoit;
As preudomes faisoit grans biens,
Ses honeroit sor toute riens,
5105 Qu'il ert molt sages et senés;
Ne n'estoit mie mal senés
Qui de lui se sot reclamer.
As bons se faisoit bien amer,
Et as mauvais criembre et douter.

---
[437] fus].
[438] voel; B]R; martyir].
[439] angoissement]BT.
[440] mere n.]BT.
[441] Parideu de Thanais]BT.

for it has taken hold of them so very close to their hearts. Yet what does it matter? Virtue will prevail and some worthy man will say, "there's no doubt that if Eracle had been believed, Laïs would never have been deceived." – Eracle, my friend, since I have no other option, so be it. I took this woman to wife in the presence of a priest and I now wish to separate from her in accordance with Church law. I wanted to make a modern martyr out of this young man, but I shall not do so. I shall give him to the lady as her husband, and if she has what she desires so much, let her do without the rest. **5050** I shall set her up with all her pleasures and I shall end up in a sorry state, for it will be difficult to live without her.[83] However, I shall take this much revenge: she will no longer have claim to imperial property, but I grant her unrestricted use of the land that belonged to her father and a hundred marks annual income. Paridés's father is a very wealthy man, there is none more comfortably off in the whole of Rome. He is a rich man and they will be too, and they will have a very comfortable standard of living.' Paridés bowed deeply to him and the lady did the same. The emperor was very upset and distressed when he parted from the empress, and the young man took her, overjoyed in his love for her. I doubt that his happiness was greater than the emperor's distress; the latter was sad and deeply regretted that he had, in everyone's opinion, lost through his own folly the most worthy, virtuous and most wise lady who had ever been born in Rome, the birthplace of many a rogue. **5080** It has often been said and reported that you can find none worse than in that city. Yet she was the flower of womankind, and since then there has never been a woman as excellent as she was, as far as I can tell. She was esteemed above all other creatures. Whether for better or for worse the emperor then let her go. It is not relevant to my subject for me to say any more about Laïs, Paridés and Athanaïs; we shall now leave them in peace and we shall tell you about Eracle from now on. You already know that he was a knight, noble, loyal and just, generous and mild towards his friends and cruel towards his enemies;[84] and so he was much loved in Rome. There was no powerful man anywhere in the empire who, if he challenged him, did not pay dearly for it. **5101** He humbled and mercilessly brought down all those who were arrogant; but rewarded the virtuous richly and honoured them above all others, for he was very wise and prudent. And whoever was able to call him his friend was no fool. He won the love of the righteous and the fear and trepidation of the wicked.

---

83   Note the extended *annominatio* on *port* and its cognates.
84   These are the qualities typically associated with kingship in the Middle Ages.

5110 Se bon vous ert a escouter,
Bon me seroit huimais a dire
Coment fu puis et rois et sire,
Et par quele aventure avint
Que il Coustantinoble tint,
5115 Et le veraie Crois conquist [c]
Sor Cordroé, que il ocist,⁴⁴²
Primes le fil et puis le pere,
Et fist dolante mainte mere.
   Signor, nos lisons en latin⁴⁴³
5120 Qu'Elaine, mere Coustentin,
Trouva icele vraie Crois
U nostre sire fu en crois.
Judas, cui Damedix bien face,
Que l'en dit or saint Cyriache,
5125 Li ensigna, ce est la voire.
Trois crois i ot, ce dist l'estoire:
As deus larons furent les deus,
La tierce a Diu le glorïeus,
Et par grant sens fu esprovee
5130 La tierce qui i fu trouvee,
Si vos dirai en quel maniere:
Illuec gisoit uns mors en biere.⁴⁴⁴
L'une des crois fu sor lui mise,
Ne li valut une cherise,
5135 Que ne fu pas del voir ciprés.⁴⁴⁵
L'autre crois i fu mise aprés,
Mais riens ne valut c'on l'i mist,
Ne que li premeraine fist.
Elaine dist: «Or voi ge bien
5140 Que ces deus crois ne valent rien.
Or ça, le tierce, el non Cestui
Qui la soufri paine et anui.
Se li voirs fus i fust eüs,

Li mors fust pieça revescus,
5145 Ce croi je bien et ce querrai,
Et se Diu plaist, je le verrai.»
Et Judas, qui jugiés estoit,
Qui le crois ensegnie avoit,
Li dist: «Dame, se Dix tant fait
5150 Que cis revive por nul plait
Par le vertu de ceste crois,
Dont querrai je que sainte fois⁴⁴⁶
Et sains baptesmes m'aidera
Quant Damedix nos jugera,
5155 Et crestïens devenrai lués, [d]
Por qu'il i a mestier et oeus.»
Le Crois ont sor le mort coucie,
Se bouce en ont primes touchie
Et puis les ix et les orelles;
5160 Puis virent avenir mervelles,
C'or cil qui mors avoit esté
Une nuit et un jor d'esté
Voiant eus tous i revesqui,
Sains con al jor con il veski,
5165 Si que tout cil de la cité
Virent le mort ressuscité;
Et droitement que ce fu fait,
Diables sailli d'un agait,
Et cuide engignier tot le monde,
5170 Si dist: «Judas, Dix te confonde!
Li autre Judas entendi
A moi servir quant il vendi
Son signor lige en traïson
Por estre en me subjection;
5175 Molt par se mist en bas degré
Trestout por moi servir a gré;
Et tu deviens mes anemis

---

⁴⁴² Sous C.; B]T; que il conquist]BT.
⁴⁴³ au matin]BT.
⁴⁴⁴ briere].
⁴⁴⁵ aprés]B.

⁴⁴⁶ ceste f.]BT.

If you would like to listen I would be happy to tell you now how he later became king and emperor, and by what good fortune he came to rule over Constantinople and then won back the Holy Cross from Chosroes, whom he killed – first the son, then the father – and made many a mother grieve.

My lords, we can read in the Latin sources how Helena, the mother of Constantine, found the True Cross on which Our Lord was crucified.[85] May God bless Judas, whom we now call Saint Cyriacus, who led her to it, and that is a fact. **5126** According to my source, there were three crosses: two of them belonged to the two thieves, the third belonged to Our Glorious Lord. The third that was found there was authenticated in a very clever way, and I shall tell you how: a dead man was lying there in his coffin. One of the crosses was placed on him, but it did not help him a fig,[86] for it was not made of the true cypress wood. The second cross was then placed on him, but there was no point placing it on him any more than there had been with the first. Helena said: 'Now I can see that these two crosses are worthless. Bring me the third, in the name of Him who suffered pain and torment on it. If we had had the true wood here, the dead man would have already been revived. This is what I believe and shall continue to believe, and if it pleases God, I shall see this come to pass.' **5147** And Judas, who was a condemned criminal and who had led her to the cross, said to her: 'My lady, if God manages to revive this man somehow or other through the power of this cross, then I shall believe that holy faith and holy baptism will come to my aid when the Lord God judges us, and I shall become a Christian straight away, for it will be both necessary and to my advantage.' They lay the Cross down on the corpse, touching his mouth with it first, then his eyes and his ears; they then witnessed a miracle, for now the man who had been dead for a night and a long summer's day, came to life again before their very eyes and was as healthy as the day when he was still alive. Thus all those from the city witnessed the resuscitation of the dead man. And as soon as this had happened, the devil leapt from his hiding-place and hoped to deceive everyone by saying: 'Judas, may God confound you. The other Judas was keen to serve me when he treacherously sold his liege-lord in order to be subject to me; **5175** he abased himself greatly to serve my every need. Yet you are now becoming my enemy

---

[85] From now on Gautier's main source is a Latin *Passionarius*, amplified through the addition of epic diction and motifs. For details on how Gautier has modified his sources, see my Introduction, pp. xviii-xxiii.

[86] Literally, a cherry.

Por estre haltement assis;
Et cil Judas enfrainst se loi
5180 Et traï son signor por moi,
Et tu m'as del tout enhaï
Et por Diu avoir m'as traï.
Molt laidement m'as engignié
Quant tu le fust as ensegnié
5185 Que je avoie fait reponre
Por le gent honir et confondre.
Mais or nel tenés a escar;
G'iere encor vengiés de te car:
Se je en t'ame n'ai pooir,
5190 Tes cors le comperra por voir:
Te cars sera por Diu vermelle!»
Molt par en orent grant mervelle
Icil qui cieste vois oïrent
El ciel et nule rien ne virent.
5195 Judas, a cui li vois parvint, [e]
Voiant tous, crestïens devint;
Si l'apielerent Cyriace.
Puis en ot il vers Diu tel grasce⁴⁴⁷
Qu'il en est el ciel courounés;
5200 Molt bons loiiers l'en est donnés,
Mais martyrs fu li Diu amis,
Si con li dist li anemis.
A le joie de cele crois
Ot molt canté a haute vois;
5205 Helaine molt s'i travilla,
Car mil fois s'i agenoulla,
Puis si le fist en deus soiier⁴⁴⁸
Et l'une moitié envoiier
A Coustentin, present l'en fist;
5210 Le moitié el sepulchre mist.

Et puis qu'Elaine fu finee,
Qui molt ot bone destinee,
Li terre u Dix prist naissement
Afebloia molt durement,
5215 Por le pecié as crestïens,
Et Cosdroé, uns rois paiens,
Vint a la chité par effors
U Damedix fu vis et mors.
Gent ot molt fiere et molt estoute.
5220 Jherusalem destruist trestoute⁴⁴⁹
Et tous les crestïens ocist,
Et le Crois el sepuchre prist,
Et si le fist porter en Perse,
A cele fole gent averse.
5225 Un chiel ot fait faire li fols,
A cieres pieres et a clos;
Molt ricement l'ot fait ouvrer.⁴⁵⁰
Illuec se faisoit aourer
A le caitive fole gent,
5230 Qui croit et mescroit por noient,
Con li popelican caitif.
Tuit i venoient a estrif,
Que par engien, si con je truis,
Faisoit plovoir par un pertruis
5235 Qu'il ot fait faire el ciel dessus; [f]
Encor i ot il assés plus:
Li terre estoit dessous cievee⁴⁵¹
Et bien planchie et bien levee;
Uns fols i ot fait por soner,
5240 Con il voloit faire touner.
Tout el i ot: venter faisoit,
Et plus assés, quant li plaisoit.
Le Crois, u fu mis Nostre Sire

---
⁴⁴⁷ crasce]BT.
⁴⁴⁸ crois s.]BT.
⁴⁴⁹ destruit]T.
⁴⁵⁰ le f.]BT.
⁴⁵¹ dessus]BT; crevee]H, *cf.* 4400 (B: cavee).

in order to sit on high. The other Judas contravened his law and betrayed his lord for me, while you have conceived a great hatred for me and have betrayed me in order to win God's favour. You tricked me most vilely when you revealed the whereabouts of the wood which I had hidden to bring shame and ruin on these people. But don't underestimate me, I shall yet take my revenge on your body: even if I have no power over your soul, your body will pay for it, I can assure you; your body will be scarlet for God!'[87] Those who heard this voice coming from an invisible source in the sky were full of amazement. Judas, to whom the voice was addressed, became a Christian before their very eyes and they called him Cyriacus. Then he received such grace from God that he was crowned in heaven. **5200** He was richly rewarded, but this man who loved God was martyred, as the devil told him he would be. From joy at the discovery of this cross there was much singing at the tops of their voices. Helena mortified herself greatly by kneeling a thousand times before it; then she had it sawn in two and sent one half to Constantine as a present; the other half was placed in the Holy Sepulchre. Once Helena, who was destined for great things, had died, the land where God took human form became much weaker as a result of Christian sinfulness. Chosroes, a pagan king, fought his way to the city where our Lord God had lived and died. His men were very fierce and proud. He destroyed Jerusalem completely and killed all the Christians and took the True Cross from the Holy Sepulchre and sent it to Persia, to that heathen enemy race. **5225** The heathen had a heaven constructed out of precious stones and studs. He commissioned splendid workmanship. There he forced his wretched heathen subjects, who, like wretched heretics, change their beliefs at the drop of a hat, to worship him.[88] They all vied with one another to go there, for, according to my sources, he had devised a mechanism for making rain fall through an opening made at the top of the heaven. And there was much more: underneath a pit had been dug and covered with boards expertly shored up and in it he had placed some bellows to be played when he wished to simulate thunder. And that was not all: he made wind blow and lots more things too, when the mood took him. The Cross on which Our Lord was hung

---

[87] This refers to the bloody torments suffered by Judas Cyriacus, a saint especially venerated in Provins; see Fourrier 1960, 253-54.

[88] A reference here, as in *Ille et Galeron*, 1247, to the Cathar heresy.

Quant il soufri por nos martire,
5245 Fist metre el ciel el plus biel leu,
Por faire, espoir, honor a Deu
Selonc le siu entendement,[452]
U por le crestïene gent[453]
Qui i venoient jor et nuit
5250 Le Crois aourer par conduit;
S'i donoit cascuns un besant,[454]
Et cuidoient li fol Persant
Qu'il aouraissent Cordroé,[455]
Le fol, le caitif avoué.
5255 As crestïens faisoit grans maux
Cis empereres desloiaus;
Il les ardoit, il les pendoit
Et trestos vis les porfendoit;
Les uns faisoit fort ensierer,
5260 Les autres tos vis entierer.
L'empereor qui lors tenoit
Coustantinoble, et Diu creoit,
Fist il ocire en traïson;
Foucars ot l'emperere non.
5265   Cil de le cité consel prisent,
Et li preudome Eracle eslirent.
Lonc d'els estoit, qu'il ert a Rome;
Mais qu'il le sorent a preudome.
Un autre eslisent, preu et sage,
5270 Qui en Aufrique ot iretage;
Non por ice que li comun[456]
Ne s'acordassent bien a un,
Ne mais sans avoué estoient
Et Cordroé forment doutoient;
5275 Et por soufraite de singnor   [149 a]
Eslisent double empereor;

Li quex que primes i venist
L'empire eüst, l'onor tenist.
Eracles i vint premerains,
5280 Et ce pesa molt as Roumains;
Ne mais se Rome en fu irie,
Coustantinoble en devint lie.
Eracle assisent en l'onor,
Jamais, je cuiç, n'aront millor.
5285 N'ot pas set ans, ne mie sis,
Puis qu'il fu en l'onor assis,
Que il acointa les contrees
Que Cordroé ot desertees;
Car cuite furent li cemin
5290 A le coustume Coustentin.
Or se crient molt li fel kenus
Que mals sordens li soit venus.
Eracles est et rois et sire,
Molt maintient vivement l'empire.
5295 Molt a grant duel, ainc n'ot grignor,
De cele Crois Nostre Signor
Que Cosdroé tient en viuté[457]
Et tenir le cuide en cierté
Por ce qu'en son ciel l'a assise;
5300 Mais ne va pas a le devise
Le bon empereor Eracle,
Et Dix en face apert miracle!
    Rois Cordroés son fil apiele:
Amis, fait il, trop se reviele
5305 Cil fols qui tient Costantinoble.
Molt s'en fait orgilleus et noble;
Il croit en autre diu qu'en moi.
Assanle gent, ge t'i envoi;
Pren le, sel giete en un vil leu.

---

452 le fin e.] (B: sien).
453 U. par] B.
454 donent]BT.
455 Cordore].
456 Ne]BT.

457 tent en viite]BT.

when he suffered martyrdom for our sakes was placed in the finest spot in the heaven, perhaps because he wanted to honour God in his own misguided way or on account of the Christians, who were permitted to come day and night to worship the Cross and who each gave a *besant* for the privilege. **5252** And the foolish Persians thought that they were worshipping Chosroes, the heathen, their wretched lord. This treacherous emperor treated the Christians abominably; he burned them, hanged them and hacked them in two while still alive. Some he had imprisoned, others were buried alive. He had the emperor who then ruled over Constantinople and who believed in God killed treacherously; the emperor's name was Phocas.

The inhabitants of the city took counsel and the elders elected Eracle. He was far away from them, though, for he was in Rome, but they knew him to be a worthy man. They also elected another man, who was brave and wise, and who came from Africa,[89] not because the common people could not agree on one person, but because they were without a protector and feared Chosroes greatly. **5275** So, because they were without a lord they elected two emperors. Whoever arrived there first would have the empire and rule over the land. Eracle arrived first, but this upset the Romans deeply. Yet if Rome had cause for regret, Constantinople had equal cause for joy. They bestowed the title on Eracle and, in my view, they will never have a better emperor. Barely seven years or even six after having the title bestowed upon him, he inspected the regions that Chosroes had devastated, for the custom of Constantine allowed free movement on the roads. The treacherous old heathen then became very afraid that his luck had run out. Eracle was both emperor and lord, and was ruling the empire energetically. He was very distressed, however, and had never been more so, about the Cross of Our Lord that Chosroes was treating with disrespect, even though he thought he was honouring it by placing it in his heaven. **5300** But this was not acceptable to Eracle, the good emperor, and may God perform a clear miracle to remedy this!

King Chosroes called his son to him and said: 'My friend, the madman who holds Constantinople in his sway has overstepped the mark by a long chalk. He is full of arrogance and ideas above his station; he believes in a god other than me. Muster your troops, for I am sending you against him; capture him and throw him in a dungeon.

---

[89] Interestingly, Heraclius's father came from Africa.

5310 Pren le païs, passe Mongeu
Et Normendie et France et Flandre,
C'onques ne fist rois Alixandres.
Tout cil qui en moi ne querront,
Si tost con il ton cors verront,
5315 Mes fai decoler a esploit. [b]
– Biax sire, a vostre plaisir soit!»
Si grans gens ne fu mais veüe
Con cis maufés a esmeüe.
Tramet ses briés en orïent,
5320 Qu'aler en velt en ocident
Les crestïens tous encalcier
Et le loi son pere essaucier.
Le nuit que cil rouva son fil[458]
Les crestïens metre a eschil,
5325 Vint li angles Nostre Signor
A nostre bon empereor;
Dist li: «Eracle, esvelle toi!
Dix te mande salus par moi
Si te requiert par moi un don.[459]
5330 Eü en as le guerredon,[460]
Qu'il t'a doné sens et savoir,
Honor et hautece a avoir.
Amis, ne l'oublier tu pas,
Car tout est de par Diu que t'as.
5335 Or si te mande Nostre Sire
Que tu assanles ton empire,
Quanc'onques on puet assanler.
Cil qui le terre fait tranler,
Rois Cordroés, li fel, li fiers,
5340 Mande sergans et chevaliers
Et trestous cex qui de lui tienent;
Mort sont en fin s'a lui ne vienent.
Son fil qu'assamble en felonie

Reuve et conmande qu'il les guie.[461]
5345 Jherusalem destruist pieça;
Or velt envoiier par deça[462]
Son fil destruire et faire anui
Tous ceus qui ne querront en lui.
Eracle, amis, or t'esvertue,
5350 Qu'il fiert et trence et prent et tue
Quanqu'il aconsiut et ataint.
S'il et si fil ne sont estaint,[463]
Ne mais uns seus, qui gist en bers,
Mains crestïens en ert cuivers,
5355 En buies mis, en crois pendus; [c]
Mains hom en sera confondus.
A Diu s'afaite et agencist
Qui felon home adevancist
Ançois qu'il soit passés le lice
5360 A faire l'uevre de malisse.
Qui soesfre felon mal a faire,
Quels que il soit, provos u maire,
Parçouniers est de canqu'il fait,
Por qu'oster l'en puist par nul plait.
5365 Cestui poras tu bien oster;
Or tost, amis, n'i a qu'ester,
Or tost, n'i a que demourer,
Que li leus velt tout devourer.
Contre se gent le toie maine
5370 Et bien aras sauve te paine;
Dix le te sara bien merir,
Qui ert as premiers cols ferir.
Et quant li cose ert acomplie,
Li Crois qui tant est covoitie
5375 Pren, porte le en Jherusalem.
Cil qui fu nés en Belleem
Le te mande del ciel lassus.

---

[458] trouva]BT.
[459] requier].
[460] Eeu].

[461] assanle]BT.
[462] volt]BT.
[463] son fil]L (BT: ses fieus).

Take possession of the land, press on through the St Bernard Pass to Normandy, France and Flanders, further than King Alexander ever reached. For my sake, have all those who refuse to believe in me decapitated on the spot as soon as they set eyes on you. – Fair lord, may it be as you wish.' This devil mustered a huge army the like of which has never been seen since. He sent his letters to the East, saying that he intended to move westwards to expel all the Christians and to promote his father's religion. **5323** The very night that he asked his son to banish the Christians, the angel of Our Lord came to our good emperor and said to him: 'Eracle, wake up! God sends you greetings via me and requests a favour of you. You have already received a gift from Him in that He gave you wisdom and knowledge with which to obtain honour and high status. My friend, do not forget Him, for all that you have is from God. Now Our Lord sends word to you to mobilise all the men of your empire, as many men as you can muster. King Chosroes the treacherous and fierce, who makes the earth tremble, is summoning his footsoldiers and his knights and all those who hold land from him; they will be killed if they do not go to his aid. He has asked and commanded his son, who is united with him in treachery, to lead them. He destroyed Jerusalem a while ago, now he plans to send his son over here to kill and persecute all those who will not believe in him. **5349** Eracle, my friend, gather up your strength, for he strikes, hacks to pieces, captures and kills everything he finds in his path and can lay his hands on. If he and his sons are not killed (except for the one who is still in his cradle), many a Christian will be reduced to slavery, chained or crucified; many a man will be slain. A man recommends himself to God and wins his favour if he intercepts a treacherous man before he transgresses and commits an act of wickedness. Whoever allows a traitor to commit evil, whoever he may be, magistrate or mayor, is an accomplice to the deed, if he could have stopped him in any way from doing it. You will be able to stop this man effectively. So hurry, my friend, there's no time to delay; hurry, don't tarry, for the wolf is keen to devour everything. Lead your troops against his and your efforts will not be wasted; God, who will be present when the first blows are struck, will know how to reward you for it. And when you have accomplished the task, seize the Cross which is so coveted and take it to Jerusalem. **5376** He who was born in Bethlehem is sending you this message from heaven above.

O toi ne puis demorer plus.»
Aprés cest mot s'esvanuist.[464]
5380 Eracles Diu en beneïst
Et loe de cest mandement,
Et fait lués son coumandement.
Ses briés a fait en cire metre
Et largement les fait trametre.
5385 Li messagier par tot espandent;
Les uns proient, autres conmandent;[465]
Li un preecent et semonnent
Et de par Damediu sermonent
Les amis Diu c'or s'aparellent,
5390 Qu'or s'esberucent et esvellent,[466]
C'ainc mais n'en fu si grans mestiers;
Qu'en abeïes n'en moustiers
N'iert mais Dix servis con il selt
Se li fel fait que faire veut:[467]
5395 Car le non Diu cuide esfacier [d]
C'ainc mais n'osa nus embrachier.
Cil cui on fait cest oevre entendre[468]
Se voelent mix aler desfendre[469]
Qu'en lor païs soient soupris
5400 Et mort et malbailli et pris.
Li messagier s'en vont batant.[470]
Hardie gent et combatant
Ot l'emperere a jor nonmé,[471]
Et maint ceval destrecomé
5405 Et maint escu et mainte lance
Et mainte biele conissance
Et maint hauberc menu maillié,

Maint hiaume a or bien entaillié.[472]
Vers Dunoe ont lor cemin pris,[473]
5410 La se sont trait, con ont apris;
Cele part prendent lor cemin.
Ne ciessent ne ne prendent fin
Entreus qu'il vienent a Dunoe,
Que nus soussiel ne le tresnoe:
5415 Rade est et fors et molt parfonde;
Un pont i a, n'a tel el monde
Si grant, si haut, si lonc, si lé;
Quarante chevalier armé
S'i soloient bien encontrer,
5420 Emmi, a l'issir, a l'entrer.[474]
Droitement con li crestïen
I sont venu, et li paiien;
Li crestïen sont par deça
Et li felon paiien dela;
5425 D'ambes deus pars sont grans les os.
Li paiien voient bien les nos,
Et il ne pueent faire rien
Que li nostre ne voient bien.[475]
Li un ne font rien cele nuit
5430 K'as autres d'autre part anuit,
Car l'aige est molt grans entre deus,
Et li passers est perilleus.
Li cief del pont sont si gaitié
N'i a chevalier si haitié,
5435 Si orgillous ne plain de rage, [e]
Qui del passer ait grant corage.
Ne mais quant l'aube est esclarchie,

---

464 Aprés mot]B.
465 proie a. conmande].
466 Q'or].
467 Se li fait]B.
468 Cix]BT.
469 delfendre].
470 Lun]BT.
471 O l.]B.

472 bor]B.
473 V. une oe o.]BT, *cf.* 5413.
474 E. asseir a larmer]B.
475 noe]BT.

I can't stay with you any longer.' After saying this he disappeared. Eracle thanked and praised the Lord for this message and immediately obeyed his command. He had letters sealed with wax and sent them out far and wide. His messengers went off in all directions, beseeching some and commanding others; some preached and exhorted, and in God's name urged those who loved God to make themselves ready, to summon their courage and be vigilant, because never before had the danger been so great. For God would no longer be worshipped as He had been in abbeys and in monasteries if the traitor were allowed to do what he planned: since he hoped to remove the name of God from the earth, so that no one would dare embrace Christianity again.

Those to whom these plans were explained preferred to go forth and defend themselves rather than be the victims of a surprise attack in their own country and to be killed, tortured or taken captive. **5401** The messengers set off at top speed. On the appointed day the emperor had brave and battle-hardened troops, many horses with their manes combed to the right, many a shield and many a lance, many a splendid coat of arms, many a hauberk of fine mail and many a helmet beautifully inlaid with gold. They set off towards the Danube, making their way to it by a familiar route. They took themselves off in that direction and did not stop or give up until they came to the Danube, which no one on earth could swim across. It was fast-flowing, had a strong current and was very deep. There was no bridge on earth as huge, high, long and wide as the one over it. It was not unusual for forty armed knights to stand face to face on it, in the middle, at the exit and at the entrance. The pagans arrived at exactly the same time as the Christians; the Christians were on one side and the treacherous pagans on the other. **5425** The armies were huge on both sides; the pagans had a good view of our troops and they could do nothing without our men seeing it clearly. Neither side did anything that night to harm the others on the opposite side, for there was a huge expanse of water between them and it was dangerous to cross it. Both ends of the bridge were so well guarded that no knight was fit, rash or foolhardy enough to be keen to cross it. However, once the sun had risen

Que l'emperere a messe oïe,
Si traist ses barons d'une part:
5440 «Signor, fait il, par vostre esgart
Voel je tout faire en ceste voie,
Que je de rien blamés ne soie,
Ne plus loés, ne plus proisiés
De nul de vos; si eslisiés
5445 Le mix, le plus biel tout ensanle;
Die cascuns ce qu'il li sanle
Et dient «Bons est cis conseus,[476]
Et cis est miudres; cis n'est prex».
Signor, voiés de ces cuivers
5450 Con li païs en est couvers;
Dis tans sont plus que nos ne somes,
Ne mais que millors gens avomes,
Et foi et baptesme et creance,
Et je le sai bien sans faillance,
5455 Nostre ert l'onors, ce verrés vos,[477]
Et si sont dis tans plus que nous.
Se nos volons l'eve passer,
Jan i verrés mil entasser
Que tuit en bevront plus qu'assés
5460 Ains qu'en i ait deus mil passés.
Contre un des nos i aroit mil:
Se cil estoient li plus vil
Que on peüst a esme eslire,
Si les poroient il ocire.
5465 Nos n'i poons nul bien coisir[478]
S'il ont deça venir loisir.
L'issir del pont et le descendre
Comment lor poriens nos desfendre?
Nos somes ci en un pendant

5470 Si venront sor nos descendant.
Nel di por vos desconforter,
Issi me doinst Dix deporter
De mes peciés au grant besoig,
Mais ce saciés, je ai grant soig.
5475 Preudom qui aime bien et pais   [f]
Redoute plus que li malvais.
Sans noise faire et sans tenchier
Doit on si l'uevre commenchier
C'al mains de mescief que on puet
5480 Soit traite a fin; et moi estuet,
Por ce que on me tient a sage,[479]
D'eschiver le conmun damage.
Nus ne doit metre trop, por voir,
En ce qu'il puet por poi avoir.[480]
5485 Je douç le mescief de nos homes,[481]
Se nos as paiens assanlomes.
Se Cordroés tel se savoit
Et tant de hardement avoit
Qu'a moi se mesist cors a cors
5490 Desor ce pont, si que dehors
Fussent nos gens si qu'il sont ore,
Biel me seroit, et si encore
Que nus de nos ne se meüst[482]
Por nul besoig qui nos creüst[483]
5495 Et fesist l'uns l'autre seür
Que cil cui Dix donroit l'eür
De son per vaintre, si fust sire
D'ansdeus les os sans contredire,
Ice me seroit a creant,
5500 Se il plaisoit au mescreant
Et a vous tos coumunement;

---

[476] bon]BT.
[477] verre].
[478] Nus]BT.
[479] assage]. *The double consonant is a common feature of Scribe* 1, *cf.* 1461, 2088, 2198, 4342, *etc.*
[480] por Diu a.]BT.
[481] mescies].
[482] nos de nos]BT.
[483] nus c.]R (B: ke il; T: que on).

and the emperor had heard mass, he drew his barons to one side and said: 'My lords, in this matter I wish to act solely on your advice so that I am not criticised for anything, or more praised or esteemed than any of you; so together choose the best, the most appropriate course of action and let everyone speak their mind, by saying: "This advice is good, this is better, this is not a good idea." **5449** My lords, you can see how the countryside is covered in these vile wretches. There are ten times more of them than there are of us, although we have better men and we also have our faith and beliefs as baptised Christians, and I know for sure that we shall triumph, as you will see; yet they do outnumber us tenfold. If we attempt to cross the river, you will see a thousand of us piled up who will all have drunk more than our fill before two thousand of us manage to get across. And against one of us there would be a thousand of them, and even if they were the most cowardly men you could possibly select, they would still be able to kill our men. We can see no good coming from it if they have the opportunity to cross over to this side; how could we then prevent them from rushing down from the bridge? We are here on a slope and they will attack us from above. I'm not saying this to discourage you; may God grant me remission of my sins in my hour of need, but I have to tell you that I am very worried. **5475** A good man who loves virtue and peace fears more readily than an evil man. Without making a fuss or quarrelling one should approach a task in such a way that it can be completed with the minimum of harm possible; and it behoves me, since I am considered to be wise, to avoid wholesale slaughter. Indeed, no one should risk a great deal if he can achieve his aim with a small wager. If we engage in battle with the pagans, I fear our men will come to grief. Now if Chosroes had the confidence in himself and enough courage to fight man-to-man against me on this bridge with our men remaining on the banks as they are now, it would be fine by me. And if, moreover, neither of us were to abandon the fight whatever danger we find ourselves in and were to swear to each other that the man to whom God granted the good fortune of beating his opponent should be the unopposed leader of both armies, I would be willing to agree to this, if it pleased the heathen and all of you.

Et je vos di veraiement
Que il n'i a tant de si buen,
Se il le voloit et li suen.
5505 Je n'i cuiç nul, tant i soit fiers,
Qui ne le voelle volentiers,
Que il ne sont por el meü
Se por lui non, bien l'ai seü;
Il est molt fel et orgilleus,
5510 Et fel et fiers et destrainneus,
Et orgilleus n'aime nului,
Et nus hom ne puet amer lui.
Mais or i aillent li plus sage,
U troi u quatre, en cest message,
5515 Se vous cuidiés que ce soit
              biens. [150 a]
– Biax sire ciers, se li paiens
Le voloit ausi come vous,
Ja ne seroit desdit par nous.»
Li messagier sont esleü;
5520 Vers le riviere sont meü.
Illuec se font li messagier
En une nef outre nagier.
Ne voelent pas passer au pont,
Qu'il ert plus d'une liue amont;[484]
5525 Ne voelent lor cevax lasser,
Por ce les font illuec passer.
Quant d'autre part sont arivé,
Montent et sont tuit abrievé.
Trespassent cele gent menue;
5530 Onques n'i ot resne tenue
Entreus qu'il vienent a celui
Qu'il vont querant, et pres de lui
Sont trestout quatre descendu.

Cil qui le mix a entendu
5535 L'afaire, en son sarrasinois
Dist en oiant: «Biau sire rois,
Eracles li prex et li sages
Nos tramist ci en cest message,[485]
Ne il nul salu ne te mande,
5540 Ne je, des puis qu'il ne conmande,
Ne te voel mie saluer,
Car tu viens occire et tuer
Et lui et se crestiienté,
Mais n'iert mie a te volenté;
5545 Tu penses un et il pense el,[486]
Sel comperont ne sai li quel.
Ensi me face Dix merci,[487]
Se il trouvé ne t'eüst ci,[488]
Tant te quesist et sus et jus
5550 Qu'il te trovast; or n'i a plus,
Mais ce te mande l'emperere:
Se tel cuer a li fix ton pere
Que cors a cors se combatist,
Eracles bien s'en aatist
5555 Que sor le pont se combatra, [b]
Et chil qui son per abatra
U qui vaintra, se n'ait regart
C'on l'assaille de nule part,
Ains soit sire d'ansdeus les os,
5560 U il des tiens ou tu des nos,
Et faite soit la seürtance
De tenir ceste covenance.
A ton plaisir le cose atire;
Mix voelt c'uns seus soit a martire[489]
5565 Que tante gens i muire a duel,[490]
Mais ja n'i morra c'uns, sien voel.»

[484] l. lonc]B (5523-24 *absent from* T).
[485] 5538-46 *Scribe* 2.
[486] un et penses el]BT.
[487] 5547-6568 *Scribe* 1.
[488] m'eust ci]BT.
[489] voel] (BT: est).
[490] tantes gens]B (T: tant de g.).

5502 And I can tell you truly that there is no better solution, provided that he and his men were to agree to it. I don't believe there is anyone amongst them, however brave, who would not willingly accept this, for they only embarked on this campaign because of him, I have always known this; he is very treacherous and proud, a treacherous proud bully, and the proud do not love anyone, nor is it possible for anyone to love them. So, if you think this is a good idea, let three or four of our wisest men go to him with this message. – Fair dear lord, if the pagan wished for this as much as you, we would certainly not veto it.'

The messengers were chosen and went off to the river. There the messengers were taken across in a boat; they crossed there rather than crossing at the bridge, because it was over a league upstream and they did not want to tire out their horses. **5527** When they arrived on the other side they mounted their horses, eager to press on. They rode past the footsoldiers and did not rein in their horses until they reached the man they were seeking. All four dismounted in his presence. The one who had best understood the situation spoke publicly in his best Saracen: 'Fair lord and king, Eracle the brave and wise has sent us to you as messengers, but sends you no greeting. And I, since he does not command it, do not wish to greet you either, for you have come here to kill and murder him and his Christian people, but you will not have your way. You have your plan, but he has quite another and I don't know which of you will suffer for it. May God have mercy on me, but if he had not found you here, he would have searched high and low until he found you; **5550** now there is no need, but this is the emperor's message: if your father's son has the heart to fight man-to-man, Eracle pledges to fight you in single combat on the bridge, and whoever kills or defeats his opponent, let him not be afraid of being attacked by anyone from either side, but let him be commander of both armies, either he of your troops or you of ours. And let guarantees be given that this agreement will be honoured. Arrange the matter to your liking; he prefers one of the two of you to be sacrificed rather than allow so many people to die in pain; no, if he has his way, only one person will die here.'

Et Cordroés, qui l'entendi,
Oiant trestous li respondi:
«Se j'en ai l'otroi de mes homes,
5570 Bien voel qu'ensi nos combatomes.»
Cascuns, qui paor a de soi,
Li a dit: «Sire, par ma foi,
Nous le loons bien entre nous,
Car ja n'assamblera a vous;[491]
5575 Ne cuidiés ja que il i viegne,
Et s'il i vient, que ja s'i tiegne.»
Icil ot dite se folie
Si ne s'en pot retraire mie.
El mont n'a home si haï,
5580 Fors sen pere; ce l'a traï;
Molt par est caitis entresait
Qui a sa gent haïr se fait,
C'uns jors venra, fiers et estous,[492]
Qui bien nos vengera de tous.
5585 Teus fu li descreans esgars:
Qu'ostages donront d'ambes pars,
Puis le metront al couvenir,
Et jurent donques a tenir
Quanqu'ot mis en le couvenance.
5590 N'i font pas longe demorance;
Li messagier atant s'en tornent,
Li notonnier lor nes atornent,
Et il passent illuec endroit.
A lor signor en vienent droit,
5595 Et se li prendent a conter [c]
Que il n'i a fors del monter;
Ostages prenge, ostages livre;[493]
Et il si fait tout a delivre.
Armer se fait molt bien li rois,
5600 Au pié del pont, atot son cois;
Ses cauces lacent doi baron,

Cascuns li cauce un esperon;
Hauberc li vestent erraument,
El mont n'a tel, mon ensïent;
5605 Puis ont mis en son cief un hialme,
Il n'a millor en un roiaume;
Çainte a l'espee al puig d'or fin
Qui ot esté roi Coustentin.
Ses cevax fu bon et aates,
5610 As piés grans et as gambes plates;
Miudres de lui ne puet nus estre.
Il monte par l'estrer seniestre,
Saisist l'escu, prent son espié,
Et proie Diu par se pitié
5615 Qu'en cest jor face demostrance
Que paien ont fole creance.
Li rois, qui gaires n'est amés,
S'est d'autre part molt bien armés;
Proie son pere molt forment
5620 Qu'il le garisse de torment;
En autre diu ne croit qu'en lui,
Mix li venist croire en Celui
Et en son saint conmandement,
Sans cui nus n'a amendement.
5625 Andoi li roi vienent au pont;
A ceval vienent contremont;
Des esperons les cevax brocent;
Enmi le pont droit s'entraprocent.
Eracles parla tous premiers,
5630 Con li plus sages chevaliers
Qui onques montast en ceval:
«Ahi! rois, fait il, con grant mal
Se tu pers ci t'ame et ton cors!
Tu nen as loi ne k'a uns pors,
5635 Et tu morras ci par mon fer; [d]
T'ame en ira droit en infer,

---

[491] n'assamblerai].
[492] f. iestous]B.
[493] prendre]T (B: prent).

Chosroes, on hearing this, gave his reply for everyone to hear: 'If I have the agreement of my men, I'm very happy to fight in this way.' Each one of them, who feared for his own safety, said to him: 'My lord, by my faith, we very much advise you to agree to this, for he will not dare to join you in combat; **5575** don't for one moment believe that he will come, and if he does, that he will stand his ground.' Chosroes had spoken foolishly and now he could not get out of it. No man on earth, apart from his father, was so hated; this was his downfall. A man who makes his people hate him will end up very wretched, for a harsh and violent day will come, which will avenge us on everyone. The following incredible pact was thus reached: both sides would provide hostages and would see what the outcome of their arrangements was. Then they swore an oath that they would observe all the terms of their agreement. Without further delay the messengers left. The ferrymen prepared their boats and they crossed at that very spot. They went straight to their lord and began to tell him that there was nothing for it but to mount his horse; he should take hostages and supply hostages; and he did this straight away. At the foot of the bridge the king armed himself splendidly in armour of his choosing. **5601** Two barons laced on his leggings and each attached a spur; they quickly put on his hauberk, the like of which has never been seen on earth, to my knowledge; there is no better helmet to be found in any kingdom than the one they then placed on his head; they girded on the sword with the pure gold pommel which had belonged to King Constantine. Eracle's horse was excellent and fast with huge feet and straight legs; there could never be a better one. He mounted by the left stirrup, seized his shield and took up his lance, and prayed to merciful God that he would demonstrate on that day that pagan beliefs are false. The king who was loved by practically no one had put on equally splendid armour; he was praying earnestly to his father to protect him from harm; he did not believe in any other god apart from him, yet he would have done better to believe in Him and his holy commandments without whom no one gains salvation. **5625** Both kings arrived at the bridge; they rode up the slope, spurring on their steeds. They met right in the middle of the bridge, Eracle, the wisest knight who had ever mounted a horse, spoke first: 'Oh king,' he said, 'what a great pity it will be if you lose your body and soul here. Your faith is worth no more than a pig's and you are going to die here by my iron blade; your soul will go straight to hell

Et a ce ne fauras tu mie
Se tu ne gerpis ta folie;
Car le gerpis, si croi en Diu.»
5640 Li rois respondi: «En quel diu
Diva! por coi me dis tu çou?
Ne mais en quel diu querrai jou?
Je croi celui qui m'engenra,
Qui contre toi me gardera.
5645 Il fait tout par droit estovoir[494]
Venter et negier et plovoir.
– Diva! c'est fantosme et engiens.
De ton pere ne vient nus biens,
Mais de Celui qui tout cria,
5650 Et ciel et terre et quanqu'i a,
Descent toute bone aventure.
Si va cascune creature:
Pluisor en usent conme sage,
Et li pluisor a lor damage.
5655 Qui Diu en sert, si fait savoir,
Et qui d'autrui le cuide avoir
Ne puet mie a bon cief venir.
Que valt lons sermons a tenir?
Mais croi en Celui fermement
5660 Qui soustient cel biel firmament,
Qui ne canciele ne ne ciet;
Cil est bien sire qui i siet.[495]
Vois les estoiles qui i luisent,
Vois les signes qui riens n'i nuisent,
5665 Vois le lune, con est vermelle.
Se il n'avoit plus de mervelle,
Sel devroit on bien aourer.
Vois le solel, qui demourer
Ne puet en un liu tel pieça,
5670 Si naist, et couce par decha
Et puis revient a l'ajorner;
Nus nel peüst si atorner

Fors Nostre Sire, Jhesu Crist,
Qui por le pecié k'Eve fist
5675 Dedens le Virge descendi [e]
Et soufri puis c'on le pendi.
En le Crois fu a mort penés
Que Cordroés, li mal senés,
Prist en Jherusalem jadis,
5680 Si le mist en son paradis.
U ele m'iert par toi rendue,
U ele t'iert molt cier vendue;
Porter le voel en Belleem,
Et puis tresqu'en Jherusalem,
5685 Illuec endroit ou Nostre Sire,
Qui soufri por nos le martire,
De cele mort ressuscita,
Dont ses amis d'infer gieta.
Car croi le cose en tel maniere
5690 Con je te di, si met ariere
Le fole loi que tient tes pere.[496]
– Ne ses que dis, fols emperere![497]
Il n'est pas liux de sermoner,
Mais de combatre et cols douner,
5695 Et d'assaiier par grant vertu
Li quex croit mix, u jou u tu.
Sermons ne t'ara ja mestier
Que de ton sanc n'aie un sestier
Ains que nos ja nos departons.
5700 Or n'i vaut riens onques sermons,
Ne rien ne te valt te manace.
Au mix que cascuns puet, si face,
Au quel que soit l'estuet couster.»
Atant s'eslongent por jouster;
5705 Hurtent cevax des esperons
Et s'entrefierent es blasons
Issi que nul mal ne se font,
Et les lances en pieces vont.

---

[494] par tout droit]BT.
[495] cui il s.]BT.

[496] perere].
[497] f. en emperere].

and you won't be able to escape this fate unless you abandon your foolish faith. Abandon your faith and believe in God!' The king replied: 'In which god? Come on, tell me, why are you saying this to me? Or at least say which god I am supposed to believe in? I believe in him who fathered me and who will protect me against you. As his will dictates, he controls the wind, snow and rain. – Come off it, that's an illusion and a trick. No good comes from your father, but all good fortune comes down to us from Him who created everything: heaven and earth and all that exists in them. **5652** This is how each of his creatures behaves: many use the gifts of fortune wisely, but most use them to their detriment. Those who use them to serve God act wisely, but those who think they receive them from someone else cannot but come to a sticky end. What's the point of my preaching at length? Just believe steadfastly in Him who supports this splendid heaven, neither faltering nor falling; he who resides there is a great lord indeed. Look at the stars that shine there, look at the constellations, which cause no harm, look at how red the moon is. If there were no other marvels than these, one would still have to worship Him. Look at the sun, which since time immemorial cannot stay in one place, but rises and then sets over there and then returns at dawn. No one could have arranged it that way except for Our Lord Jesus Christ, who, because of the sin committed by Eve, came down to earth in the Virgin's womb and then allowed us to hang him; **5677** he was tortured to death on the Cross which foolhardy Chosroes seized some time ago in Jerusalem and placed in his heaven. Either you will return it to me or you will pay dearly for it; I intend to take it to Bethlehem and from there to Jerusalem, to the place where Our Lord, who suffered martyrdom for us, triumphed over eternal death, from which he delivered his friends in hell. Accept the belief as I have outlined it for you here and reject the foolish religion which your father practises. – You don't know what you are saying, foolish emperor! This is not the place to preach, but to fight and exchange blows, and to put to the test in a show of force which of us has the better faith, you or I. Preaching will in no way protect you from my spilling a gallon of your blood before we part from each other; **5700** preaching is now of no use at all, nor are your threats. Let each of us do the best he can, whoever has to pay for it.' They then rode off in different directions to prepare for the lance attack; they spurred their horses on and struck each other on the shield, not doing each other any harm, but shattering their lances.

Outre s'en vont andoi molt tost;
5710 Esgardé sont de ceus de l'ost.
Les mains ont mises as espees,
Dont s'entredonent grans colees.
Cevax guencissent a droiture,
Si revinrent grant aleüre.
5715 Ichil fu plus amanevis [f]
Qui en Diu creïst a envis.
L'empereor molt tost requiert
Et dessor l'aume a or le fiert;
Un si grant cop li a doné
5720 Que a poi l'a tout estouné;
Al col se prent de son ceval,[498]
Poi faut qu'il ne trebuce aval.
A molt grant paine s'est tenus,
Et quant un poi est revenus
5725 Le cuer a mix sené et sage.
Se li ramembre del message
Que li angles li a porté,
Et ce l'a molt reconforté.
«Biax Dix, fait il, par te merci,
5730 Giete moi a honor de ci
Que cis malfés ne me puist nuire,[499]
Qui velt de tout te loi destruire.
S'ocire me puet cis paiens,
Li remanans des crestïens
5735 En mesquerra molt durement,
Et trestot cil conmunement
Qui sont ensanle o moi venu
Sont pris et mort et retenu.»
Reprent l'espee et se li vient;
5740 De le Crois Diu li ressovient,
Ice l'enasprist et atise.
Le paien el plus halt avise
Sel fiert et li cals li descent
Desor l'espaule droitement;

5745 Trença le guice de l'escu;
Si l'en a fait molt irascu,
Et puis se li a dit: «Paiens,
Car devien, por Diu, crestïens,
Si croi en Diu, le fil Marie;
5750 Si en sera t'ame garie.
Vers Diu te pués bien adrechier!»[500]
Et li paiens a courecier;
Ice l'a plus d'ire esmeü
Que li cops qu'il a receü,
5755 Et si en a honte et despit [151 a]
Plus qu'en dirai; sans nul respit
Revint vers lui, si l'a feru
De l'espee sor son escu
Qu'a terre vole quanqu'ataint,
5760 Et puis l'a durement empaint.
Ceval ot bon, si le sorporte.
Eracles molt se desconforte,
Et si a durement douté
Que Dix ne l'ait pas escouté
5765 Ne se proiere n'ait oïe;
Vers Damediu molt s'umelie,
Reprie Diu par se douçor
Qu'il en tel jor li doinst honor
Et que ses pix iex li aoevre.
5770 Atant revient et cuer recuevre,
En Diu a toute se pensee;
Vient vers celui, hauce l'espee
Et fiert a guise de vassal;
Trence le col de son ceval
5775 Tres par devant s'afeutreüre.
Li paiens pas ne s'asseüre;
Li cevax ciet et cil trebuce
De desous lui, et crie et huce:
«Ahi! peres qui m'engendras,
5780 U tu del tout me maintenras,

---

[498] le p.]BT.
[499] ne ne p.]BT.

[500] puet]BT.

They quickly rode on in opposite directions, watched by their armies. They drew their swords, ready to exchange terrible blows. They steered their horses round immediately and returned at high speed. The man who was reluctant to believe in God was the more experienced fighter. He galloped towards the emperor and struck him on his gilded helmet. Chosroes struck him such a hefty blow that he nearly stunned him. Eracle grabbed hold of his horse's neck and very nearly fell off onto the ground. He only just managed to hold on, but when he had recovered a little, his heart was all the wiser and more prudent. **5726** He remembered the message the angel had brought him, which comforted him greatly. 'Fair Lord,' he said, 'have mercy on me and help me to survive this situation honourably. Do not allow this devil, who wishes completely to destroy your law, to kill me. If this pagan succeeds in killing me, the rest of the Christians will definitely stop believing in it, and all those who came with me will be taken, killed or held prisoner.' He took up his sword again and went on the attack, remembering God's Cross, which inspired and fired him up. He aimed at the pagan from as high as he could reach, struck him and the blow landed straight on his shoulder; he cut through the strap on his shield and angered him greatly, then he said to him: 'Pagan, for God's sake, become a Christian and believe in God, the son of Mary, then your soul will be saved. **5751** You can still make amends before God.' The pagan then flew into a rage; these words moved him more to anger than the blow he had received; indeed, he was more ashamed and humiliated than words can express. Without pausing he rode towards him and hit him so hard with his sword on his shield that everything he struck flew to the ground. Then he thrust at him violently. His horse was strong and carried him safely away. Eracle was full of despair and really feared that God had not listened to him or heard his prayer. He humbled himself greatly before the Lord God and prayed to God again, asking Him in His kindness to grant him an honourable victory on that day and to look upon him with merciful eyes. Immediately, he came to his senses and regained his vigour. With all his thoughts concentrated on God he rode towards Chosroes, raised his sword and struck a blow worthy of a fine warrior; he sliced through the horse's neck just in front of his padded saddle. **5776** The pagan could do nothing to keep his balance; his horse collapsed and he fell off, sliding under it. He cried out and shouted: 'Ah, father who gave me life, either protect me from everything

U je querrai en Mahomet,
Qui as caitis consel tramet.
Pere, car vien, et si m'alasque!»
Li cevax atant se soufasque;
5785 Cil a se gambe a soi retraite
Et saut em piés l'espee traite.
Un cop gietast, se lui leüst,
Et s'un poi de loisir eüst;
Mais cil ne vait pas atendant,
5790 Ains vient vers lui tot destendant;
Empaint le del pis del ceval,
Qu'il le fait trebucier aval;
Petit en faut que ne l'afole[501]
Et li hiaumes du cief li vole.
5795 Or est il durement bleciés,   [b]
Porquant s'est en estant dreciés;
Voi le sans hiaume et sans escu!
Et cil dist qu'il a trop vescu,
Et vient vers lui s'espee traite,
5800 Sel cuide ferir de retraite;
Mais li paiens fu molt legiers,
Hardis et preux, aidans et fiers;
Guencist quant il le dut ferir,
Et se li cuide bien merir
5805 Tout quanqu'il li a fait de honte.
Que vos feroie plus lonc conte?[502]
Sor l'escu li a tel donee
Que il ne pot ravoir s'espee.
Eracles ne se targe mie,
5810 Hauce son cop, fiert sor l'oïe,
Et se coife de fer li fausse.
Ainc n'usa mais si aigre sausse,
Car cil li baigne l'alemelle

Parmi le tiés en le cervelle.
5815 A tierre ciet, mort l'a soupris.
Eracles par les piés l'a pris,
Sel giete par dessous le pont
En l'eve aval el plus parfont.
Joie a, c'ainc mais nen ot grignor,[503]
5820 Et loe Diu, Nostre Signor,
De l'onor qu'il li a donee.
Or n'iert mais si abandonee
Crestïentés que il cuida,
Qui tout son païs en vuida
5825 Por le destruire et mal baillir;
Mais or i puet il bien faillir.
Or sont icil de l'ost molt lié[504]
Et vers Diu molt humelïé;
Prendent escus par les enarmes,
5830 Au pont en vienent tuit as armes,[505]
De lor signor grant joie en font.
Outre Dunoe en oirre en vont
Que par le pont, que par les nés,[506]
N'en i a mie un seul remés.
5835 As paiens vienent, ses baptisent; [c]
As autres le vie apetisent,
Qui bonement ne voelent croire.
Au baptisier sont tout provoire
Et portent l'eve encontre mont[507]
5840 Si l'espandent par tot le mont.
  Quant baptisiés les ont trestos,
Estre les fals et les estous,
Bien en i a cent mil et plus;
Et cil s'en fuient sus et jus
5845 Qui nen ont cure del baptesme:
Bien en i a vint mil a esme.[508]

---

501   qui]B.
502   feroi].
503   A *omits* a.]B (T: ot).
504   lot]BT.
505   vient]BT.
506   p. q. p. le gues]BT.
507   porte].
508   esmes]B (5845-46 *absent from* T).

or I shall believe in Mohammed, who sends help to the wretched. Father, come and deliver me.' His horse then got up and he pulled his leg free and leapt to his feet, with sword drawn. He would have landed a blow if he had been allowed to and if he had been given the time to do so; however, Eracle did not delay, but approached him at a gallop, his horse's chest colliding with him and knocking him down. He nearly killed him and his helmet flew off his head. Now he was badly wounded, yet he got to his feet again. Just imagine him without helmet or shield! And Eracle declared that he had lived too long, and rode towards him with drawn sword, intending to strike him as he rode back. **5801** However, the pagan was very agile, brave, valiant, resourceful and fierce; he ducked when Eracle was about to strike him and hoped to make him pay for all the humiliation he had caused him. What would be the point of dragging out my story? Chosroes struck his shield with such force that he lost his grip on his sword. Eracle did not delay, he raised his sword, struck him on his ear and cut through his chain-mail hood. Never before had Chosroes tasted such a bitter sauce, for Eracle plunged his blade into his head, right into his brain. Overcome by death, he fell to the ground. Eracle grabbed him by the feet and hurled him down from the bridge into the deepest part of the river. Never before had he been as joyful as at that moment and he praised God, Our Lord, for the honour He had bestowed upon him. Now the Christian faith would no longer be abandoned in the way that Chosroes had expected when he rid his whole country of it in order to destroy and eradicate it. **5826** But now it was very likely that he would fail. The members of Eracle's army were now very happy and humbly prostrated themselves before God. They took up their shields by the straps and they all came to the bridge fully armed. They made a great fuss of their lord; then they quickly crossed the Danube, either by the bridge or by boat,[90] not a single one of them remaining behind. They caught up with the pagans and baptised them; those who did not wish to believe in the true faith had their lives cut short. Everyone became priests for the purpose of baptising them, carrying water up from the river and sprinkling it over everyone.

When they had baptised all of them, there were in total more than a hundred thousand men, not counting the approximately twenty thousand or more foolish and recalcitrant pagans, who fled in all directions, refusing to be baptised.

---

90 Although MS *A* has *gues* (fords) in l. 5833, the *BT* reading must be original given Gautier's description of the Danube as unfordable.

Cil les ocient tuit a tire
Qui ont receü baptestire;
N'i espargne li fix le pere.
5850 Et puis s'en vait li emperere
Dusc'a Persë u cil estoit
Qui tous de fin or se vestoit.
U ciel qu'il ot fait d'or ouvrer,
Le millor qu'il pot recovrer,
5855 Seoit et disoit qu'il ert seus,
Qu'estre lui seul n'estoit nus
     deus.[509]
Vers Diu a longes estrivé.[510]
Il n'a el monde si privé
Qui li ost dire l'aventure
5860 De cele grant desconfiture:
Plains iert de si grant felonie
Qu'il gietast maintenant de vie
Celui qui li desist nouviele
Qui ne li fust et bone et biele.
5865 Mais tels i venra ja, espoir,
Qui bien li dira tout le voir.
N'atarga gaire que cil vient
Cui Dix aconduist et maintient.
El ciel est montés maintenant,
5870 Qui dure bien en un tenant
Cent piés ou plus a la reonde,
Et sanle que tos l'ors del monde
I soit aportés por mervelle.
L'uevre en est molt clere et
     vermelle,[511]
5875 Que por les pieres que por l'or; [d]
El mont nen a si fort tresor.
Tels cose ou seroit recovree?
Mais qu'ele fust por Diu usee!

Les cieres pieres seulement
5880 Valent tout l'or et tout l'argent
Au roi englés, qui molt en a.
De grant folie se pena
Icil qui tant i mist d'or fin,
Car riens n'est preus sans bone fin.
5885 Sor uns degrés d'or qu'il i a
Se siet qui l'uevre edefia,
En le caiere ou riens ne faut;[512]
Le cose el mont qui mains i vaut,
Çou est fins ors qui tient les pieres,
5890 Si con li plons fait les verrieres.
Eracles voit le mescreant
Et le Crois Diu, dont li creant
Sont molt dolant qui l'ont perdue.
A terre ciet, si le salue
5895 Sifaitement con vous orrés,
Et con vos oïr ci porés:
«Crois, beneoite soies tu!
Dix beneïe ta vertu!
Par toi ai fait et esploitié
5900 Ce que g'ai le plus covoitié.
Sainte Crois, molt t'ai goulousee,
Que tu fus du sanc arousee
Dont Dix racata tout le monde;
Lavee fus de la sainte onde.
5905 Molt ricement fus atornee,
Et des sains membres aournee
Diu, nostre verai Sauveor,
Par cui sont sauf li peceor.
Crois prescïeuse, u li saint membre
5910 Furent pendu por nos raembre,
Tous jors seras en me memoire
Por l'onor grant, por le victoire

---

[509] dels]BT.
[510] dix a l. destrive]BT.
[511] Lore]T: Tant est l'uevre bielle et v. (B: L'une e.).
[512] Et le c.]B.

Those who had been christened killed them in one fell swoop, sons not sparing their fathers. **5850** Then the emperor went off to Persia, where the man resided who dressed himself from head to toe in pure gold. He was seated in his heaven, which he had ordered to be constructed from the finest gold obtainable. He said that he was unique, for there was no other god apart from himself. He had contested God's position for a long time. He had no confidant in the world who dared to give him the bad news about their great defeat; he was so full of treachery that he would have killed on the spot anyone who gave him news that was not favourable and welcome. But perhaps someone would come one day who would tell him the whole truth. Not long afterwards, the man who was guided and supported by God arrived there. He immediately went up into the heaven, fashioned in one piece with a circumference of a hundred feet or more. And it seemed that all the gold in the world had been brought there to astonish the onlooker. The edifice was very shiny and red, as much because of the precious stones as because of the gold. **5876** There was no greater treasure in the whole world. Where else could you have found an object of such value? If only it had been in the service of God! The precious stones alone were worth all the gold and all the silver owned by the King of England, and he is very rich indeed.[91] Whoever employed so much pure gold in its construction foolishly wasted his efforts, for nothing is of value if it is not in a good cause. Inside, at the top of a flight of steps, the man who had commissioned this edifice was seated on a throne, which lacked nothing in splendour. The least valuable part of it was the pure gold which provided a setting for the precious stones, just as lead does for stained glass. Eracle set eyes on the heathen and on the Lord's Cross, whose loss had greatly distressed the true believers. He fell to the ground and greeted it with the following words, exactly as you are about to hear: 'Oh Blessed Cross, may the Lord bless your power.[92] With your aid I have achieved and accomplished what I have most desired to do. **5901** Holy Cross, I have so longed for you, because you were splashed with the blood with which God atoned for the sins of humankind; you were washed with the holy fluid. The holy limbs of God, our true Saviour, through whom all sinners are saved, adorned and embellished you most splendidly. Oh Precious Cross, on which the holy limbs were hung to redeem us, I shall never forget you because of the great honour and victory

---

[91] Henry II, whose wealth was legendary.
[92] Eracle's speech to the Cross is reminiscent of the liturgy; cf. 'O crux benedicta' in the antiphon used for the Feast of the Exaltation of the Cross on the 14th of September.

Que de par toi m'a Dix doné.
Molt ai grant cose conquesté
5915 Quant revenras el liu par moi [e]
U li Fix Diu pendi en toi.
N'est hom el mont si embarnis,
Se il de toi nen est garnis,
Qui puisse gaires esploitier.
5920 Por ce doit cascuns covoitier
Qu'il en soit garnis et signiés,
U il est mors et engigniés.
Crois, tu sauves as tiens le vie,
S'en a diables grant envie;
5925 Tu iés as tiens joie et confors,
Tu fais adiés les tiens plus fors.
Crois, tu m'as aidié et valu.
En nule maison n'a salu
S'on ne garnist de toi l'entree.
5930 Bone aventure ai encontree
Quant je te voi sifaitement;
Mais je te venrai autrement
A molt cort terme, se je vif.
Malgré en aient cist caitif
5935 Qui de lor creator n'ont cure,
Ains aourent se creature;
Ce fait cis caitis que je voi,
Qui vit sans raison et sans loi,
Et as gens se fait aourer.
5940 Diables le puist enporter
S'il autrement ne se contient.
De le folie qu'il maintient
Savoir m'estuet qu'il en dira.»
Dont si li dist: «Que fais tu la?
5945 Diva! caitis mal eürés?
Por toi aront molt endurés

Mal et traval li crestïen.
Car croi en Diu, si feras bien.
Croi en Celui qui fu pendus,
5950 Et mains et piés ot estendus
En cele Crois deseur ton cief.
Reçoif de moi te terre en fief,
Si fai te gent crestïener.
Je ne te quier a plus mener:[513]
5955 Vivre poras sifaitement, [f]
U ja ne vivras autrement,
Ains t'ocirai si con ton fil.
O soi sera t'ame en escil,
En infer ert ja avalee
5960 La ou li siue en est alee.
Li siue est en infer pieça;
Je l'ocis, voir, puis m'en vinç ça;
N'i voil trametre autre mesage.[514]
Tu iés mais bien de tel eage
5965 Que tu dois mais bien aperçoivre
Que tu ne fais el que deçoivre
Toi meïsme et le tiue gent.
Il ne m'est pas ne biel ne gent
Que tu renes en tel maniere.
5970 Car croi en Diu, si met ariere[515]
La folie ou tu as vescu.» [516]
Cil a le cuer molt irascu,
Et dist: «Por coi me dis tu çou?
Est il dont autres dix que jou?
5975 Je faiç tout, venter et negier.
Iés me tu venus assaiier
El grignor pooir que j'oi onques?
– Te deïtés valt petit donques,
Quant il t'est caoit ambesas
5980 El grignor pooir que tu as.

---

[513] q. ja p.]BT.
[514] voel].
[515] After 5970 A repeats 5949-52 almost verbatim.
[516] Tu as molt folement v.]BT.

God has granted me through you. My achievement will be great if, through my efforts, you return to the place where the Son of God hung from you. No man on earth, however courageous, can succeed in much at all if he does not have your support. Therefore everyone should strive to be protected by the sign of the Cross, otherwise they will die and be damned. Oh Holy Cross, you procure eternal life for your followers, much to the envy of the devil. **5925** You are a joy and a comfort to your people, making them ever stronger. Oh Cross, you have helped and strengthened me. No house can be a safe haven unless its threshold is protected by you. I have met with good fortune in being allowed to see you in this way. But in a very short while, if I live long enough, I shall see you in a different place, even if it angers these wretches who care nothing for their creator, worshipping instead His creature. This wretch whom I see before me is making the same mistake, for he lives a foolish, irreligious life, and forces his people to worship him. If he does not mend his ways, let the devil carry him off. But I must learn what he has to say about the folly he is pursuing.' So Eracle said to him: 'Tell me, what do you think you are doing there, miserable wretch? Because of you, Christians have suffered much pain and hardship. Believe in God and you won't regret it. **5949** Believe in Him who was crucified, whose hands and feet were stretched out on this Cross which is now above your head. Receive your land from me as a fief and have your people converted to Christianity. That is all I ask of you: you can either live in this way or you will not live at all, for I shall kill you as I did your son. Your soul will be in torment with him, as it is soon to descend into hell where his soul has already gone. His has been in hell a while already, for in truth I killed him before coming here. I did not wish to send another messenger to you. You have now reached an age when you ought to be able to recognise that you are merely deceiving yourself and your people. It does not seem right and proper to me that you should rule in this way. Come on, believe in God and put behind you the life of folly you have been leading.' Chosroes was very angry in his heart and said: 'Why are you saying such things to me? Do any other gods exist apart from me? **5975** I produce everything, the wind and the snow. Have you come to challenge me when I am at the height of my powers? – But your divinity is of little value since even at the height of your powers you have thrown only two aces.[93]

---

[93] This is the lowest score in dice – two ones.

Onques selonc m'entention
Ne vi un seul si tres felon;
Ains mais ne fu si orgillex.
Tu ne vois goute, si as ex;
5985 Orelles, si ne pués oïr.
Se de te vie vels joïr,
Guerpir t'estuet te grant folie;
Mais peciés te destraint et lie,
Tant as a Diu fait honte et lait.
5990 Ne pués el faire que t'as fait?[517]
Di moi, feras tu autre cose?[518] [152 a]
– Tai, fols, dist il, si te repose!
La fors te ferai decoler;
Ne te voel pas ci decauper,
5995 Que je sui dix et en mon ciel
Ne doit on pas espandre fiel,
Ne cose qui i soit contraire,
Qu'il i a molt de saintuaire.
– C'est voirs que molt en a çaiens,
6000 Ne mais de toi est il noiens.[519]
Endroit de toi n'en a riens chi
Dont Damedix ait ja merchi;
Mais se tu de le Crois disoies
Et toi et ton ciel despisoies,
6005 Auques i poroit on attendre.
– Je ne voel pas issi entendre;
Le crois ne pris je un bouton.
Orains cuidoie, fel glouton,
Que tu aourer me venisses
6010 Et a ton signor me tenisses.
– Fols, or voit on molt bien de plain
Que tu ses bien cuidier en vain!
Fols dix, con malement t'aquites!
Or as tu les ensegnes dites
6015 Que tu maines malvaise vie:
Que li miens Dix ne cuide mie,
Ains set des le commencement
Del siecle le definement,[520]
Et si connoist et set et voit
6020 Quels iert li cose ains qu'ele soit.
Il done tous biens a plenté
Et fait tout a se volenté:
Et ciel et air et terre et mer;
Por ce le doit on molt amer.
6025 Fols caitis, plains de vilenie,
Tu morras en te felounie,
Mais que li Crois en soit ostee
Que tu as tant jors acostee;
Ce est grans dués del saint ciprés
6030 Que tu li fus onques si prés.»
Eracles monte et prent le Crois, [b]
Baisie l'a plus de cent fois.
Portee l'a enmi le court,
Et tous li pules i acourt;
6035 Vont et li nostre et li paien
Qui sont devenu crestïen.
A genillons le Crois aourent[521]
Et si le baisent et honorent;
Et l'emperere el ciel remonte,
6040 Por celui faire tant de honte
Con il onques plus puet avoir.
Por demoustrer son nonsavoir,
Lassus vait celui acorer
U il se seut faire aourer;
6045 Le teste en prent, et depart l'or
Que cil avoit en son tresor:
Dona le tout a povre gent;
As chevaliers done l'argent;

---

517 el dire]BT.
518 A *omits* moi]BT.
519 moiens]BT.

520 commencement]BT.
521 aurent].

Never, as far as I can remember, have I seen such a treacherous person. Never before was there such an arrogant man. You have eyes yet you cannot see, ears yet you cannot hear.[94] If you wish to enjoy life further, you must abandon your great folly; but sin constrains and fetters you, since you have committed such shameful crimes against God. Can you not mend your ways? Tell me, will you behave differently? – 'Shut up, fool,' he said, 'give it a rest! Not wishing to decapitate you here, I shall have your head cut off outside, for I am god and one should not spread bitterness in my heaven or desecrate such a holy place. – It is true that there is much holiness here, but it has nothing to do with you. **6001** Here there is nothing associated with you that would deserve God's mercy; but if you were referring to the Cross, while scorning yourself and your heaven, then one might expect a little mercy. – That's not what I have in mind at all. I don't care a button for the Cross. At first I believed, treacherous scoundrel, that you had come to worship me and were acknowledging me as your lord. – Fool, now we can see quite clearly how misguided your belief is. Foolish god, how badly you acquit yourself. Now you have given us verbal proof that you are leading an evil life: for my God does not believe erroneously,[95] rather He knows from the beginning of the world what the end will be. Indeed, He is aware, knows and foresees what will come to pass before it happens. He is generous with all his gifts and creates everything according to His designs: the heavens, the air, the land and the sea. For this reason we should love Him dearly. **6025** Foolish wretch, full of wickedness, you will die a traitor to the true faith; but first let the Cross, which has been in your presence for so long, be taken away; it's a great pity that you ever came so close to the holy cypress wood.' Eracle climbed up, took the Cross and kissed it more than a hundred times. He then carried it into the courtyard and everyone ran towards it; our people as well as the pagans who had just converted to Christianity all approached it. They worshipped the Cross on bended knee, kissing and honouring it; and the emperor returned to the heaven to inflict the greatest possible humiliation on Chosroes. To show him how misguided he had been Eracle went up to kill him in the very place where he used to have himself worshipped. He cut off his head and distributed the gold stored in his treasury: he gave it all to the poor and gave the silver to his knights.

---

[94] See Mark 8: 18: 'Oculos habentes non videtis? et aures habentes non auditis'.
[95] Gautier is punning on *cuidier* ('to believe', often erroneously) in ll. 6008, 6012, 6016.

As barons a fait departir
6050 Les pieres c'a fait dessartir
Del ciel u eles furent mises;[522]
Diversement les a tramises.
Et quant li cose est esmondee,
Une glise a illuec fondee:
6055 U li ciex ert droit en cel liu,
La sera sacrés li cors Diu.
Une autre en i a fait de moines,
Mais en cesti a mis canoines;
Assiet i rentes a plenté
6060 Et partout met crestïenté.
Li Crois Diu buer i venist onques,
Que quanque cil esploita donques
Fu par ce qu'ele i fust portee.
Es vous gent molt reconfortee
6065 De ce dont furent ains dolant;
Or voient il apertemant
Que li Crois, qui i vint premiere,
Fu de ceste oeuvre messagiere:
Cil l'i aporta par se rage,
6070 Mais ce ne fu el que message
De ceste grant bone aventure. [c]
Cil ot un fil a noureture,
Dont l'angles dist l'empereor
Que il le gardast a honor;
6075 Por ce l'en fait o lui mener.
Cestui vaura il assener,
Mais qu'il soit ains crestïennés,[523]
A quanque tint li mal senés.
    Li emperere a departie
6080 En deus moitiés se compaignie,
Et vers Coustantinoble envoie
Une moitié, si tient se voie.

O lui en vait l'autre moitiés,
Et puis si s'est tant esploitiés
6085 O le vraie Crois qu'il enporte
Qu'il est venus pres de la porte
U Dix vint a porcession
Ains qu'il venist a passion;
Et cil qui lisent les estoires[524]
6090 L'ont apielee Portes Oires.
Cil qui fu nés en Belleem
Vint par la en Jherusalem
Le jor de le Pasque florie.
Ce fu li fix sainte Marie,
6095 Et li enfant encontre alerent,[525]
Et rains d'olives i porterent.
Cantant vinrent li enfançon
A haute vois ceste cançon:
Osona, filio Davi!
6100 Et plus encor, car je le vi
En un livre dont me souvient,
Beneois soit icil qui vient
El non de Diu, Nostre Signor!
Ice cantoient a s'ounor.
6105 Les rains prisent a entasser
Par la ou il devoit passer,
Et li pluisor qui illuec erent
Lor vestimens illuec gieterent;
Et si cevalca Nostre Sire
6110 Le plus vil bieste c'on puist dire,
Por demoustrer humelité[526]   [d]
Qui doit estre en humanité:
Ce fu de l'ane le femiele.
Senefïance i a molt biele
6115 Et de le mere et del faon
Qui le sivoit; or si l'oon:[527]

---

[522] U c.]B.
[523] M. ains quil s.]H, cf. 6421-25 for the order of events.
[524] estoire]BT.
[525] encontre].
[526] demoustre]BT.
[527] Que]B.

6049 He had the precious stones prised out of the heaven where they had been set and shared them amongst his barons; thus they were distributed by him in different lots. And when the place had been purified, he founded a church there: on the very spot where the heaven had been the body of Christ would be celebrated during mass. He also founded a monastery, but in the other foundation he placed canons; everything was generously endowed and he introduced Christianity everywhere. How fortunate that the Lord's Cross had ever been there, for all that Eracle subsequently accomplished was because it had been taken there. Imagine how the people now derived great consolation from what had earlier caused them much dismay. Now they could see clearly that the Cross had come there first to herald this great deed: Chosroes had brought it there in his folly, yet it was none other than a messenger announcing this wonderful good news. Chosroes had an infant son. The angel told the emperor to look after him honourably, so Eracle took him with him. **6076** His intention was to hand over to him everything owned by his misguided father, once he had become a Christian.

Having divided his followers into two groups, the emperor sent half of them on their way to Constantinople, and then continued on his way. The other half accompanied him, and he made such good progress, carrying the True Cross with him, that he arrived at the gate to which God processed just before His passion. Those who read the sources have called it the Golden Gate.[96] The man who was born in Bethlehem entered Jerusalem by that route on Palm Sunday. This was, of course, the son of Blessed Mary, whom the children ran to greet carrying olive branches. The little children approached singing these words at the tops of their voices: 'Hosanna to the son of David'. **6100** And that was not all, for I can remember seeing written in a book: 'Blessed is he that cometh in the name of our Lord God'.[97] They sang these words in his honour. They began to strew his path with branches and the majority of those present threw their garments on the ground. Our Lord was riding the most lowly animal imaginable, a female ass, thus demonstrating the humility that mankind should possess. The symbolic significance of the mare and her foal, which was following her, is very enlightening, so let us hear what it is:

---

[96] Gautier adds to the *Passionarius* account the detail that Eracle entered Jerusalem by the 'Portes Oires', a reference to the gate built by the Emperor Justinian in the sixth century which was always walled up, except for twice a year on Palm Sunday and the Feast of the Exaltation of the Cross.

[97] In this passage Gautier quotes the Bible, first in Latin, then in the vernacular. The book in question is Matthew 21: 9.

Li mere al faon senefie
Cele viés loi avant oïe,
Et par le faon entendons
6120 Le loi noviele u nos tendons.
Ce n'afiert pas ici a dire,
Se por ce non que Nostre Sire
Vint par chi si tres humlement,
Et cis i vint si fierement
6125 Sor un ceval d'Espaigne sor,
Qui valt plus de cent onces d'or;[528]
Et entor lui tel generasce
Qui li rendent et gré et grasce
De l'onor grant, de le victore,
6130 C'on devroit faire au Roi de Glore
Par coi li victore est eüe.
Et le Crois c'ont illuec veüe
Eracles le porte en se destre.
Il en est liés, si doit il estre;[529]
6135 Ne prise paiens deus festus.
D'uns dras de soie estoit vestus;
D'ermine est fourés li mantiaus
Dessi as piés des les tassiaus,
Et le cote toute autressi.
6140 Or est il liés, ainc ne fu si,
Mais sempres orra tes novieles
C'ainques n'oï nus hom mains bieles,
Ne dont il fust si coureciés[530]
Ne si dolans ne si iriés;
6145 Si sera cent tans plus honteus
Qu'iriés, dolans, ne coreceus,
Ains qu'en le porte soit entrés
U Damedix fu encontrés.
Et vint cevalcant tout le pas
6150 Et souavet, qu'il est molt las,

Et les gens grant presse li font [e]
Qui entor lui vienent et vont;
Molt le detrient et demeurent
Por cele Crois u il aeurent.
6155 Par ce est auques detenus,
6156 Tant c'a la porte est parvenus;[531]
6159 Et quant il volt entrer laiens
6160 Ne li valut, ce fu noiens.
Oiés, signor, confait miracle
Et quel vergoigne a oeus Eracle:
Defors remest, ce li covint;
Oiés por coi et qu'i avint:
6165 Li mur se sont ensanle joint
Li uns a l'autre, point a point,
Si qu'en cest monde n'a maçon,
Tant sace d'uevre et de façon,
Qui les joinsist si biel, si bien;
6170 C'a Damediu ne set nus rien.
Li murs est joins et si sierés
Que jamais nul mix ne verrés.
    Signor, ce nen est mie fable,
Ançois est cose veritable;
6175 N'a home en tout le mont si baut
Qui l'oseroit si metre en haut
Se il de verté nel savoit,
Et il des clers tesmoig n'avoit.
Eracles a grignor vergoigne
6180 Que li livres nes ne tesmoigne,
Ne mais encor l'ara grignor,
Que de par Diu, Nostre Signor,
Vint uns angles del ciel molt tost,
Et dist, oiant tous cex de l'ost:
6185 «Eracle, molt as bien ouvré
Quant tu as le fust recouvré

---

[528] ondes]B.
[529] Il en est il l.]BT.
[530] Se dont i f.]T (B: Et si sera molt c.).

[531] *After 6156 A repeats 6147-48, inverted. I have retained R's eccentric system of line-numbering here to avoid confusion over references to his edition in the secondary literature.*

the foal's mother represents the Old Law which used to be obeyed, whilst the foal should be interpreted as the New Law we now strive to keep.[98] The only reason why I am mentioning it here is that Our Lord came that way in all humility, yet Eracle arrived there very proudly, mounted on a chestnut Spanish steed worth more than a hundred ounces of gold. **6127** He was also surrounded by such a huge crowd of grateful people thanking him for the great honour his victory had bestowed upon them. Yet they should have been thanking the King of Glory, who had granted him this victory. And the Cross which they had once seen there was being carried by Eracle in his right hand. He was delighted with it, as was only natural; he did not care a fig for the pagans.[99] He was clad in silk cloth; his mantle was lined with ermine from the clasps at the top to the hem at his feet and his tunic was the same. He had never been as joyful as he was then, but he was soon to hear worse news than any man had ever heard before, and which would make him so very angry, upset and distressed. And yet he would be a hundred times more ashamed than distressed, upset or angry before he had entered the gate at which Our Lord was welcomed.[100] **6149** Eracle rode up at a gentle walking pace, for he was very weary, and the people thronged closely around him as they came and went; they delayed him and held up his progress because of the Cross that they were worshipping. Thus he was somewhat delayed before reaching the gate. Yet when he tried to enter the city, it was to no avail; he got nowhere. My lords, hear what a shameful miracle was designed for Eracle. He was forced to remain outside; you will now hear why and what happened next: the two walls came together until they were perfectly joined with no gap between them. No stonemason on earth is so skilful at his craft that he could have joined them so perfectly and expertly, for compared to God's expertise, man's is worthless. The walls were joined so seamlessly that you would never see a better fit.

My lords, this is no fiction, but the truth. **6175** There is no one in the whole world so bold that he would dare to spread this story unless he knew it to be true and had it on clerical authority. Eracle was more ashamed than even the book relates, and yet his shame was about to increase further as an angel sent by Our Lord God suddenly came down from heaven and said to him, within the hearing of his whole army: 'Eracle, you did very well when you recovered the wooden Cross

---

[98] This interpretation is based on Origen's commentary on St John's Gospel, Book X, chapter 18. See http://www.newadvent.org/fathers/101510.htm (last accessed on 6 May 2007).
[99] Literally 'two straws'.
[100] Ll. 6143-46 contain a good example of chiasmus.

U Damedix fu clauficiés,
Ne mie por les siens peciés
(Ainc n'ot pecié el fil Marie,
6190 Ni en se bouce trecerie),
Mais por le mont, qui perdus ert, [f]
Pendi el fust qu'ileuques pert.
Onques n'i volt envoiier angle
El liu de lui, ne nul archangle;
6195 Et si n'ot pas li Sire tort,
C'angles ne puet pas sofrir mort;
Li moie cars n'est pas mortels,
Ançois est cose espiriteus;
Et li mons iert a mort dampnés[532]
6200 Si ne pot estre racatés[533]
Se par mort non et par martire.
Et estre volt tel Nostre Sire[534]
Que il morir puist a delivre,
Et par soi meïme revivre;
6205 Et fors Dix nus ne puet ce faire.
Por ce vint il a cest afaire;
A le mort vint, home aquita,
Et puis de mort ressuscita.
Grant merci ot de se faiture,
6210 Qu'en home a gente creature.[535]
Or as tu ceste Crois aquise
U se cars fu pendue et mise;
N'est mie toie ceste glore,
Mais Diu qui fist ceste victore;[536]
6215 Dix a l'afaire te nouma,
Mais il meïmes l'assoma;
Ce saces tu veraiement.
Por coi viens tu sifaitement?

Orgilleuse est te vesteüre,
6220 Et fiere te cevauceüre;
Tes conrois est molt orgilleus[537]
A porter cest fust prescïeus.
Tout autrement vint ja par ci
Cil Dix qui plains est de merci;
6225 Tout autrement vint vers cest fust
Quint jor ains que se cars i fust,
Qu'il cevauca une vil bieste
Devant le pule a haute feste,
Trestous descaus et tous en langes.
6230 Eracles, trop par iés estranges
Quant tu ensi t'iés contenus;[538] [153 a]
U est tes grans sens devenus?»
Atant se teut et plus ne dist
Et voiant tos s'esvanuist.
6235 Et cil descent devers senestre,[539]
Por mil mars d'or n'i vausist estre;
Ains ne se tint mais a si fol.
Giete le mantiel de son col,
A un povre home l'abandone.
6240 A un autre le bliaut done;
N'i remaint braie ne cemise.
En son dos a le haire mise,
Quant il l'ot fait, se car derompre;
Folie a fait et si le compre;
6245 Qui bien reconnoist se folie,
Vers Damediu molt s'umelie.
Pluisors de cels qui o lui furent
Tel dessepline o lui reçurent;
De haire sont trestout viestu,
6250 Lor cors ne prisent un festu.

---

[532] amor]BT.
[533] puet; BT]L.
[534] Et metre v.] (B: Et teus vot iestre nostre sire; T: Itelz vot estre n. s.).
[535] Quant on a]L (B: Grant honte a g. c.; T: Quant pour li devint c.).
[536] Dix]B.

[537] est o.]BT.
[538] n'ies c.]T (B: ensi ies c.).
[539] senistre].

on which Our Lord God was nailed, not to atone for His own sins (the son of Mary was without sin and incapable of speaking a word of treachery), but in order to save humankind from damnation He was hung on the Cross you see before you.[101] He did not wish to send an angel or an archangel in his stead, nor was Our Lord wrong in this, for an angel cannot suffer death. I am not made of mortal flesh, but of pure spirit. The world was condemned to eternal death and it could only be redeemed by death and suffering. **6202** So Our Lord decided to become a being that could die at will and then resurrect Himself, and God alone can do this. This is the reason why He became involved in this matter. In dying He redeemed mankind, then rose from the dead. He showed great mercy towards His creation, for man is a noble creature.[102] Now you have won back the Cross on which His very flesh was hung and placed. Yet this glory is not yours, but God's, for He brought about the victory. God designated you to the task, but He Himself brought it to a successful completion; you should be in no doubt of this. Why have you come here in this manner? Your clothing smacks of pride and your steed of arrogance. You are surrounded by too much pomp and circumstance to be the bearer of this precious wooden Cross. Years ago our most merciful God passed this way in a very different manner. **6225** And He approached this holy wood in a very different manner five days before His body was placed on it, for barefoot and clad entirely in coarse wool, He rode on a lowly animal before the crowds of celebrating people. Eracle, you must have changed a great deal to be behaving like this; what has happened to your great wisdom?' Then the angel fell silent and said no more, vanishing before everyone's eyes. Eracle dismounted on the left and would have given a thousand marks of gold not to be there, for he had never before felt so foolish. He pulled his cloak off from around his neck and gave it to a poor man; to another he gave his tunic. He did not even keep his breeches or his shirt. He put a hairshirt on his back; when he had done this, he mortified his flesh, for he had committed a sin and was paying for it. Whoever recognises that he has sinned must humble himself completely before God. Many of the men who accompanied him subjected themselves to similar mortification; they covered themselves with hairshirts and cared not a jot for their bodies.

---

[101] Here Gautier is quoting the first Epistle of Peter, 2: 22, and the first Epistle of John, 2: 2.
[102] Löseth's correction of l. 6210 is supported by St Bernard, *Sermo in adventu*, 1, 4 'Nobilis creatura homo'.

Eracles s'est puis trais arriere
O le Crois prescïeuse et ciere;⁵⁴⁰
O se gent fait a Diu promesses,
Et voe a faire canter messes,⁵⁴¹
6255 De povres revestir et paistre
A l'onor Diu, qui daigna naistre
De le virge sainte Marie.
En mainte guise s'umelie:
Par larmes, par afflictions
6260 Et par saintimes dictions
Qu'il dist souef et oiant tous.
N'i a si dur ne si estous
Qui n'aient grant pitié de lui.
Si genoul sainent ambedui,⁵⁴²
6265 Car il est forment travilliés,
Et tantes fois agenoulliés
Que nus n'en puet savoir le conte.
Pleurent et crient duc et conte,
Ne mais a la soie dolor
6270 Ne montent rien ne cri ne plor;
Dont dist «Dix, plains de passïence, [b]
Si voirement con negligense
M'a encombré ains que orguels,
Garde vers moi de tes pius oeus;
6275 Oevre tes ieus, si me regarde,
Car certes ne m'en donai garde.
Fontaine de misericorde,
A cui toute bontés s'acorde,
Pardone l'outrage au caitif;
6280 Ne prendre mie a moi estrif.
Tant de vertu me tramesis
Que celui vaintre me fesis
Qui son ciel fist d'or esteler,

Et dix se faisoit apieler.
6285 Et tout ce, Sire, que me vaut
Se t'ire m'argüe et assaut?⁵⁴³
Sire, por voir le puis jurer,
Qu'a toi ne poroit nus durer
S'a son mesfait garde prennoies
6290 Et se tu pitié n'en avoies.
Sire, se jou ai fait folie,
Je ne fis nule felonnie,
Mien ensïent, ne nul orguel;
Et se fait l'ai, forment m'en duel
6295 Et molt m'en poise voirement.
Biax sire Dix, a toi apent
Que tu soies de pitié plains;
T'en as tous jors plaines tes mains;
Bien sai que tu autant en as
6300 Que adont quant tu pardounas
Ses peciés a le Mazelaine.
Si con li rius de le fontaine,
Sort et descent pitiés de toi.
Pius Dix, aies merci de moi,
6305 Que je puisse entrer en le vile.
Il est escrit en l'evangile,
Qui de proier en est engrés,⁵⁴⁴
Qui n'entre lués, il en est prés;
Engrés ne fui ainc, mais or l'ere,⁵⁴⁵
6310 Que s'on de ci ne m'oste en biere,
N'en partirai por nule perte, [c]
Tresque le porte estra ouverte
Et ressoient arriere trait
Li mur, qu'il ne me soit retrait.⁵⁴⁶
6315 Ci aroit molt estrainne cose
Se por moi ert li porte close

---

⁵⁴⁰ U]BT.
⁵⁴¹ volt]BT.
⁵⁴² goul].

⁵⁴³ tressaut]B (T: mais ce que monte que me vaut).
⁵⁴⁴ parler]R, *cf.* Luke 11: 9-10 (B: Ki cuide par lonc iestre engriés).
⁵⁴⁵ En fui ainc, m.]BT.
⁵⁴⁶ que il me]L.

6251 Eracle then stepped aside with the precious, Holy Cross, and in the presence of his men he made promises to God, vowing to arrange for masses to be sung and to clothe and feed the poor in order to honour God, who had deigned to be born of the Holy Virgin Mary. He humbled himself in various different ways, weeping, falling to his knees and uttering holy prayers, which he whispered quietly to himself or spoke for all to hear. There was no one so hard or arrogant who was not moved to pity him deeply. Both his knees were bleeding, for he had punished himself so harshly and knelt down so frequently that no one could say just how often. Dukes and counts wept and cried out, but their crying and weeping was nothing in comparison with his pain, which he expressed thus: 'Oh Lord full of forbearance, since I have truly been brought down by a momentary lapse rather than by pride, look on me with your merciful eyes. **6275** Open your eyes and look carefully into my soul, for in truth I was not paying attention. Oh fount of compassion, in whom all virtues are united, pardon a wretch's sins. Do not pick a quarrel with me. You gave me such powers that you enabled me to defeat the man who had his heaven covered in golden stars and who had himself called a god. What good is all this to me, my Lord, if I am assailed and persecuted by your wrath? My Lord, I can vouch for the fact that once you have noticed a person's misdeed he would not be able to remain in your favour unless you took pity on him. My Lord, if I have committed a foolish act, I did not do so, as far as I am aware, out of wickedness or pride. And if that was the case, it grieves me greatly and I sincerely regret it. Fair Lord God, it is in your nature to be full of pity; you dispense it every day in handfuls; I know that you have as much pity now as you had when you forgave Mary Magdalen her sins. **6302** Just as the river flows from its source, so mercy originates and flows down from you. Compassionate Lord, have mercy on me and allow me to enter this town. It is written in the Gospel[103] that whoever persists in asking is allowed to enter, if not straightaway, then shortly afterwards. I have never been persistent, but I shall be now. Unless I am carried off in a coffin, I shall not leave here, whatever the risk to me, until the gate opens and the walls have parted again, so that there is no cause to reproach me. It would be a terrible thing if because of me the gate were barred

---

[103] Luke 11: 5-13.

A ceus qui laiens entrer seulent[547]
Et au mains ceus qui entrer voelent.
Cil qui por moi perdroit l'entree
6320 Maudiroit adiés le ventree
Celi qui fu de moiençainte,
Qui fu si bone dame et sainte,
Et maudiroit qui m'engenra.[548]
Mais, se Diu plaist, ja n'avenra
6325 Que li autre perdent par moi
L'entree; Dix! mais il, por coi?
Il n'ont coupe de cest afaire,
Et ja est Dix si deboinaire
Que n'ert ja que je merci n'aie.
6330 En Damediu a grant manaie
Si con el verai Sauveor;[549]
Ne velt pas mort de peceor,
Ains velt qu'il se repente et vive.
S'orelle a tos jors ententive
6335 A oïr ceus qui se recroient
De lor peciés et merci proient.
Molt tost vient lor proiere amont,
Por qu'ele naisse de parfont.»
Eracles quiert a Diu merci;
6340 Il l'avra ains qu'il part de chi,
Que Dix aiue a bone foi
Celui qui a pitié de soi.
Eracles forment se demente,
En merci querre a grant entente.
6345 Ne por avoir ne por riquece

N'a mie un point plus de perece.
Icil sont molt d'estrainne fuer
Qui por riquece ont plus dur cuer,[550]
Que mains de pitié ont en eus[551]
6350 Et mains de merci ont de ceus[552]
Sor cui il ont point de justice,[553] [d]
Car mar virent lor manantise.[554]
Qui plus a, miels doit croire en Diu,[555]
Et reconnoistre en cascun liu
6355 Que de Diu est quanqu'il en a;
Et se de rien li mesesta,
Qui plus a, plus de crieme i monte
Coment il puist venir a conte
A Damediu des grans honors
6360 Qu'il tient de lui: c'est le paors
Que cascuns princes doit avoir,
Por qu'en lui ait point de savoir;
Meïmement quant lui mesciet,
Que l'ire Diu sor lui s'assiet,
6365 Dont se doit cremir li peciere
S'aucuns peciés de en arriere
A tel pecié le trait et tire
U Damedix li mostre s'ire,[556]
Com il a fait l'empereor,
6370 Qui reconnoist molt bien s'onor,[557]
Et bien le doit, et sel tesmoigne
Que ceste noviele vergoigne
Li vient et naist de viés peciés
Dont li diables l'a touciés.

---

[547] entre].
[548] q. engenra]BT.
[549] Si el v.]B.

[550] r. a p.]B.
[551] Q. mais de p. o. enclos e. e.] (B: Et mains de p.).
[552] o. en eus]BT.
[553] coi]BT.
[554] mantise]BT.
[555] droit]BT.
[556] D. li nostre sire]B (T: Li moustre s'ire nostre sire).
[557] m. s'onor]B (T: r. bien son signour).

to those who are accustomed to enter here, or at least to those who wish to enter. Anyone who lost the right to enter here because of me would always curse the child in the womb of the lady who bore me and was so virtuous and pious, and he would curse the man who begat me. But, if it pleases God, never will others forfeit the right to enter here because of me. For, in God's name, why should they? **6327** They are not responsible for this sorry state of affairs and God is so magnanimous that he will not fail to have mercy on me. The Lord God possesses great compassion, as our True Saviour should. He does not wish for the death of a sinner, preferring him to mend his ways and continue to live.[104] His ear is always straining to hear those who renounce sin and pray for mercy.[105] Their prayer reaches heaven very rapidly, provided it comes from the depths of their hearts.' Eracle asked for God's forgiveness and he was granted it before he left there, for God helps in good faith whoever takes pity on his own soul. Eracle lamented greatly, striving with all his might for forgiveness. Neither his wealth nor his power made him falter any more. They are made of strange stuff indeed, those people whose hearts are harder because they hold positions of power, for they are less forgiving and show less mercy towards those over whom they have some jurisdiction. Woe betide those who ever became so powerful. **6353** The more one has, the more one should believe in God and acknowledge on all occasions that everything one has comes from God. And if the successful man suffers some misfortune, he should be all the more anxious to account before our Lord God for the great honours he has received from Him: every prince with an ounce of intelligence should be anxious to do this. Above all when things go wrong and the wrath of God is turned against him, then the sinner should be afraid in case an earlier sin has induced and forced him to commit the sort of sin for which Almighty God shows him His wrath.[106] This is what happened to the emperor, who clearly acknowledged the honour bestowed on him, and rightly so, and admitted to himself that this recent shameful occurrence resulted from and originated in an old sin instigated by the devil.

---

[104]   Ezekiel 18: 23 and 33: 11.
[105]   Psalms 130: 2.
[106]   John 3: 36.

6375 Molt s'est jugiés li emperere,
Et Damedix, li verais pere,
I a fait si apert miracle
Por son empereor Eracle
Que li doi mur, qui enssanle erent,
6380 Se sont retrait si con il erent;
La don il vinrent la revont,[558]
Voiant tous ceus qu'illeuques sont;
Tuit se descuevrent li degré
Et li porte oevre de son gré.
6385 Cil a le cuer molt esjoï
De ce que Dix l'a si oï;
Torné li est a grant honor
Ce c'ains li fu a deshonor
Et dont il fu au cuer dolans
6390 Et soupirans et gemissans;
Et il est liés et esjoïs, [e]
Tesmoins a cex dont est joïs.
Puis s'abaissë et prent le Crois,
Qui des autres iert sire et rois,
6395 Et en Jherusalem se met;
Tout son pooir a Diu proumet.
Et cil qui çou ont regardé
Dient: «Cis hom est de par Dé;
Dix ne li est ne mols ne durs.
6400 Les portes li clost et les murs,
Et par son angle a lui tença;[559]
Or li retrait le mur en ça
Et par de la, com il ains iert,
Le porte oevre con il i piert.
6405 Estraigne plait li a basti
Quant il, apriés son biel casti,
I met tel assouagement.»[560]
Parlé en ont sauvagement
Et li estraigne et li privé;

6410 En demendant ont estrivé:
«Que li rent Dix bon loiier hui
de tout ce qu'il a fait por lui!
Bon fait a son service entendre,
Car molt set bien ses mains estendre
6415 Al gueredon de son servise.»
Eracles a le Crois Diu mise[561]
Illuec ou Cordroé l'osta,
Qui nule rien n'i conquesta;
Mors en est pardurablement,
6420 Et ses fix, l'aisnés, ensement.
Le mainné, le petit paien,
Fist il faire bon crestïen,
Et n'i pert vaillant un festu
Que il ne l'ait lués revestu
6425 De quanque tint li fel, ses pere;[562]
Son non li dona l'emperere.
Eracles a le Crois conquise,
Et a le merci Diu remise
La u li cors Diu fu penés.
6430 Li biax, li preus, li alosés
Fist molt grant feste, ce fu drois, [f]
A l'onor de le vraie Crois.
La fu li feste adont trovee
Qui en septembre est celebree.
6435 Je l'ai leü, si m'en ramembre,
Que ce fu tout droit en septembre,
Et dont fu li essaucemens
Del fust ou Dix pendi sanglens.
Icis trova le feste adonques,
6440 Qui devant ce n'ot esté onques;
Icis le trova tous premiers,
Or en est cascuns coustumiers
Que il le face a icel jor.

---
[558] il i v.] (B: La dont il vienent s'en revont).
[559] angle lui tempta]T (B: tenta).
[560] Et m.]T (B: I vient).
[561] mis]BT.
[562] quaque]BT.

6375 The emperor judged himself very harshly and our Lord God, the true father, performed such a clear miracle for his emperor Eracle that the two sections of wall which were joined together went back to where they were before; witnessed by all present, they returned to their original positions. All the steps were visible once more and the gate opened of its own accord. Eracle was overjoyed in his heart that God had responded to him in this way, for He had transformed into a great honour what had previously been to Eracle's dishonour, making his heart heavy with sighing and lamenting; yet now he was jubilant and overjoyed, as was clear to those who were his supporters. Then the man who was their lord and ruler bent down, picked up the Cross and entered Jerusalem, promising to dedicate all his power to the service of God. Those who had witnessed these events said: 'This man is chosen by God. God has been neither indulgent nor harsh with him. **6400** He closed the gates and the walls before him and upbraided him through his angel; but now He has parted the walls, returning them to their former positions, as is evident from the open gate. What a strange sequence of events He has set in motion, first reprimanding him roundly, then consoling him in this way.' Everyone, both friends and strangers, debated the situation passionately, rivalling one another with their questions: 'What a generous reward God has given him today for all he has done for Him. It is wise to dedicate oneself to His service, for He can be relied upon to stretch out his hands and reward those who serve Him.' Eracle replaced the Lord's Cross in the spot from which Chosroes had snatched it. Yet it profited the latter nothing, for he was in a state of eternal damnation, along with his older son. The younger pagan boy became a good Christian thanks to Eracle, and he lost nothing at all by it, since he was subsequently invested with everything his treacherous father had possessed. **6426** He even took the emperor's name.[107] Eracle had won back the Holy Cross and with God's grace returned it to the place where God's body was made to suffer. Our handsome, valiant, illustrious hero organised, as was only right and proper, a huge celebration in honour of the True Cross. Thus the feast day we celebrate in September was instituted.[108] I remember reading somewhere that it was indeed in September, and since then we have celebrated the exaltation of the Cross on which God was hung, covered in blood. Thus it was that Eracle founded the feast day which had not existed before. He was its founder; now it is customary for everyone to celebrate it on that very day.

---

[107] In fact Heraclius was succeeded by his own sons Heraclius-Constantine and Heraklonas.
[108] The Feast of the Exaltation of the Cross on 14th September.

Eracles sans autre sejor,
6445 Quant il le Crois ot essaucie,
S'est molt tost mis en le caucie
Qui vers Coustantinoble vait;
Tous li païs grant joie en fait.
Coustantinoble le reçoit
6450 A grant honor quant l'aperçoit,
Car nul jor n'aront mais signor
Qui les maintiegne a tele honor
N'a tel francise n'a tel pais;
Comment l'aroient il jamais?[563]
6455 Molt par ama justice et foi,
Et molt essauça nostre loi;
Grans biens fist tant con il vesqui.
Benoit soit l'eure qu'il nasqui!
Benoite soit l'ame son pere!
6460 En paradis l'ame se mere!
Nule gens mix ne se contint
Tant con cis siecles le detint.[564]
Une maison edefïerent[565]
U il, des puis qu'il dessevrerent,
6465 Ont mes et manront tos jors mais,
En paradis, el haut palais.
Et quant li fix en ot pooir,
Por aus dona molt grant avoir,
Mais por noient: n'orent besoing;
6470 A lui ala; n'ala plus loing.
Je ne sui pas de çou en doute [154 a]
Que il n'en ait l'aumosne toute,
C'aumosne vient, et venir doit,
Coment que onques mise soit;
6475 Quanques cis a por eus ouvré,
En paradis l'a recouvré,

Et le siue ame en secourut.
Quant avint cose qu'il morut,
Costantinoble en fist grant duel;
6480 Fondue fust al jor, son voel.[566]
Grant duel i ot, grant duel en fisent,
Et ricement l'enseveliren.
Oiés c'ont fait li ancien,
Et gardés s'il le fisent bien:
6485 Tres en mi liu de le cité,
Qui est de grant antiquité,
Ont un molt grant piler drecié[567]
Qu'il ont a paines porcachié;
Molt i aroit a traire uns hom
6490 Del pié desous desci en son.
Par deseure ont mis une ymage,[568]
Itel de vis et de corage
Con li preudom qui tint l'empire.
Sor un ceval seoit li sire
6495 Tel con il ot quant il venqui[569]
Le fil au fol qui relenqui
Diu, si se cuida essaucier
Por le loi Diu toute abaissier.
Gentement est l'image assise,
6500 Et faite l'ont par tel devise
Que jamais jor ne dequerra;
La pert et tos jors mais parra.
De biel tor est, et doit bien estre:
Vers paienime tent se destre
6505 Et fait sanlant de manecier
Et de l'onor Diu porcacier.
Si fist li sire en son vivant;
Et s'il vesquist deus ans avant,[570]
Il moustrast bien se grant poissance[571]

---

[563] C. l'en tienent il]BT.
[564] se contint]T (B: les d.).
[565] dedefierent]B.

[566] sor v.]BT.
[567] O. il molt piler]H (B: Ot un; T: p. ot d.).
[568] a m.]BT.
[569] vesqui; BT]L.
[570] sis v.]BT.
[571] moustrat]BT.

Once he had exalted the Cross, Eracle soon set off without delay on the road to Constantinople. Everyone throughout the country rejoiced. **6449** As he came into view, the people of Constantinople greeted him with full honours; for they were never again to have a lord who would procure for them such a period of success, freedom and peace. How could they ever enjoy such a period again? He was a great defender of justice and faith, and he promoted our religion enthusiastically. He achieved a great deal of good during his lifetime; blessed be the hour when he was born! Blessed be the soul of his father, and may his mother's soul rest in heaven. No couple ever behaved better than they did while they remained on this earth. They built an abode for themselves in a heavenly palace on high, where they have resided since they parted from this life and will reside for ever.[109] And when their son was in a position to do so, he gave away huge sums of money for their sakes; but this was not necessary, for they did not need it. So his charity reverted to him; it did not go any further. I have no doubt that he had the whole benefit of his alms-giving, for charity returns to the giver, and so it should, however it is distributed. **6475** Whatever good works Eracle performed for his parents, he reaped the benefits in heaven and thereby saved his own soul. When it came to pass that he died, the whole of Constantinople mourned him; they would not have cared if the city had fallen into ruin that day. There was great lamenting and great mourning, and they buried him with due pomp and ceremony. Listen to what people used to do in the past and decide if they behaved properly: right in the heart of the city, which is very ancient, they erected a huge column, which took an enormous effort to achieve; it must have been a great struggle to get from the base right to the summit. On top they placed a statue which captured exactly the features and disposition of the hero who had governed the empire.[110] Their ruler was mounted on a horse similar to the one he was riding when he defeated the son of the miscreant who had deserted God and thought that he could elevate himself by denigrating God's law. **6499** They carefully placed the statue on the column, positioning it in such a way that it would never fall off. It is still to be seen there and always will be seen. It is very impressive, and so it should be: Eracle is pointing towards pagan territory with his right hand, seeming to threaten them and to pursue God's honourable cause. Thus he lived his life, and had he lived two more years he would have demonstrated further his great strength,

---

[109] 2 Corinthians, 5: 1.
[110] The statue to be found in Constantinople in the twelfth century was, in fact, of the emperor Justinian.

6510 Et se vertu et se vaillance;
Et si fist il ains qu'il morust [b]
Ne que le mors sor lui courust,
Et par se grant cevalerie
Est sainte Glise el mont florie.
6515 Vers Damediu l'esperitable
Nous soit li sainte Crois aidable
Dont Vautiers d'Arras a traitié!
Tuit li cortois, li afaitié,
Le doivent bien a Diu proiier,
6520 Et que ge si puisse emploiier[572]
Ceste oevre que je bien i aie
Et qu'ele en males mains ne kaie.[573]
Li quens Tiebaus ou riens ne faut,
Li fix au boin conte Tiebaut,
6525 Me fist ceste oevre rimoiier.
Par lui le fis, nel quier noiier,
Et par le contesse autressi,
Marie, fille Loëy.
Faite m'en a mainte assaillie
6530 Cil qui a Hainau en baillie,
Que je traitasse l'uevre en fin.
Jel sai si preudome et si fin[574]
Que je l'aim plus que prince el monde,
Et se je menç, Dix me confonde.
6535 Et se por lui ne le faisoie,
Ce que por autrui ne feroie,
Jugier poroit tres bien en lui[575]
Que je ne l'aim pas plus c'autrui.
De riens nule c'amis a ciere[576]
6540 Ne doit nus hom nes faire ciere

Que mais le voele retenir;
C'on doit son bon ami tenir.
En dis et set ans et demi
Ne treuve on pas un bon ami;
6545 S'ame consaut sains Esperis!
Trestous mes pooirs est petis
A mon signor servir a gré;
Molt par montai en haut degré,[577]
Et ricement bien m'empointai[578]
6550 Le jor que premiers l'acointai;
Esleü l'ai en mon aumaire, [c]
Et se nus hom por nul afaire
En desfaisoit le serreüre,
Ja ne trouverai troveüre[579]
6555 Ne ne me querrai mais en home.[580]
Il est tous seus, c'en est la some,[581]
Nen a ne per ne compaignon,[582]
Ne ja n'ara se par lui non.
Quens Bauduïn, a vos l'otroi;
6560 Ains que passent cinc an u troi,
Metrai aillors, espoir, m'entente.
Sire, je sui de bone atente,
Mais gardés que n'i ait engan;
Se me promesse n'est auvan,
6565 Dont gardés qu'ele soit en tens.
Vos savés assés que je pens.
Dix me doinst gré de mon signor,
De ce et d'el adiés grignor.
Amen. amen. amen. amen.
Explicit d'Eracle.

---

572 pusse]BT.
573 male m.; T]R (B: male main).
574 Je s.]BT.
575 e lui]T.
576 c'a mis ariere]T.

577 monta]T.
578 m'empoitai]L (T: me prouvai).
579 Jamais ne trovai t.]L.
580 Ne ne ne me q.]T.
581 Il a t. s. c. e. lassome]T.
582 a le p.]T.

valour and courage.[111] Yet he managed this before he died and before death overtook him. It is thanks to his excellent chivalry that Holy Church has flourished throughout the world. May the Holy Cross, the subject of this work by Gautier d'Arras, intercede on our behalf before our heavenly Lord God. All courtly and educated men should pray to God for this, and also that I might use this work for my benefit and that it does not fall into the wrong hands. **6523** Count Thibaut, who is perfect in every way and is the son of good Count Thibaut, asked me to compose this work in verse. I do not wish to deny that I did it for him and for the countess as well, Marie, the daughter of Louis.[112] The lord of Hainault has exhorted me repeatedly to complete this work.[113] I know him to be such a worthy, fine gentleman that I love him more than any other lord on earth. And if I am lying, may God punish me! If I had not done for him what I would not do for anyone else, then he would be entitled to draw the conclusion that I do not love him any more than anyone else. No one should so much as give the impression that they wish to hold on to something that their friend is keen to have, for one should do anything to keep a good friend. It takes more than seventeen and a half years to find a good friend. May the Holy Spirit save his soul! The sum total of my skill is insufficient to serve my lord as befits him. I improved my standing greatly and placed myself in a splendid position the day I first met him; I have chosen him to be the keeper of my treasures, and if anyone, for any reason, were to break the lock on this chest, I would never again compose a work, nor would I ever trust anyone again.[114] **6556** He is one of a kind, that is the long and the short of it, for he has neither equal nor companion, and never will have unless he produces one himself. Count Baudouin, I am handing over this work to you. Before five or even three years have elapsed, I shall perhaps apply myself to something new. My lord, I am a patient man, but mind there is no trickery in all this, for if the promise you have made to me is not fulfilled this year, let it be so soon. You are well aware of my thoughts on this matter. May God grant me my lord's favour now, and even more so in the future.

Amen, amen, amen, amen.

Here ends the story of Eracle.

---

[111] According to Fourrier 1960, 210, this is a reference to the seizing of the Holy Cross by the Arab Emir Omar in 644.

[112] Thibaut V of Blois and his sister-in-law Marie de Champagne, daughter of King Louis VII.

[113] Baudouin IV or V of Hainault; see my Introduction, pp. viii-ix.

[114] An *aumaire* was a place where valuables were stored, but also a book cupboard. Gautier has thus decided not only to give Baudouin his 'treasure' *Eracle* for safe-keeping, but also to write more works for him, if the bond between them is not broken. The phrase 'eslir en son aumaire' is used by Guillaume le Clerc in his *Joies Notre Dame* when describing God's choice of the Virgin Mary as a vessel for a precious object: 'E esleue a son armaire/Por nostre delivrance faire' (433-34). Thus, Gautier is implying a special relationship with his favoured patron. However, if Baudouin does not keep his 'promise', the poet threatens to change patrons again, as is implied by the secondary meaning of l. 6561: 'I shall, perhaps, turn my attentions elsewhere'.

Variants & Textual Notes

A = Paris, Bibliothèque Nationale de France, fr. 1444; B = Paris, Bibliothèque Nationale de France, fr. 24430; T = Turin, Biblioteca Nazionale, L. I. 13.; H = Hayes; L = Löseth; O = *Eraclius*, Meister Otte's Middle High German adaptation of *Eracle*; R = Raynaud de Lage.

Line numbers from my edition are followed by significant variants from the other manuscripts and relevant information from other editions. Readings shared by *A* are abbreviated to save space; e.g. in l. 3, T: e. = estuet as in *A*.

3 B: esteut il traire et faire; T: e. tel cose faire.
4 BT: Ki sour toutes ses euvres paire.
6 B: Por coi il a cest euvre empris.
15-18 *absent from* B; 17-50 *absent from* T.
26 B: Ki donne adiés et goie et rit.
29 B: mescante.
39-40 B: tencier/Car ne sevent consentier.
42 B: escarcon.
45 B: Se on veut goie entraus mener.
55 B: Maugré m.; T: Maugret mien savra tout le pire.
After 60 BT *have 6 extra lines*; B: Ses peres voit dieu en la face/Son non li laisa et sa grase/Con fist Ysaac Ysau/Ne fust Jacop ki l'ot peu/D'un kievreul tenre de saison/Qu'il li douna por garison. *Their inauthenticity is indicated by the fact that the last couplet is followed by a further one (61-62) on the same rhyme. The information about Thibaut's father is not vital as it appears in the epilogue in all MSS (6524), but see* Fourrier 1960, 190.
64 B: que il se membre.

After 74 BT *have 2 extra lines*: Ne mais li avoirs li anuie (T: Car li avoirs si lui anuie)/Qu'il onkes autrement estruie (T: Onques autrement nel estuie).
79 BT: Q. het les boins (T: le bien).
90 B: Povre fameleus et d.
95 BT: en romans.
102 B: el roumans lire; T: en roumanch dire.
127 B: Andoi ensi au s. ahiersent.
135 B: reclaimment; T: reclama.
139 B: proie; T: prierent.
146 T: D. te mande salus par moy, *cf.* 5328, 5539.
147 BT: te proiiere; O, 236: gebet *reflects* BT.
154 *Here and elsewhere the scribes of* A *and* B *do not always distinguish between* qui *and* que, *subject and object case; no correction has been made.*
157-60 *absent from* B.
170 B: falir.
176 BT: dieus d.; O, 256: got *reflects* BT.
191 B: vilouniee; T: lecherie.
192 BT: legerie.

193 B: ce n'en iert ja; T: non fera ja.
195-96 B: D. coumande a f./Ne puet t. a nul c.
197 B: A. s'esvelle.
198 BT: Qui Mereados avoit non.
201-02 *inverted in* BT.
244 B. por lire; T: sans ire; O, 372: versigelter brief *reflects* A.
266-67 B: Et des cevaus likeus iert pires/ savra, teus sera sa matiere.
275-76 T: Et que cascunne estuet porter/ Ki le vorrroit de cors porter; 276 B: S'il le veoit n'en doutés point.
283-84 B: ricetes/fremetes; O, 500-01: rîchtuom/veste *reflect* B.
286 BT: s. segnor s.
290 B: il la raison e.
314 B: A peu de cose vient plentez; T: De poy de cose ist grans plentés.
333 B: B. fait vait la u aler d. (*cf.* 6470).
After 342 T *has 2 extra lines*: Ainsi con il le disent firent/C'onques terme n'i atendirent.
366 BT: g. peril.
380 B: La mere et ensi l'en avint.
402 B: preu i aras; T: bien l. f.
418 B: iriés ne pesans; T: De fin or massis et pesans; BT *offer a better rhyme with* besans.
420 B: n'en i faura pas une malle.
B *has 4 lines for* 451-52: Et dient tout ma douce amie/Or me dites ne le celés mie/Di nous de cest enfant le fuer/ Que tu n'en laises en nul fuer.
469 B: n'en doutés r.
479 B: s. hastievement.
509-10 *absent from* B.
532 B: Li ques est boins ne li keus p.

544 B: une encore; T: tel cose; O, 816: noch *reflects* B.
555 B: b. me vis el j.; T: Et ber te vi en jour entrer.
570 B: en plorant.
572 B: porteure.
580 B: R. t'ent; T: Remembre t'en.
582 B: Garde m. f. maintien m'enfens. T *inverts* 581-82; 582: Biau s. dieus souvingnet en.
586 B: al daerain; T: Qu'il ne s'en lot s'il n'est dolent.
593 BT: c. cuer.
T *inverts* 611-12.
613-14 *absent from* T.
632 BT: croit.
T *inverts* 657-58.
661 B: Li emperere adont demande; T: Et li empereres manda.
664-65 B: deviner/Et faire cou dont s'est v.
669 BT: vaut.
673 B: v. con l'en a dit; T: qu'om li a dit.
681 B: pas por nient dounés; T: Le sien cuide avoir puer gieté.
703-06 B: tes parlers m. c./Plains m. s. de b. t./Q'ame ki fait faus grant proiiere/ De ce k'elle fet plus est fiere. O, 888: rede *reflects* B, 703.
708 B: Li varles ne soit baretere; T: Le vallet ne soit baretere.
750 B: Se cou est voirs ke t.
777-78 *absent from* T.
803 B: s'en pasent; T: s'en passe.
815-16 *absent from* T.
819-20 B *rhymes*: feroie/vengeroie.
836 B: poivre et autre gomme; T: povrement a R.

T *inverts* 839-40.
841-42 *absent from* T.
T *inverts* 873-74: Sen miercie dieu de lassus.
BT *invert* 877-78.
906 BT: dolans.
922 BT: balanciés.
923 B: pril; T: maus; O, 1133: merer *reflects* A (pïeur).
929-30 *absent from* T.
943-44 BT: nos t./Qui cuidons q.; 943 T: Fol sommes et il nous t.
T *inverts* 977-78: Ki garanti l'ot de morir.
988 B: o. de fantosmerie.
992 B: M. en si haut l.
996-97 B: Et molt liés est l. s./Au col li giete u.; 997 T: Li met au col u.
1004 BT: s'en rist.
1007-09 *absent from* B.
1013 B: fait; T: sait.
1060 B: Li envious et li f.; T: Li menchongnier et li f.
1069-70 *absent from* T.
1076 B: d. nient plus k'une e.; T: Ne que a d'un caisne l'escorche.
1120-21 B: Por le feu ki si l'anguisa/Nes k'il fust une lieue en sus.
1163 B: e. un femier.
BT *invert* 1193-94; BT: Qu'il (T: Molt) het cest varlet por nient/C'ainc (T: Ains) mes ne vit, mon enscient.
1203 B: v. cremés.
1230 B: u. gaians m.
1234 BT: Et coumande.
1253 BT: v. pis.
1254 B: Et k'il ne voist de pis en pis; T: Et preudoms a ses anemis.
1285 B: seulement.

1298 B: Or porons n. d'Eracle aprendre; T: Por ce porrons d'Eracle aprendre.
1333-34 *absent from* T.
1358 B: m. ki entour lui; T: entour celui.
1360-61 B: Qui poi prisen un tel poulain (T: p. cent poulain)/Que cest li pires au v. d.
1364 T: Sire ne vous ayrés o.
1365-66 *absent from* T.
1377-80 *absent from* T.
1390 B: Nos a il trestous enivrés; T: Vos a il trestous desjuglés.
1434 BT Ne savés v. *likely to be original, see* 1435.
1458 BT: Qu'il m'osteroit d.
1480 *absent from* B.
1491-92 *absent from* T.
T *inverts* 1493-94 *and* 1495-96.
1530-31 T: Mais je meismes qui chi sui, *then adds*: Fuisse molt liés se en seusses/Et s'en toi tant de sen eusses/Que tu e. a.
1556-60 T: Ichi vingne tout li plus c./Au chief du cor un pau aval/F. m. vostre cheval/ Et le secont en loins non prés/ Et li tiers soit encor apriés; 1560 B: A la bonne droit al cief priés. *The scribes of all three MSS found this passage problematic.*
1561-62 B: premier/Ja ne m'i verés delaiier; 1563-64 B: place/estace; 1561-66 T: Jusque au soir des le matin/Keurent et li poulains ausin/Si mouveront de c. p./Et s'il ne les vaint et estanche/Ains qu'il soient a l'autre a mi/J'otroi c'on me trenche parmi.
1579 BT: il parfait c.
1617-18 *absent from* T.

1623 B: t. fu trais; T: con trait.
1634 BT: ki les (T: ce) voit.
1637-38 *absent from* T.
1669 B: l. engrose; T: l. engroisse.
1690 B: Q. longement; T: Q. mout lonc tamps.
1693-94 *absent from* T.
1702 B: mais mestier con plus le maint; T: mais mestier que on le maint.
T *inverts* 1703-04; 1703-06 *are written in* T *after* 1722 *and are followed by 4 extra lines:* Et quant .E. l'a veü/Si atorné et recreü/Courant s'en vait parmi le val/ Tant qu'il vient vers le tierch cheval.
1736 B: f. deceüs.
1765-66 T: cheval plus ne sejourne/Mais tantos arriere tourne, *then adds* Sour le poulain que il mout aimme/Et a soi meismes se claimme.
1775-78 *absent from* T.
1777-80 *absent from* B.
1799-1802 *absent from* T.
1802-05 B: Mes quers a houni se tenroit/ Se g'en avoie retraçon/D'une sifaite mesproison/Cuidiés vous ke ce soit a ciertes; T *omits* 1799-1802, *then continues*: Que viers vous fache mesprison/ Eracle amis, bele façon/Sachiés ie ne di mie achiertes.
T *inverts* 1811-12.
T *inverts* 1815-16.
1816 BT: en R. entrai.
1826-27 B: Petit enfant et se veustu/Je frai morir de m. m.; T: Petis enfes et jouvenes es tu/Or fai m. de. m. m.
1842 B: Si fait; A: Qu'il fait *corrected to* Qu'il s'art *by later hand.*
1887-88 B: Fendre le quir la molle espandre/Jus a lor piés sour li erbe tendre; T: Fendre et la moulle espandre/Jus a ses piés sans plus atendre. *The* B *reading for* 1888, *is reflected by* O, 1680: an daz gras.
1901-02 BT: s. a cier son c./T. l. a. le veulent b.
1904 B: Tout le cierisent apriés lui.
1911-12 *absent from* B.
1951 B: C. c. aura se creance.
1951-54 *absent from* T.
1961 T: isnielement.
1992 T: e. apris.
2006 BT: Q. p. eür.
2057 B: Une traitie priés des tentes; T: A une traitie des t.
2063-64 *absent from* T.
2073 BT: afaitement.
2089-90 *absent from* T.
2103-04 *absent from* T.
2111-22 *absent from* T.
2141 BT: eslite qu'une, *but there is no need to correct* A's *reading as* R *does here and in line* 2206.
2151-52 *absent from* T.
2170 B: Jou ne nus hon teus c.; T: Ie ne voi nul tel c.
2213-14, *containing a faulty rhyme, are absent from* BT *and may be inauthentic. Cf.* B, 2211-15: Car cil ki eslit cel tresor/ Il voit le keuvre desous l'or/Et le plonc paroir s. l.
2257-58 *absent from* B.
2273-74 *absent from* T.
2298 B: Telle euvre otriera mesire; T: Telle eure n'i sera mes sire.
2374 BT: puet (*cf.* 2399, B: pevent; T: porent).

2387-92 *replaced in* T *by* Ki ses volentés en eüst/Se il requerre la seüst.
2471-72 B: Cou ke elle est de grant fiertés/ Mais trop par couste si ciertés.
2529-30 *absent from* T.
2588 BT: b. corage.
2667-68 T: il or m'entendés/Cheste meschinette gardés.
2669-70 *absent from* T.
2673-74 *absent from* B.
2721 B: t. en si con est; T: t. el p.
2751-52 *absent from* T.
B *inverts* 2817-18.
2819-20 *absent from* T.
2825-26 B: Si est del tout si afaitie/Et si sagement ensegnie.
2831-32 *absent from* B.
2833-34 B: Bien est ses quers endotrinés/A faire toutes honestés; T: Ce n'en fait mie nobletés/Bien set conquerre ses bontés.
2839 B: Por k'elle i soit le droit e.; T: Pour quoy ni s. iustiche e.
T *inverts* 2845-46.
2947 BT *omit* ce *producing hypometric lines.*
2978 B: p. demorer k'il n'i aut.
2996 BT: Ki cou m. *reflected by* O, 2548-49: swer nie herzeliep gewan,/der velschet lîhte disiu wort.
3042 BT: castoiement; casti (3044) *suggests that the* BT *reading here may be authentic.*
3058 BT: mieus estre.
3077-78 *absent from* T.
B *inverts* 3083-84.
3093 BT: l'eure k'elle vit.
3099 *absent from* B.

3103 *absent from* B; T: fait une grant folie.
3113 S'il *is acceptable in Picard for* S'ele.
T *inverts* 3125-26.
3145-46 *absent from* T.
3227 B: p. dont; T: p. soi; O, 2762: Got *reflects* A.
3236 BT: il b. a.
After 3254 B *has 4 extra lines*: Et ke g'ai maintenu en moi/Hounour et loiauté et foi/Et por cou m'est elle anemie/Que jou lor ai esté amie *and* T *has 6*: Et si ai maintenue en moi/Amour et loyauté et foi/Envie het touz jours biauté/Honeur et foi et loiauté/Et pour ce m'est elle anemie/Que je li ai esté amie.
T *inverts* 3263-64.
3273-78 *absent from* T.
3293 BT: N'est pas li miens eürs de lui.
3296 B: maus e.; T: Chiaus qui a s'amour welent tendre.
3347-48 T: Ains me rent on tout a bandon/De mon bien fait mal g.
3356 BT: m. loiier.
After 3398 BT *have 2 extra (possibly original) lines*: Ains dame ne fu si (T: plus) apierte/Ne fera mie povre pierte.
3425-28 *absent from* T.
3433-34 BT: Salent tument ballent et rotent/Balent treskent (T: dansent) cantent et notent.
3463-64 *absent from* B.
3468 BT: estour.
3483 B: Se fut mout bien laciez as las; T: S'estroit estroit lachiés a laz.
3513-14 *absent from* BT.
3525-28 (BT *invert* 3527-28) B: Amours n'a cure de tencier (T: rentier)/Se il n'a

tout le quer entier/Amours n'a cure de garçon/Ne de quer avoir a parçon. *The A reading makes sense (to fire an arrow) and is similar in meaning to B's* tencier; T *offers a richer rhyme, and may be a scribal reminiscence of Chrétien's* Cligés, 3114, *copied later in the same MS, but it makes less good sense.*

3549-50 *absent from* T.

3561 BT: Q. buer.

3568 BT: Et sel (T: Mais s'il) savoit, J. *There is no change of speaker.*

3587-90 *absent from* BT.

3593-94 *absent from* BT.

3654 T: me het *is the lessson adopted by* R, *who also accepts* L's *correction for* 3652 'te confonde' *against all the MSS.* A, *however, makes perfect sense as Eracle is being spoken about, not Athanaïs.*

3664 BT: m. dieus qui me s.

3687-88 *absent from* T.

3691-92 *absent from* T.

T *inverts* 3695-96.

3732-33 B: Mais ne se sont entrecounu/ Quatre ans tous plains m. e.

3754 BT: s'est m.

B *inverts* 3769-70.

3784 B: Con en despit bien les pluisor.

3790 BT: fel et e.

3791-92 *absent from* T.

3825-38 *absent from* T.

3831-34 B: Ne k'il puist v. cascun jour/ Que fins amans trait nuit et jour/Tant con ces amis se diout d'amour/Et con il plerent par dolour. B *then adds* U tant con il s'en veut sentier/Tant en entent sans nul mentir.

3841-42 *absent from* T.

3851-52 *absent from* T.

3867-80 *absent from* T.

B *inverts* 3883-84.

3886 BT: .v. ou .vi.

T *inverts* 3909-10.

3913-14 *absent from* T.

T *inverts* 3969-70.

3982 B: pointure.

3999 BT: mort non.

After 4010 BT *have 4 extra lines*; B: Ne m'esmervel se on s'en diut/Por bonne conse ki si meurt (T: Povre cose et s'elle se muert)/Car li tresors en iert mauvés (T: li restors i est m.)/Icil niert restorés jamés (T: Ichilz n'iert estoiés jamais).

4077-78 *absent from* T.

4083 T: nus malades n.

4084 BT: son malage.

4162 B: Cele en vaut mil mien ensient; T: Chelle vaut mieus mien essient.

4171 BT: el monde; O, 3307: ze Rome *reflects* A.

4215 BT: f. planter.

BT *invert* 4223-24.

4235-40 *absent from* B (a *saut du même au même*) .

After 4258 B *has 6 extra lines*, T *has 4*; B: Par son la ciere k'elle fait (T: Et par la chiere)/Cuidon en li el ki ni ait (T: Cuident voirs soit tout entresait)/ Car a la dame mot ne sonne (T: Que la dame nul mot n. s.)/De lor cuidier d'el l'araisonne (T: De ce dont elle l'araisonne)/Le voir contre li faus sanblant/Souavet dist et en tranblant.

4267 B: Ha flour de biauté douce rose; O, 3514: Suzziu ros *reflects* B.

4275-76 *absent from* T.
4319-20 *absent from* T.
4373-74 *absent from* T.
4390 B: Par autrui iert atrais afin; T: Par autre iert traiz li jeus a fin.
4391-92 *absent from* T.
4424 ABT *have* li sorplus (*subject case*), *which* T *later corrects to* le.
4433-34 B: t. dierverie/En quer d.
4465 B: croc a.; T: cort a.; L: crot.
4523-32 *absent from* B.
4533 B: cros; T: cort.
4540 B: crok; T: crot, BT: est ens k.
4545 B: desjuglé.
4615-17 B: Davis les m. m./Dist ke dieus a sour aus sa face/Tous iours nient pour donner sa glore; T: David les fourfaisans m./Et dist que diex donne sa grasce/As bons et leur donne sa gloire.
4644 BT: il tent.
4680 B: H. est fors; T: H. iert hors.
4773-80 *absent from* T.
4788 B: venu; T: ceü; L: cheü.
4794 B: malmet et blaice; T: malement bleche.
4806 B: N'en jovene iestre n'a l'enviellir; T: N'en ioneche n'en en viellir.
4829-30 *absent from* T.
4849-50 *absent from* T.
4865 B: prendra m. m.; T: prendra bon m. (T *corrects error shared with* B?).
4866 *The letter* t *in* Faite *has been partially erased in* A.
4871-72 *absent from* T.
After 4894 BT *has 2 extra lines*; B: Li dui criement por lor desierte/Et l'autres se plaint de sa pierte; T: Li uns se plaint mout de se perte/Li dui criement qu'a leur desserte.
4895 B: l'empenreis crient asés plus; T: Leur soit li g. r.
4900 B: Cascuns le m.; T: En feu le maufet d.
4951-52 *absent from* T.
4957-60 *absent from* B.
4959-60 *absent from* T.
After 4998 BT *have an extra couplet*: B: S'en avés abaisie men pris/Ne mais de cau ki l'a mespris; T: S'en avés abaissie mon pris/Et de tout quanqu'elle a mespris.
5003-04 *absent from* T.
5013-14 *absent from* T *and* T *inverts* 5015-16.
5033 BT: c'uns d. a. d.
5050 BT: d. a feme li d.
5091-92 BT: laroi/dirai.
5100 BT: Que chierement.
5122 B: fu destrois.
T *inverts* 5149-50.
5175-78 *absent from* B.
5181-82 *absent from* B.
5187-88 *absent from* T.
5252 B: f. parlant.
5258 BT: les escorcoit.
5260 B: v. decoler.
5315 BT: Me fait.
T *inverts* 5367-68.
5373 B: ert esploitie (*richer rhyme, cf.* 5899-5900; 5919-20).
B *inverts* 5405-06.
5410 B: t. cou m'est apris; T: t. cou m'est avis.
5415 B: R. e. et lee et m. p.; T: R. fu et noire et parfonde.
T *inverts* 5513-14.

T *inverts* 5525-26.
5536 *absent from* T.
5538 B: c. comme mesages.
5539 *absent from* T.
5585 B: Teus fu des esgardeus les gars; T: Itelz fu li communs esgars.
5592 B: la nef; T: lour nef.
5610 BT: as piés coupés (*see* Eskénazi 2002, 42-43 *and* Roques 1981, 63-64 *for a discussion of parallels with the Oxford* Roland *and the* Roman de Thèbes).
5640 B: r. en ebrieu.
5651-52 *couplet inverted in* BT; B: S'en a c. c./Tout paraison a sa mesure; T: En terre toute creature/Selonc lor sens et lor nature.
T *inverts* 5661-62.
5735-36 *absent from* T.
5836 B: la voie; T: les voies.
5855 BT: ert teus.
5877-78 *absent from* T.
5906 BT: ciers m.
5912 BT: Por l'amour.
5936 BT: lor c.
5940 BT: devorer.
T *inverts* 5959-60.
6005-06 B: entendre/entendre; T: entendre/atendre.
6051-52 *absent from* T.
6079 T: Li empereres departi, *then adds*: Et quant ce ot fait si parti, *and after* 6081: Qui mout fu bielle et signourie.
6081 B: en va; T: En C. en envoie; O: 5194 sand gein *reflects* A.
6101-04 *absent from* T.
6175 BT: haut *producing an identical rhyme with* 6176.
B *inverts* 6225-26.

6227-28 *absent from* T.
6243-44 *absent from* T.
T *inverts* 6253-54.
6304 BT: a. pité.
6308 BT: il entre apriés.
T *inverts* 6357-58.
6365-66 *absent from* T.
6390-92 *and* 6394 *absent from* BT; 6393 BT: le crois prent.
T *adds after* 6424: Et mout biel et mout richement/Et le paiien mout largement.
6434 T: Ki est en franche celebree.
6458 *cf.* 1814. *This line would be hypermetric if corrected to* 'Benoite'; B: Bient soit; T: Biens soit; L *and* R: Bien soit de l. *After* 6458 B *has two extra lines*: Bien ait de Dieu ki l'alaita/Et benois soit ki l'engenra, *then continues* 6459-60 B: Em paradis soit li siens pere/Et en repos l'arme sa mere; 6459 T: En repos soit l'ame son pere.
6470 B: A lui revint; T: A lui remest.
6492 BT: Itel (T: Telle) de cors et de visage.
6503 T: De biau t. est bielle et houneste.
6504 BT: tient/tint sa tieste (*a clear common error; see* Pratt 1987, 36).
6530 B: a ounour e. b. (B *suppresses all reference to Baudouin of Hainault and stops at line* 6536 *with* AMEN d'Eracle).
6545 T: Si me c.
6554 T: Jamais ne ferai t.
T: Explichit del enpereour eracle.